Fragrances of the World
Parfums du Monde
2001

To five evaluators, remarkable professionals
whose insights have proved so helpful.
À cinq évaluatrices, professionnelles émérites,
dont les conseils m'ont été si utiles.

Elisabeth Carre
Sylvaine Delacourte
Françoise Donche
Karyn Khoury
Elizabeth Marrone

Michael Edwards

Fragrances of the World
Parfums du Monde
2001

Guy Robert
Technical Consultant
Conseiller Technique

Isamu Sawa
Images

Avant-propos

Trouver le parfum dont on rêve - pour soi ou pour les autres - est souvent une véritable épreuve. D'autant que sont lancés sans cesse de nouveaux parfums, tous plus séduisants les uns que les autres; 312, rien que cette année! Difficile de faire son choix… Les conseillers en parfumerie risquent d'y perdre leur latin et c'est d'ailleurs pour eux qu'à l'origine j'avais imaginé ce guide des Parfums du Monde. *Mais mon projet a très vite dépassé le cercle des professionnels et je constate aujourd'hui avec plaisir que* Parfums du Monde *est une référence pour tous les amoureux du parfum.*

Cela représente pour moi la récompense de beaucoup années d'efforts consacrées à l'évaluation et à la classification de plus de 2695 parfums féminins et masculins.

Pour m'aider dans cette tâche considérable, j'ai eu la chance de travailler avec Guy Robert, l'un de nos plus grands parfumeurs contemporains, qui est l'auteur, entre autres, des fameux Calèche *et* Madame Rochas. *La complémentarité de nos compétences alliée aux multiples vérifications réalisées par les évaluateurs et les parfumeurs des marques concernées, confèrent à ce guide sa totale impartialité.*

J'espère surtout que Parfums du Monde *encouragera chacun à être plus aventureux. Le parfum peut être beaucoup plus qu'un plaisant accessoire. Il est écrit dans le Coran: « Les parfums sont des nourritures qui éveillent l'esprit ». Un grand parfum est une oeuvre d'art. Poésie silencieuse, il est l'invisible langage du corps. Il peut rendre nos jours plus heureux, hanter nos nuits et donner sa nuance à nos souvenirs.*

Le parfum est une émotion liquide.

Foreword

Finding the right fragrance can be a confusing exercise. The avalanche of new fragrances makes it difficult even for professionals and beauty advisers to make appropriate selections. *Fragrances of the World* is dedicated to the idea that discovering fragrances should be a pleasure, not a problem.

What started as a simple yet innovative reference for staff in perfumeries and department stores has now become a guide for anyone and everyone who loves fragrance.

This new edition of *Fragrances of the World* assigns 2,695 fragrances to their relevant fragrance families and includes 312 new fragrances introduced in 2000 and 2001.

It has taken eighteen years to develop and perfect the guide and to evaluate, classify and check so many fragrances. I could not have done it without the help and support of the fragrance houses and the perfumers. In recent years, I have also had the privilege of working closely with perfumer Guy Robert, a former president of the French Society of Perfumers and the celebrated composer of *Madame Rochas* and *Calèche*.

Fragrances of the World is more than a professional reference. It is a fragrance map to a world of pleasures. I hope it will encourage people to be more adventurous and spontaneous with their fragrance wardrobe. Fragrances can be so much more than just pleasant accessories; "Perfumes are foods that reawaken the spirit," as it says in the Koran. A great perfume is a work of art. It is silent poetry, invisible body language. It can lift our days, enrich our nights and create the milestones of our memories.

Fragrance is liquid emotion.

Sommaire

Contents

Comprendre le guide	6	Understanding the guide	7
Description des symboles	8	The symbols explained	10
Le Cercle des parfums	9	The Fragrance Wheel	11
Nouveautés	12	New Fragrances	12
Hespéridé	14	Citrus	14
Vert	20	Green	20
Marine	24	Water	24
Florale	28	Floral	28
Fleuri Aldéhydé	40	Soft Floral	40
Fleuri Oriental	44	Floral Oriental	44
Oriental Doux	50	Soft Floral	50
Oriental	54	Oriental	54
Oriental Boisé	58	Woody Oriental	58
Chypre Boisé	64	Mossy Woods	64
Boisé Cuir	70	Dry Woods	70
Fougère	74	Aromatic	74
Index féminin	84	Feminine Index	84
Index masculin	98	Masculine Index	98
Index des Maisons	106	House Index	106

Comprendre

Un guide exhaustif, innovateur et impartial

Parfums du Monde *est, à ce jour, le seul guide proposant une classification aussi complète des parfums actuellement disponibles sur le marché. C'est en effet l'unique ouvrage qui comprend, outre les créations des grandes marques classiques, toutes celles des « artisans parfumeurs » et autres parfumeurs indépendants, tels Annick Goutal, le Comptoir Sud Pacifique, Creed, Demeter Fragrance Library, Diptyque, Fresh, L'Artisan Parfumeur, L'Occitane, Maître Parfumeur et Gantier, Molinard.* Parfums du Monde *s'est attaché à inclure tous les parfums à édition limitée, qu'il s'agisse de large diffusion ou d'édition rare, aussi bien que les parfums de grande diffusion créés par les maisons réputées. Le guide mentionne également les parfums qui ne sont plus disponibles mais auxquels on continue à se référer.*

Par ailleurs, ce manuel offre la particularité d'indiquer, par famille de senteurs, l'accord entre les parfums féminins et masculins. Cette innovation est importante : elle donne la possibilité aux couples de s'offrir des parfums amoureusement complices, sans risque de se tromper de registre. L'occasion d'éviter de bien regrettables erreurs...

Chaque classification est vérifiée avec les évaluateurs dans les Maisons de parfum et avec les parfumeurs eux-mêmes. Vérifier prend du temps, mais c'est une étape importante de mon travail, et sans doute sa force.

Un outil pour tous

Initialement conçu pour aider le personnel des parfumeries à conseiller la clientèle de façon simple et efficace, ce guide trouve aujourd'hui une très large audience.

Résultat d'une recherche exhaustive, Parfums du Monde *est désormais considéré comme un ouvrage indispensable par les parfumeurs et les évaluateurs. C'est une véritable encyclopédie des parfums qui sert déjà de manuel pédagogique pour la formation. C'est également un outil remarquable pour les professionnels du marketing qui, en consultant l'index des Maisons, y trouvent toutes les références nécessaires. Mais cette publication ne se limite pas, loin de là, au cercle des professionnels ou des initiés. La méthode proposée est en effet si claire et si commode, que tout utilisateur de parfums - même le moins averti - y trouvera la possibilité d'épanouir ses connaissances et de multiplier les plaisirs de la découverte.*

Le classement par familles de senteurs: une méthode efficace

Si vous êtes conseiller en beauté, ce livre va vous permettre d'orienter très efficacement, et assez rapidement, le client le plus indécis. La démarche est simple. Posez à votre interlocuteur cette question : « Quels sont les parfums que vous aimez ? » Cherchez alors dans l'index alphabétique chacun des parfums mentionnés afin de savoir à quelle famille de senteurs il appartient. Nul doute qu'au moins deux de ces parfums relèveront du même groupe. Car à notre insu, et depuis toujours, nous avons tous une prédilection pour certaines fragrances, qu'elles soient fleuries ou chyprées. C'est donc dans ce registre favori que vous allez orienter votre client vers de nouveaux parfums. Vous pouvez aussi lui suggérer une senteur d'une famille différente mais, dans ce cas, choisissez obligatoirement parmi les deux familles adjacentes en vous référant au Cercle des parfums (voir page 9). Car il est vrai qu'une femme qui aime le Fleuri oriental, par exemple, portera volontiers un Oriental doux.

Les familles de parfum détiennent la clé des goûts et des rejets de chacun de nous. Chaque famille a une fragrance spécifique qui se reflète dans toutes ses différentes senteurs. Certaines sont plus riches ou plus complexes, d'autres plus fraîches ou plus légères, mais il s'agit des variations d'un même thème dans cette famille.

Il peut également arriver qu'un client n'ait, apparemment, aucune préférence marquée et indique quatre fragrances de quatre familles différentes. Ne vous inquiétez pas : c'est tout simplement un amoureux des parfums, qui aime s'aventurer dans de nouvelles senteurs. Il suffit de lui demander de donner à nouveau le nom de quelques autres parfums qu'il aurait un jour portés ou admirés. Vous parviendrez à chaque fois sans problème à déterminer un penchant pour une famille ou pour une autre. Cette méthode est, en quelque sorte, infaillible !

Encore une fois, point n'est besoin d'être professionnel pour jouer à ce jeu des familles de senteurs. Chacun peut s'y exercer avant de faire le choix d'un nouveau parfum...ou par pur plaisir, lors d'une soirée entre amis : les uns et les autres, interrogés sur leurs préférences, se lanceront sans doute joyeusement dans une de ces conversations passionnantes et embaumées.

Parfums du Monde *sera votre guide dans un monde d'émotions et de plaisirs nouveaux.*

Understanding

Select from the universe of fragrance with this innovative and easy-to-use guide

Fragrances of the World 2001 puts 2,695 fragrances at your fingertips. This comprehensive, innovative and impartial guide lists fragrances from all the major prestige and mass-market fragrance houses. It also includes niche fragrances by boutique perfumers such as Annick Goutal, Comptoir Sud Pacifique, Creed, Demeter Fragrance Library, Diptyque, Fresh, L'Artisan Parfumeur, L'Occitane, Maître Parfumeur et Gantier, Molinard, etc. And at the request of subscribers, the guide lists the long-gone fragrances that have passed from view but remain fixed in memory and desire.

Classification by fragrance families: an effective method

The fragrances families, defined by the Fragrance Wheel (page 11), hold the key to using the guide. Each family has a characteristic scent whose personality is reflected in its fragrances.

If you are passionate about fragrance you will enjoy browsing through the lists and matching your favourite perfumes to their fragrance families. You may be surprised to discover just how many fragrances you like belong to the same family. And if you are a beauty advisor or a sales associate, you'll find the classification of fragrances into their relevant fragrance families makes it easy to help your customers find new fragrances they are certain to like.

Ask the question: "What are your favourite fragrances?" Look up each fragrance in the alphabetical Index to find out the family to which it belongs. Most times, you will find that at least two of the fragrances will belong to the same family.

Occasionally, someone will give you the names of three or four fragrances that belong to quite different families. The reason this has occurred is simple - they love fragrance. Their taste is more adventurous simply because they have tried more fragrances. Don't worry. Just ask for the names of another two or three fragrances they have worn and loved. Invariably, you will discover one family that holds a special appeal.

Now select three new fragrances within that family for yourself, your friend or customer to try - one or two that are close to the fragrances worn and another one that is fresher or richer.

If you wish to try or suggest a fragrance from a different family, consider moving one family up or down on the Fragrance Wheel. Women who enjoy Floral Orientals, for example, often wear Soft Florals as well. In cooler weather, they may switch to the more sensual Soft Orientals.

An understanding of the different fragrance families makes it easy for everyone to discover new perfumes.

A guide for everyone

Created originally for beauty advisers, *Fragrances of the World* has become so comprehensive that it has attracted a wider audience. This authoritative listing has become an encyclopaedic reference for perfumers, evaluators and trainers, a valuable resource for beauty writers and an indispensable competitive reference for marketing professionals.

Fragrances of the World is independent and impartial. No charge is made for classifying and listing fragrances. Its publication is made possible each year by the thousands of subscribers.

The guide's value is enhanced by the fact that classifications are checked with the evaluators at the fragrance houses, or with the perfumers themselves. Checking takes time, but is an essential step and perhaps the greatest strength of the work.

Fragrances of the World will fascinate fragrance lovers. It makes finding new fragrances a pleasure rather than a problem. It remains the only guide to match men's and women's fragrances family by family and this unique feature makes it easy to select appropriate gifts or matching his-and-her fragrances.

Fragrances of the World is a handbook for everyone who enjoys or works with fragrance.

It will become your guide to a world of emotional pleasures.

Description des symboles

Quatre Colonnes

Dans cet ouvrage, chaque famille est elle-même subdivisée selon une « échelle de parfums » si novatrice qu'elle est à ce jour brevetée.

Cette échelle, comparable à une gamme musicale, hiérarchise les parfums d'une même famille : on passe des parfums les plus frais aux plus profonds et d'une colonne à l'autre (Frais, Pétillant, Classique, Profond) les fragrances proposées deviennent plus pénétrantes.

Frais	●	*Les parfums les plus effervescents dans cette famille*
Pétillant	●●	*Interprétation vivante avec une touche de vivacité*
Classique	●●●	*Equilibre des notes, caractéristique de cette famille*
Profond	●●●●	*Les parfums les plus profonds, les plus riches*

Notes et dominantes

Rien n'est plus difficile que d'imaginer une senteur. C'est la raison pour laquelle les quatre colonnes de l'échelle des parfums font apparaître d'autres subdivisions intitulées « hespéridé fruité », « vert », « marine », « fleurs blanches », etc. Il s'agit en fait de précisions qui vont permettre au lecteur d'avoir déjà une idée des notes dominant la fragrance concernée.

Certaines de ces notes sont immédiatement éloquentes. Ainsi les indications « mimosa », « rose » ou « œillet » qui figurent dans la famille des floraux sont aisément compréhensibles.

Même chose pour les « épicés » ou « fruités ». D'autres peut-être méritent quelques commentaires. Ainsi le « vert », par exemple, exprime une note fraîche de feuille verte ou de gazon coupé. L'« hespéridé » indique des senteurs d'huiles d'agrumes, les notes « marines » ont la fraîcheur d'une brise océane ou d'une eau vive.

Quant aux « fleurs blanches », elles conjuguent douceur soyeuse et frais accents de muguet, jasmin, gardénia, jacinthe, chèvrefeuille et freesia.

Parfums féminins, parfums masculins et parfums mixtes

Les parfums féminins sont imprimés en noir :
L'AIR DU TEMPS   Nina Ricci 1948

Les parfums masculins sont imprimés en bleu :
ROMANCE MAN   Ralph Lauren 1999

Les parfums mixtes sont marqués de ♀ et sont présents à la fois dans la liste des parfums pour femme et pour homme.

Dates

1948	*Indique l'année de lancement du parfum*
1962/95	*Lorsque deux dates apparaissent, la première est celle du lancement du parfum, la deuxième, celle de sa reprise, mise à jour ou bien nouvelle conception entièrement différente*

Symboles

*	*L'astérisque indique un parfum disparu, mentionné dans le guide parce qu'il constitue une référence ou bien parce qu'il est encore disponible dans certaines boutiques*
♀	*Indique un parfum mixte (unisexe) à la fois destiné aux femmes et aux hommes*
Ⓛ	*Indique un parfum en édition limitée*

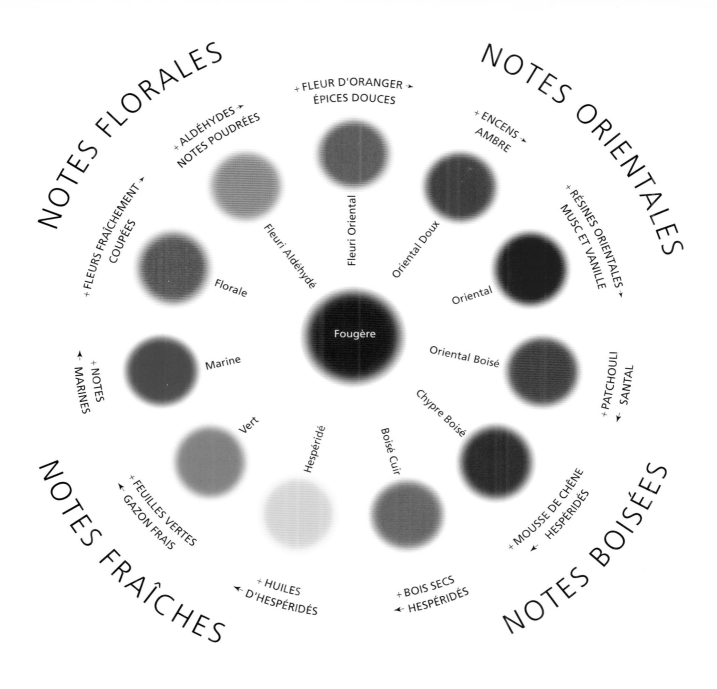

NOTES FLORALES

NOTES ORIENTALES

NOTES FRAÎCHES

NOTES BOISÉES

+ FLEUR D'ORANGER →
ÉPICES DOUCES

+ ALDÉHYDES →
NOTES POUDRÉES

+ ENCENS →
AMBRE

+ FLEURS FRAÎCHEMENT →
COUPÉES

+ RÉSINES ORIENTALES
MUSC ET VANILLE →

Fleuri Aldéhydé

Fleuri Oriental

Oriental Doux

Florale

Oriental

Fougère

↑
+ NOTES
MARINES

Marine

Oriental Boisé

+ PATCHOULI
← SANTAL

Chypre Boisé

Vert

Hespéridé

Boisé Cuir

← + FEUILLES VERTES
GAZON FRAIS

+ MOUSSE DE CHÊNE
← HESPÉRIDÉS

+ HUILES
← D'HESPÉRIDÉS

+ BOIS SECS
← HESPÉRIDÉS

Le Cercle des parfums

Les émotions ont une telle influence sur l'odorat que l'on croit souvent que le choix d'un parfum échappe à toute règle. Or il n'en est rien. Tout individu a sa propre sensibilité olfactive et nos parfums préférés appartiennent en général à une même famille.

C'est la raison pour laquelle notre guide repose entièrement sur cette classification par familles de parfums : ces diverses catégories de senteurs détiennent la clé de nos goûts et de nos rejets.

Ces familles entretiennent entre elles certaines affinités; c'est ce que le Cercle des parfums nous permet d'appréhender d'un seul coup d'oeil. On y distingue, d'abord, les 4 groupes dominants de parfums qui se répartissent en notes fraîches, florales, orientales et boisées.

Ces 4 grandes catégories sont elles-mêmes subdivisées plus finement en 12 familles distinctes, chacune d'entre elles introduisant la suivante. C'est ainsi que les Floraux deviennent des Fleuris

aldéhydés, lorsqu'on y mélange de piquants aldéhydes poudrés d'iris ou de vanille. Les Fleuris aldéhydés se transforment à leur tour en Fleuris orientaux si on leur adjoint des senteurs de fleurs d'oranger et d'épices douces. Et ainsi de suite.

On s'étonnera peut-être de la place particulière des Fougères qui occupent le centre du Cercle des parfums. C'est que cette famille synthétise toutes les caractéristiques des autres familles:

> *La fraîcheur de l'Hespéridé*
> *La note Florale de la lavande*
> *La douceur épicée du Fleuri Oriental*
> *La profondeur ambrée de l'Oriental*
> *Le Chypre Boisé aux chauds accents de santal et de mousse de chêne*

Ses senteurs universelles permettent aux parfums Fougères masculins de s'accorder avec presque tous les parfums féminins.

The symbols explained

The Four Columns

At the heart of this guide is a fragrance scale so innovative it is copyright. Think of fragrances as musical notes, with the freshest notes on the left of each family page and the richest, deepest notes on the right.

When four fragrances from the same family are compared - one a Fresh interpretation, the second a Crisp, the third a Classical and the fourth a Rich version - one's nose steps down a fragrance scale of Fresh > Crisp > Classical > Rich interpretations. With each step, the fragrance note becomes a little deeper.

Fresh	●	The most effervescent fragrances in the family
Crisp	●●	Lively interpretations with a crisp accent
Classical	●●●	Balanced notes characteristic of the family
Rich	●●●●	The richer, deeper fragrances

Citrus-Fruity, Green, Water and White Flowers

Grouping the Fresh and Crisp fragrances under the headings Citrus-Fruity, Green, Water and White Flowers makes it easier to imagine the scent of each fragrance. **Green** notes, for example, will add the sharp freshness of green leaves, crushed grass. A hint of green will make a fragrance crisp while a touch more will make it fresh.

Citrus-Fruity notes come from citrus oils, from apple and apricot, melon and peach, plum and exotic fruits. Their scent adds a tangy freshness quite different from the sharper Green notes.

Water notes, by contrast, capture the cool freshness of sea air or the pure scent of a waterfall.

The scents of fresh **White Flowers** add the sweet, soft, fresh accents of lily of the valley and jasmine, gardenia, hyacinth, white honeysuckle and freesia.

Women's, Men's and Shared fragrances

Feminine fragrances are printed in black:
L'AIR DU TEMPS   Nina Ricci 1948

Masculine fragrances are printed in blue:
ROMANCE MAN   Ralph Lauren 1999

Shared fragrances, marked ♂, are listed among both women's and men's fragrances

Dates

1948	This indicates the year in which the fragrance was introduced
1962/95	When two dates are shown, the first date is the year in which the fragrance was originally introduced, the second the year in which it was reorchestrated, updated or, on occasion, completely changed

Symbols

*	An asterisk indicates that the fragrance has been discontinued but is still included in the guide for reference or because stocks are still available in some stores
♂	Indicates a Shared fragrance
Ⓛ	Indicates a limited edition fragrance

10

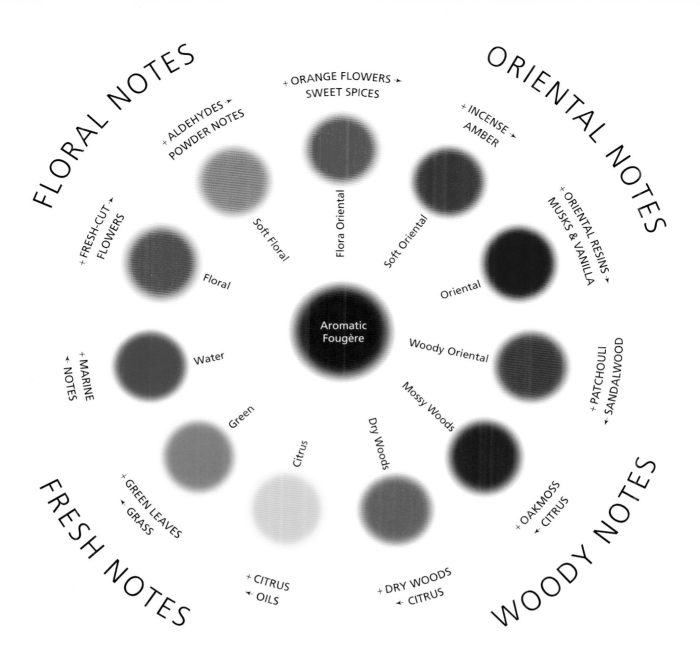

FLORAL NOTES

+ ORANGE FLOWERS →
SWEET SPICES

ORIENTAL NOTES

+ ALDEHYDES →
POWDER NOTES

+ INCENSE →
AMBER

+ FRESH-CUT →
FLOWERS

Soft Floral

Flora Oriental

Soft Oriental

+ ORIENTAL RESINS →
MUSKS & VANILLA

Floral

Aromatic
Fougère

Oriental

Water

Woody Oriental

+ PATCHOULI →
SANDALWOOD

+ MARINE →
NOTES

Green

Mossy Woods

Citrus

Dry Woods

WOODY NOTES

+ GREEN LEAVES →
GRASS

+ OAKMOSS →
CITRUS

FRESH NOTES

+ CITRUS →
OILS

+ DRY WOODS →
CITRUS

The Fragrance Wheel

Since emotions play such a large part in the sense of smell, people assume there is no logic in their choice of fragrances. Yet it's likely that at least two of their favourite fragrances belong to the same 'family'.

The fragrance families hold the key to everyone's likes and dislikes.

The Fragrance Wheel allows you to see at a glance the relationship between the different families.

To the major groups of fragrances defined by perfumers – Floral, Oriental and Woody – has been added a fourth, the Fresh notes.

Modern perfumery has transformed what were once simply light eaux de cologne into real Citrus fragrances.

The true Green fragrances and the Water fragrances are also included among the Fresh notes.

To help you pinpoint your selection more accurately, the Fragrance Wheel breaks down the four major

groups into 12 distinct families. Each family leads to the next. Florals become Soft Florals when blended with sparkling aldehydes and balanced by a soft iris or vanilla drydown. Soft Florals are transformed into Floral Orientals by adding the scents of orange flowers and sweet spices.

Positioned at the hub of the Fragrance Wheel are the Aromatic Fougères, a universal fragrance family that includes elements from many families:

The freshness of a Citrus
Floral notes of lavender
The spicy-sweetness of a Floral Oriental
The ambery depth of an Oriental
And the Mossy Woods warmth of sandalwood
and oakmoss

This universal appeal makes masculine Aromatic Fougères a perfect match to almost any feminine fragrance.

The Fragrance Wheel:
Copyright © 1992-2001 Michael Edwards

11

Citrus
Hespéridé

AGUA DE LOEWE   Loewe ♂
ARMAND BASI FEMME   Idesa
BASIL TONIC #7   Trish McEvoy
CITRUS PETALS #8   Trish McEvoy
DÉLIRIUM DE NUIT   Guépard
DOUBLE CLICK   Kesling ♂
DOUBLE FRAÎCHEUR POUR ELLE   Molinard
EAU DE DIOR COLORESSENCE ENERGISANTE
EAU DE DIOR COLORESSENCE RELAXANTE
   Christian Dior
EAU DE THÉ VERT   Roger & Gallet ♂
FIG TEA   Patricia de Nicolaï
GINGER ESSENCE   Origins
HIGH ... (Cerise)   Patrick Cox
I AM CLEAR   Danica Aromatics
INDEX GRAPEFRUIT MUSC   Fresh ♂
LAGERFELD FEMME   Lagerfeld
LAVENDER INSPIRATIONS: GINGER & LIME
   Yardley
LES FLORALIES GREEN TEA   Les Floralies
LES FLORALIES WHITE GINGER   Les Floralies
OBLIQUE PLAY   Givenchy
OYÉDO   Diptyque ♂
O•ZONE WOMAN   Sergio Tacchini
RECTOVERSO MANDARIN MUSC
   Ulric de Varens
SKINLIGHTS   Revlon
YSEULT   Pierre Cardin
DOUBLE FRAÎCHEUR POUR LUI   Molinard
FUNTASTIC BOY   Benetton
GRAND SLAM   My Very Own
INDIGO   Gant
MASCULIN EXTRÊME   Bourjois
O•ZONE MAN   Sergio Tacchini

Green
Vert

BODY POWER   Estée Lauder
CERRUTI IMAGE WOMAN   Cerruti

Water
Marine

I AM COOL   Danica Aromatics
LAUNDROMAT   Demeter Fragrance Library ♂
LAVENDER INSPIRATIONS: SEAWEED & ALOE
   Yardley
ALEGRIA HOMBRE   Adolfo Domínguez
BERNINI VODA   Bernini
GOAL   My Very Own
JEAN LUC AMSLER HOMME   Jean Luc Amsler
METAL JEANS MEN   Versace
ROOTS FOR HIM   Coty

Floral
Florale

2000 FLEURS   Creed
ADIDAS WOMAN ACTIVE   Adidas
ADIDAS WOMAN ENERGY   Adidas
ADIDAS WOMAN FITNESS   Adidas
À LA NUIT   Serge Lutens
AMERICAN ORIGINAL:
   STETSON FOR WOMEN   Coty
ANNAYAKÉ POUR ELLE   Annayaké
AURA FOR WOMEN   Jacomo
AUTOUR DU THÉ CLASSIQUE   Molinard
AUTOUR DU THÉ ROMANTIQUE   Molinard
BETTY BARCLAY WOMAN N° 3
   Mäurer & Wirtz
BOSS WOMAN   Hugo Boss
BUTTERFLY KISSES   My Very Own
CHALEUR D'ANIMALE   Parlux
CHAMPS-ÉLYSÉES TOO MUCH   Guerlain
CHIEMSEE WOMAN TWO   Chiemsee
CHRISTIAN BRETON POUR FEMME
   Christian Breton
COEUR DE RAISIN   Comptoir Sud Pacifique
DALIFLOR   Salvador Dali
DANIEL HECHTER SPORT POUR ELLE
   Daniel Hechter
DÉLIRIUM OCEANE   Guépard
DÉLIRIUM ROSE   Guépard
DÉLIRIUM TEA   Guépard
DONNA   Compagnia Delle Indie
DONNA NAUTILUS   Nautilus
DREAM ANGELS HALO   Victoria's Secret
DUO POUR ELLE   Vuarnet
EAU D'IVOIRE   Pierre Balmain
ESPÍRITU DE MONTESINOS   Dana
FAÇONNABLE   Façonnable
FLEUR   Floris
FLEUR   Lenthéric
FLORA NEROLIA   Guerlain
FUNTASTIC GIRL   Benetton
GARDENIA MUSK #4   Trish McEvoy
GUESS (New)   Guess
HEART   Herbalife
HERITAGE ROSE   Perfumers Guild
I AM LOVE   Danica Aromatics
INDEX JASMINE LYS   Fresh ♂
JEAN LUC AMSLER FEMME   Jean Luc Amsler
LAMBORGHINI POUR FEMME   Lamborghini
LAVENDER INSPIRATIONS: JUNIPER & ROSE
   Yardley
LILY CHIC* Ⓛ   Escada
L'INSTANT JASMIN   Maria Galland
LUCE   Creative Universe ♂
LUCKY YOU FOR WOMEN   Lucky Brand
MANDARIN & GINGER LILY #6   Trish McEvoy
MANIFESTO   Isabella Rossellini
MAT;   Masakï Matsushima
MÉTÉORITES   Guerlain
MEXX WOMAN   Mexx: Star
MICHAEL   Michael Kors
MICK MICHEYL   Mick Micheyl
MIRACLE   Lancôme
MONTANA BLU   Montana
NARCISSUS   Yardley
NAZARENO POUR FEMME
   Nazareno Gabrielli
OBLIQUE FAST FORWARD   Givenchy
OH! MY DOG   Dog Generation
PAUL SMITH WOMEN   Paul Smith
PERRY ELLIS PORTFOLIO   Perry Ellis

PRESCRIPTIVES POTION   Prescriptives
PRIORITÉ EAU BLEU   Dana
PURPLE FANTASY Ⓛ   Guerlain
RALPH   Ralph Lauren
RECTOVERSO SUN SEA   Ulric de Varens
RECTOVERSO SWEETY FRUITY
   Ulric de Varens
RÊVERIE PURE   Gloria Vanderbilt
ROSE D'ARGENT   Rosine
RYKIEL ROSE   Sonia Rykiel
S pour FEMME   Francesco Smalto
SA MAJESTÉ LA ROSE   Serge Lutens
SAMOURAÏ WOMAN   Alain Delon
SCENT OF ROMANCE UNFORGETTABLE
   Perfumers Guild
SECRET INTENTION Ⓛ   Guerlain
SENTIMENT   Escada
SHI   Alfred Sung
SO...? WILD   So Cosmetics
SUMMER   Gabriela Sabatini
SUNSHINE   My Very Own
TROPICAL PUNCH Ⓛ   Escada
TUBEROSE   Floris
URBAN ENERGY   Revlon
VARIATIONS   Carven
VERS LE JOUR   Worth
VERSACE ESSENCE ETHEREAL   Versace
VERSACE ESSENCE EXCITING   Versace
WATT YELLOW   Cofinluxe

Soft Floral
Fleuri Aldéhydé

AUTOUR DU THÉ EXOTIQUE   Molinard
BLUMARINE II   Blumarine
BULGARI BLU   Bulgari
CLOSE   Gap
DREAM ANGELS DIVINE   Victoria's Secret
I AM RICH   Danica Aromatics
LE FEU D'ISSEY LIGHT   Issey Miyake
LUMIÈRE (New)   Rochas
MILLENNIUM ROSE   Perfumers Guild
OXYGÈNE   Lanvin
REBEL WOMEN   Kraft International
SO PRETTY EAU FRUITÉE   Cartier
TOUJOURS L'AIMANT   Coty
VERS TOI   Worth
VERSACE ESSENCE EMOTIONAL   Versace

Floral Oriental
Fleuri Oriental

BIJAN WITH A TWIST   Bijan
BURBERRY TOUCH FOR WOMEN   Burberry
BYBLOS BREEZA / BREEZE   Byblos
CHINA ROSE   Floris
DREAM ANGELS HEAVENLY   Victoria's Secret
FLOWER BY KENZO   Kenzo
GHOST   Ghost

I AM POWER   Danica Aromatics
INTUITION   Estée Lauder
IRENA GREGORI   Succès de Paris
MAHORA   Guerlain
MCM ROUGE   MCM
METAL JEANS WOMEN   Versace
METALLICA Ⓛ   Guerlain
NAOMAGIC   Naomi Campbell
PERLE D'AUBUSSON   Aubusson
PREMIER JOUR   Nina Ricci
PURE MOMENT   Alfred Sung
PURE WISH   Chopard
ROUGE DE REVLON   Revlon
ROUGE HERMÈS   Hermès
SENSATIONS   Jil Sander
SIGNATURE POUR FEMME   S.T.Dupont
THAT'S AMORE! LEI   Gai Mattiolo
UN AIR D'HABANITA   Molinard
YES FOR WOMEN   Lomani

Soft Oriental
Oriental Doux

OLIVIER STRELLI   Olivier Strelli
TRÈS CHIC   Holzman & Stephanie

Oriental
Oriental

BELLE DE MINUIT   Nina Ricci
BYBLOS URAGANO / HURRICANE   Byblos
FORUM   Tufi Duek
INITIAL   Boucheron
JUST MUSK (New)   Lenthéric
MONTE CARLO   Pierre Cardin
SUI DREAMS   Anna Sui
VANILLE AMBRE   Molinard
YES FOR MEN   Lomani

Woody Oriental
Oriental Boisé

ARABIE   Serge Lutens ♂
AROMACALM   Lancôme
BASI FEMME   Idesa
BLACKBERRY & VANILLA MUSK #9
   Trish McEvoy
COUTURE POUR ELLE   Philippe Venet
DANS LA NUIT   Worth
DESNUDA   Ungaro
DOUCE AMÈRE   Serge Lutens ♂
EAU DE PIVER   L.T.Piver
ECLIX   La Perla
ELLEN TRACY   Ellen Tracy
EXTASE PURE PASSION WOMAN   Muelhens
FLUID ICEBERG WOMAN   Iceberg
HELMUT LANG WOMAN   Helmut Lang

HOT COUTURE   Givenchy
JEAN LUC AMSLER PRIVÉ FEMME
   Jean Luc Amsler
L'OR DES BOURBON   Marina de Bourbon
MASQUERADE   Bob Mackie
MAUBOUSSIN   Mauboussin
MORGANE LE FAY BLUE   Morgane Le Fay
NIKE WOMAN   Nike
OBLIQUE REWIND   Givenchy
RECTOVERSO LOLLIPOP TOFFEE
   Ulric de Varens
SAMBA HEAT WOMAN
   Perfumer's Workshop
SIROCCO DONNA   Dana
TEA FOR TWO   L'Artisan Parfumeur
TRUTH CALVIN KLEIN   Calvin Klein
WATT RED   Cofinluxe
WINTER DELICE Ⓛ   Guerlain
ARMAND BASI HOMME   Idesa
BODY KOUROS   Yves Saint Laurent
BRUNO BANANI   Bruno Banani
CHIEMSEE MAN TWO   Chiemsee
COUTURE POUR LUI   Philippe Venet
CRISTOBAL POUR HOMME   Balenciaga
DAKS   Daks
DESIRE   Alfred Dunhill
DUÉ WILD   Lomani
EXTASE PURE PASSION MAN   Muelhens
GMV HOT   Gian Marco Venturi
LALIQUE POUR HOMME BLEU   Lalique
LAMBROSIO   Lomani
LOLITA LEMPICKA AU MASCULIN
   Lolita Lempicka
MAN.AUBUSSON   Aubusson
MUST DE CARTIER POUR HOMME   Cartier
S pour HOMME   Francesco Smalto
SAMBA HEAT MAN   Perfumer's Workshop
SIGNATURE POUR HOMME   S.T.Dupont
SIROCCO UOMO   Dana
THAT'S AMORE! LUI   Gai Mattiolo
TOUCH GRIGIOPERLA   La Perla
V/S MAN   Versace
VANDERBILT FOR MEN   Gloria Vanderbilt
WATT FOR MEN GREEN   Cofinluxe

Mossy Woods
Chypre Boisé

ACQUA DI PARMA PROFUMO
   Acqua di Parma
AGENT PROVOCATEUR   Agent Provocateur
ANGEL SCHLESSER FEMME   Idesa
APERÇU   Houbigant: Claire
AQUA DI AQUA   Marina de Bourbon
BAÏMÉ   Maître Parfumeur et Gantier ♂
BOHÈME   Napa Valley
CAFÉ-CAFÉ ADVENTURE POUR FEMME
   Cofinluxe
FLEUR DE CAROTTE Ⓛ   L'Artisan Parfumeur
LADY CARON   Caron
LIBERTINE   Vivienne Westwood
OPÔNÉ   Diptyque ♂
RIZIÈRES   Comptoir Sud Pacifique ♂
VERSACE WOMAN   Versace
ZEN (New)   Shiseido
AURA FOR MEN   Jacomo
BASI HOMME   Idesa
BURBERRY TOUCH FOR MEN   Burberry
CHAUMET HOMME   Chaumet
DUO POUR HOMME   Vuarnet
GENTLEMAN GUÉPARD   Guépard
GUCCI RUSH FOR MEN   Gucci

LUCKY YOU FOR MEN   Lucky Brand
PURE VÉTIVER   Azzaro
THEOREMA UOMO   Fendi
UN AIR DE JAVA   Decléor
UOMO   Compagnia Delle Indie
VETIVER   Floris

Dry Woods
Boisé Cuir

AIR DE ... CABOCHARD   Grès
BONFIRE   Demeter ♂
ODEUR 71   Comme de Garçons ♂
PASSION DE FEMME   Rodier
AIGNER POUR HOMME   Etienne Aigner
EAU DU FIER   Annick Goutal
FLUID ICEBERG MAN   Iceberg
JEAN LUC AMSLER PRIVÉ HOMME
   Jean Luc Amsler
MONTECRISTO   Perfumes y Diseño
PONTACCIO 21   Gianfranco Ferré
TOUCHDOWN   Mäurer & Wirtz
TRISTAN   Pierre Cardin

Aromatic
Fougère

ADIDAS MOVES FOR HER   Adidas
LAVENDER SPICE #10   Trish McEvoy
ADIDAS TEAM   Adidas
ALAIN DELON POUR HOMME   Alain Delon
AMAZING FOR MEN   Bill Blass
ANNAYAKÉ POUR LUI   Annayaké
ARROGANCE POUR HOMME   Arrogance
ASPEN DISCOVERY   Aspen
BLACK LABEL   Lenthéric
BLUE SILVER MEN   MCM
BOGNER SNOW   Bogner
CAFÉ-CAFÉ ADVENTURE POUR HOMME
   Cofinluxe
CHALEUR D'ANIMALE POUR HOMME   Parlux
CLARTÉ FOR MEN   E.Coudray
DKNY MEN   Donna Karan
DUÉ CLASSIC   Lomani
ENDURANCE   Ted Baker
FERRARI YELLOW EAU DE TOILETTE   Ferrari
HELMUT LANG MAN   Helmut Lang
HIGH ... (Turquoise)   Patrick Cox
L'ANARCHISTE   Caron
LATITUDE LONGTITUDE   Nautica
LE BLEU   Les Copains
L'ORIGINAL   Decléor
MEXX MAN   Mexx: Star
NAZARENO POUR HOMME
   Nazareno Gabrielli
REBEL MEN   Kraft International
SO MAX   So Cosmetics
SOUL   Herbalife
SWISH   My Very Own
PAUL SMITH MEN   Paul Smith
TABAC MAN   Mäurer & Wirtz
TOUCH DOWN   My Very Own
U de V FUN   Ulric de Varens
VERINO POUR HOMME   Roberto Verino

Citrus

From the zest of lemons, mandarins, bergamot, oranges and grapefruit come the citrus oils that lend these fragrances their distinctive, tangy aroma. Floral, spicy and woody notes transformed the light, refreshing eaux de cologne into real fragrances. A new generation of musk and tea accents adds an interesting dimension to the oldest fragrance family.

Tonique et fruitée, la famille des hespéridés emprunte aux écorces d'agrumes une vigueur pétillante. Ces fraîches senteurs de citron, mandarine, bergamote, orange ou pamplemousse sont à l'origine de nos plus anciens « parfums » : les eaux de Cologne. Associées aux notes florales, épicées et boisées, ces eaux légères prennent corps et deviennent plus tenaces. Elles se sont en outre enrichies, dernièrement, de tout nouveaux accents de musc et de thé.

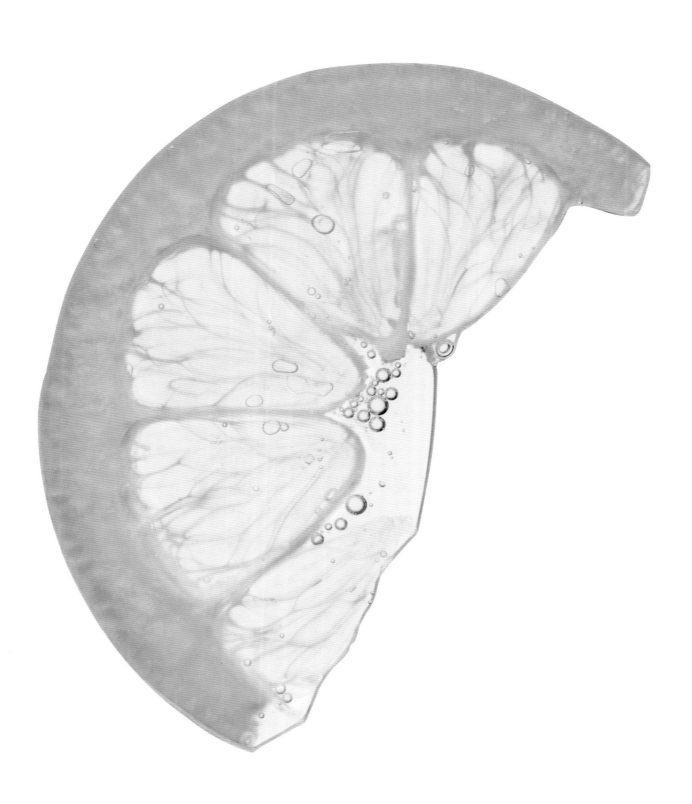

Fresh / Frais ●

AGUA DE LOEWE   Loewe 2000 ♂
ARMAND BASI FEMME   Idesa 2000
AROMATONIC   Lancôme 1999
BASIL TONIC #7   Trish McEvoy 2000
BULGARI EAU PARFUMÉE   Bulgari 1993 ♂
BULLES DE FRAÎCHEUR   Molinard 1999
CANNELLE ORANGE   L'Occitane 1996/99 ♂
CHANSON DE VIE   Coty 1999
CITRON VERT*   Molinard 1993 ♂
cK ONE   Calvin Klein 1994 ♂
CROWN ESS BOUQUET   Crown 1872
DALIMIX   Salvador Dali 1996 ♂
DOUBLE CLICK   Kesling 2000 ♂
EARL GREY TEA   Demeter Fragrance Library 1996 ♂
EAU BELLE   Azzaro 1995
EAU DE DIOR COLORESSENCE ENERGISANTE   Christian Dior 2000
EAU DE THÉ VERT   Roger & Gallet 2000 ♂
EAU DE VARENS N° 2   Ulric de Varens 1997 ♂
EAU D'ORLANE   Orlane 1992
ESCADA SPORT SPIRIT   Escada 1996 ♂
EX'CLA.MA'TION EAU   Coty 1996
EXTASE BODY TALK   Muelhens 1996 ♂
FEUILLE DE VERVEINE   L'Occitane 1999 ♂
FIRE & ICE COOL   Revlon 1996
FRENCH CONNECTION   French Connection 1997
FUJIYAMA   Succès de Paris 1995 ♂
GIEFFEFFE   Gianfranco Ferré 1995 ♂
GOLD JEANS FEMME   Roccobarocco 1997
GOURMANDISE DE RODIER   Rodier 1999
GREEN TEA   Elizabeth Arden 1999
I AM ENERGY   Danica Aromatics 1999
ICEBERG TWICE ICE   Iceberg 1998
IMPOSIBLE (sic)   Dana 1950/99 ♂
INDEX BERGAMOT CITRUS   Fresh 1996 ♂
INDEX POMEGRANATE ANISE   Fresh 1997 ♂
L'EAU DE KOOKAÏ   Kookaï 1996
LES FLORALIES WHITE GINGER   Les Floralies 2000
NETWORK   Lomani 1996 ♂
O₂XYGEN WOMAN   California North 1996
PACO   Paco Rabanne 1996 ♂
QUERCUS   Penhaligon's 1996 ♂
REYNALD KATZ   Reynald Katz 1998 ♂
ROUTE DU THÉ   Barneys New York 1986 ♂
SANGUINE MUSKISSIME   Maître Parfumeur et Gantier 1988 ♂
SKINLIGHTS   Revlon 2001
SOLO SOPRANI   Luciano Soprani 1995 ♂
SUMMER SPLASH   Lilian Barony 1998
TÉ   Creative Universe 1996 ♂
THÉ POUR UN ÉTÉ   L'Artisan Parfumeur 1996 ♂
VERY M.C.   MCM 1996 ♂
WEIL EAU DE FRAÎCHEUR   Weil 1961/93 ♂
X LIMITED   Etienne Aigner 1997 ♂

♂ Shared *mixte*

Crisp / Pétillant ●●

CARRIÈRE   Gendarme 1996
CÉDRAT POMELO   L'Occitane 1999 ♂
CEYLON   Isabell 1996
CRISTALLE   Chanel 1974
DIORELLA   Christian Dior 1972
EAU D'ÉTÉ   Patricia de Nicolaï 1997
EAU DE VARENS N° 3   Ulric de Varens 1997 ♂
EAU DU SUD   Annick Goutal 1995 ♂
EAU FRAÎCHE   Molinard 1992 ♂
EAU VITAMINÉE   Biotherm 1997
EAU VIVE   Carven 1966/95
ESPRIT DU ROI   Penhaligon's 1989 ♂
ESTIVALIA   Antonio Puig 1975
ÉTIQUETTE BLEUE   d'Orsay 1908 ♂
FRAÎCHE PASSIFLORE   Maître Parfumeur et Gantier 1988
GOLDEN DELICIOUS   Demeter Fragrance Library 1999 ♂
GRAPEFRUIT   Jo Malone 1992 ♂
HIGH... (Cerise)   Patrick Cox 2000
I AM CLEAR   Danica Aromatics 2000
INDEX HONEYSUCKLE GRAPEFRUIT   Fresh 1999 ♂
INDEX MOROCCAN MINT TEA   Fresh 1997 ♂
KUMQUAT   Comptoir Sud Pacifique 1998 ♂
LAVENDER INSPIRATIONS: GINGER & LIME   Yardley 2000
L'EAU BY LAURA   Laura Ashley 1995
LOVIN' GIRL   Un Monde Nouveau 1995/98
MANDARINE   Comptoir Sud Pacifique 1976 ♂
NATURE SYSTEM   Roger & Gallet 1992 ♂
NOI MISSONI   Missoni 1993
PACO ENERGY   Paco Rabanne 1998 ♂
PAMPLEMOUSSE   Comptoir Sud Pacifique 1985 ♂
PARFUM ALLIÉ SPLASH 24   Shu Uemura 1988/99
PRIORITÉ   Dana 1949/98
RECTOVERSO MANDARIN MUSK   Ulric de Varens 2000
SCAPA   Scapa of Scotland 1991
SOUTHERN EXPOSURE   Terry Ellis 1997
SUGAR   Fresh 1999 ♂
THÉ VERT   L'Occitane 1999 ♂
VOCALISE   Maître Parfumeur et Gantier 1988

* Discontinued *non disponible*

Classical / Classique ●●●

4711 ORIGINAL   Muelhens 1792 ♂
ACQUA CLASSICA DI BORSARI   Borsari 1880 ♂
ACQUA DI PARMA COLONIA   Acqua di Parma 1916 ♂
ATKINSON GOLD MEDAL   Atkinson 1799 ♂
BOIS DE CÉDRAT   Creed 1875 ♂
CHANSON D'EAU   Coty 1995
CITRUS BIGARRADE   Creed 1901 ♂
CLASSIC   Banana Republic 1995 ♂
CLÉMENTINE   Molinard 1993
CLUB COLOGNE   Perfumers Guild 1981 ♂
COLOGNE SOLOGNE   Patricia de Nicolaï 1989 ♂
CROWN ESTERHAZY   Crown 1874
EAU DE COLOGNE   Penhaligon's 1927 ♂
EAU DE FLEURS DE CÉDRAT   Guerlain 1920 ♂
EAU DE GUERLAIN   Guerlain 1974 ♂
EAU DE LANCASTER   Lancaster 1977
EAU DE MÛRE   Maître Parfumeur et Gantier 1988
EAU DE PATOU   Jean Patou 1976
EAU DE ROCHAS   Rochas 1970
EAU D'HADRIEN   Annick Goutal 1981 ♂
EAU DU COQ   Guerlain 1894 ♂
EAU DU GANTIER   Maître Parfumeur et Gantier 1988 ♂
EAU DYNAMISANTE   Clarins 1987 ♂
EAU FRAÎCHE   Caron 1997 ♂
EAU FRAÎCHE   Christian Tortu 1997
EAU FRAÎCHE   Léonard 1974
EAU FRANCE   Molinard 1949 ♂
EAU IMPÉRIALE   Guerlain 1853 ♂
ENGLISH FINE COLOGNE   Yardley 1984 ♂
GIN & TONIC   Demeter Fragrance Library 1997 ♂
GIVRINE (SICILE)   E.Coudray 1950 ♂
JEAN-MARIE FARINA   Roger & Gallet 1806 ♂
L'EAU DE L'ARTISAN   L'Artisan Parfumeur 1993 ♂
Ô de LANCÔME   Lancôme 1969
PENHALIGON'S CASTILE   Penhaligon's 1999 ♂
PETIT GUERLAIN   Guerlain 1994 ♂
ROGER & GALLET EXTRA-VIEILLE   Roger & Gallet 1991 ♂
SPECIAL N° 127   Floris 1910 ♂
VERBENAS OF PROVENCE   Jo Malone 1995 ♂
VERVEINE   Le Jardin Retrouvé 1978 ♂

Rich / Profond ●●●●

ALPONA   Caron 1939
BOUQUET IMPÉRIAL   Roger & Gallet 1991 ♂
BYBLOS GHIACCIA   Byblos 1998
CITRUS PETALS #8   Trish McEvoy 2000
COLD   Benetton 1997 ♂
DAY   Gap 1994 ♂
DÉLIRIUM DE NUIT   Guépard 2000
DOUBLE FRAÎCHEUR POUR ELLE   Molinard 2000
EAU DE CARON FORTE   Caron 1999 ♂
EAU DE COURRÈGES   Courrèges 1977
EAU DE DIOR COLORESSENCE RELAXANTE   Christian Dior 2000
EAU DE VARENS N° 4   Ulric de Varens 1998 ♂
EAU DE VERVEINE   Penhaligon's 1949 ♂
EAU D'ORANGE VERTE   Hermès 1979 ♂
EXTRACT OF LIMES   Penhaligon's 1963 ♂
FIG TEA   Patricia de Nicolaï 2000
FRAÎCHEUR MUSKISSIME   Maître Parfumeur et Gantier 1988 ♂
FRUITS SAUVAGES   Comptoir Sud Pacifique 1987
GINGERALE   Demeter Fragrance Library 1997 ♂
GINGER ESSENCE   Origins 2000
GRAPEFRUIT & YELLOW FREESIA #1   Trish McEvoy 1998
INDEX GRAPEFRUIT MUSC   Fresh 2000 ♂
INDEX SANDALWOOD PETITGRAIN   Fresh 1997 ♂
INTENSE DE SCAPA   Scapa of Scotland 1999
LAGERFELD FEMME   Lagerfeld 2000
LES FLORALIES GREEN TEA   Les Floralies 2000
LIME, BASIL & MANDARIN   Jo Malone 1991 ♂
LIMES   Floris 1832 ♂
MIEL ORANGE   E.Coudray 1995
MÛRE / BLACKBERRY   Molinard 1993
MÛRE ET MUSC   L'Artisan Parfumeur 1978
MÛRE ET MUSC EXTRÊME   L'Artisan Parfumeur 1993
OBLIQUE PLAY   Givenchy 2000
ORANGE CAFÉ   Molinard 1999
OYÉDO   Diptyque 2000 ♂
O•ZONE WOMAN   Sergio Tacchini 2000
PAMPLELUNE   Guerlain 1999 ♂
PATCHOULI   L'Artisan Parfumeur 1979 ♂
TURQUOISE   Morabito 1992
TWENTY ONE   Perfumers Guild 1990 ♂
YSEULT   Pierre Cardin 2000
ZESTE MANDARINE PAMPLEMOUSSE   Creed 1975 ♂
ZIGZAG   Dana 1949/99

Ⓛ Limited edition *édition limitée*

1947 Launch *lancement*   1947 / 92 Reorchestration *recréation*

Citrus

feminine

17

Hespéridé

masculin

Fresh / Frais ●

AGUA DE LOEWE   Loewe 2000 ♂
AQUA-FITNESS   Biotherm 1999
BULGARI EAU PARFUMÉE   Bulgari 1993 ♂
CANNELLE ORANGE   L'Occitane 1996/99 ♂
CITRON VERT*   Molinard 1993 ♂
cK ONE   Calvin Klein 1994 ♂
CLAIBORNE FOR MEN*   Liz Claiborne 1989
DALIMIX   Salvador Dali 1996 ♂
DOUBLE CLICK   Kesling 2000 ♂
EARL GREY TEA   Demeter Fragrance Library 1996 ♂
EAU DE THÉ VERT   Roger & Gallet 2000 ♂
EAU DE VARENS N° 2   Ulric de Varens 1997 ♂
EAU POUR LE JEUNE HOMME   Maître Parfumeur et Gantier 1990
ESCADA SPORT SPIRIT   Escada 1996 ♂
EXTASE BODY TALK   Muelhens 1996 ♂
FEUILLE DE VERVEINE   L'Occitane 1999 ♂
FUJIYAMA   Succès de Paris 1995 ♂
FUNTASTIC BOY   Benetton 2000
GAI MATTIOLO UOMO   Gai Mattiolo 1998
GIEFFEFFE   Gianfranco Ferré 1995 ♂
GRAND SLAM   My Very Own 2000
HAPPY FOR MEN   Clinique 1999
HERBISSIMO TÉ VERDE   Dana 1996
HILFIGER ATHLETICS   Tommy Hilfiger 1998
IMPOSIBLE (sic)   Dana 1950/99 ♂
INDEX BERGAMOT CITRUS   Fresh 1996 ♂
INDEX POMEGRANATE ANISE   Fresh 1997 ♂
NETWORK   Lomani 1996 ♂
NOI UOMINI   Missoni 1997
O₂XYGEN   California North 1994
PACO   Paco Rabanne 1996 ♂
QUERCUS   Penhaligon's 1996 ♂
REYNALD KATZ   Reynald Katz 1998 ♂
ROUTE DU THÉ   Barneys New York 1986 ♂
SANGUINE MUSKISSIME   Maître Parfumeur et Gantier 1988 ♂
SOLO SOPRANI   Luciano Soprani 1995 ♂
TÉ   Creative Universe 1996 ♂
THÉ POUR UN ÉTÉ   L'Artisan Parfumeur 1996 ♂
VERY M.C.   MCM 1996 ♂
WEIL EAU DE FRAÎCHEUR   Weil 1961/93 ♂
X LIMITED   Etienne Aigner 1997 ♂

♂ Shared mixte

Crisp / Pétillant ●●

ADIDAS SPORT   Adidas 1994
BOOSTER   Lacoste 1996
CAPUCCI POUR HOMME   Roberto Capucci 1968
CÉDRAT POMELO   L'Occitane 1999 ♂
CERRUTI 1881 POUR HOMME   Cerruti 1990
CHROME   Azzaro 1996
EAU DE VARENS N° 3   Ulric de Varens 1997 ♂
EAU DU BADIAN   L'Occitane 1999
EAU DU SUD   Annick Goutal 1995 ♂
EAU FRAÎCHE   Molinard 1992 ♂
ESPRIT DU ROI   Penhaligon's 1989 ♂
ÉTIQUETTE BLEUE   d'Orsay 1908 ♂
GOLDEN DELICIOUS   Demeter Fragrance Library 1999 ♂
GRAPEFRUIT   Jo Malone 1992 ♂
GREEN WATER   Jacques Fath 1947/67/93
INDEX HONEYSUCKLE GRAPEFRUIT   Fresh 1999 ♂
INDEX MOROCCAN MINT TEA   Fresh 1997 ♂
KUMQUAT   Comptoir Sud Pacifique 1998 ♂
L'EAU PAR KENZO POUR HOMME   Kenzo 1999
M   Banana Republic 1995
MANDARINE   Comptoir Sud Pacifique 1976 ♂
MASCULIN EVASION   Bourjois 1996
NATURE SYSTEM   Roger & Gallet 1992 ♂
NEIGES POUR HOMME   Lise Watier 1997
PACO ENERGY   Paco Rabanne 1998 ♂
PAMPLEMOUSSE   Comptoir Sud Pacifique 1985 ♂
POUR L'HOMME   Roger & Gallet 1993
QUARTZ POUR HOMME   Molyneux 1996
SÉLECTION VERTE   Creed 1970
SILVER LIGHT   Escada 1997
SPORT DE PACO RABANNE   Paco Rabanne 1986
SUGAR   Fresh 1999 ♂
THÉ VERT   L'Occitane 1999 ♂
ZIPPED   Perfumer's Workshop 1998

* Discontinued non disponible

18

Classical / Classique ●●●

4711 ORIGINAL Muelhens 1792 ♂
ACQUA CLASSICA DI BORSARI Borsari 1880 ♂
ACQUA DI PARMA COLONIA Acqua di Parma 1916 ♂
ATKINSON GOLD MEDAL Atkinson 1799 ♂
BABY BLUE JEANS Versace 1995
BLENHEIM BOUQUET Penhaligon's 1902
BOIS DE CÉDRAT Creed 1875 ♂
CITRUS BIGARRADE Creed 1901 ♂
CLASSIC Banana Republic 1995 ♂
CLUB COLOGNE Perfumers Guild 1981 ♂
COLOGNE SOLOGNE Patricia de Nicolaï 1989 ♂
EAU DE COLOGNE Penhaligon's 1927 ♂
EAU DE FLEURS DE CÉDRAT Guerlain 1920 ♂
EAU DE GUERLAIN Guerlain 1974 ♂
EAU DE QUININE Crown 1890
EAU DES PRINCES L.T.Piver 1850
EAU DES TROPIQUES Comptoir Sud Pacifique 1988
EAU D'HADRIEN Annick Goutal 1981 ♂
EAU DU COQ Guerlain 1894 ♂
EAU DU GANTIER Maître Parfumeur et Gantier 1988 ♂
EAU DYNAMISANTE Clarins 1987 ♂
EAU FRAÎCHE Caron 1997 ♂
EAU FRANCE Molinard 1949 ♂
EAU IMPÉRIALE Guerlain 1853 ♂
EAU SAUVAGE Christian Dior 1966
ENGLISH FINE COLOGNE Yardley 1984 ♂
FERRARI YELLOW COLOGNE WATER Ferrari 1998
GIN & TONIC Demeter Fragrance Library 1997 ♂
GIVRINE (SICILE) E.Coudray 1950 ♂
HERBISSIMO CEDRO Dana 1978
HUNGARY WATER* Crabtree & Evelyn 1975
INDIGO Gant 2001
JEAN-MARIE FARINA Roger & Gallet 1806 ♂
L'EAU DE L'ARTISAN L'Artisan Parfumeur 1993 ♂
LE PETIT PRINCE Antoine de Saint-Exupéry 1998
MESSIRE Jean d'Albret 1961/96
MONSIEUR DE GIVENCHY Givenchy 1959
PENHALIGON'S CASTILE Penhaligon's 1999 ♂
PETIT GUERLAIN Guerlain 1994 ♂
ROGER & GALLET EXTRA-VIEILLE Roger & Gallet 1991 ♂
SIGNORICCI Nina Ricci 1975
SPECIAL N° 127 Floris 1910 ♂
VERBENAS OF PROVENCE Jo Malone 1995 ♂
VERVEINE Le Jardin Retrouvé 1978 ♂
VERVEINE Molinard 1949
VORAGO ACTION California Fragrances 1992

Rich / Profond ●●●●

ACTION SPORT Trussardi 1993
ARMANI POUR HOMME Giorgio Armani 1984
BOUCHERON POUR HOMME Boucheron 1991
BOUQUET IMPÉRIAL Roger & Gallet 1991 ♂
CAMP BEVERLY HILLS FOR MEN* CBH 1988
CHEVALIER D'ORSAY d'Orsay 1914
COLD Benetton 1997 ♂
CROWN IMPERIAL Crown 1905
CROWN SPICED LIMES Crown 1921
D&G MASCULINE Dolce & Gabbana 1999
DAY Gap 1994 ♂
DOUBLE FRAÎCHEUR POUR LUI Molinard 2000
EAU DE CARON FORTE Caron 1999 ♂
EAU DE COLOGNE EXTRA FINE L'Occitane 1990
EAU DE ROCHAS HOMME Rochas 1993
EAU DE VARENS N° 4 Ulric de Varens 1998 ♂
EAU DE VERVEINE Penhaligon's 1949 ♂
EAU D'ORANGE VERTE Hermès 1979 ♂
EAU POUR HOMME L.T.Piver 1995
EAU SAUVAGE EXTRÊME Christian Dior 1984
ELITE Floris 1980
EXTRACT OF LIMES Penhaligon's 1963 ♂
FRAÎCHEUR MUSKISSIME Maître Parfumeur et Gantier 1988 ♂
GENDARME Gendarme 1991
GINGERALE Demeter Fragrance Library 1997 ♂
ICEBERG HOMME Iceberg 1991
INDEX GRAPEFRUIT MUSC Fresh 2000 ♂
INDEX SANDALWOOD PETITGRAIN Fresh 1997 ♂
LIME, BASIL & MANDARIN Jo Malone 1991 ♂
LIMES Floris 1832 ♂
LORDS Penhaligon's 1911
MASCULIN EXTRÊME Bourjois 2000
MISSONI SPORT Missoni 1990
MONSIEUR BALMAIN Pierre Balmain 1964/90
NAVEGAR L'Artisan Parfumeur 1998
NÉROLI SAUVAGE Creed 1994
OYÉDO Diptyque 2000 ♂
O•ZONE MAN Sergio Tacchini 2000
PAMPLELUNE Guerlain 1999 ♂
PATCHOULI L'Artisan Parfumeur 1979 ♂
PINO SILVESTRE EXTREME Pino Silvestre: Mavive 1998
SAMBA FOR MEN Perfumer's Workshop 1990
SANTOS EAU DE SPORT Cartier 1989
SUMARE Crown 1925
TED BAKER SKINWEAR Ted Baker 1998
THAT MAN Revlon 1958/89
TROPHÉE LANCÔME* Lancôme 1982
TWENTY ONE Perfumers Guild 1990 ♂
YSL POUR HOMME Yves Saint Laurent 1971
ZESTE MANDARINE PAMPLEMOUSSE Creed 1975 ♂

Citrus

Green

Vert

Green fragrances capture the sharp scent of fresh-cut grass and violet leaves. Despite the outdoors imagery, the impact of the classic resinous galbanum accord is so potent that many green fragrances have a formal rather than sporty personality. In recent years, a palette of softer, lighter green notes has given this fragrance family fresh appeal.

Fusants et vifs, les parfums « verts » suggèrent l'herbe fraîchement coupée et la feuille de violette. Mais bien qu'évoquant le plein air, ces fragrances - marquées de l'empreinte puissante du galbanum - ont un style très élégant et très « couture ». Depuis quelques années, avec l'introduction de notes vertes plus douces et légères, ces parfums connaissent un rafraîchissant renouveau.

Vert

Fresh / Frais ●

ANNABELLA   Annabella 1997
CHÈVREFEUILLE ORIGINAL Creed 1982 ♂
DALIMIX GOLD   Salvador Dali 1997 ♂
FEUILLE D'HERBE FRAÎCHE & HERBACÉE   L'Occitane 1999
GREENHOUSE   Demeter Fragrance Library 1997 ♂
JASMINE & ROSE HONEY #2   Trish McEvoy 1998
MENTHE FROISSÉE   L'Occitane 1999
RICHARDSON BAY   California North 1991 ♂
SONOMA VALLEY   Crabtree & Evelyn 1999
SUNG SPA   Alfred Sung 1992

Crisp / Pétillant ●●

ACTION*   Trussardi 1989
CERRUTI IMAGE WOMAN   Cerruti 2000
GRAIN DE FOLIE   Grès 1999
HERBA FRESCA   Guerlain 1999 ♂
INDEX CHINA GREEN TEA   Fresh 1997 ♂
INDISCRET   Lucien Lelong 1935/97
JONES NEW YORK   Jones New York 1996
LETTUCE   Demeter Fragrance Library 1998 ♂
PARFUM ALLIÉ BEATS 14   Shu Uemura 1988/99
TOMATO   Demeter Fragrance Library 1996 ♂
VIRGILIO   Diptyque 1990 ♂

CHÈVREFEUILLE ORIGINAL Creed 1982 ♂
DALIMIX GOLD   Salvador Dali 1997 ♂
GREENHOUSE   Demeter Fragrance Library 1997 ♂
RICHARDSON BAY   California North 1991 ♂
TIFFANY FOR MEN SPORT   Tiffany 1998

HERBA FRESCA   Guerlain 1999 ♂
INDEX CHINA GREEN TEA   Fresh 1997 ♂
LETTUCE   Demeter Fragrance Library 1998 ♂
Ô pour HOMME   Lancôme 1996
TOMATO   Demeter Fragrance Library 1996 ♂
VIRGILIO   Diptyque 1990 ♂

Classical / Classique ●●●

AIRE LOEWE   Loewe 1985
ALIAGE / ALLIAGE   Estée Lauder 1972
BODY POWER   Estée Lauder 2000
DI BORGHESE*   Borghese 1978
EAU DE CAMPAGNE   Sisley 1974 ♂
GRASS   Demeter Fragrance Library 1996 ♂
GRASS   Gap 1994 ♂
I AM SERENE   Danica Aromatics 1999
INOUÏ   Shiseido 1976
VACANCES   Jean Patou 1936
VENT VERT   Pierre Balmain 1947/90
WEIL DE WEIL   Weil 1971

Rich / Profond ●●●●

CAMÉLIA CHINOIS   Maître Parfumeur et Gantier 1997
JEAN-LOUIS SCHERRER   Jean-Louis Scherrer 1979
PHÉROMONE   Marilyn Miglin 1978
PRIVATE COLLECTION   Estée Lauder 1973
SABI   Henry Dunay 1998
SILENCES   Jacomo 1978
WITH PLEASURE   Caron 1949

EAU DE CAMPAGNE   Sisley 1974 ♂
GRASS   Demeter Fragrance Library 1996 ♂
GRASS   Gap 1994 ♂
GREEN IRISH TWEED   Creed 1985
HALSTON 1-12   Halston 1976
HERBISSIMO ENEBRO   Dana 1978

DEVIN   Aramis 1978
MILA SCHÖN UOMO   Mila Schön 1986
NINO CERRUTI   Cerruti 1979
TACTICS   Shiseido 1979

Water

Redolent of the scent of soft sea breezes,
the marine notes were created in 1990.
The early water notes captured the ozonic
aroma of wet air after a thunderstorm.
Today, the water notes are more often used
as an accent to enliven florals, orientals
and woody fragrances.

*Les notes marines, embuées d'iode et de
brise océane, sont apparues en 1990.
À l'origine, elles évoquaient cette fraîche
senteur d'ozone que l'on respire les soirs
d'orage. Aujourd'hui, ces parfums d'eau
sont le plus souvent destinés à vivifier les
compositions florales, orientales ou boisées.*

▶

Fresh / Frais ●

AQUAFLORE   Carolina Herrera 1996
CHARLIE WHITE   Revlon 1994
CYBERSP@CE   Mäurer & Wirtz 1997 ♂
DUENDE   J. del Pozo 1992
EAU DE MER   Lise Watier 1999
EAU PURE   Caron 1996 ♂
GHOST MYST   Coty 1995
INIS   Fragrances of Ireland 1998 ♂
MOTU   Comptoir Sud Pacifique 1992
MUST DE CARTIER II   Cartier 1993
ROOTS UNISCENT   Coty 1996 ♂
WRAPPINGS   Clinique 1990

▶

Crisp / Pétillant ●●

CARITA   Carita 1996
FLEUR DE LOTUS   L'Occitane 1996/99
FUN WATER WOMAN   De Ruy 1998
I AM COOL   Danica Aromatics 2000
INDEX CURRANT MARINE   Fresh 1996 ♂
LAUNDROMAT   Demeter Fragrance Library 2000 ♂
LAVENDER INSPIRATIONS: SEAWEED & ALOE   Yardley 2000
L'EAU D'ISSEY   Issey Miyake 1992
L'EAU LILIAN   Lilian Barony 1995
MARE   Creative Universe 1999 ♂
MONSOON EAU   Monsoon 1997
ODEUR 53   Comme des Garçons 1998 ♂
POLO SPORT WOMAN   Ralph Lauren 1996
SAMBA NATURAL   Perfumer's Workshop 1996
SANS ADIEU   Worth 1925/95
SERGIO TACCHINI DONNA   Sergio Tacchini 1998
WILD WIND   Gabriela Sabatini 1999

CYBERSP@CE   Mäurer & Wirtz 1997 ♂
EAU PURE   Caron 1996 ♂
EROLFA   Creed 1992
INIS   Fragrances of Ireland 1998 ♂
KENZO POUR HOMME   Kenzo 1991
METAL JEANS MEN   Versace 2000
NAUTICA   Nautica 1992
ROOTS UNISCENT   Coty 1996 ♂

ACQUA DI GIÒ POUR HOMME   Giorgio Armani 1996
ALEGRIA HOMBRE   Adolfo Dominguez 2000
BERNINI VODA   Bernini 2000
GOAL   My Very Own 2000
INDEX CURRANT MARINE   Fresh 1996 ♂
LAUNDROMAT   Demeter Fragrance Library 2000 ♂
L'EAU SPORT MEN   Lilian Barony 1999
MARE   Creative Universe 1999 ♂
ODEUR 53   Comme des Garçons 1998 ♂
ROOTS FOR HIM   Coty 2001
SILVER MOUNTAIN WATER   Creed 1995

Classical / Classique ●●●

ASPEN FOR WOMEN   Coty 1990
BEST OF CHEVIGNON   Chevignon 1996 ♂
NEW WEST FOR HER*   Aramis 1990
PROFUMO DI MONTECATINI   Borghese 1993 ♂
SUNFLOWERS   Elizabeth Arden 1993

Rich / Profond ●●●●

ESCAPE   Calvin Klein 1991
HOLY WATER   Demeter Fragrance Library 1999 ♂
MILLÉSIME IMPÉRIAL   Creed 1995 ♂
VANILLE MARINE   Molinard 1998

BEST OF CHEVIGNON   Chevignon 1996 ♂
JEAN LUC AMSLER HOMME   Jean Luc Amsler 2000
LATITUDE SPORT   Olivier de Kersauson 1997
L'EAU D'ISSEY POUR HOMME   Issey Miyake 1994
MOLINARD HOMME III   Molinard 1996
PROFUMO DI MONTECATINI   Borghese 1993 ♂

HOLY WATER   Demeter Fragrance Library 1999 ♂
MILLÉSIME IMPÉRIAL   Creed 1995 ♂
NAUTILUS AQUA   Nautilus 1998
NEW WEST FOR HIM*   Aramis 1988

Floral

Florals remain the most popular fragrance family. Their repertoire is vast, ranging from concertos on the theme of a single floral note to mighty symphonies of heady mixed bouquets. Headspace technology has given perfumers an avalanche of exciting new floral notes: it allows them to identify and clone the scent of blooms from which no oil can be extracted by traditional methods. Each year, unusual new notes are found, revitalising the traditional floral theme.

Les parfums floraux restent les plus appréciés. Suaves variations autour d'une fleur unique ou capiteuses symphonies de corolles mêlées : leur répertoire est inépuisable. D'autant que la technologie dite du « headspace » permet aujourd'hui aux parfumeurs d'élargir à l'infini leur palette florale. Ce procédé permet en effet de capturer les senteurs des fleurs les plus délicates et jusqu'ici rebelles à toute technique d'extraction ou de distillation. C'est ainsi que, chaque année, le beau jardin des floraux s'enrichit de notes délicieusement inédites.

Fresh / Frais ●

Lily of the Valley / Muguet

CROWN ALPINE LILY   Crown 1879
DIORISSIMO   Christian Dior 1956
ÉAU FRAÎCHE   Elizabeth Arden 1986
FLORE   Caroline Herrera 1994
JESSICA McCLINTOCK   Jessica McClintock 1987
LE MUGUET DE ROSINE   Rosine 1996
LILY* ℗   Christian Dior 1999
LILY OF THE VALLEY   Crabtree & Evelyn 1970
LILY OF THE VALLEY   Floris 1847
LILY OF THE VALLEY   Penhaligon's 1976
LILY OF THE VALLEY   Perfumers Guild 1981
LILY OF THE VALLEY   Woods of Windsor 1978
LILY OF THE VALLEY   Yardley 1980/94
MUGUET / LILY OF THE VALLEY   Molinard 1994
MUGUET DES BOIS   Coty 1942
MUGUET DU BONHEUR   Caron 1952
WILD MUGUET   Jo Malone 1995

Lime blossom / Fleur de tilleul

FRENCH LIME BLOSSOM   Jo Malone 1995
TILLEUL   d'Orsay 1955/95 ♂

Crisp / Pétillant ●●

Freesia

ANTONIA'S FLOWERS   Antonia's Flowers 1984
FREESIA   Crabtree & Evelyn 1993
FREESIA   Woods of Windsor 1999

Gardenia / Gardénia

ADIEU SAGESSE   Jean Patou 1925
CLASSIC GARDENIA   Dana 1995
EAU DE TOUCH   Tocca 1998
GARDÉNIA   Chanel 1925
GARDENIA   Crabtree & Evelyn 1974
GARDENIA   Demeter Fragrance Library 1997
GARDENIA   Floris 1997
GARDENIA   Jo Malone 1995
GARDENIA   Penhaligon's 1976
GARDENIA MUSK #4   Trish McEvoy 2000
JUNGLE GARDENIA   Tuvaché / Coty 1950/95
TIARÉ   Chantecaille 1997
TIARÉ   Comptoir Sud Pacifique 1984

Honeysuckle / Chèvrefeuille

CHÈVREFEUILLE   Le Jardin Retrouvé 1977
CHÈVREFEUILLE*   Molinard 1993
HONEYSUCKLE   Demeter Fragrance Library 1998

Lilac / Lilas

LILAC   Demeter Fragrance Library 1998

Lily / Lys

LYS   Le Jardin Retrouvé 1989

Mimosa

CALYPSO MIMOSA   Calypso St Barth 1998
CHAMPS-ÉLYSÉES   Guerlain 1904/96
CHAMPS-ÉLYSÉES TOO MUCH   Guerlain 2000
FARNESIANA   Caron 1947
LA BASE FOR HER   Magic Helvetia 1994
MIMOSA   Molinard 1994
MIMOSA   Woods of Windsor 1997
MIMOSA POUR MOI   L'Artisan Parfumeur 1992
MIMOSAÏQUE   Patricia de Nicolaï 1992
UN MATIN D'ÉTÉ   Morabito 1997

Rose

AGUA FRESCA DE ROSAS   Adolfo Dominguez 1995
CE SOIR OU JAMAIS   Annick Goutal 1999
HERITAGE ROSE   Perfumers Guild 2000
ROSA MAGNIFICA   Guerlain 1999
SA MAJESTÉ LA ROSE   Serge Lutens 2000
VERSACE ESSENCE EXCITING   Versace 2000

Sweet pea / Pois de senteur

FLORET   Antonia's Flowers 1995
IN LOVE*   Hartnell 1946
SWEETPEA   Demeter Fragrance Library 1998

Wisteria / Glycine

WISTERIA   Chantecaille 1997

♂ Shared *mixte*

* Discontinued *non disponible*

Classical / Classique ●●●

Boronia

BORONIA   Déco 1976

Jasmine / Jasmin

À LA NUIT   Serge Lutens 2000
CALYPSO JASMIN   Calypso St Barth 1999
JASMAL   Creed 1959
JASMIN   Le Jardin Retrouvé 1977
JASMIN   Maître Parfumeur et Gantier 1988
JASMIN   Molinard 1994
JASMIN DE PROVENCE*   Crabtree & Evelyn 1970
LA HAIE FLEURIE DU HAMEAU   L'Artisan Parfumeur 1982
L'INSTANT JASMIN   Maria Galland 2000
NUAGES D'EAU   Marc de la Morandière 1994
OZBEK   Rifat Ozbek 1995

Lavender / Lavande

ACQUA DI PARMA LAVANDA TONICA   Acqua di Parma 1999 ♂
AGUA LAVANDA   Antonio Puig 1940 ♂
ARÔME 3   d'Orsay 1943 ♂
EAU DE LAVANDE   Annick Goutal 1981 ♂
EAU DE PROVENCE   Patricia de Nicolaï 1992 ♂
ENGLISH LAVENDER   Atkinson 1910 ♂
ENGLISH LAVENDER   Yardley 1873
LAVANDA   Myrurgia 1916 ♂
LAVANDE ROYALE   Roger & Gallet 1991
LAVANDE VELOURS   Guerlain 1999 ♂
LAVENDER   Crabtree & Evelyn 1970 ♂
LAVENDER   Demeter Fragrance Library 1995 ♂
LAVENDER   Floris 1828 ♂
LAVENDER   Woods of Windsor 1974
LUCE   Creative Universe 2000 ♂
PROVENCE LAVENDER   Perfumers Guild 1981

Rose

CROWN ROSE   Crown 1873
DARBY ROSE   Chantecaille 1999
EAU DE MURANO   Kare 1994
ELISABETHAN ROSE   Penhaligon's 1984
ENGLISH ROSE   Perfumers Guild 1981
ENGLISH ROSE   Yardley 1997
EVELYN   Crabtree & Evelyn 1993
FLEURS DE BULGARIE   Creed 1845/1980
MARÉCHALE ORIGINAL   Crown 1669/1994
PARIS   Yves Saint Laurent 1983
PRIMROSE   Penhaligon's 1976
QUELQUES ROSES   Claire 1997
RED ROSES   Jo Malone 1996
ROSE   Caron 1949
ROSE   Molinard 1994
ROSE ABSOLUE   Annick Goutal 1984
ROSE D'ARGENT   Rosine 2000
ROSE NÉROLI   L'Occitane 1999
ROSE OPULENTE   Maître Parfumeur et Gantier 1988
ROSE-PIVOINE   Patricia de Nicolaï 1998
ROSE SANTAL   Molinard 1999
ROSE THÉ   Le Jardin Retrouvé 1989
ROSES AND MORE   Priscilla Presley 1998
SOIR DE PARIS (New)   Bourjois 1928/91
TEA ROSE   Perfumer's Workshop 1972
WILD ROSE   Woods of Windsor 1974

Ylang-ylang

INDEX YLANG-YLANG HIBISCUS   Fresh 1999 ♂
YLANG & VANILLE   Guerlain 1999

Rich / Profond ●●●●

Carnation / Oeillet

BELLODGIA   Caron 1927
MALMAISON   Floris 1830/1999
NIGHT SCENTED STOCK   Penhaligon's 1976
OEILLET*   Molinard 1993

Frangipani / Frangipane

FRANGIPANE   Chantecaille 1997

Lavender / Lavande

ARÔME 3 TRADITION   d'Orsay 1998 ♂
LAVANDE   Molinard 1925/96 ♂
LAVENDER INSPIRATIONS: JUNIPER & ROSE   Yardley 2000

Orange flower / Fleur d'oranger

BASILIC FLEUR D'ORANGER   Molinard 1999
FLORA NEROLIA   Guerlain 2000
MANDARIN   Isabell 1996
NARCISSE BLANC   Caron 1923
NARCISSE NOIR   Caron 1911
ORANGE BLOSSOM   Penhaligon's 1976
STEPHANOTIS   Floris 1786

Tuberose / Tubéreuse

CAROLINA HERRERA   Carolina Herrera 1988
CHIARA BONI   Chiara Boni 1990
CHLOÉ   Chloé 1975
DREAM ANGELS HALO   Victoria's Secret 2000
ENJOLI   Revlon 1978
FRACAS   Robert Piguet 1948
FRAGILE   Jean Paul Gaultier 1999
GARDÉNIA PASSION   Annick Goutal 1989
JONTUE   Revlon 1975
MADELEINE DE MADELEINE   Madeleine Mono 1978
MICHAEL   Michael Kors 2000
MICHELLE   Balenciaga 1979
PAVLOVA   Payot / Five Star 1977
TUBÉREUSE   Annick Goutal 1984
TUBÉREUSE   L'Artisan Parfumeur 1978
TUBÉREUSE   Le Jardin Retrouvé 1980
TUBÉREUSE   Maître Parfumeur et Gantier 1988
TUBEROSE   Floris c1870/2000
TUBEROSE   Jo Malone 1991
VANILLE FLEURIE   Molinard 1998
VERSACE'S BLONDE   Versace 1995

Violet / Violette

APRIL VIOLETS   Yardley 1913
CALYPSO VIOLETTE   Calypso St Barth 1999
CHARTREUSE DE PARME   Stendhal 1960
MÉTÉORITES   Guerlain 2000
QUELQUES VIOLETTES   Claire 1996
VIOLET   Woods of Windsor 1998
VIOLETTA   Penhaligon's 1976
VIOLETTA DI PARMA   Borsari 1870
VIOLETTE   Molinard 1994
VIOLETTE PRÉCIEUSE   Caron 1918

1947 Launch *lancement*   1947 / 92 Reorchestration *recréation*

Florale

Fresh / Frais ●

Bouquet Citrus fruity / Hespéridé fruité

100% PURE CHIPIE GREEN   Coty 1998
ADIDAS WOMAN ACTIVE   Adidas 2000
ADIDAS WOMAN SPORT   Adidas 1997
AMERICA FOR WOMEN   Perry Ellis 1996
AMULETI   Mariella Burani 1999
ANDY WARHOL FOR WOMEN   Andy Warhol 1999
AUBUSSON COULEURS   Aubusson 1997
BABY DOLL PARIS   Yves Saint Laurent 1999
BENETTON SPORT WOMAN   Benetton 1999
BLUE N° 655 HER   Gap 1997
BOUTON D'OR*   L'Artisan Parfumeur 1994
CALYX   Prescriptives 1986
CHANSON D'AIR   Coty 1997
CHARLIE SILVER   Revlon 1998
CHARLIE SUNSHINE   Revlon 1997
CHEAP & CHIC   Moschino 1995
CHERISH*   Revlon 1996
CHERRY BLOSSOM   Guerlain 1999
CLAIRE DE NILANG   Lalique 1997
CLEAR DAY LIGHT   Etienne Aigner 1999
COEUR DE RAISIN   Comptoir Sud Pacifique 2000
CURVE FOR WOMEN   Liz Claiborne 1996
DALIFLOR   Salvador Dali 2000
DANIEL HECHTER SPORT POUR ELLE   Daniel Hechter 2000
DÉLIRIUM OCEANE   Guépard 2000
DUÉ DAY   Lomani 1999
DUO POUR ELLE   Vuarnet 2000
EAU DE CHARLOTTE   Annick Goutal 1982
EAU DE CORIANDRE   Jean Couturier 1996
EAU DE DALI   Salvador Dali 1995
EAU DE DOLCE VITA   Christian Dior 1998
EAU DE FATH   Jacques Fath 1996
EAU DE GIVENCHY   Givenchy 1980
EAU POUR SOI   Roger & Gallet 1999
EAU SVELTE   Christian Dior 1995
ELYSIUM   Clarins 1993
ESCADA EN FLEURS   Escada 1997
ESSENZA DI MEDITERRANEÒ DONNA   Parah 1999
EX'CLA.MA'TION BLUSH   Coty 1996
FABULEUSE   Léonard 1998
FIORI DI KRIZIA*   Krizia 1995
FLEUR DE WEIL*   Weil 1995
FRUITS & FLOWERS   The Cross 1996
FUNTASTIC GIRL   Benetton 2000
GÉNÉRATION COURRÈGES   Courrèges 1996
GREEN GENERATION HER   Pino Silvestre: Mavive 1998
GUESS (New)   Guess 1990/99
HAPPY   Clinique 1997
HEAD OVER HEELS   Ultima II 1994
HIGH TECH WOMEN   Lomani 1999
I AM LOVE   Danica Aromatics 2000
ICEBERG   Iceberg 1989
IL BACIO   Borghese 1993
ÎLES D'OR   Molinard 1929/93
I LOVE YOU   Molyneux 1998
INCLINATION   L.T.Piver 1998
INDEX AMARYLLIS CASSIS   Fresh 1998 ♂
IN LOVE AGAIN*   ℒ   Yves Saint Laurent 1998
J'ADORE   Christian Dior 1999
JOVAN FRESH MUSK   Jovan 1996
LAMBORGHINI POUR FEMME   Tonino Lamborghini 2000
L'EAU DE SONIA RYKIEL   Sonia Rykiel 1998
LIBERTÉ ACIDULÉE (LES BELLES DE RICCI)   Nina Ricci 1996
LILIAN   Lilian Barony 1997
LIZ CLAIBORNE   Liz Claiborne 1986
LUCKY YOU FOR WOMEN   Lucky Brand 2000
LYRA 3   Alain Delon 1998
MANDARIN & GINGER LILY #6   Trish McEvoy 2000

Crisp / Pétillant ●●

Bouquet Citrus fruity / Hespéridé fruité

360° FOR WOMEN   Perry Ellis 1993
À LA FRANÇAISE   Marina de Bourbon 1999
ALEGRIA   Adolfo Dominguez 1999
AMAZONE   Hermès 1974/89
AMERICAN ORIGINAL: STETSON FOR WOMEN   Coty 2001
AMOUR D'AMANDIER   Nina Ricci 1999
ARIA MISSONI   Missoni 1987
ARROGANCE POUR FEMME   Arrogance 1982
AURA FOR WOMEN   Jacomo 2000
AZZURA   Azzaro 1999
BAMBOU   Weil 1984/91
BE BOP   Kesling 1991
BEAUTIFUL   Estée Lauder 1985
BIRMANE   Van Cleef & Arpels 1999
BOLERO   Gabriela Sabatini 1997
BOSS WOMAN   Hugo Boss 2000
BUTTERFLY KISSES   My Very Own 2000
BYBLOS*   Byblos 1990
CELEBRATE   Coty 1996
CERRUTI 1881 POUR FEMME   Cerruti 1995
C'EST MAGIQUE   Kesling 1997
CHARLIE RED   Revlon 1993
CHELSEA DREAMS   Old England 1999
CHERRY MUSK   Un Monde Nouveau 1993/98
CHEVIGNON 57 FOR HER   Chevignon 1999
CHIEMSEE WOMAN TWO   Chiemsee 2000
CHRISTIAN BRETON POUR FEMME   Christian Breton 2000
CLARTÉ   L.T.Piver 1998
CLEAR DAY   Etienne Aigner 1997
COURRÈGES 2020   Courrèges 1997
DALISSIME   Salvador Dali 1994
DAZZLING GOLD   Estée Lauder 1998
DE BERCHELAI   Edgar de Berchelai 1997
DÉLIRIUM ROSE   Guépard 2000
DONNA NAUTILUS   Nautilus 2000
DUÉ NIGHT   Lomani 1999
EAU D'INFINITIF   Infinitif 1996
EAU LES COEURS*   Molinard 1995
FANTASIA   Fendi 1996
FASCINATION   Holzman & Stephanie 1990
FIORILU EN FLEURS   Pupa 1996
FIORUCCI   Fiorucci 1978/99
FLEUR   Lenthéric 1991/2001
FOLIE DOUCE   Grès 1997
FOU D'ELLE   Ted Lapidus 1997
GATTINONI À PORTER   Gattinoni 1999
GENNY (New)   Genny 1987/98
GIORGIO HOLIDAY*   ℒ   Giorgio Beverly Hills 1998
INDEX PEAR CASSIS   Fresh 1999 ♂
INDEX RED CURRANT BASIL   Fresh 1998 ♂
JAÏPUR   Boucheron 1994
KENZO   Kenzo 1988
KITON DONNA   Palladio 1997
KOOKAÏ OUI-NON   Kookaï 1993
L de LOEWE   Loewe 1972/88
LAIT SUCRÉ   Comptoir Sud Pacifique 1999
LASTING   Revlon 1995
LAUREN   Ralph Lauren 1978
L'EAU DE SUCCÈS*   Succès de Paris 1997
LE BAISER   Lalique 1999
LIGHT HER   Trussardi 1997
LILY CHIC*   ℒ   Escada 2000
L'INSAISISSABLE   Stéphanie de Monaco 1991
MADLY   Ultima II 1996
MCM   MCM 1999
MCM BLUE PARADISE   MCM 1989
MILLENNIUM HOPE WOMAN   Jivago 1999
MIRACLE   Lancôme 2000

32

▶

Classical / Classique ●●●

Bouquet

273 RODEO DRIVE   Fred Hayman 1989
BARYSHNIKOV POUR FEMME   Mikhail Baryshnikov 1995
BELLE DE RAUCH   Madeleine de Rauch 1998
BEST LADY   Succès de Paris 1995
BETTY BARCLAY WOMAN N° 3   Mäurer & Wirtz 2000
BULGARI POUR FEMME   Bulgari 1994
CANDIE'S   Liz Claiborne 1999
CAPRICCI   Nina Ricci 1961
CHANEL N° 22   Chanel 1922
CROWN STEPHANOTIS   Crown 1921
FLEURS DE ROCAILLE   Caron 1933
GIANFRANCO FERRÉ 20   Gianfranco Ferré 1998
JASMIN IMPÉRATRICE EUGÉNIE   Creed 1870/1989
JOY   Jean Patou 1930
L'AIR DU TEMPS   Nina Ricci 1948
LÊ DE*   Givenchy 1957
N'AIMEZ QUE MOI   Caron 1916
OMAR SHARIF*   Omar Sharif 1989
ORVAL   Molinard 1900/93
QUELQUES FLEURS   Houbigant: Claire 1912/87
ROMANCE   Ralph Lauren 1998
ROSE VANILLE   Comptoir Sud Pacifique 1989
SCENT OF ROMANCE UNFORGETTABLE   Perfumers Guild 2000
SISSI   Marc de la Morandière 1991
SORENZA   Fragonard 1996
TRAMP   Lenthéric 1975
WHITE SHOULDERS   Evyan 1945
WIND SONG   Prince Matchabelli 1952
ZEN (Original)   Shiseido 1964

▶

Rich / Profond ●●●●

Bouquet

1000   Jean Patou 1972
AMOUR AMOUR   Jean Patou 1925
ASPHALT FLOWER   MAC 1999
AZZARO 9   Azzaro 1984
BILL BLASS   Bill Blass 1978
BLACK JEANS FEMME   Roccobarocco 1998
BLUE GRASS   Elizabeth Arden 1934/89
CAESARS WOMAN   Caesars World 1988
COURRÈGES IN BLUE   Courrèges 1983
CRUISER FOR WOMEN   Lomani 1998
DILYS   Laura Ashley 1991
ÉCOUTE-MOI   Molinard 1997
ESP STAYFAST   Yardley 1982/88
ESTÉE   Estée Lauder 1968
EXPERIENCES   Priscilla Presley 1993
FABERGÉ IMPERIAL   Fabergé 1996
FANTASIA DE FLEURS   Creed 1862/1983
FREEZIA D'OR   Maître Parfumeur et Gantier 1988
GIÒ   Giorgio Armani 1992
IVANA   Ivana Trump 1995
JARDINS DE BAGATELLE   Guerlain 1983
JESS   Jessica McClintock 1995
JIVAGO 24k WOMEN   Jivago 1994
LA PRAIRIE   La Prairie 1993
L'EAU DE MONTEIL   Monteil 1995
MADAME CARVEN*   Carven 1979
MISS BE BOP   Kesling 1993
MISS WORTH   Worth 1977
MOMENT SUPRÊME   Jean Patou 1929
MOONDROPS   Revlon 1970
OMBRE BLEUE*   Jean-Charles Brosseau 1987
PARAH   Parah 1996
RED DOOR   Elizabeth Arden 1989
ROMANCE   Royal Secret 1990
SAND & SABLE   Coty 1983
SENSES   Les Floralies 1994
SENTIMENT   Escada 2000
SOCIETY   Perfumers Guild 1982
TATIANA   Diana von Furstenberg 1975
TIFFANY   Tiffany 1987
TWEED   Lenthéric / FFC 1924/92
VICKY TIEL ORIGINALÉ   Vicky Tiel 1990
VICTORIAN POSY   Penhaligon's 1979
VIVID   Liz Claiborne 1993
WINGS*   Giorgio Beverly Hills 1992

Floral

feminine

33

▶ Fresh / Frais ●

Bouquet Citrus fruity / Hespéridé fruité

MARBERT WOMAN RED   Marbert 1999
MELODIE D'AMOUR   Marc de la Morandière 1996
MEXX WOMAN   Mexx: Star 2000
MISS ARPELS   Van Cleef & Arpels 1994
MISS HABANITA   Molinard 1994
MODERN QUARTZ   Molyneux 1999
MON BOUQUET   Marina de Bourbon 1998
MUST DE CARTIER (JOUR)*   Cartier 1981
OMBRE ROSE FRAÎCHE   Jean-Charles Brosseau 1997
Ô OUI   Lancôme 1998
PASSION FLOWER*   Crabtree & Evelyn 1996
PASTEL DE CABOTINE   Grès 1996
PAUL SMITH WOMEN   Paul Smith 2000
PENNY BLACK WOMAN   Penny Black 1999
PETITE CHÉRIE   Annick Goutal 1998
PLUMES   Pupa 1997
PURE   Alfred Sung 1997
QUARTZ   Molyneux 1977
RALPH   Ralph Lauren 2000
RECTOVERSO SWEETY FRUITY   Ulric de Varens 2000
ROSE MUSKISSIME   Maître Parfumeur et Gantier 1988
SHAHI AQUA   Chypron 1998
SHI   Alfred Sung 2000
SILVER JEANS FEMME   Roccobarocco 1995
SO DE LA RENTA   Oscar de la Renta 1997
SO...? INSPIRED   So Cosmetics 1997
SO...? WILD   So Cosmetics 2000
SPRING FLOWER   Creed 1996
S.T.DUPONT FEMME   S.T.Dupont 1998
SUMMER   Gabriela Sabatini 2000
SUNSHINE   Chiara Boni 1998
TALISMAN EAU TRANSPARENTE   Balenciaga 1996
TROPICAL PUNCH ⓛ   Escada 2001
U   Natio 1999
UNE TOUCHE DE NAF NAF   Naf Naf 1991
UNZIPPED SPORT   Perfumer's Workshop 1999
URBAN ENERGY   Revlon 2000
VERS LE JOUR   Worth 1925/2000
V/S WOMAN   Versace 1998
WHITE CHANTILLY   Dana 1995
WOMAN   Herbalife 1996
YELLOW JEANS*   Versace 1996

Bouquet Green / Vert

5th AVENUE   Elizabeth Arden 1996
2000 FLEURS   Creed 2000
ADIDAS WOMAN   Adidas 1988/97
ADIDAS WOMAN FITNESS   Adidas 2000
ANNAYAKÉ POUR ELLE   Annayaké 2000
ANOUCK   Antonio Puig 1989
APRIL FIELDS   Coty 1999
AROMANTIC   Decléor 1999
ASPEN SENSATION   Coty 1998
AUTOUR DU THÉ CLASSIQUE   Molinard 2000
BLUEBELL / WOODLAND HYACINTH   Penhaligon's 1978
BOBBI   Bobbi Brown 1998
BYBLOS MARE / SEA   Byblos 1997
CASCAYA SUMMER   Gabriela Sabatini 1998
CASSISSIER   L'Occitane 1999
CATALYST   Halston 1993
CHALEUR D'ANIMALE   Parlux 2000
CHAUMET   Chaumet 1999
DÉLIRIUM TEA   Guépard 2000
EAU DE CAMILLE   Annick Goutal 1983
EAU D'IVOIRE   Pierre Balmain 2000
ESCADA FEELING FREE   Escada 1996

▶ Crisp / Pétillant ●●

Bouquet Citrus fruity / Hespéridé fruité

MISS BALAHÉ   Léonard 1996
MON PARFUM   Bourjois 1925/95
MONTAIGNE   Caron 1986
MYSTIC   Marilyn Miglin 1998
NAZARENO POUR FEMME   Nazareno Gabrielli 2000
ON AIR FEMME   Morabito 1998
PARFUM ALLIÉ MELLOW 51   Shu Uemura 1988/99
PATOU FOR EVER   Jean Patou 1998
PRIVATE NUMBER FOR WOMEN*   Etienne Aigner 1991
PURPLE FANTASY ⓛ   Guerlain 2000
REALITIES*   Liz Claiborne 1990
RED JEANS   Versace 1994
RÉMY FOR WOMAN   Rémy Marquis 1999
ROCCOBAROCCO TRE   Roccobarocco 1994
ROMEO   Romeo Gigli 1989
RYKIEL ROSE   Sonia Rykiel 2000
S pour FEMME   Francesco Smalto 2001
SALVATORE FERRAGAMO   Salvatore Ferragamo 1998
SAMBA   Perfumer's Workshop 1987
SAMOURAÏ WOMAN   Alain Delon 2001
SCAASI   Scaasi 1989
SCARF TAORMINA   Marbert 1996
SCHÖN   Mila Schön 1997
SECRET INTENTION ⓛ   Guerlain 2001
SENSO   Ungaro 1987/92
SHADES BY NAVY*   Dana 1998
SHE*   Revlon 1997
SPRING FEVER   Origins 1995
SUGGESTION EAU D'OR*   Montana 1994
SUN SPIRIT*   Marbert 1995
TOCADILLY*   Rochas 1997
TRÈS JOURDAN*   Charles Jourdan 1992
TRIANGLE   Myrurgia 1996
TRIBÙ   Benetton 1993
U de V POUR ELLE   Ulric de Varens 1999
VALENTINO   Valentino 1977/86
VARIATIONS   Carven 2000
VICE VERSA* ⓛ   Yves Saint Laurent 1999
WATT YELLOW   Cofinluxe 2000
WHITE LAVENDER   Yardley 1995
YIN   Jacques Fath 1999
ZARA WOMAN   Antonio Puig 1999
ZOA   Régine's 1992

Bouquet Green / Vert

AUTOUR DU THÉ ROMANTIQUE   Molinard 2000
BURBERRY WEEK END FOR WOMEN   Burberry 1997
CABOTINE DE GRÈS   Grès 1990
CHARLIE   Revlon 1973
CROWN BOUQUET   Crown 1936
DANDELION   Demeter Fragrance Library 1998 ♂
DIVINA   Diana de Silva 1996
EAU DU CIEL   Annick Goutal 1985
FAÇONNABLE   Façonnable 2000
FASHION FAIR N° 1   Fashion Fair 1977
FLEUR DE ROCAILLE   Caron 1993
FLIRT   Prescriptives 1998
GEOFFREY BEENE   Geoffrey Beene 1998
GFF F   Gianfranco Ferré 1997
LANCETTI EAU DE JOIE   Lancetti 1997
L'EFFLEUR   Coty 1990
L'OMBRE DANS L'EAU   Diptyque 1983
MARJOLAINE   Jean Couturier 1997
MICK MICHEYL   Mick Micheyl 2000
MODERN   Banana Republic 1997
MOLINARD DE MOLINARD   Molinard 1979
MONSOON   Monsoon 1994

Classical / Classique ●●●

Rich / Profond ●●●●

Floral

feminine

Florale *féminin*

▶ ## Fresh / Frais ●

Bouquet Green / Vert

ÉTHÉRÉ   Vicky Tiel 1999
EXTRAVAGANCE D'AMARIGE   Givenchy 1998
FACE À FACE FEMME   Façonnable 1996
FIDJI   Guy Laroche 1966
FLEUR   Floris 2000
FLORE AUBUSSON   Aubusson 1998
FREE WORLD WOMAN   Mäurer & Wirtz 1999
HEART   Herbalife 2000
I AM PASSION   Danica Aromatics 1999
LACOSTE FOR WOMEN   Lacoste 1999
LE MONDE EST BEAU   Kenzo 1997
LE TEMPS D'UNE FÊTE   Patricia de Nicolaï 1989
LIZSPORT   Liz Claiborne 1997
LONG AGO / WISTFUL   Amway 1997
LOVING BOUQUET* Ⓛ   Escada 1999
MANIFESTO   Isabella Rossellini 2000
MAT;   Masakï Matsushima 2000
MONTANA BLU   Montana 2000
MORGANE LE FAY   Morgane Le Fay 1997
MV   Madeleine Vionnet 1998
OBLIQUE FAST FORWARD   Givenchy 2000
OFRÉSIA   Diptyque 1999
PARFUM ALLIÉ CRYSTAL 32   Shu Uemura 1988/99
PARFUM D'ÉTÉ   Kenzo 1993
PEOPLE DONNA   Luciano Soprani 1999
PIAZZA DI SPAGNA   Roccobarocco 1997
PLEASURES   Estée Lauder 1995
PRINCESS GRACE DE MONACO   Fabergé 1998
PRIORITÉ EAU BLEU   Dana 2000
PRUNING SHEARS   Demeter Fragrance Library 1998 ♂
RELAXING FRAGRANCE   Shiseido 1997
RÊVERIE PURE   Gloria Vanderbilt 2000
ROOTS FOR HER   Coty 1998
ROSE D'ÉTÉ   Rosine 1997
SERINGA   Floris 1993
SNOWDROP & CRYSTAL FLOWERS #3   Trish McEvoy 1999
THE SPIRIT OF SWITZERLAND   Michel Jordi 1999
SPRING RAIN   Crabtree & Evelyn 1979
SUNSHINE   My Very Own 2000
SUNWATER   Lancaster 1997
TOMMY GIRL   Tommy Hilfiger 1996
UN AMOUR DE PATOU   Jean Patou 1998
VERSACE ESSENCE ETHEREAL   Versace 2000
VÔTRE*   Charles Jourdan 1978
W   Banana Republic 1995

Bouquet Water / Marine

ACQUA DI FIORI   De Ruy 1999
ACQUA DI GIÒ   Giorgio Armani 1995
ADIDAS WOMAN ENERGY   Adidas 2000
BETTY BARCLAY WOMAN   Mäurer & Wirtz 1998
CHIEMSEE WOMAN   Chiemsee 1999
"DELICIOUS" FEELINGS   Gale Hayman 1996
DIAMONDS & SAPPHIRES*   Elizabeth Taylor 1993
DONNA   Compagnia Delle Indie 2000
DREAMS BY TABU*   Dana 1996
EAU D'EDEN   Cacharel 1996
EAU DE RÉVILLON   Révillon 1998
EAU DE VERINO   Roberto Verino 1995
EAU MARINE   Les Copains 1999
ESENCIA DE DUENDE   J. del Pozo 1995
FEMINA*   Alberta Ferretti 1993
FETISH   Dana 1997
FLEUR D'EAU   Rochas 1996
FLEUR DE DIVA   Ungaro 1997
FLEUR D'INTERDIT   Givenchy 1994
FOREVER   Alfred Sung 1995

▶ ## Crisp / Pétillant ●●

Bouquet Green / Vert

MOODS*   Krizia 1989
NORELL   Norell 1968
PARFUM ALLIÉ SWING 36   Shu Uemura 1988/99
POPY MORENI DE FÊTE   Popy Moreni 1998
ROYAL PAVILLON   Etro 1989 ♂
SARCANTHUS   Crown 1931
SAVANNA   Isabell 1996
SCENT OF ROMANCE WITH LOVE   Perfumers Guild 1992
SI FLEURI   Rémy Latour 1994
SOLEIL   Fragonard 1995
TENDRE POISON   Christian Dior 1994
TOUCH   Fred Hayman 1993
VALERIA   Valeria Mazza 1998

Bouquet Water / Marine

AV   Adrienne Vittadini 1994
COOL WATER WOMAN   Davidoff 1996
EXTASE EXOTIC NATURE WOMAN   Muelhens 1997
FERRARI DONNA   Ferrari 1995
HALLOWEEN   J. del Pozo 1997
HAVANA POUR ELLE   Aramis 1995
HUGO WOMAN   Hugo Boss 1997
JEAN LUC AMSLER FEMME   Jean Luc Amsler 2000
MISS JAGUAR   Jaguar 1993
OH! MY DOG   Dog Generation 2000
PRESCRIPTIVES POTION   Prescriptives 2000
SUGGESTION EAU D'ARGENT*   Montana 1994

36

▶ **Classical / Classique** ●●●

▶ **Rich / Profond** ●●●●

Floral

feminine

37

▶

Fresh / Frais ●

Bouquet Water / Marine

GALA DE DIA   Loewe 1996
ICEBERG TWICE   Iceberg 1994
INDIVIDUELLE   Charles Jourdan 1996
LAURA   Laura Biagiotti 1994
L'EAU PAR KENZO   Kenzo 1996
MISS MORABITO   Morabito 1996
OCEAN DREAM   Giorgio Beverly Hills 1996
PARFUM ALLIÉ PASTEL 43   Shu Uemura 1988/99
PERRY ELLIS PORTFOLIO   Perry Ellis 2000
RECTOVERSO SUN SEA   Ulric de Varens 2000
SONG DE CHINE*   Crabtree & Evelyn 1997
THAÏS   Antonio Puig 1996
TRIBÙ ACQUA FRESCA   Benetton 1995
WATT PINK   Cofinluxe 1993

Bouquet White flowers / Fleurs blanches

ACACIOSA   Caron 1924
ACQUA DI MIELE   Fresh 1997 ♂
ANAÏS ANAÏS   Cacharel 1978
ARROGANCE ME   Arrogance 1997
BABY ROSE JEANS   Versace 1995
CASUAL   Paul Sebastian 1995
CHLOÉ INNOCENCE*   Chloé 1996
DESTINY   Marilyn Miglin 1990
DREAM   Gap 1995
EAU DE GUCCI*   Gucci 1982/93
EDWARDIAN BOUQUET   Floris 1901/84
EMOZIONI FOR WOMAN   Fila 1997
ENVY   Gucci 1997
ESPÍRITU DE MONTESINOS   Dana 2000
ETERNITY   Calvin Klein 1988
EX'CLA.MA'TION DARE   Coty 1996
FLEURISSIMO   Creed 1972
FLEURS   Morabito 1998
FLEURS DE CHIARA BONI   Chiara Boni 1999
FLEURS D'ORLANE   Orlane 1983
FREEDOM FOR HER   Tommy Hilfiger 1999
GIANFRANCO FERRÉ   Gianfranco Ferré 1984
INDEX JASMINE LYS   Fresh 2000 ♂
JACINTHE ROSE (ROMANTICA)   E.Coudray 1983
JONTUE MOONLIGHT*   Revlon 1996
KISS & TELL   Fragrance International 1999
LAILA   Geir Ness 1995
LE JARDIN   Max Factor / H&BF 1983
LUCKY BRAND WOMEN'S*   Lucky Brand 1997
LUMIÈRE (Original)*   Rochas 1984
NARCISSUS   Yardley 2000
NAUTICA WOMAN   Nautica 1997
NEIGES   Lise Watier 1993
NICOLE   Nicole Miller 1998
ODALISQUE   Patricia de Nicolaï 1989
PAPERWHITES   Isabell 1998
POUR UNE FEMME   Roger & Gallet 1993
SCENT OF FLOWERS   Perfumers Guild 1990
SHEER TIFFANY   Tiffany 1999
SPLENDOR   Elizabeth Arden 1998
SUMMER HILL   Crabtree & Evelyn 1988
SUNG   Alfred Sung 1986
WHITE CAMELLIA   St John 1998
WHITE SPELL   Un Monde Nouveau 1993/98
XS POUR ELLE   Paco Rabanne 1994
ZINNIA   Floris 1990

ACQUA DI MIELE   Fresh 1997 ♂
INDEX AMARYLLIS CASSIS   Fresh 1998 ♂
INDEX JASMINE LYS   Fresh 2000 ♂
PRUNING SHEARS   Demeter Fragrance Library 1998 ♂
TILLEUL   d'Orsay 1955/95 ♂

▶

Crisp / Pétillant ●●

Bouquet White flowers / Fleurs blanches

24, FAUBOURG   Hermès 1995
BLU BLUMARINE   Blumarine 1995
DÉCADENCE*   Parlux 1985
DIAMONDS & EMERALDS*   Elizabeth Taylor 1993
ÉLÀ NONCHALANCE   Mäurer & Wirtz 1999
GIORGIO   Giorgio Beverly Hills 1981
HONEYSUCKLE & JASMINE   Jo Malone 1996
INDIANA / TUBERÉUSE INDIANA   Creed 1980
JARDIN BLANC   Maître Parfumeur et Gantier 1988
LA CHASSE AUX PAPILLONS   L'Artisan Parfumeur 1999/2000
MEA CULPA   Rosine 1994
MON CLASSIQUE   Morabito 1987
NO REGRETS   Alexandra de Markoff 1994
NUMBER ONE   Patricia de Nicolaï 1989
OLÈNE   Diptyque 1988
PASSION   Annick Goutal 1983
SPIRIT OF ZEN   Shiseido 1986

DANDELION   Demeter Fragrance Library 1998 ♂
INDEX PEAR CASSIS   Fresh 1999 ♂
INDEX RED CURRANT BASIL   Fresh 1998 ♂
INSENSÉ   Givenchy 1993
JARDIN DU NIL   Maître Parfumeur et Gantier 1988
ROYAL PAVILLON   Etro 1989 ♂

Classical / Classique ●●●

Rich / Profond ●●●●

Floral

ACQUA DI PARMA LAVANDA TONICA   Acqua di Parma 1999 ♂
AGUA LAVANDA   Antonio Puig 1940 ♂
ARÔME 3   d'Orsay 1943 ♂
EAU DE LAVANDE   Annick Goutal 1981 ♂
EAU DE PROVENCE   Patricia de Nicolaï 1992 ♂
ENGLISH LAVENDER   Atkinson 1910 ♂
INDEX YLANG-YLANG HIBISCUS   Fresh 1999 ♂
LAVANDA   Myrurgia 1916 ♂
LAVENDER   Crabtree & Evelyn 1970 ♂
LAVENDER   Demeter Fragrance Library 1995 ♂
LAVENDER   Floris 1828 ♂
LAVANDE VELOURS   Guerlain 1999 ♂
LUCE   Creative Universe 2000 ♂
ROYAL SCOTTISH LAVENDER   Creed 1856

ARÔME 3 TRADITION   d'Orsay 1998 ♂
HOMBRE DE FLORES POLIANTHES TUBEROSE   Fresh 1999
LAVANDE   Molinard 1925/96 ♂
LAVANDE DES PRINCES   L.T.Piver 1991
POUR UN HOMME   Caron 1934
TÉNÉRÉ   Paco Rabanne 1988

Soft
Floral

The marriage of sparkling aldehydes and delicate flowers creates a family of soft, often powdery, abstract florals. Aldehydes are found naturally in rose and citrus oils, but in such minute amounts that they have to be re-created in the laboratory. Their natural scent is not pleasant: some have a sharp, metallic fragrance, others the burnt, waxy aroma of a just-snuffed candle. Add them to flowers, however, and their subtle magic makes the blossoms sing. Their soprano notes are muted by the powdery accents of iris and vanilla to create a fragrance that is both soft and flowery.

Ces parfums de séduction proposent de beaux bouquets abstraits. Leur secret réside dans les aldéhydes, composants naturels des senteurs de rose ou d'agrumes mais en quantités si infimes qu'il faut les synthétiser en laboratoire.
Isolés, ils ont une curieuse odeur de métal ou de brûlé. Mais qu'on les mêle aux fleurs et, aussitôt, ils font chanter et fuser les parfums. Leur prodigieux pouvoir de diffusion, poudré d'iris et de vanille, caractérise ces compositions fleuries, tendres et de pure élégance.

Fresh / Frais ●

Citrus fruity / Hespéridé fruité

212   Carolina Herrera 1997
BLUMARINE II   Blumarine 2000
CAMÉLIA IRIS (BLEU)   E.Coudray 1946
CLOSE   Gap 2000
COLORS   Alexander Julian 1993
DESIGN   Paul Sebastian 1985
DKNY WOMEN   Donna Karan 1999
EAU ROSÉE   Mariella Burani 1997
G   Giorgio Beverly Hills 1999
G GIGLI*   Romeo Gigli 1994
GIORGIO AIRE*   Giorgio Beverly Hills 1996
HANAE MORI HAUTE COUTURE   Hanae Mori 1998
IMPLICITE   Sea World 1998
JOOP! BERLIN   Joop! 1991
LAURA ASHLEY N° 1   Laura Ashley 1989
OMBRE D'OR*   Jean-Charles Brosseau 1994
OXYGÈNE   Lanvin 2000
PARESSE DE RODIER   Rodier 1999
SO PRETTY EAU FRUITÉE   Cartier 2000
SPARKLING WHITE DIAMONDS   Elizabeth Taylor 1999
TED BAKER WOMAN   Ted Baker 1999
TRUESTE   Tiffany 1995
VENEZIA PASTELLO*   Laura Biagiotti 1995
WHITE LINEN BREEZE   Estée Lauder 1996

Green / Vert

ALABASTER   Mary McFadden 1996
CALVIN KLEIN*   Calvin Klein 1978
CHANEL N° 19   Chanel 1971
CIALENGA   Balenciaga 1973
EXCITING ARROGANCE   Arrogance 1999
HEURE EXQUISE   Annick Goutal 1984
IVOIRE   Pierre Balmain 1980
JIL SANDER WOMAN PURE*   Jil Sander 1980
JOSEPH DE JOUR   Joseph 1997
LÉONARD DE LÉONARD*   Léonard 1989
MURASAKI   Shiseido 1980
NUDE   Bill Blass 1990
SAFARI   Ralph Lauren 1990
SI TENDRE   Rémy Latour 1989
SO PRETTY   Cartier 1995

Water / Marine

CHARLIE WHITE MUSK   Revlon 1997
LE CIRQUE DE POPY MORENI   Popy Moreni 1999
OH! DE MOSCHINO   Moschino 1996

White flowers / Fleurs blanches

ANNE KLEIN*   Parlux 1984
FLEUR DE FLEURS   Nina Ricci 1980/82
FLEURS DE PÊCHER   Comptoir Sud Pacifique 1976
GUIRLANDES*   Carven 1982
HEAVEN   Gap 1994
I AM RICH   Danica Aromatics 2000
MÉTAL   Paco Rabanne 1979
TILLEUL CHÈVREFEUILLE   L'Occitane 1999
TRUE LOVE*   Elizabeth Arden 1994

Iris

HIRIS   Hermès 1999
INÈS DE LA FRESSANGE   Inès de la Fressange 1999

Crisp / Pétillant ●●

Citrus fruity / Hespéridé fruité

ANNA SUI   Anna Sui 1999
AUTOUR DU THÉ EXOTIQUE   Molinard 2000
BLUMARINE*   Blumarine 1988
CAFÉ-CAFÉ   Cofinluxe 1996
CHIARA BONI LIGHT   Chiara Boni 1997
COUNTRY ROAD WOMAN   Country Road 1999
DREAM ANGELS DIVINE   Victoria's Secret 2000
FIRENZE   Enrico Coveri 1993
FLEUR DE DÉSIRADE   Aubusson 1995
FOLAVRIL   Annick Goutal 1981
K de KRIZIA   Krizia 1981
LE CHIC*   Molyneux 1932/95
LUMIÈRE (New)   Rochas 1984/2000
MARIELLA BURANI   Mariella Burani 1992
MUKKI   Fresh 1996 ♂
NINA   Nina Ricci 1987
PALACE   Régine's 1995
ROUGE FORMIDABLE   Kesling 1998
ROYALISSIME   Henri d'Orléans 1997
SAMBA RED WOMAN   Perfumer's Workshop 1999
SOCIETY*   Burberry 1991
SWEET COURRÈGES   Courrèges 1993
TOUJOURS L'AIMANT   Coty 2000
WOMENSWEAR   Alexander Julian 1992

Green / Vert

CALANDRE   Paco Rabanne 1969
CÂLINE   Jean Patou 1964
CHRISTIAN LACROIX   Christian Lacroix 1999
DAZZLING SILVER   Estée Lauder 1998
DRÔLE DE ROSE   L'Artisan Parfumeur 1996
ENERGIZING FRAGRANCE   Shiseido 1999
FAROUCHE   Nina Ricci 1974
FLEURAGE   Visari 1999
FLORISSA   Floris 1978
GUCCI N° 1*   Gucci 1974
PANACHE   Lenthéric / FFC 1979
RIVE GAUCHE   Yves Saint Laurent 1971
ROSEBERRY   Rosine 1997
TAMANGO   Léonard 1977
TRIGÈRE   Pauline Trigère 1973
VERSACE ESSENCE EMOTIONAL   Versace 2000
VIVRE   Molyneux 1971

Water / Marine

ACTE 2   Escada 1995
EAU DE BIARRITZ   Comptoir Sud Pacifique 1995
V   Gloria Vanderbilt 1994

White flowers / Fleurs blanches

AMAZING   Bill Blass 1999
CAMP BEVERLY HILLS*   CBH 1986
DAMASK ROSE   Crabtree & Evelyn 1976/91
DEAUVILLE   Michel Germain 1999
INTRIGUE*   Carven 1986
LA PARISIENNE   Holzman & Stephanie 1989
PARFUM ALLIÉ DREAM 45   Shu Uemura 1988/99
PERRY ELLIS FOR WOMEN   Perry Ellis 1985/96
REALLY PARAH   Parah 1998
WHITE DIAMONDS   Elizabeth Taylor 1991
WHITE LINEN   Estée Lauder 1978
WHITE SATIN   Yardley / FFC 1985

MUKKI   Fresh 1996 ♂
TABAC ORIGINAL (EdC)   Mäurer & Wirtz 1959

►

Classical / Classique ●●●

CHANEL N° 5   Chanel 1921
COEUR-JOIE   Nina Ricci 1946
ÉCUSSON   Jean d'Albret 1947
FERRÉ BY FERRÉ   Gianfranco Ferré 1991
FLEUR D'IRIS   Maître Parfumeur et Gantier 1988
FORGET-ME-NOT   Woods of Windsor 1982
GALANOS   Galanos 1979/96
JASMIN MANDARINE   L'Occitane 1999
L'AIMANT   Coty 1927
LANCETTI   Lancetti 1998
L'INTERDIT   Givenchy 1957
LIÙ   Guerlain 1929
LOVE'S BABY SOFT   Mem / Dana 1974
NONCHALANCE   Mäurer & Wirtz 1960
OPHÉLIE   Pierre Cardin 1995
PARCE QUE!*   Roberto Capucci 1963
SCENT OF ROMANCE ST VALENTINE   Perfumers Guild 1991
TURQUOISE   Comptoir Sud Pacifique 1991

►

Rich / Profond ●●●●

AIMEZ-MOI   Caron 1996
ALYSSA ASHLEY MUSK   Alyssa Ashley 1992
AMOUAGE   Amouage 1983
ARPÈGE   Lanvin 1927/93
BLASÉ   Max Factor / H&BF 1975
BULGARI BLU   Bulgari 2000
CALIFORNIA   Jaclyn Smith / Dana 1989
CLIMAT   Lancôme 1967
D&G FEMININE   Dolce & Gabbana 1999
"DELICIOUS"   Gale Hayman 1993
DEMI-JOUR   Houbigant / Dana 1988
DETCHÉMA   Révillon 1953/94
DI ROMEO GIGLI   Romeo Gigli 1999
DNA*   Bijan 1993
DOLCE & GABBANA   Dolce & Gabbana 1992
EAU DE COUTURE   Philippe Venet 1998
FIRST   Van Cleef & Arpels 1976
GRAND AMOUR   Annick Goutal 1996
HOPE   Frances Denney 1952
INFINI   Caron 1912/70
JE REVIENS   Worth 1932
JOVAN MUSK   Jovan 1972
LADY STETSON   Coty 1986
LA ROSE DE ROSINE   Rosine 1991
LE DIX   Balenciaga 1947
LE FEU D'ISSEY LIGHT   Issey Miyake 2000
MADAME ROCHAS   Rochas 1960/89
MILLENNIUM ROSE   Perfumers Guild 2000
NAJ-OLEARI   Naj-Oleari 1989/99
NOA   Cacharel 1998
NOCTURNES   Caron 1981
NUAGE D'OR   Marc de la Morandière 1994
REBEL WOMEN   Kraft International 2001
RÊVE D'OR   L.T.Piver 1889/1926
SOIR DE PARIS (Original)   Bourjois 1928
SOLILOQUY   Amway 1997
SORTILÈGE*   Le Galion 1937
TOSCA   Muelhens 1921
TOVA   Tova Borgnine 1982
VERS TOI   Worth 1934/2000
YENDI*   Roberto Capucci 1974

AMOUAGE GENTLEMEN   Amouage 1983
JOVAN MUSK FOR MEN   Jovan 1973

Soft Floral

Floral
Oriental

Soft, spicy orange flower notes meld with piquant aldehydes and sweet spices to create the heart of a Floral Oriental fragrance. Born in the 1900s, Floral Orientals came back to life again in the 1970s. In the past decade, lively, fruity interpretations dominated the Floral Oriental category, but recent fragrances have developed a more subtle, muted personality.

Pour créer le cœur d'un parfum Fleuri oriental, il faut les notes suaves et poivrées de la fleur d'oranger, de piquants aldéhydes et une pincée d'épices douces. Très en vogue à la Belle Époque, ces accords grisants réapparurent dans les années 1970. Depuis, ils n'en finissent pas de séduire : tour à tour pétillants et fruités ou, plus récemment, subtils et très tendres.

Fresh / Frais ●

Citrus fruity / Hespéridé fruité

ALLURE   Chanel 1996
ALVIERO MARTINI DONNA   Alviero Martini 1997
ANTHRACITE   Jacomo 1991
AURA LOEWE   Loewe 1994
BELLA FIRENZE   Tosca-Muelhens 1998
BERNINI WOMEN   Bernini 1996
BIJAN WITH A TWIST   Bijan 2001
BLACK PEARLS*   Elizabeth Taylor 1996
BOGNER WOMAN   Bogner 1999
BURBERRY FOR WOMEN   Burberry 1995
BYBLOS BREEZA / BREEZE   Byblos 2000
CHARLIE GOLD   Revlon 1995
CHIPIE   Coty 1995
COLORS OF BENETTON   Benetton 1987/93
CONTRADICTION   Calvin Klein 1997
CONVICTION   Omar Sharif 1998
GAI MATTIOLO   Gai Mattiolo 1997
GOLDEN MOMENT   Priscilla Presley 1999
GOODLIFE WOMAN   Davidoff 1999
HOT   Benetton 1997
I AM POWER   Danica Aromatics 2000
I EX'CLA.MA'TION   Coty 1998
INDIAN SUMMER   Priscilla Presley 1996
INSPIRATION   Charles Jourdan 1998
JIL SANDER N° 4   Jil Sander 1990
JUNGLE: LE TIGRE   Kenzo 1997
KASHÂYA   Kenzo 1994
LAGUNA   Salvador Dali 1991
LES COPAINS   Les Copains 1988/97
L'ÉTÉ DE VENTILO   Ventilo 1998
LONGING   Coty 1994
MAGNETIC   Gabriela Sabatini 1992
MCM ROUGE   MCM 2001
ORGUEIL DE RODIER   Rodier 1999
PATTI LaBELLE   Flori Roberts 1996
PERHAPS   Bob Mackie 1997
PERLE D'AUBUSSON   Aubusson 2000
POLEMIC!   Succès de Paris 1999
PREMIER JOUR   Nina Ricci 2001
PURE MOMENT   Alfred Sung 2000
PURE WISH   Chopard 2000
RED 2*   Giorgio Beverly Hills 1996
ROBERTA DI CAMERINO   Roberta di Camerino 1998
RUBIS D'OR*   Kristal Saint Martin 1996
SENSATIONS   Jil Sander 2000
SÉXUAL   Michel Germain 1994
SINAÏ   Kesling 1997
SUMATRA RAIN WOMAN   Muelhens 1999
SUN MOON STARS   Lagerfeld 1994
ULTRAVIOLET   Paco Rabanne 1999
UN AIR D'HABANITA   Molinard 2000
UNZIPPED UNIVERSE   Perfumer's Workshop 1999
VALENTIN YUDASHKIN   Valentin Yudashkin 1999
VERANDA   Crabtree & Evelyn 1990
VOCALISE   Shiseido 1997
YES FOR WOMEN   Lomani 2000
ZAHAROFF   Zaharoff 1997

Green / Vert

BURBERRY TOUCH FOR WOMEN   Burberry 2000
C'EST LA VIE*   Christian Lacroix 1990
INTUITION   Estée Lauder 2000
LP N° 9   Penhaligon's 1998
MAXIM'S DE PARIS*   Maxim's 1984
NAOMAGIC   Naomi Campbell 2000
STYLE   Gale Hayman 1999
THAT'S AMORE! LEI   Gai Mattiolo 2000

Crisp / Pétillant ●●

Citrus fruity / Hespéridé fruité

ALCHIMIE   Rochas 1998
ANIMALE ANIMALE   Parlux 1993
ATREVIDA   De Ruy 1998
BAROQUE   Yardley 1996
BONJOUR   Bonjour 1994
BYBLOS TERRA / EARTH   Byblos 1997
CASCAYA   Gabriela Sabatini 1994
CHLOÉ NARCISSE   Chloé 1992
CIARA FEMME FATALE*   Revlon 1995
DALIMANIA   Salvador Dali 1999
DÉSIRADE   Aubusson 1990
DIAMANT D'OR*   Kristel Saint Martin 1996
DONNA BORSALINO   Borsalino 1995
DOULTON   Royal Doulton 1998
DREAMING PRINCESS   Succès de Paris 1994
ENFANTS DU SOLEIL   Comptoir Sud Pacifique 1999
ERUPTION WOMAN   Mäurer & Wirtz 1997
ESSENTIALLY JAGUAR   Jaguar 1998
EX'CLA.MA'TION   Coty 1988
FANTASME   Ted Lapidus 1992
FASHION   Léonard 1970/93
FLOWER BY KENZO   Kenzo 2000
GALICE   Paris Bleu 1995
GENNY SHINE*   Genny 1993
GHOST   Ghost 2000
GODDESS   Marilyn Miglin 1999
ICI   Coty 1995
INCOGNITO   Cover Girl / Dana 1992
JEAN PAUL GAULTIER   Jean Paul Gaultier 1993
JIN ABE   Jin Abe 1998
JIVAGO 7 NOTES   Jivago 1998
LA COUPE D'OR   Rosine 1993
L'ÉLUE   Rémy Latour 1998
MACKIE   Bob Mackie 1985/91
NAZARENO GABRIELLI POUR FEMME   Nazareno Gabrielli 1996
NICOLE MILLER   Nicole Miller 1993
NOI DONNA   Missoni 1997
NOKOMIS   Coty 1997
PANTHÈRE   Cartier 1987
RED PEARL   Red Pearl 1999
REVOLUTION À VERSAILLES*   Jean Desprez 1989
SHIMÓ   Monsoon 1996
SIGNATURE POUR FEMME   S.T. Dupont 2000
SIRÈNE   Vicky Tiel 1994
SOLYTIS   Lomani 1996
STARDUST   Llewelyn 1998
TRÉSOR   Lancôme 1990
UNFORGETTABLE TOO   Revlon 1999
URVÂSHI   Gandh Sugandh 1999
VAN CLEEF   Van Cleef & Arpels 1993
VENTILO   Ventilo 1997
VERSUS DONNA*   Versace 1991
VOLUPTÉ   Oscar de la Renta 1992
ZAHRA   Fashion Fair 1993
ZILLION   Herbalife: Parfums Vitessence 1995

Green / Vert

CHAMADE   Guerlain 1969
DREAM ANGELS HEAVENLY   Victoria's Secret 2000
GALA LOEWE   Loewe 1991
GMV DONNA   Gian Marco Venturi 1999
NANTUCKET BRIAR   Crabtree & Evelyn 1985
PARFUM D'HERMÈS   Hermès 1984
ROUGE DE REVLON   Revlon 2000
VERINO   Roberto Verino 1992
XI'A XI'ANG*   Revlon 1987

Classical / Classique ●●●

BALAHÉ   Léonard 1983
BÂL À VERSAILLES   Jean Desprez 1962/95
BOUCHERON   Boucheron 1988
BOUDOIR   Vivienne Westwood 1998
BOUVARDIA*   Floris 1996
CHALDÉE   Jean Patou 1927
CORNUBIA   Penhaligon's 1991
DANIEL DE FASSON   Daniel de Fasson 1990
DÉLICE D'ÉPICES   Nina Ricci 1999
DIVINE FOLIE   Jean Patou 1933
EMPORIO ARMANI SHE / ELLE   Giorgio Armani 1998
ESCADA   Escada-Margaretha Ley 1990
FABULOUS   Jan Moran 1996
FERENTINA   Caesars World 1994
FÉTICHE   E.Coudray 1998
FOREVER KRYSTLE   Revlon-Carrington 1984
FORMIDABLE   Kesling 1994
GALORÉ   Germaine Monteil / Royal Secret 1964
GLAMOUR   Gale Hayman 1999
HELIOTROPE   Etro 1989 ♂
HERVÉ LÉGER   Hervé Léger 1999
ICEBERG UNIVERSE FEMME   Iceberg 1997
INITIATION*   Molyneux 1990
JE T'AIME   Holzman & Stephanie 1987
JIL SANDER SUN   Jil Sander 1989
LATA   Gandh Sugandh 1999
L'HEURE BLEUE   Guerlain 1912
L'ORIGAN*   Coty 1905
LUSCIOUS   Herbalife: Parfums Vitessence 1995
MADELEINE VIONNET   Madeleine Vionnet 1925/96
MAROUSSIA   Slava Zaïtsev 1992
MCM 1900   MCM 1991
METALLICA ①   Guerlain 2000
OR ET NOIR   Caron 1949
OSCAR   Oscar de la Renta 1977
PARFUM SACRÉ   Caron 1990
POÊME   Lancôme 1995
RAFFINÉE   Houbigant / Dana 1982
RAVELLO   Ravello 1997
RÊVERIE   Gloria Vanderbilt 1999
ROUGE HERMÈS   Hermès 2000
SACREBLEU!   Patricia de Nicolaï 1993
SHAHI GOLDEN SUN   Chypron 1997
SPAZIO KRIZIA DONNA   Krizia 1998
SPELLBOUND   Estée Lauder 1991
SUGGESTION EAU CUIVRÉE   Montana 1994
TANGLEWOOD BOUQUET   Crown 1932
THIARA   Marc de la Morandière 1994
TIGRESS*   Fabergé 1938
TOCADE   Rochas 1994
TRULY LACE   Coty 1992
VALLÉE DES ROIS   Mira Takla 1990
VANDERBILT   Gloria Vanderbilt 1982
VENET   Philippe Venet 1965/96
VÉNUS DE L'AMOUR   Vicky Tiel 1997
VIVA DI TOSCA   Muelhens 1997
VOICE BY BETTY BARCLAY   Mäurer & Wirtz 1995
VOILE D'ÉTÉ   Guerlain 1999
WATERPERRY   Perfumers Guild 1989

Rich / Profond ●●●●

CHINA ROSE   Floris 2000
CLANDESTINE*   Guy Laroche 1986
DARK VANILLA   Coty 1998
EN AVION   Caron 1930
JOOP! LE BAIN   Joop! 1988
LE JARDIN D'AMOUR   Max Factor / HB&F 1987
LOVE STORY   Louis Féraud 1997
LUTÈCE   Parquet / Dana 1984
MAHORA   Guerlain 2000
NAHÉMA   Guerlain 1979
NAVY   Cover Girl / Dana 1990
OMBRE ROSE   Jean-Charles Brosseau 1981
POISON   Christian Dior 1985
ST JOHN   St John 1994
UNINHIBITED*   Cher 1989

▶

Fresh / Frais ●

Water / Marine

AUTHENTIC MAROUSSIA   Slava Zaïtsev 1996
DIESEL PLUS PLUS FEMININE   Diesel 1997
EDEN   Cacharel 1994
NILANG   Lalique 1995
PARADOX   Jacomo 1998
SCULPTURE   Nikos 1994
SHEER HALSTON   Halston 1998
VICOLO FIORI   Etro 1996 ♂

White flowers / Fleurs blanches

ACCENTI   Gucci 1995
APRÈS L'ONDÉE   Guerlain 1906
BETTY BARCLAY WOMAN N° 2   Mäurer & Wirtz 1999
BYZANTINE*   Rochas 1995
ESCADA TENDER LIGHT   Escada-Margaretha Ley 1999
IRENA GREGORI   Succès de Paris 2000
METAL JEANS WOMEN   Versace 2000
PARFUM ALLIÉ MARIA 66   Shu Uemura 1988/99
VANILLA   Crabtree & Evelyn 1994

▶

Crisp / Pétillant ●●

White flowers / Fleurs blanches

AMARIGE   Givenchy 1991
ANTICIPATE / SULTRY   Amway 1998
BYZANCE   Rochas 1987
FRENCH CANCAN   Caron 1936
GABRIELA SABATINI   Gabriela Sabatini 1989
LALIQUE   Lalique 1992
LOULOU BLUE*   Cacharel 1995
MATSUKITA   Crown 1929
PHANTOM OF THE OPERA*   Parlux 1988
RUFFLES*   Oscar de la Renta 1983
SCHERRER 2   Jean-Louis Scherrer 1986
SUNSET BOULEVARD   Gale Hayman 1998

VICOLO FIORI   Etro 1996 ♂

▶ **Classical / Classique** ●●●

▶ **Rich / Profond** ●●●●

HELIOTROPE   Etro 1989 ⚥

Soft Oriental

Incense adds sensual overtones to fragrant flowers, spices and amber to create a softer style of Oriental. The base notes of a modern Soft Oriental are not as sweet or as heavy as a true Oriental and the result - a mélange of flowers and spices - is distinctly softer.

L'Oriental doux modère les ardeurs de l'Oriental « pur ». Ce n'est pas ici l'Orient des sérails mais celui des petits jardins embaumés de Damas. Beaucoup de douceur et de tendresse dans ces parfums qui cultivent les fleurs odorantes auxquelles se mêlent l'ambre, les épices et les vapeurs d'encens.

Fresh / Frais ●

Citrus fruity / Hespéridé fruité

INDEX ORANGE CHOCOLATE   Fresh 1997 ♂
KL   Lagerfeld 1982
ROYAL BAIN DE CHAMPAGNE   Caron 1941 ♂

Green / Vert

REALM WOMEN   Human Pheromone Sciences 1993
TRÈS CHIC   Holzman & Stephanie 2000

Water / Marine

MARIELLA   Mariella Burani 1996
PERLE DE SILENCES   Jacomo 1996

White flowers / Fleurs blanches

CRISTAL DE MUSC   Comptoir Sud Pacifique 1986
JOVAN WHITE MUSK   Jovan 1992

Crisp / Pétillant ●●

Citrus fruity / Hespéridé fruité

CARAMEL PAIN D'ÉPICE   Molinard 1999
L'EAU   Diptyque 1968 ♂
LE ROY SOLEIL   Salvador Dali 1997
OH LÀ LÀ   Azzaro 1993
OLIVIER STRELLI   Olivier Strelli 2000
ORANGE-CANNELLE   Molinard 1993
SUGAR COOKIE   Demeter Fragrance Library 1996 ♂
THEOREMA ESPRIT D'ÉTÉ   Fendi 1999

Green / Vert

COTONNADE   Comptoir Sud Pacifique 1988 ♂

INDEX ORANGE CHOCOLATE   Fresh 1997 ♂
JIL SANDER FEELING MAN   Jil Sander 1989
PIERRE CARDIN POUR MONSIEUR   Pierre Cardin 1972
ROYAL BAIN DE CHAMPAGNE   Caron 1941 ♂
SAMOURAÏ   Alain Delon 1995
SCOTT McCLINTOCK   Jessica McClintock 1992

COTONNADE   Comptoir Sud Pacifique 1988 ♂
L'EAU   Diptyque 1968 ♂
M de M   Marc de la Morandière 1998
MONSIEUR CARVEN*   Carven 1978
SUGAR COOKIE   Demeter Fragrance Library 1996 ♂

► Classical / Classique ●●●

ALEXANDRA   Alexandra de Markoff 1979
AMBRE CANNELLE   Creed 1949
ANGEL FOOD   Demeter Fragrance Library 1997 ♂
ANNÉ PLISKA   Anné Pliska 1987
ASJA   Fendi 1992
BULGARI PETITS ET MAMANS   Bulgari 1998
CAFÉ   Cofinluxe 1978
CALLA   Isabell 1996
CINNABAR   Estée Lauder 1978
COCO   Chanel 1984
DIORESSENCE   Christian Dior 1969/79
ENJOLI MIDNIGHT   Revlon 1984
ENRICO COVERI   Enrico Coveri 1987
GALANOS DE SERENE   Galanos 1979
HYPERSOUK   MAC 1999
J'AI OSÉ   Guy Laroche / J'Ai Osé 1977
JUNGLE: L'ÉLÉPHANT   Kenzo 1996
MAJA   Myrurgia 1921
MULBERRY   Mulberry 1997
NOHIBA (TULIPE NOIRE)   E.Coudray 1922
NORMANDIE   Jean Patou 1935
OPIUM   Yves Saint Laurent 1977
ORIENT   Déco 1981
POIS DE SENTEUR   Caron 1927
PRÉLUDE   Balenciaga 1982
SALVADOR DALI   Salvador Dali 1983
SCENT OF ROMANCE ORIGINAL   Perfumers Guild 1990
SOPHIA*   Coty 1980
SUBLIME   Jean Patou 1992
TEATRO ALLA SCALA*   Krizia 1986
THEOREMA   Fendi 1998
VANILLE   L'Occitane 1999 ♂
YOU'RE THE FIRE FOR WOMEN   Yardley 1973
YOUTH-DEW   Estée Lauder 1953

► Rich / Profond ●●●●

AMBRE SULTAN   Serge Lutens 1993 ♂
BLEU DE CHINE   Marc de la Morandière 1987/94
ETRA   Etro 1999 ♂
LOULOU   Cacharel 1987
POIVRE   Caron 1954
ROYAL DELIGHT   Creed 1993 ♂

ANGEL FOOD   Demeter Fragrance Library 1997 ♂
GRABAZZI   Gendarme 1995
J.H.L.*   Aramis 1982
OLD SPICE   Shulton / P&G 1937
PS   Paul Sebastian 1979
VANILLE   L'Occitane 1999 ♂

AMBRE SULTAN   Serge Lutens 1993 ♂
ETRA   Etro 1999 ♂
ROYAL COPENHAGEN MUSK   Royal Copenhagen 1976
ROYAL DELIGHT   Creed 1993 ♂

Soft Oriental

Oriental

*Orientals are the exotic queens of
perfumery. Sensual, often heavy, blends of
oriental resins, opulent flowers, sweet
vanilla and musks are introduced by
refreshing citrus, green or fruity top notes.
The new 'sheer' Orientals gained some
ground in the late 1990s, but the appeal of
the full-bodied, take-no-prisoners
Orientals endures.*

*Les parfums orientaux comblent, depuis
toujours, nos rêves d'exotisme et de
sensualité. Opulentes et tenaces, ces
formules offrent, en prélude, de fraîches
notes vertes, fruitées ou hespéridées, avant
de dérouler leurs effluves balsamiques,
fleuris, vanillés et musqués.
Les nouveaux Orientaux témoignent d'un
éternel attrait pour ces fragrances,
accessoires privilégiés de la séduction pure
… et des passions fatales.*

Fresh / Frais ●

Citrus fruity / Hespéridé fruité

ADRIENNE VITTADINI   Adrienne Vittadini 1999
BOND   James Bond 1997
I AM WILD   Danica Aromatics 1999
MAGOT   Etro 1996 ♂
OBSESSION   Calvin Klein 1985
OZBEK 1001   Rifat Ozbek 1999
VANILLE ABRICOT   Comptoir Sud Pacifique 1994
VANILLE AMANDE   Comptoir Sud Pacifique 1994
VANILLE CERISE   Comptoir Sud Pacifique 1997

Green / Vert

ANNE KLEIN II*   Parlux 1986
AYAKO   Marc de la Morandière 1999
DIONNE   Dionne Warwick 1986
MCM OBELISK   MCM 1985
MUST DE CARTIER   Cartier 1981
VERY VALENTINO   Valentino 1997

White flowers / Fleurs blanches

LANCASTER BODY & BATH   Lancaster 1987
VANILLE TIARÉ   Comptoir Sud Pacifique 1989

MAGOT   Etro 1996 ♂

Crisp / Pétillant ●●

Citrus fruity / Hespéridé fruité

AMOUR DE CACAO   Comptoir Sud Pacifique 1993
BELLE DE MINUIT   Nina Ricci 2000
BYBLOS URAGANO / HURRICANE   Byblos 2000
CHOCOLAT MENTHE   Molinard 1999
EAU DE CARON   Caron 1980
FATH DE FATH   Jacques Fath 1953/93
FIRE & ICE   Revlon 1994
FORUM   Tufi Duek 2000
KRAZY KRIZIA*   Krizia 1991
MONTE CARLO   Pierre Cardin 2000
SUI DREAMS   Anna Sui 2000
VANILLE FRAÎCHEUR   Molinard 1998
VANILLE FRUITÉE   Molinard 1998
YOHJI   Yohji Yamamoto 1996

Green / Vert

JAÏPUR SAPHIR   Boucheron 1999
ROMA   Laura Biagiotti 1988

White flowers / Fleurs blanches

JACQUELINE   Jean-Jacques Diener 1998
VANILLE   Comptoir Sud Pacifique 1978

EAU DE RUSSE   Crown 1911
HABIT ROUGE   Guerlain 1965
VERSAILLES   Jean Desprez 1980
YES FOR MEN   Lomani 2000

▶

Classical / Classique ●●●

AMBRA   Etro 1989 ♂
AMBRE   Molinard 1993
ANGÉLIQUE ENCENS   Creed 1933
ASMERA   Herbalife: Parfums Vitessence 1995
CHANTILLY   Houbigant / Dana 1941
EAU LENTE   Diptyque 1986 ♂
ÉMERAUDE   Coty 1921
EXTASE MUSK WOMAN   Muelhens 1976
INITIAL   Boucheron 2000
INTERLUDE   Frances Denney 1965
L'EAU D'AMBRE   L'Artisan Parfumeur 1978
LYRA   Alain Delon 1993
MALABAR   Crown 1919
MARBERT WOMAN   Marbert 1987
MISUKI   Holzman & Stephanie 1987
MOSCHINO   Moschino 1987
NUITS INDIENNES   Jean-Louis Scherrer 1994
OR DES INDES   Maître Parfumeur et Gantier 1988
ROYAL SECRET   Monteil / Royal Secret 1958
SAVANNAH GARDENS   Crabtree & Evelyn 1984
SHALIMAR   Guerlain 1925
SHOCKING   Schiaparelli 1937/97
VANILIA   L'Artisan Parfumeur 1978
VANILLE   E.Coudray 1986
VANILLE   Molinard 1993
VANILLE AMBRE   Molinard 2000
VANILLE CAFÉ   Comptoir Sud Pacifique 1987 ♂
VANILLE CANNELLE   E.Coudray 1935
VANILLE-TONKA   Patricia de Nicolaï 1997
VANISIA   Creed 1987

▶

Rich / Profond ●●●●

AMBRE PRÉCIEUX   Maître Parfumeur et Gantier 1988 ♂
ATTAR   Isabell 1996
CIARA   Revlon 1973
GINGERBREAD   Demeter Fragrance Library 1998 ♂
JUST MUSK   Lenthéric 1992/2000
KÉORA   Jean Couturier 1983
MESSE DE MINUIT   Etro 1994 ♂
MOLTO MISSONI   Missoni 1990
SECRÈTE DATURA   Maître Parfumeur et Gantier 1992
TABU   Dana 1932
UNTAMED MUSK   Déco 1994
WILD MUSK   Coty 1973

AMBRA   Etro 1989 ♂
EAU LENTE   Diptyque 1986 ♂
KL HOMME*   Lagerfeld 1986
VANILLE CAFÉ   Comptoir Sud Pacifique 1987 ♂

AMBRE PRÉCIEUX   Maître Parfumeur et Gantier 1988 ♂
EXTASE MUSK MAN   Muelhens 1985
GINGERBREAD   Demeter Fragrance Library 1998 ♂
MESSE DE MINUIT   Etro 1994 ♂
MONSIEUR MUSK   Parquet / Dana 1973

Oriental

Woody Oriental

The liaison of rich Oriental notes and the potent scents of patchouli and sandalwood produced some of the most original perfumes of the 1990s. This family emphasises the woody character of Floral Orientals. The key difference is that their flowers and spices play second string to the dominant sandalwood and/or patchouli notes. The Oriental influence is more noticeable, too, and balances the deep wood notes.

Si l'on associe de riches notes orientales aux puissantes senteurs du patchouli et du santal, on obtient certains des plus beaux parfums qui aient été créés ces dernières années. Cette famille exalte le caractère boisé des Fleuris orientaux; mais ici fleurs et épices jouent en sourdine tandis que s'épanouissent les essences de bois précieux. L'influence orientale, très évidente, équilibre ces résonnances boisées, intenses et profondes.

Fresh / Frais ●

Citrus fruity / Hespéridé fruité

100% PURE CHIPIE PURPLE   Coty 1998
ALL ABOUT EVE   Joop! 1996
ALYSSA ASHLEY VANILLA   Alyssa Ashley 1996
ANGEL   Thierry Mugler 1992
ANGEL INNOCENT   Thierry Mugler 1998
BASI FEMME   Idesa 2000
BLACKBERRY & VANILLA MUSK #9   Trish McEvoy 2000
BYBLOS CIELO / SKY   Byblos 1997
COLÈRE DE RODIER   Rodier 1999
COUTURE POUR ELLE   Philippe Venet 2000
CRISTOBAL   Balenciaga 1998
DESTINY WOMAN   Harley-Davidson 1999
DIESEL ZERO PLUS FEMININE   Diesel 1999
DULCE VANILLA   Coty 1999
ECLIX   La Perla 2000
ESCADA COLLECTION   Escada 1997
FIRE & ICE SMOULDER FOR HER   Revlon 1999
GATTINONI COUTURE   Gattinoni 1998
GOLD   Mary McFadden 1996
GOSSIP   Cindy Adams 1997
GUET-APENS* ℓ   Guerlain 1999
LOLITA LEMPICKA   Lolita Lempicka 1997
L'OR DES BOURBON   Marina de Bourbon 2000
MARINA DE BOURBON   Marina de Bourbon 1994
NIKE WOMAN   Nike 2000
NIRMALA   Molinard 1955/93/2000
OPERA III   Roberto Capucci 1999
PLEINE LUNE   Ulric de Varens 1995
POPY MORENI   Popy Moreni 1996
PRINCESSE CHIPIE   Coty 1997
RODIER   Rodier 1998
SIROCCO DONNA   Dana 1942/2000
SONIA RYKIEL   Sonia Rykiel 1997
SOPRANI 2   Luciano Soprani 1994
TODD OLDHAM*   Todd Oldham 1995
UNZIPPED   Perfumer's Workshop 1998
VANILLE COCO   E.Coudray 1989
WISH   Chopard 1997
WITH LOVE*   Fred Hayman 1991
ZUT   Schiaparelli 1937/97

Green / Vert

EXTASE DEVOTION WOMAN   Muelhens 1994
JIL   Jil Sander 1997
TRUTH CALVIN KLEIN   Calvin Klein 2000
TUSCANY PER DONNA   Aramis / Estée Lauder 1992
UN AIR DE SAMSARA   Guerlain 1995

Water / Marine

DUNE   Christian Dior 1991
LA PLAGE   Marc de la Moriandière 1999

White flowers / Fleurs blanches

25   Aubusson 1994
BEVERLY HILLS   Gale Hayman 1990
BLACK TIE   Oleg Cassini 1998
COEUR D'OR   Paris Bleu 1998
ENCHANTÉ   Déco 1987
E.N.C.O.R.E   Alfred Sung 1990
GERANI   Gerani 1998
LUNE D'ÉTÉ   Rémy Latour 1993
MARQUIS POUR FEMME   Rémy Marquis 1999
MASQUERADE   Bob Mackie 2000
ROUGE   Annabella 1999
VENDETTA*   Valentino 1991
YSATIS   Givenchy 1984

Crisp / Pétillant ●●

Citrus fruity / Hespéridé fruité

AMBUSH   Dana 1955/97
CASMIR   Chopard 1991
CHAOS*   Donna Karan 1996
DESNUDA   Ungaro 2001
DOLCE VITA   Christian Dior 1995
DOUCE AMÈRE   Serge Lutens 2000 ♂
FRENCH VANILLA   Dana 1994
HANAE MORI   Hanae Mori 1968/95
HOLLYWOOD   Fred Hayman 1998
HONEYMOON   Gloria Vanderbilt 1996
HOT COUTURE   Givenchy 2000
JUST ME   Montana 1997
LE PARFUM   Sonia Rykiel 1993
L'INSOLENT*   Charles Jourdan 1995
MAUBOUSSIN   Mauboussin 2000
MIRA BAÏ   Chopard 1998
OBLIQUE REWIND   Givenchy 2000
RECTOVERSO LOLLIPOP TOFFEE   Ulric de Varens 2000
SCARF   Marbert 1993
TEMPORE DONNA   Laura Biagiotti 1999
WATT RED   Cofinluxe 2000

Green / Vert

GUCCI RUSH   Gucci 1999
JOLIE MADAME   Pierre Balmain 1953/92
LAPIS   Napoleon 1999
MAGIE NOIRE   Lancôme 1978
MYSTÈRE   Rochas 1978
NUTMEG & GINGER   Jo Malone 1990 ♂
ORGANZA   Givenchy 1996
ORMOLU   Penhaligon's 1987
ROYAL SECRET II   Royal Secret 1999
SAVAGE VANILLA   Un Monde Nouveau 1993
SYNTHETIC NIRVANA   MAC 1999
VOL DE NUIT   Guerlain 1933

White flowers / Fleurs blanches

CAPUCCI DE CAPUCCI   Roberto Capucci 1987
GRAFFITI VANILLA   Naf Naf 1995
GUESS (Original)*   Guess (Georges Marciano) 1990
JUSTE UN RÊVE   Patricia de Nicolaï 1996
LYRA 2   Alain Delon 1995
VANILLA FIELDS   Coty 1993

A*MEN / ANGEL MEN   Thierry Mugler 1996
ARMAND BASI HOMME   Idesa 2000
BACKGROUND   Jil Sander 1993
BLACK JEANS HOMME   Roccobarroco 1998
BLUE JEANS   Versace 1994
BOSS   Hugo Boss 1998

► Classical / Classique ●●●

AMBER & LAVENDER Jo Malone 1995 ♂
AROMACALM Lancôme 2000
BIJAN Bijan 1987
BOIS DES ÎLES Chanel 1926
BYBLOS FUOCO / FIRE Byblos 1998
BY WOMAN Dolce & Gabbana 1997
CROWN HELIOTROPE Crown 1939
DANS LA NUIT Worth 1924/85/2000
DIAMONDS & RUBIES* Elizabeth Taylor 1993
DIESEL Diesel 1996 ♂
EAU DE PIVER L.T.Piver 2000
ELLEN TRACY Ellen Tracy 1992/2000
ENIGMA Alexandra de Markoff 1972
EUNECE Fashion Fair 1985
EXTASE PURE PASSION WOMAN Muelhens 2000
FABLE Hope Diamond Collection 1999
FEMINITÉ DU BOIS Shiseido 1992
FLUID ICEBERG WOMAN Iceberg 2000
GRAIN DE SOLEIL Fragonard 1999
GUÉPARD Guépard 1997
HELMUT LANG WOMAN Helmut Lang 2000
I AM ETERNAL Danica Aromatics 1999
INTOXICATION D'AMOUR d'Orsay 1942/97
JEAN LUC AMSLER PRIVÉ FEMME Jean Luc Amsler 2001
JOOP! NUIT D'ÉTÉ* Joop! 1990
KIRI Kiri Te Kanawa 1999
LE FEU D'ISSEY Issey Miyake 1998
LELONG POUR FEMME Lucien Lelong 1999
L'HEURE ATTENDUE Jean Patou 1946
MANIA Giorgio Armani 1999
MOMENTS Priscilla Presley 1990
MORGANE LE FAY BLUE Morgane Le Fay 2000
MUSC Molinard 1995
NUBIADE* Omar Sharif 1994
NUIT DE NOËL Caron 1922
OM Gap 1996 ♂
ONLY Julio Iglesias 1989
PAIN D'ÉPICES Comptoir Sud Pacifique 1986
PARFUM ALLIÉ DELICIOUS 62 Shu Uemura 1988/99
PASSION Elizabeth Taylor 1987
PATCHOULY Etro 1989 ♂
PYTHON Trussardi 1999
RÉGINE'S Régine's 1989
ROCOCO Joop! 1999
SAMBA HEAT WOMAN Perfumer's Workshop 2000
SAMSARA Guerlain 1989
SANDALWOOD Yardley 1996 ♂
SANTAL IMPÉRIAL Creed 1850 ♂
SECRET DE VÉNUS Weil 1933/96
SMALTO DONNA* Francesco Smalto 1993
SO...? So Cosmetics 1994
SOLEIL LEVANT Comptoir Sud Pacifique 1975
SOTTO VOCE* Laura Biagiotti 1996
STÉPHANIE Stéphanie de Monaco 1989
TENTATIONS* Paloma Picasso 1996
THÉ Comptoir Sud Pacifique 1997 ♂
VANILLA MUSK Coty 1994
VANILLE PATCHOULI Molinard 1998
VENEZIA* Laura Biagiotti 1992
WOODHUE* Fabergé 1944

► Rich / Profond ●●●●

ARABIE Serge Lutens 2000 ♂
FENDI Fendi 1985
FEUILLE D'HERBE FRAÎCHE & EPICÉE L'Occitane 1999
GEM Van Cleef & Arpels 1987
HABANITA Molinard 1921
HYPNOTIC POISON Christian Dior 1998
JOOP! Joop! 1987
NAOMI CAMPBELL Naomi Campbell 1999
ORGANZA INDÉCENCE Givenchy 1999
SANDALO Etro 1989 ♂
SHAAL NUR Etro 1997 ♂
SHAHI Chypron 1995
TEA FOR TWO L'Artisan Parfumeur 2000
TOUJOURS MOI Corday / Dana 1921
UNFORGETTABLE Revlon 1990
UNGARO Ungaro 1977/90
WINTER DELICE ⓛ Guerlain 2000

▶

Fresh / Frais ●

ALLURE HOMME   Chanel 1998
ANIMALE ANIMALE FOR MEN   Parlux 1994
BEST MAN   Succès de Paris 1995
BLEU MARINE   Pierre Cardin 1965/86
BODY KOUROS   Yves Saint Laurent 2000
BRUNO BANANI   Bruno Banani 2000
CASRAN   Chopard 1999
CASUAL FRIDAY   Escada 1999
CHEVIGNON 57 FOR HIM   Chevignon 1999
CHIEMSEE MAN TWO   Chiemsee 2000
COLORS FOR MEN   Benetton 1988
CONTRADICTION FOR MEN   Calvin Klein 1998
COUTURE POUR LUI   Philippe Venet 2000
DESIRE   Alfred Dunhill 2000
DIESEL PLUS PLUS MASCULINE   Diesel 1997
DUNE POUR HOMME   Christian Dior 1997
ENVY FOR MEN   Gucci 1998
FERRARI RED   Ferrari 1996
GENGIS KHAN   Marc de la Morandière 1989
GERANI UOMO   Gerani 1999
H.M.   Hanae Mori 1997
ICEBERG UNIVERSE HOMME   Iceberg 1997
IMPROV   Herbalife: Parfums Vitessence 1995
JORDAN BY MICHAEL   Bijan 1999
JOVAN WHITE MUSK FOR MEN   Jovan 1992
KITON NAPOLI   Palladio 1998
LALIQUE POUR HOMME BLEU   Lalique 2000
LAND   Lacoste 1991
LIGHT HIM   Trussardi 1997
MASCULIN OURAGAN   Bourjois 1997
MOLINARD HOMME II   Molinard 1996
OBSESSION FOR MEN   Calvin Klein 1986
PARADOX FOR MEN   Jacomo 1999
PEOPLE UOMO   Luciano Soprani 1999
PERIPHERY / OPPORTUNE   Amway 1998
RAW VANILLA   Coty 1996
RÉGINE'S FOR MEN   Régine's 1993
REPLAY   Morris 1996
S pour HOMME   Francesco Smalto 2001
SAMBA HEAT MAN   Perfumer's Workshop 2000
SANTA FE FOR MEN   Tsumura 1988
SÉXUAL POUR HOMME   Michel Germain 1996
SIGNATURE POUR HOMME   S.T.Dupont 2000
TEMPORE UOMO   Laura Biagiotti 1999
THAT'S AMORE! LUI   Gai Mattiolo 2000
TOUCH GRIGIOPERLA   La Perla 2000
ULYSSE   Vicky Tiel 1998
UOMO? MOSCHINO   Moschino 1997
VANDERBILT FOR MEN   Gloria Vanderbilt 2000
VERSUS UOMO*   Versace 1990
V/S MAN   Versace 2000
X   Mäurer & Wirtz 1998
XXL   Daniel Hechter 1997
YANG   Jacques Fath 1999

▶

Crisp / Pétillant ●●

BURBERRYS FOR MEN (Original)*   Burberry 1992
BY MAN   Dolce & Gabbana 1998
CATALYST FOR MEN   Halston 1994
CENTAURE CUIR AMBRE   Pierre Cardin 1996
CIGAR   Rémy Latour 1996
CONVICTION MEN   Omar Sharif 1999
DAKS   Daks 2001
DNA FOR MEN*   Bijan 1993
DOUCE AMÈRE   Serge Lutens 2000 ♂
DUÉ WILD   Lomani 2000
THE DREAMER   Versace 1996
ERUPTION MAN   Mäurer & Wirtz 1997
ESCADA POUR HOMME   Escada 1993
EXTASE PURE PASSION MAN   Muelhens 2000
FORCE MAJEURE   Jacques Bogart 1998
GIGLI PER UOMO   Romeo Gigli 1991
GINSENG N.R.G   Jovan 1998
GMV HOT   Gian Marco Venturi 2000
GRAVITY   Coty 1992
HÉRITAGE   Guerlain 1992
HÉROS   Didier Calvo-Uomo 1995
HERRERA FOR MEN   Carolina Herrera 1991
JACOMO DE JACOMO   Jacomo 1980
JAGUAR MARK II   Jaguar 1995
JAÏPUR HOMME   Boucheron 1997
JAKO   Lagerfeld 1997
JIMMY'Z   Régines 1991
JIVAGO 7 ELEMENTS   Jivago 1998
JOHNNY LAMBS   Schiapparelli Pikenz 1995
JUNGLE POUR HOMME   Kenzo 1998
KIPLING   Weil 1986
LALIQUE POUR HOMME   Lalique 1997
LE MÂLE   Jean Paul Gaultier 1995
LOLITA LEMPICKA AU MASCULIN   Lolita Lempicka 2000
MAN.AUBUSSON   Aubusson 2000
MANÈS   Rémy Latour 1990
MINOTAURE*   Paloma Picasso 1992
MONTANA POUR HOMME   Montana 1989
NAUTICA COMPETITION   Nautica 1997
NEMO   Cacharel 1999
NEW YORK   Patricia de Nicolaï 1989
NICOLE MILLER FOR MEN   Nicole Miller 1994
NUTMEG & GINGER   Jo Malone 1990 ♂
OPIUM POUR HOMME   Yves Saint Laurent 1995
PASSION D'HOMME   Rodier 1999
PATCHOULI   Crabtree & Evelyn 1970
POUR L'HOMME   Jacques Fath 1998
REALM MEN   Human Pheromone Sciences 1993
RELAX   Davidoff 1990
RÉMY   Rémy Marquis 1999
RICCI-CLUB   Nina Ricci 1989
ROCHAS MAN   Rochas 1999
ROMA UOMO   Laura Biagiotti 1994
ROYAL SECRET FOR MEN*   Royal Secret 1999
SABLES   Annick Goutal 1985
SAFRANIER   Comptoir Sud Pacifique 1996
SALVADOR DALI POUR HOMME   Salvador Dali 1987
SAMBA NOVA HOMME   Perfumer's Workshop 1993
SCULPTURE HOMME   Nikos 1995
SIROCCO UOMO   Dana 2000
SUMATRA RAIN WOOD   Muelhens 1997
SYBARIS   Antonio Puig 1988
TED   Ted Lapidus 1999
TYCOON   Marbert 1997
U de V N° 2   Ulric de Varens 1999
VENEZIA UOMO*   Laura Biagiotti 1995
VERY VALENTINO POUR HOMME   Valentino 1999
WATT FOR MEN GREEN   Cofinluxe 2000
XERYUS ROUGE   Givenchy 1995
ZIPPED UNIVERSE   Perfumer's Workshop 1999

▶

Classical / Classique ●●●

▶

Rich / Profond ●●●●

π   Givenchy 1998
AMBER & LAVENDER   Jo Malone 1995 ⚥
AMBRO DE JACOMO   Jacomo 1996
BAIE DE GENIÈVRE   Creed 1982
CHAPS   Ralph Lauren 1979
CHAPS MUSK   Ralph Lauren 1985
COTY MUSK FOR MEN   Coty 1974
CRISTOBAL POUR HOMME   Balenciaga 2000
DERRICK   Orlane 1978/80
DIESEL   Diesel 1996 ⚥
DIESEL ZERO PLUS MASCULINE   Diesel 1999
EAU DE SANDALWOOD   Le Jardin Retrouvé 1977
ÉGOÏSTE / L'ÉGOÏSTE   Chanel 1990
EXTASE MAGMA MAN   Muelhens 1993
FERRÉ FOR MAN   Gianfranco Ferré 1986
G2   Gant 1999
HAMMAM BOUQUET   Penhaligon's 1872
JOOP! HOMME   Joop! 1989
KANØN   Scannon 1966
LAGERFELD   Lagerfeld 1978
LAMBROSIO   Lomani 2000
LP N° 9 FOR MEN   Penhaligon's 1999
MCM 24 EVENING*   MCM 1993
MOODS UOMO*   Krizia 1989
MUST DE CARTIER POUR HOMME   Cartier 2000
OM   Gap 1996 ⚥
PASSION FOR MEN   Elizabeth Taylor 1989
PATCHOULY   Etro 1989 ⚥
PATOU POUR HOMME   Jean Patou 1980
ROI SANTAL   Comptoir Sud Pacifique 1988
ROYAL COPENHAGEN   Royal Copenhagen 1970
SANDALWOOD   Crabtree & Evelyn 1970
SANDALWOOD   Yardley 1996 ⚥
SANDRINGHAM   Crown 1873
SANTAL IMPÉRIAL   Creed 1850 ⚥
STETSON   Coty 1981
THÉ   Comptoir Sud Pacifique 1997 ⚥
TIFFANY FOR MEN   Tiffany 1989
VERDI 800   Pol 1995
VERSACE L'HOMME   Versace 1984
ZIZANIE   Fragonard / Marimar 1932

ARABIE   Serge Lutens 2000 ⚥
BALENCIAGA POUR HOMME*   Balenciaga 1990
BOIS DU PORTUGAL   Creed 1987
BURL   Sulka 1998
FURYO*   Jacques Bogart 1988
HOMBRE DE FLORES NARCISSUS   Fresh 1999
M de MORABITO   Morabito 1989
MAN DE RAUCH   Madeleine de Rauch 1998
MAXIM'S POUR HOMME*   Maxim's 1988
SANDALO   Etro 1989 ⚥
SHAAL NUR   Etro 1997 ⚥
ZAHAROFF POUR HOMME   Zaharoff 1999
ZINO DAVIDOFF   Davidoff 1986

Woody Oriental

masculine

63

Mossy Woods

Perfumers call these forest notes of oakmoss, woods and citrus Chypre fragrances. The family takes its name from the first significant mossy-woody fragrance, *Chypre de Coty*, created by François Coty in 1917. Chypre is the French name for the island of Cyprus, birthplace of Venus, the legendary goddess of love. From Cyprus, too, comes the oakmoss that is at the heart of all Chypre fragrances.

Ces accords que l'on dit « chyprés » sont pleins de senteurs automnales et de parfums de sous-bois que relèvent des fraîcheurs hespéridées. C'est le Chypre de Coty, *premier parfum moussu-boisé créé par François Coty en 1917, qui est à l'origine de cette famille de senteurs. Le nom lui est resté, d'autant qu'il évoque l'île mythique où serait née Vénus et où l'on récolte la mousse de chêne, indispensable ingrédient des chyprés boisés.*

Chypre Boisé

féminin

▶ Fresh / Frais ●

Citrus fruity / Hespéridé fruité

AQUA DI AQUA   Marina de Bourbon 2000
CHOC   Pierre Cardin 1981
CIELO   Napa Valley 1998
FEUILLE D'HERBE FLORALE & FRUITÉE   L'Occitane 1999
FIG LEAF   Demeter Fragrance Library 1996 ♂
FLEUR DE FIGUIER   Molinard 1999
HALSTON   Halston 1975
INDEX FIG APRICOT   Fresh 1997 ♂
LIBERTINE   Vivienne Westwood 2000
MAGIC   Céline 1996
NIKI DE SAINT PHALLE   Niki de Saint Phalle 1982
PHILOSYKOS   Diptyque 1996 ♂
PREMIER FIGUIER   L'Artisan Parfumeur 1994
YVRESSE (CHAMPAGNE)   Yves Saint Laurent 1993

Green / Vert

ARMANI   Giorgio Armani 1982
BAÏMÉ   Maître Parfumeur et Gantier 2000 ♂
BALMAIN   Pierre Balmain 1998
COCKTAIL   Jean Patou 1930
COMME DES GARÇONS 2   Comme des Garçons 1999 ♂
DENEUVE*   Catherine Deneuve 1986
EARTH   Gap 1994 ♂
GAULOISE*   Molyneux 1980
GIVENCHY III   Givenchy 1970
GRAIN DE PLAISIR   Maître Parfumeur et Gantier 1998 ♂
GREEN VALLEY   Creed 1999 ♂
INDEX GALBANUM PATCHOULI   Fresh 1999 ♂
INTIMATE*   Revlon 1955
MISS DIOR   Christian Dior 1947
U II SHEER SCENT   Ultima II 1990
Y   Yves Saint Laurent 1964
ZEN (New)   Shiseido 2000

Water / Marine

EASY KRIZIA   Krizia 1999
MONTANA PARFUM D'ELLE*   Montana 1990

White flowers / Fleurs blanches

CONSIDERATIONS / CONFIDENT   Amway 1998
CRÉATION   Ted Lapidus 1984
LACE   Yardley / FFC 1984
SAMBA NOVA   Perfumer's Workshop 1992

♂ Shared *mixte*

▶ Crisp / Pétillant ●●

Citrus fruity / Hespéridé fruité

ANOUCHKA   Révillon 1994
CAFÉ-CAFÉ ADVENTURE POUR FEMME   Cofinluxe 2000
CASSINI   Oleg Cassini 1990
CHAPEAU BLEU   DC Design 1994
COLONY   Jean Patou 1938
DECI DELÀ   Nina Ricci 1994
FLEURS DES COMORES   Maître Parfumeur et Gantier 1988
INDEX CEDAR ARMOISE   Fresh 1999 ♂
IO   La Perla 1995
IQUITA*   Alain Delon 1996
JARDIN SECRET   Patricia de Nicolaï 1992
ORO POUR FEMME   Renata Balestra 1997
PARFUM D'OR   Kristel Saint Martin 1995
PAVAROTTI DONNA   Pavarotti 1995
POMME CANNELLE   Molinard 1999
RACINE   Maître Parfumeur et Gantier 1988 ♂
RED   Giorgio Beverly Hills 1989
RIVIERA PALACE   L'Artisan Parfumeur 1990
RUE PEROGLÈSE   Ulric de Varens 1996
SHU UEMURA   Shu Uemura 1989
TALISMAN   Balenciaga 1994
VARENSIA   Ulric de Varens 1994
VERSACE WOMAN   Versace 2001
V'E VERSACE*   Versace 1989
VETYVER HAITI   Comptoir Sud Pacifique 1977 ♂
YOHJI ESSENTIAL   Yohji Yamamoto 1998

Green / Vert

APHRODISIA*   Fabergé 1938
BOHÈME   Napa Valley 2000
CHANT D'ARÔMES   Guerlain 1962
CRÊPE DE CHINE*   Millot 1925
DIRT   Demeter Fragrance Library 1996 ♂
FLEUR DE CAROTTE Ⓛ   L'Artisan Parfumeur 2000
FLORAMYE   L.T.Piver 1905/91
INDEX VIOLET MOSS   Fresh 1997 ♂
MA GRIFFE   Carven 1946
VETYVER   Jo Malone 1995 ♂

Water / Marine

SNOW   Demeter Fragrance Library 1999 ♂

White flowers / Fleurs blanches

ANGEL SCHLESSER FEMME   Idesa 2000
EXPLOSIVE*   Etienne Aigner 1986
GUCCI N° 3*   Gucci 1985
JIL SANDER WOMAN II*   Jil Sander 1982
LADY CARON   Caron 2000

* Discontinued *non disponible*

► **Classical / Classique** ●●●

ACQUA DI PARMA PROFUMO   Acqua di Parma 2000
AGENT PROVOCATEUR   Agent Provocateur 2000
ANTILOPE   Weil 1945
APERÇU   Houbigant: Claire 2000
APOGÉE   Les Senteurs 1991
AZZARO   Azzaro 1975
CALÈCHE   Hermès 1961/92
CHYPRE DE COTY*   Coty 1917
CROWN OF GOLD   Crown 1910
DIORAMA   Christian Dior 1949
DONNA TRUSSARDI   Trussardi 1993
EAU DU SOIR   Sisley 1990
EAU FRAÎCHE   Christian Dior 1953
EXC'LA.MA'TION NOIR   Coty 1998
FEMME   Rochas 1944/89
FILLE D'EVE   Nina Ricci 1952
FLEURS DE LA FORÊT   Jo Malone 1995
HALSTON COUTURE*   Halston 1988
HISTOIRE D'AMOUR   Aubusson 1984
IMPERIAL VETYVER   Yardley 1996 ♂
INDEX OLIVE MUSCADE   Fresh 1999 ♂
INFINITIF   Infinitif 1994
INSTINCT D'ANIMALE   Parlux 1997
JIL SANDER BATH & BEAUTY   Jil Sander 1981
KNOWING   Estée Lauder 1988
LANCETTI MADAME   Lancetti 1995
L'ARTE DI GUCCI*   Gucci 1991
LE TEMPS D'AIMER   Alain Delon 1981
MARÉCHALE 90   Crown 1994
MILA SCHÖN   Mila Schön 1980
MITSOUKO   Guerlain 1919
OPÔNÉ   Diptyque 2001 ♂
PAGAN   Picot / Lenthéric 1967
PALOMA PICASSO   Paloma Picasso 1984
PARFUM PRIVÉ*   La Perla 1998
PARURE   Guerlain 1975
PATCHOULI   Molinard 1993 ♂
PURE SILK   Lenthéric 1982
QUADRILLE   Balenciaga 1955
QUE SAIS-JE?   Jean Patou 1925
RÉPLIQUE*   Raphaël 1947
RIZIÈRES   Comptoir Sud Pacifique 2001 ♂
ROSE CARDIN   Pierre Cardin 1990
SAWDUST   Demeter Fragrance Library 1999 ♂
SOIR D'ÉTÉ   Morabito 1995
TIEMPE PASSATE   Antonia's Flowers 1999
TUXEDO*   Ralph Lauren 1979
UBAR   Amouage 1995
VIE DE CHATEAU (CHEVERNY)   Patricia de Nicolaï 1992 ♂
WHITE JEANS*   Versace 1997
ZIBELINE   Weil 1928

► **Rich / Profond** ●●●●

ANIMALE   Parlux 1987
CHIQUE   Yardley / FFC 1976
COMME DES GARÇONS   Comme des Garçons 1994 ♂
CORIANDRE   Jean Couturier 1973
DIVA   Ungaro 1983
GIANNI VERSACE   Versace 1982
INDEX MANDARINE AMBER   Fresh 1999 ♂
MAROC*   Revlon 1985
MISHA   Mikhail Baryshnikov 1989
MISSONI   Missoni 1981
TURBULENCES   Révillon 1981

Fresh / Frais ●

212 MEN   Carolina Herrera 1999
BAÏMÉ   Maître Parfumeur et Gantier 2000 ♂
BURBERRY TOUCH FOR MEN   Burberry 2000
CHAMADE POUR HOMME* ⓛ   Guerlain 1999
CHAUMET HOMME   Chaumet 2001
COMME DES GARÇONS 2   Comme des Garçons 1999 ♂
EARTH   Gap 1994 ♂
EAU DE GREY FLANNEL   Geoffrey Beene 1996
EAU GRISE   Comptoir Sud Pacifique 1976
FAHRENHEIT   Christian Dior 1988
FIG LEAF   Demeter Fragrance Library 1996 ♂
GENTLEMAN GUÉPARD   Guépard 2000
GRAIN DE PLAISIR   Maître Parfumeur et Gantier 1998 ♂
GREEN VALLEY   Creed 1999 ♂
GREY FLANNEL   Geoffrey Beene 1976
HUGO DARK BLUE   Hugo Boss 1999
HUNTSMAN   Perfumer's Guild 1999
INDEX FIG APRICOT   Fresh 1997 ♂
INDEX GALBANUM PATCHOULI   Fresh 1999 ♂
IRIS BLEU GRIS   Maître Parfumeur et Gantier 1988
KITON MEN   Palladio 1996
MARBERT MAN PURE   Marbert 1989
PHILOSYKOS   Diptyque 1996 ♂
R   Révillon 1995
SALVATORE FERRAGAMO POUR HOMME   Ferragamo 1999
UOMO   Compagnia Delle Indie 2000
VOYAGEUR   Jean Patou 1995

Crisp / Pétillant ●●

AQUA VELVA ICE BLUE   Williams 1935
AUBUSSON HOMME   Aubusson 1992
BASI HOMME   Idesa 2000
BURBERRY WEEK END FOR MEN   Burberry 1997
CENTAURE CUIR BLANC   Pierre Cardin 1996
CHEVIGNON   Chevignon 1992
CORIOLAN   Guerlain 1998
DIRT   Demeter Fragrance Library 1996 ♂
DUO POUR HOMME   Vuarnet 2000
EAU DE VÉTYVER   Le Jardin Retrouvé 1977
EMPORIO ARMANI HE / LUI   Giorgio Armani 1998
FERRARI BLACK   Ferrari 1999
FIRE & ICE SMOULDER FOR HIM   Revlon 1999
FRAÎCHE BADIANE   Maître Parfumeur et Gantier 1994
GREENERGY   Givenchy 1999
GUCCI RUSH FOR MEN   Gucci 2000
GUÉPARD HOMME   Guépard 1998
HALSTON Z   Halston 1998
HALSTON Z-14   Halston 1976
HIGH TECH MEN   Lomani 1999
HOMBRE DE FLORES JASMINUM   Fresh 1999
IMPLICITE HOMME   Sea World 1998
INDEX CEDAR ARMOISE   Fresh 1999 ♂
INDEX VIOLET MOSS   Fresh 1997 ♂
IRISCH MOOS / IRISH MOSS   Muelhens 1935
LE ROY SOLEIL HOMME   Salvador Dali 1998
LES COPAINS L'HOMME   Les Copains 1998
LIFE ESSENCE   Fendi 1996
LUCKY YOU FOR MEN   Lucky Brand 2000
MADRIGAL   Molinard 1935/93
MARBERT GENTLEMAN   Marbert 1986
METROPOLIS   Estée Lauder 1987
MOUSTACHE   Rochas 1948
OPERA IV   Roberto Capucci 1999
PRIVATE NUMBER FOR MEN*   Etienne Aigner 1992
PURE VÉTIVER   Azzaro 2000
RACINE   Maître Parfumeur et Gantier 1988 ♂
SAMBA RED MAN   Perfumer's Workshop 1999
SIENNA   Crabtree & Evelyn 1990
SMALTO   Francesco Smalto 1987/98
SNOW   Demeter Fragrance Library 1999 ♂
STETSON COUNTRY   Coty 1998
THEOREMA UOMO   Fendi 2001
TOWN & COUNTRY   Crown 1925
UN AIR DE JAVA   Decléor 2000
VERSION HOMME*   Ulric de Varens 1995
VETIVER HOMBRE   Adolfo Dominguez 1998
VETYVER   Jo Malone 1995 ♂
VETYVER HAITI   Comptoir Sud Pacifique 1977 ♂

Shared *mixte*

* Discontinued *non disponible*

Classical / Classique ●●●

ACQUA DI SELVA   Victor 1949
AGUA BRAVA   Antonio Puig 1968
AGUA FRESCA   Adolfo Dominguez 1996
ARGENTO POUR HOMME   Renato Balestra 1997
AURA FOR MEN   Jacomo 2000
CHANEL POUR MONSIEUR   Chanel 1955
CLASSIC   Yardley / Parfums Bleu 1985
DESTINY   Harley-Davidson 1999
EAU DE MONSIEUR   Annick Goutal 1981
FOR GENTLEMEN   Woods of Windsor 1981
IMPERIAL VETYVER   Yardley 1996 ♂
INDEX OLIVE MUSCADE   Fresh 1999 ♂
OPÔNÉ   Diptyque 2001 ♂
PATCHOULI   Molinard 1993 ♂
PINO SILVESTRE ORIGINAL   Pino Silvestre: Mavive 1955
RIZIÈRES   Comptoir Sud Pacifique 2001 ♂
ROUTE DU VÉTIVER   Maître Parfumeur et Gantier 1988
SAWDUST   Demeter Fragrance Library 1999 ♂
SILVESTRE   Victor 1946
TIMBERLINE   Mem / Dana 1968
VÉTIVER   Carven 1957
VETIVER   Creed 1948
VETIVER   Floris c1870/2000
VETIVER   Guerlain 1959
VÉTYVER   L.T.Piver 1991
VETYVER   Molinard 1984
VÉTYVER   Roger & Gallet 1974/91
VIE DE CHATEAU (CHEVERNY)   Patricia de Nicolaï 1992 ♂

Rich / Profond ●●●●

ACIER ALUMINIUM   Creed 1973
BOIS PRÉCIEUX   Molinard 1995
BOURBON HOMME   Marina de Bourbon 1999
COMME DES GARÇONS   Comme des Garçons 1994 ♂
GIORGIO MEN*   Giorgio Beverly Hills 1984
GIVENCHY GENTLEMAN   Givenchy 1974
INDEX MANDARINE AMBER   Fresh 1999 ♂
IQUITOS*   Alain Delon 1987
MCM SUCCESS*   MCM 1986
SANTAL NOBLE   Maître Parfumeur et Gantier 1988

Ⓛ Limited edition *édition limitée*

1947 Launch *lancement*   1947 / 92 Reorchestration *recréation*

Dry Woods

A mossy-woody fragrance takes on a drier character with the addition of cedar, tobacco and burnt wood notes. The Dry Woods family is often called Leather, after the dry, smoky scent of Russian leather. Fresh citrus notes play an important role in most Dry Woods fragrances, lightening the deep, almost animalic heart notes.

Cette famille un peu particulière associe aux senteurs moussues-boisées des notes de cèdre, de tabac et de bois brûlé. Il en résulte des parfums dont l'odeur très sèche et fumée rappelle un peu celle du cuir de Russie. Ces notes profondes, presque animales, sont en général éclaircies et rafraîchies de touches hespéridées.

▶

Fresh / Frais ●

Citrus fruity / Hespéridé fruité

AIR DE ... CABOCHARD   Grès 2000

Green / Vert

AROMATICS ELIXIR   Clinique 1971
EAU DE CÈDRE   Comptoir Sud Pacifique 1975 ♂
GENNY (Original)   Genny 1987
PASSION DE FEMME   Rodier 2000
VOLEUR DE ROSES   L'Artisan Parfumeur 1993 ♂

Water / Marine

ODEUR 71   Comme de Garçons 2000 ♂

White flowers / Fleurs blanches

CASHMERE MIST   Donna Karan 1994

ARAMIS 900   Aramis 1973
BE BOP MAN   Kesling 1995
DÉCLARATION   Cartier 1998
DK MEN UNLEADED*   Donna Karan 1995
EAU DE CÈDRE   Comptoir Sud Pacifique 1975 ♂
ESSENZA DI MEDITERRANEÒ UOMO   Parah 1999
FLUID ICEBERG MAN   Iceberg 2000
LE DANDY   d'Orsay 1925/98
ODEUR 71   Comme de Garçons 2000 ♂
SPAZIO KRIZIA UOMO   Krizia 1993
SPRINGFIELD   Antonio Puig 1993
VETIVER   L'Artisan Parfumeur 1978
VOLEUR DE ROSES   L'Artisan Parfumeur 1993 ♂

▶

Crisp / Pétillant ●●

Citrus fruity / Hespéridé fruité

BULGARI BLACK   Bulgari 1998 ♂
JITROIS   Jean-Claude Jitrois 1989
RUMBA   Balenciaga 1988
SOIE ROUGE   Maître Parfumeur et Gantier 1988

Green / Vert

COEUR DE PARFUM*   Jacomo 1987
JIL SANDER WOMAN III   Jil Sander 1986
L'EAU TROIS   Diptyque 1975 ♂

White flowers / Fleurs blanches

PASSAGE D'ENFER   L'Artisan Parfumeur 1999

273 RODEO DRIVE FOR MEN   Fred Hayman 1990
ACTEUR   Azzaro 1989
ADIDAS CLASSIC   Adidas 1986
AIGNER POUR HOMME   Etienne Aigner 2000
BASILE UOMO   Basile 1987
BOSS SPIRIT*   Hugo Boss 1989
BULGARI BLACK   Bulgari 1998 ♂
CARACTÈRE   Daniel Hechter 1989
CARLO CORINTO   Carlo Corinto 1984
CARVEN HOMME   Carven 1999
CROWN PARK ROYAL   Crown 1929
DK MEN*   Donna Karan 1994
EAU DE CUIR DE RUSSIE   Le Jardin Retrouvé 1977
ENGLISH LEATHER   Mem / Dana 1949
ESENCIA LOEWE   Loewe 1987
JEAN LUC AMSLER PRIVÉ HOMME   Jean Luc Amsler 2001
L'EAU TROIS   Diptyque 1975 ♂
LEGENDARY   Harley-Davidson 1994
L'HOMME   Comptoir Sud Pacifique 1993
LORD MOLYNEUX*   Molyneux 1988
MARBERT HOMME   Marbert 1988
MARK BIRLEY FOR MEN   Mark Birley 1996
MONTECRISTO   Perfumes y Diseño 2000
MOSCHINO POUR HOMME   Moschino 1991
MULBERRY FOR MEN   Mulberry 1966
NIAGARA   Courrèges 1995
OSCAR DE LA RENTA POUR LUI   Oscar de la Renta 1980
OSCAR FOR MEN   Oscar de la Renta 1999
PHEROMONE FOR MEN   Marilyn Miglin 1999
POLO   Ralph Lauren 1978
POLO CREST   Ralph Lauren 1991
POLO SPORT EXTREME   Ralph Lauren 1998
PONTACCIO 21   Gianfranco Ferré 2000
QUORUM   Antonio Puig 1982
SEAWARD   Herbalife: Parfums Vitessence 1995
TOUCHDOWN   Mäurer & Wirtz 2000
TRUSSARDI UOMO FRESH   Trussardi 1999
VENDETTA POUR HOMME*   Valentino 1991

►

Classical / Classique ●●●

AZURÉE   Estée Lauder 1969
BANDIT   Robert Piguet 1944
CABOCHARD   Grès 1959
CACHET (Original)   Prince Matchabelli 1970
CUIR DE RUSSIE   Chanel 1924
CUIR DE RUSSIE   L.T.Piver 1939 ♂
DIORLING   Christian Dior 1963
DONNA KARAN   Donna Karan 1992
EAU D'HERMÈS   Hermès 1951 ♂
EMPREINTE   Courrèges 1971/92
IMPRÉVU   Coty 1966
INDEX TOBACCO CARAMEL   Fresh 1999 ♂
LA PERLA   La Perla 1987
MISS BALMAIN   Pierre Balmain 1967
POMPEÏA   L.T.Piver 1907
TABAC BLOND   Caron 1919
THIS IS NOT A PIPE   Demeter Fragrance Library 1998 ♂
TRUSSARDI   Trussardi 1982
VETIVER   Etro 1989 ♂

►

Rich / Profond ●●●●

BONFIRE   Demeter Fragrance Library 2000 ♂
DZING!   L'Artisan Parfumeur 1999
GOMMA   Etro 1989 ♂
LA NUIT   Paco Rabanne 1985
L'AUTRE   Diptyque 1973 ♂
MONTANA PARFUM DE PEAU   Montana 1986
PALAIS JAMAIS   Etro 1989 ♂

ARAMIS   Aramis 1965
ARAMIS GOLD   Aramis 1998
ATMAN   Atman 1998
BALADIN   Patricia de Nicolaï 1994
BARBIER DES ISLES   Comptoir Sud Pacifique 1978
CENTAURE CUIR ÉTALON   Pierre Cardin 1996
ᶜN   California North 1995
CRABTREE & EVELYN FOR MEN*   Crabtree & Evelyn 1984
CUIR DE RUSSIE   L.T.Piver 1939 ♂
DUNHILL   Alfred Dunhill 1934
EAU D'HERMÈS   Hermès 1951 ♂
ETIENNE AIGNER N° 1*   Etienne Aigner 1975
IGNIS*   Omar Sharif 1994
INDEX TOBACCO CARAMEL   Fresh 1999 ♂
KNIZE TEN   Knize 1924
LANCETTI MONSIEUR   Lancetti 1995
LUCIANO PAVAROTTI   Pavarotti 1994
MISSONI UOMO   Missoni 1983
NOIR   Network 1982
PERRY ELLIS FOR MEN   Perry Ellis 1985/96
PIROGUIER   Comptoir Sud Pacifique 1990
ROYAL ENGLISH LEATHER   Creed 1781
SANTAL   L'Artisan Parfumeur 1978
SIESTE   Fragonard 1999
TECK   Molinard 1989
THIS IS NOT A PIPE   Demeter Fragrance Library 1998 ♂
VÉTIVER   Annick Goutal 1985
VETIVER   Etro 1989 ♂
YOU'RE THE FIRE FOR MEN   Yardley 1989

ANTAEUS   Chanel 1981
BEL AMI   Hermès 1986
BONFIRE   Demeter Fragrance Library 2000 ♂
CIGARILLO   Rémy Latour 1996
DAVIDOFF   Davidoff 1984
DAVINCI UOMO   Davinci 1991
DEEP FOREST*   Bogner 1995
DERBY   Guerlain 1985
EAU DES ÎLES   Maître Parfumeur et Gantier 1988
EAU DU FIER   Annick Goutal 2000
FENDI UOMO   Fendi 1988
FRENCH LINE*   Révillon 1984
GOMMA   Etro 1989 ♂
HO HANG CLUB*   Balenciaga 1986
HOMME DE GRÈS   Grès 1996
JIL SANDER MAN PURE*   Jil Sander 1981
KRIZIA UOMO   Krizia 1984
L'AUTRE   Diptyque 1973 ♂
LA BASE FOR HIM   Magic Helvetia 1994
L'EAU DU NAVIGATEUR   L'Artisan Parfumeur 1982
LÉONARD POUR HOMME*   Léonard 1980
L'HOMME DE VENTILO   Ventilo 1998
MACASSAR   Rochas 1980
MÉCHANT LOUP   L'Artisan Parfumeur 1997
ONE MAN SHOW   Jacques Bogart 1980
PALAIS JAMAIS   Etro 1989 ♂
PARFUM D'HABIT   Maître Parfumeur et Gantier 1988
ROCABAR   Hermès 1998
S.T.DUPONT HOMME   S.T.Dupont 1998
TABAROME   Creed 1875/1999
TRISTAN   Pierre Cardin 2000
VAN CLEEF & ARPELS POUR HOMME   Van Cleef & Arpels 1978
VANITECK   Molinard 1996
YATAGAN   Caron 1976

Fougère

Aromatic

This is the universal fragrance family, with sexy cool-warm notes of citrus and lavender, sweet spices and oriental woods. It takes its name from a fragrance long since discontinued: *Fougère Royale*, introduced by Houbigant in 1882. Men grew up on Fougères. Most of the key men's fragrances developed since the mid-1960s have come from this family; their zesty, masculine character makes men feel comfortable. Most women, too, find the blend of Fresh, Floral, Oriental and Woody notes appealing. It is a winning combination.

Curieuse famille de parfums baptisée du nom d'une plante - la fougère - dénuée de toute odeur spécifique ! Ce nom, en fait, rappelle celui d'un parfum masculin aujourd'hui disparu : Fougère Royale *créé par Houbigant en 1882. Ce type de formule - mariant hespéridés, lavande, épices douces et bois orientaux - fut longtemps réservé aux hommes. Cependant ses qualités traditionnellement « viriles » ont su aussi séduire les femmes qui, aujourd'hui, apprécient ce « chaud et froid » combinaison de notes fraîches, florales, orientales et boisées. Cette famille de parfums très « sexy » est désormais l'une des plus universellement appréciées.*

Fresh / Frais ●

ADIDAS MOVES FOR HER   Adidas 2000
AQUA RELAX   Biotherm 1999
cK BE   Calvin Klein 1996 ♂
ESPRIT DE LAVANDE   Penhaligon's 1976 ♂
LEMON SORBET   Etro 1989 ♂
MERGE   Xan Kim 1999 ♂
SHU UEMURA 029   Shu Uemura 1999 ♂
SOLO SOPRANI BLU   Luciano Soprani 1998 ♂
WILKES SAN FRANCISCO   Wilkes Bashford 1998 ♂

Aromatic / Aromatique

ADVENTURE QUASAR   J. del Pozo 1999
ALAIN DELON POUR HOMME   Alain Delon 2000
ANDY WARHOL FOR MEN   Andy Warhol 1999
ARROGANCE POUR HOMME   Arrogance 2000
ASPEN DISCOVERY   Aspen 2000
AVATAR   Coty 1997
AZZARO POUR HOMME   Azzaro 1978
CASSINI FOR MEN   Oleg Cassini 1995
CENTAURE CUIR FOUGÈRE   Pierre Cardin 1996
CHAPEAU   Borsalino 1997
CLARTÉ FOR MEN   L.T.Piver 2000
CURVE FOR MEN   Liz Claiborne 1996
DANIEL HECHTER SPORT   Daniel Hechter 1999
DEAUVILLE POUR HOMME   Michel Germain 1999
DUÉ CLASSIC   Lomani 2000
ELEMENTS   Hugo Boss 1993
ENDURANCE   Ted Baker 2000
ESPRIT DE LAVANDE   Penhaligon's 1976 ♂
GANT CLASSIC   Gant 1999
GOLD   Yardley / Parfums Bleu 1983
GREEN GENERATION HIM   Pino Silvestre: Mavive 1998
INSATIABLE*   Pierre Cardin 1995
JAZZ   Yves Saint Laurent 1988
JB BLEND   Perfumers Guild 1984
JIVAGO 24k MEN   Jivago 1995
LATITUDE LONGTITUDE   Nautica: Unilever Cosmetics 2000
MICHAEL JORDAN   Bijan 1996
MOLTO SMALTO*   Francesco Smalto 1992
ON AIR HOMME   Morabito 1998
PERRY ELLIS PORTFOLIO FOR MEN   Perry Ellis 1999
PINSTRIPE   Herbalife: Parfums Vitessence 1995
PREFERRED STOCK   Coty 1990
ROBERTA DI CAMERINO POUR HOMME   R di Camerino 1998
ROUTE 66 COLORADO RAIN   Coty 1997
SAFARI FOR MEN   Ralph Lauren 1992
SECRET MÉLANGE   Maître Parfumeur et Gantier 1988
SERGIO TACCHINI   Sergio Tacchini 1987
SILVER JEANS HOMME   Roccobarocco 1995
SOLO SOPRANI BLU   Luciano Soprani 1998 ♂
SPORT 2000   Davinci 1997

Crisp / Pétillant ●●

BLACK SILVER   MCM 1998 ♂
EAU SANS PAREIL   Penhaligon's 1992 ♂
ESCADA COUNTRY WEEKEND   Escada 1996 ♂
GREEN GENERATION   Pino Silvestre: Mavive 1996 ♂
INDEX CORIANDER LAVENDER   Fresh 1997 ♂
LAVENDER SPICE #10   Trish McEvoy 2000
ORANGE SPICE   Creed 1950 ♂
ORPHÉE   Maxim's 1998 ♂
PARFUM ALLIÉ FOREST 02   Shu Uemura 1988/99

Aromatic / Aromatique

ADIDAS ACTIVE BODIES   Adidas 1990
AMAZING FOR MEN   Bill Blass 2000
ARROGANCE UOMO   Arrogance 1987
BARYSHNIKOV   Mikhail Baryshnikov 1991
BE BOP POUR HOMME   Kesling 1992
BIJAN FOR MEN   Bijan 1981
BLACK JEANS*   Versace 1997
BLACK SILVER   MCM 1998 ♂
BOGNER MAN II*   Bogner 1988
BOSS NUMBER ONE   Hugo Boss 1985
BRISTOL BLUE   Applewoods 1996
BRUT INSTINCT   Fabergé 1997
BUCKINGHAM   Crown 1880
BURBERRY FOR MEN (New)   Burberry 1992/95
CAESARS MAN   Caesars World 1988
CAFÉ-CAFÉ ADVENTURE POUR HOMME   Cofinluxe 2000
CALIFORNIA FOR MEN   Jaclyn Smith / Dana 1990
CALVIN   Calvin Klein 1981
CAPTAIN*   Molyneux 1975
CENTAURE DIAMANT NOIR   Pierre Cardin 1998
CENTAURE TÊTE D'OR   Pierre Cardin 1998
C'EST MAGIQUE HOMME   Kesling 1997
CRUISER FOR MEN   Lomani 1998
DISCOVER   Juvena 1994
DRAKKAR NOIR   Guy Laroche 1982
DUC DE VERVINS   Houbigant: Claire 1991
EAU SANS PAREIL   Penhaligon's 1992 ♂
EL PASO   Lomani 1993
ENGLISH BLAZER   Yardley / Parfums Bleu 1989
EXTASE EXOTIC NATURE MAN   Muelhens 1997
GARRIGUE   Maître Parfumeur et Gantier 1988
HERBISSIMO MEJORANA   Dana 1978
HOLLYWOOD FOR MEN   Fred Hayman 1998
INSTINCT   Les Floralies 1993
LATITUDE   Olivier de Kersauson 1992
L'HOMME   Roger & Gallet 1980
LOMANI   Lomani 1987
MANDATE   Shulton / H&BF 1976
MASERATI   Italart 1989
MEXX MAN   Mexx: Star 2000

Classical / Classique ●●●

CROWN COURT BOUQUET   Crown 1882
EAU D'ÉLIDE   Diptyque 1988 ♂
ENGLISH FERN   Penhaligon's 1911 ♂
GINGHAM   Innoxa 1970
HEAVEN SENT   Mem / Dana 1941
JEAN NATÉ   Ritz 1935
JICKY   Guerlain 1889 ♂
MA LIBERTÉ*   Jean Patou 1987
OPOPONAX   Comptoir Sud Pacifique 1992

Rich / Profond ●●●●

INDEX GERANIUM PEPPER   Fresh 1998 ♂
LAVANDE   L'Occitane 1996/99 ♂

THE BARON   Evyan / LTL 1961/96
BLACK LABEL   Lenthèric 1967/2000
BRITISH STERLING   Mem / Dana 1965
BRUT   Fabergé 1964
CANOÉ   Dana 1935
CENTAURE   Maître Parfumeur et Gantier 1991
CROWN FOUGÈRE   Crown 1885
DOLCE & GABBANA POUR HOMME   Dolce & Gabbana 1994
EAU D'ÉLIDE   Diptyque 1988 ♂
EAU DU CONTADOUR   L'Occitane 1994
ENGLISH FERN   Penhaligon's 1911 ♂
FOUGÈRE ROYALE*   Houbigant 1882
HELMUT LANG MAN   Helmut Lang 2000
JADE EAST   Swank / Regency 1964
JICKY   Guerlain 1889 ♂
MASCULIN EQUATEUR   Bourjois 1993
MENNEN SKIN BRACER   Mennen 1931
MONSIEUR ROCHAS   Rochas 1969
MOUCHOIR DE MONSIEUR   Guerlain 1904
N° 89   Floris 1950
ONLY FOR MEN   Julio Iglesias 1991
PATOU POUR HOMME PRIVÉ   Jean Patou 1994
POLICE   Police 1998
PUB   Revlon 1965
RACQUETS FORMULA   Penhaligon's 1989
SILVER*   Mem / Dana 1989
TOUCH FOR MEN*   Fred Hayman 1995

BASALA   Shiseido 1993
CIGAR AFICIONADO   Cigar Aficionado 1997
ÉQUIPAGE   Hermès 1970
ETIENNE AIGNER N° 2   Etienne Aigner 1976
GUESS FOR MEN*   Guess (Georges Marciano) 1991
HAVANA   Aramis 1994
INDEX GERANIUM PEPPER   Fresh 1998 ♂
JAGUAR   Jaguar 1988
JULES   Christian Dior 1980
KOUROS   Yves Saint Laurent 1981
L'ANARCHISTE   Caron 2000
LAPIDUS POUR HOMME   Ted Lapidus 1987
LAVANDE   L'Occitane 1996/99 ♂
L'EAU DU CAPORAL   L'Artisan Parfumeur 1985
MONSIEUR LÉONARD   Léonard 1992
PERSONALITY   Marbert 1995
PIERRE CARDIN MUSK*   Pierre Cardin 1987
ROCCOBAROCCO*   Roccobarocco 1989
ROYAL WATER   Creed 1997
TABAC MAN   Mäurer & Wirtz 2000
TENAZ   Daniel de Fasson 1994
THIRD MAN / 3ᵉ HOMME / N° 3   Caron 1985
VAN GILS   Van Gils 1988
YOHJI HOMME   Yohji Yamamoto 1999

Aromatic

▶ Fresh / Frais ●

STATEMENT FOR MEN* Etienne Aigner 1994
STETSON SIERRA Coty 1993
TABAC EXTREME Mäurer & Wirtz 1991
TSAR Van Cleef & Arpels 1989
TUSCANY PER UOMO Aramis 1984
U de V Ulric de Varens 1993
UNGARO POUR L'HOMME III Ungaro 1993
UNIVERSO Coty 1994
WATERPERRY GENTLEMEN Perfumers Guild 1990
XS POUR HOMME Paco Rabanne 1993

Citrus / Hespéridé

ASPEN FOR MEN Coty 1989
BENETTON SPORT MAN Benetton 1999
BERNINI SPORT Bernini 1999
BETWEEN SHEETS Van Gils 1997
BOGNER SNOW Bogner 2000
BROOKSFIELD ROYAL BLUE Brooksfield 1998
BUGATTI Ettore Bugatti 1992/99
BULGARI POUR HOMME Bulgari 1995
CANDIE'S MEN Liz Claiborne 1999
cK BE Calvin Klein 1996 ♀
CLEAR DAY FOR MEN Etienne Aigner 1998
DKNY MEN Donna Karan 2000
EAU DES 4 VOLEURS L'Occitane 1991
EAU FRESH Jacques Bogart 1993
ÉGOÏSTE PLATINUM Chanel 1993
FERRARI YELLOW EAU DE TOILETTE Ferrari 2000
FREE WORLD MAN Mäurer & Wirtz 1999
FUN WATER FOR MEN De Ruy 1996
GFF M Gianfranco Ferré 1997
GREEN JEANS* Versace 1996
HÉROS SPORT Didier Calvo-Uomo 1997
HIGH... (Turquoise) Patrick Cox 2000
HORIZON* Guy Laroche 1993
LACOSTE 2000 Lacoste 1999
LANVIN L'HOMME Lanvin 1997
LEMON SORBET Etro 1989 ♀
M pour MONSIEUR Marc de la Morandière 1992
MAN Herbalife 1996
MANÈS ICE Rémy Latour 1997
MERGE Xan Kim 1999 ♀
NAVIGATOR Dana 1996
NAZARENO GABRIELLI POUR HOMME Nazareno Gabrielli 1996
OLYMPIOS Missoni 1994
R de CAPUCCI* Roberto Capucci 1985
ROLAND GARROS Coty 1992
SOCIETY GENTLEMEN Perfumers Guild 1988
SO MAX So Cosmetics 2000
SUMATRA RAIN FRESH Muelhens 1998
SWISH My Very Own 2000
TOMMY Tommy Hilfiger 1995
VUARNET Vuarnet 1999
WILD WIND FOR MEN Gabriela Sabatini 1999
WILKES SAN FRANCISCO Wilkes Bashford 1998 ♀

▶ Crisp / Pétillant ●●

MODERN FOR HIM Banana Republic 1997
MR J Fashion Fair 1975
NICKI LAUDA Florbath 1978
PACO RABANNE POUR HOMME Paco Rabanne 1973
PARFUM D'HOMME Kristel Saint Martin 1995
PASHA Cartier 1992
RAFALE Molinard 1977/94
RAPPORT Shulton / H&BF 1988
REBEL MEN Kraft International 2001
RED FOR MEN Giorgio Beverly Hills 1990
ROUTE 66 Coty 1995
SANDER FOR MEN Jil Sander 1999
SANTOS Cartier 1981
SCAPA POUR HOMME* Scapa of Scotland 1994
SERGIO TACCHINI UOMO Sergio Tacchini 1996
SUNG HOMME Alfred Sung 1988
VERINO POUR HOMME Roberto Verino 2000
VORAGO California Fragrances 1987
WATT FOR MEN BLUE Cofinluxe 1991
WORTH POUR HOMME Worth 1981
XERYUS Givenchy 1986
ZEGNA Ermenegildo Zegna 1992

Citrus / Hespéridé

BOGART Jacques Bogart 1975
BOWLING GREEN Geoffrey Beene 1987
BYBLOS UOMO* Byblos 1993
EAU DE SPORT* Alain Delon 1997
ÉBÈNE Pierre Balmain 1983
FORMIDABLE HOMME Kesling 1995
FREEDOM FOR HIM Tommy Hilfiger 1999
GALILEO DE VIENTO Muelhens 1995
GREEN GENERATION Pino Silvestre: Mavive 1996 ♀
HEAVEN Chopard 1994
INDEX CORIANDER LAVENDER Fresh 1997 ♀
KOUROS FRAÎCHEUR Yves Saint Laurent 1993
LACOSTE Lacoste 1984
LAMBORGHINI POUR HOMME Tonino Lamborghini 1999
LANCETTI POUR HOMME Lancetti 1999
LAUDER FOR MEN Estée Lauder 1987
LE BLEU Les Copains 2000
PHOTO Lagerfeld 1990
RÄKS André Barnwell 1998
TABAC ORIGINAL (Aftershave) Mäurer & Wirtz 1959

▶

Classical / Classique ●●●

▶

Rich / Profond ●●●●

Aromatic

masculin

Fresh / Frais ●

Fruity / Fruité

360° FOR MEN   Perry Ellis 1995
ACTION UOMO*   Trussardi 1990
ADIDAS MOVES   Adidas 1999
ADIDAS TEAM   Adidas 2000
ADOLFO DOMINGUEZ*   Adolfo Dominguez 1991
AMERICA FOR MEN   Perry Ellis 1996
ANIMALE FOR MEN   Parlux 1993
ANNAYAKÉ POUR LUI   Annayaké 2000
BARYSHNIKOV SPORT   Mikhail Baryshnikov 1996
BROOKS BROTHERS   Brooks Brothers 1998
CARRÉ D'AS   Patricia de Nicolaï 1995
CERRUTI IMAGE POUR HOMME   Cerruti 1998
CHEMISTRY   Clinique 1995
CHIEMSEE MAN   Chiemsee 1999
COOL WATER   Davidoff 1988
D   Alfred Dunhill 1996
DEEP BLUE   Lomani 1994
DESIGN FOR MEN   Paul Sebastian 1995
EAU DU TSAR   Van Cleef & Arpels 1998
ETERNITY FOR MEN   Calvin Klein 1989
FIRE & ICE FOR MEN   Revlon 1994
GMV UOMO   Gian Marco Venturi 1997
GRANITE BLUE   Granite 1996
ICEBERG TWICE HOMME   Iceberg 1995
J.F.   Floris 1993
KYRIAZ   Rémy Latour 1994
LUCKY BRAND MEN'S*   Lucky Brand 1997
MACKIE FOR MEN   Bob Mackie 1992
MARBERT MAN TOO   Marbert 1998
MARQUIS   Crown 1928
MARQUIS   Rémy Marquis 1999
MCM 24 MORNING*   MCM 1993
NAVY FOR MEN   Cover Girl / Dana 1996
NIGHTFLIGHT   Joop! 1992
NIKE   Nike Cosmetics 1991
NOMAD   Crabtree & Evelyn 1999
PERRY ELLIS RESERVE   Perry Ellis 1997
PHAROS   Alain Delon 1997
PLEASURES FOR MEN   Estée Lauder 1997
REBEL ... JAMES DEAN   Kraft International 1998
ROMANCE MEN   Ralph Lauren 1999
ROYAL GREEN   Seve Ballesteros 1992
SOUL   Herbalife 2000
SPORTIF   Pierre Cardin 1996
U de V FUN   Ulric de Varens 2000
VIKING   Royal Copenhagen 1999
WINGS FOR MEN   Giorgio Beverly Hills 1994
YARDLEY ORIGINAL   Yardley 1992

Green / Vert

ADIDAS ACTION   Adidas 1998
ALVIERO MARTINI UOMO   Alviero Martini 1997
BLUE N° 655 HIM   Gap 1997
BLUE STRATOS   Shulton / Parfums Bleu 1975
BOGNER MAN   Bogner 1985/90/99
CAFÉ-CAFÉ POUR HOMME   Cofinluxe 1996
CHIARA BONI UOMO   Chiara Boni 1997
COUNTRY ROAD MAN   Country Road 1999
CROSSROADS   Amway 1997
DRAKKAR DYNAMIK   Guy Laroche 1999
HUGO   Hugo Boss 1995
LUCIANO   Pavarotti 1999
SWISS ARMY   Swiss Army 1996
WHAT ABOUT ADAM   Joop! 1997
ZIPPED SPORTS   Perfumer's Workshop 1999

Crisp / Pétillant ●●

Fruity / Fruité

BOSS SPORT*   Hugo Boss 1987
BROOKSFIELD FOR MEN   Brooksfield 1993
GLOBE*   Rochas 1990
GOODLIFE   Davidoff 1998
JOSEPH ABBOUD   Euroltalia 1993
OLD SPICE WHITEWATER   Shulton / P&G 1996
OMAR SHARIF POUR HOMME*   Omar Sharif 1992
ORPHÉE   Maxim's 1998 ♂
PENNY BLACK   Penny Black 1999
PUMA CHALLENGE   Muelhens 1998
SOPRANI ACTIVE MAN   Luciano Soprani 1994
VÉTIVER DRY*   Carven 1988

Green / Vert

CENTAURE CUIR CASAQUE   Pierre Cardin 1996
ESCADA COUNTRY WEEKEND   Escada 1996 ♂
GUCCI NOBILE*   Gucci 1988
MASCULIN ACIER   Bourjois 1988
MOLINARD HOMME I   Molinard 1996
NAZARENO POUR HOMME   Nazareno Gabrielli 2000
PAUL SMITH MEN   Paul Smith 2000
SUMATRA RAIN MEN   Muelhens 1993

Classical / Classique ●●●

Rich / Profond ●●●●

▶

Fresh / Frais ●

Water / Marine

ADIDAS DYNAMIC   Adidas 1997
AQUA QUORUM   Antonio Puig 1994
BLUE   Parfums Bleu 1997
BLUE SILVER MEN   MCM 2000
BRUT ACTIF BLUE   Fabergé 1994
CLAIBORNE SPORT   Liz Claiborne 1997
CULTURE by TABAC BLUE   Mäurer & Wirtz 1999
ESCAPE FOR MEN   Calvin Klein 1993
FACE À FACE HOMME   Façonnable 1996
FAÇONNABLE   Façonnable 1994
GALILEO 21st CENTURY   Muelhens 1997
GMV ENERGY   Gian Marco Venturi 1998
GRANITE ORIGINAL   Granite 1992
GRIGIOPERLA   La Perla 1991
ICE WATER*   Pino Silvestre: Mavive 1992
INSENSÉ ULTRAMARINE   Givenchy 1994
JAGUAR SPECIAL EDITION   Jaguar 1998
LIVE JAZZ   Yves Saint Laurent 1998
L'ORIGINAL   Decléor 2000
MILLENNIUM HOPE MAN   Jivago 1999
MONSIEUR MORABITO   Morabito 1994
NK   Nike Cosmetics 1997
POLO SPORT   Ralph Lauren 1994
PUMA INDEPENDENCE   Muelhens 1997
QUASAR   J. del Pozo 1994
ROYAL COPENHAGEN SPORT*   Royal Copenhagen 1996
SAMBA NATURAL MAN   Perfumer's Workshop 1997
SO HIM   So Cosmetics 1998

Spicy / Epicé

BLEU FORMIDABLE   Kesling 1998
CHALEUR D'ANIMALE POUR HOMME   Parlux 2000
EMOZIONI FOR MAN   Fila 1997
GENTRY   Dana 1971/99
L'UOMO TRUSSARDI   Trussardi 1995
PEN DUICK   Eric Tabarly 1998
PIAZZA DI SPAGNA UOMO   Roccobarroco 1998
RYKIEL HOMME   Sonia Rykiel 1999
SERGIO TACCHINI SPORT EXTREME*   Sergio Tacchini 1993
SHU UEMURA 029   Shu Uemura 1999 ♂
SUD EST   Romeo Gigli 1995
TOUCH DOWN   My Very Own 2000
VOLCANO HOMME   Lomani 1999

▶

Crisp / Pétillant ●●

Water / Marine

BERNINI MEN   Bernini 1994

Spicy / Epicé

ADIDAS ADVENTURE   Adidas 1992
ANTHRACITE POUR L'HOMME   Jacomo 1991
ARROGANCE YOU   Arrogance 1997
BORSALINO   Borsalino 1984
BOSTON MAN   Antonio Puig 1989
CACHAREL POUR L'HOMME   Cacharel 1981
CULTURE by TABAC   Mäurer & Wirtz 1996
DUNHILL EDITION   Alfred Dunhill 1985
ELEMENTS AQUA   Hugo Boss 1996
ENIGME   Pierre Cardin 1992
EPICÉA   Creed 1965
GALE HAYMAN MAN   Gale Hayman 1997
GOLD JEANS HOMME   Roccobarocco 1997
HO HANG   Balenciaga 1971
JIL SANDER MAN III*   Jil Sander 1987
LOEWE POUR HOMME   Loewe 1974
M de BOURBON   Marina de Bourbon 1997
MARBERT MAN   Marbert 1977
OPEN   Roger & Gallet 1985
ORANGE SPICE   Creed 1950 ♂
PRESSURE   Rémy Latour 1999
SALVADOR   Salvador Dali 1992
WEIL POUR HOMME   Weil 1980/97

Classical / Classique ●●●

Rich / Profond ●●●●

Aromatic

masculine

Index féminin

5th AVENUE *Floral / Florale* 34 ●
24, FAUBOURG *Floral / Florale* 38 ●●
25 *Woody Oriental / Oriental Boisé* 60 ●
57 FOR HER ➛ CHEVIGNON 57 FOR HER
100% PURE CHIPIE GREEN *Floral / Florale* 32 ●
100% PURE CHIPIE PURPLE *Woody Oriental / Oriental Boisé* 60 ●
212 *Soft Floral / Fleuri Aldéhydé* 42 ●
273 RODEO DRIVE *Floral / Florale* 33 ●●●
360° FOR WOMEN *Floral / Florale* 32 ●●
1000 *Floral / Florale* 33 ●●●●
2000 FLEURS *Floral / Florale* 34 ●
2020 ➛ COURRÈGES 2020
4711 ORIGINAL ⚥ *Citrus / Hespéridé* 17 ●●●

A

ACACIOSA *Floral / Florale* 38 ●
ACCENTI *Floral Oriental / Fleuri Oriental* 48 ●
ACQUA CLASSICA DI BORSARI ⚥ *Citrus / Hespéridé* 17 ●●●
ACQUA DI FIORI *Floral / Florale* 36 ●
ACQUA DI GIÒ *Floral / Florale* 36 ●
ACQUA DI MIELE ⚥ *Floral / Florale* 38 ●
ACQUA DI PARMA COLONIA ⚥ *Citrus / Hespéridé* 17 ●●●
ACQUA DI PARMA LAVANDA TONICA ⚥ *Floral / Florale* 31 ●●●
ACQUA DI PARMA PROFUMO *Mossy Woods / Chypre Boisé* 67 ●●●
ACTE 2 *Soft Floral / Fleuri Aldéhydé* 42 ●●
ACTION Trussardi* *Green / Vert* 22 ●●
ADIDAS MOVES FOR HER *Aromatic / Fougère* 76 ●
ADIDAS WOMAN *Floral / Florale* 34 ●
ADIDAS WOMAN ACTIVE *Floral / Florale* 32 ●
ADIDAS WOMAN ENERGY *Floral / Florale* 36 ●
ADIDAS WOMAN FITNESS *Floral / Florale* 34 ●
ADIDAS WOMAN SPORT *Floral / Florale* 32 ●
ADIEU SAGESSE *Floral / Florale* 30 ●●
ADRIENNE VITTADINI *Oriental / Oriental* 56 ●
AGENT PROVOCATEUR *Mossy Woods / Chypre Boisé* 67 ●●●
AGUA DE LOEWE ⚥ *Citrus / Hespéridé* 16 ●
AGUA FRESCA DE ROSAS *Floral / Florale* 30 ●●
AGUA LAVANDA ⚥ *Floral / Florale* 31 ●●●
AIMANT – L' *Soft Floral / Fleuri Aldéhydé* 43 ●●●
AIMEZ-MOI *Soft Floral / Fleuri Aldéhydé* 43 ●●●●
AIR DE ... CABOCHARD *Dry Woods / Boisé Cuir* 72 ●
AIR DE SAMSARA – UN *Woody Oriental / Oriental Boisé* 60 ●
AIR D'HABANITA – UN *Floral Oriental / Fleuri Oriental* 46 ●
AIR DU TEMPS – L' *Floral / Florale* 33 ●●●
AIRE ➛ GIORGIO AIRE*
AIRE LOEWE *Green / Vert* 23 ●●●
ALABASTER *Soft Floral / Fleuri Aldéhydé* 42 ●
À LA FRANÇAISE *Floral / Florale* 32 ●●
À LA NUIT *Floral / Florale* 31 ●●●
ALCHIMIE *Floral Oriental / Fleuri Oriental* 46 ●●
ALEGRIA *Floral / Florale* 32 ●●
ALEXANDRA *Soft Oriental / Oriental Doux* 53 ●●●
ALIAGE / ALLIAGE *Green / Vert* 23 ●●●
ALL ABOUT EVE *Woody Oriental / Oriental Boisé* 60 ●
ALLURE *Floral Oriental / Fleuri Oriental* 46 ●
ALPONA *Citrus / Hespéridé* 17 ●●●●
ALVIERO MARTINI DONNA *Floral Oriental / Fleuri Oriental* 46 ●
ALYSSA ASHLEY MUSK *Soft Floral / Fleuri Aldéhydé* 43 ●●●●
ALYSSA ASHLEY VANILLA *Woody Oriental / Oriental Boisé* 60 ●
AMARIGE *Floral Oriental / Fleuri Oriental* 48 ●●
AMAZING *Soft Floral / Fleuri Aldéhydé* 42 ●●
AMAZONE *Floral / Florale* 32 ●●
AMBER & LAVENDER ⚥ *Woody Oriental / Oriental Boisé* 61 ●●●
AMBRA ⚥ *Oriental / Oriental* 57 ●●●
AMBRE *Oriental / Oriental* 57 ●●●
AMBRE CANNELLE *Soft Oriental / Oriental Doux* 53 ●●●
AMBRE PRÉCIEUX ⚥ *Oriental / Oriental* 57 ●●●●
AMBRE SULTAN ⚥ *Soft Oriental / Oriental Doux* 53 ●●●●
AMBUSH *Woody Oriental / Oriental Boisé* 60 ●●
AMERICA FOR WOMEN *Floral / Florale* 32 ●
AMERICAN ORIGINAL: STETSON FOR WOMEN *Floral / Florale* 32 ●●
AMOUAGE *Soft Floral / Fleuri Aldéhydé* 43 ●●●●
AMOUR AMOUR *Floral / Florale* 33 ●●●●
AMOUR D'AMANDIER *Floral / Florale* 32 ●●
AMOUR DE CACAO *Oriental / Oriental* 56 ●●
AMOUR DE PATOU – UN *Floral / Florale* 36 ●
AMULETI *Floral / Florale* 32 ●
ANAÏS ANAÏS *Floral / Florale* 38 ●
ANDY WARHOL FOR WOMEN *Floral / Florale* 32 ●
ANGEL *Woody Oriental / Oriental Boisé* 60 ●
ANGEL FOOD ⚥ *Soft Oriental / Oriental Doux* 53 ●●●
ANGEL INNOCENT *Woody Oriental / Oriental Boisé* 60 ●
ANGÉLIQUE ENCENS *Oriental / Oriental* 57 ●●●
ANGEL SCHLESSER FEMME *Mossy Woods / Chypre Boisé* 66 ●●
ANIMALE *Mossy Woods / Chypre Boisé* 67 ●●●●
ANIMALE ANIMALE *Floral Oriental / Fleuri Oriental* 46 ●●
ANNABELLA *Green / Vert* 22 ●
ANNA SUI *Soft Floral / Fleuri Aldéhydé* 42 ●●
ANNAYAKÉ POUR ELLE *Floral / Florale* 34 ●
ANNE KLEIN* *Soft Floral / Fleuri Aldéhydé* 42 ●
ANNE KLEIN II* *Oriental / Oriental* 56 ●
ANNÉ PLISKA *Soft Oriental / Oriental Doux* 53 ●●●
ANOUCHKA *Mossy Woods / Chypre Boisé* 66 ●●
ANOUCK *Floral / Florale* 34 ●
ANTHRACITE *Floral Oriental / Fleuri Oriental* 46 ●
ANTICIPATE / SULTRY *Floral Oriental / Fleuri Oriental* 48 ●●
ANTILOPE *Mossy Woods / Chypre Boisé* 67 ●●●
ANTONIA'S FLOWERS *Floral / Florale* 30 ●●
APERÇU *Mossy Woods / Chypre Boisé* 67 ●●●
APHRODISIA* *Mossy Woods / Chypre Boisé* 66 ●●
APOGÉE *Mossy Woods / Chypre Boisé* 67 ●●●
APRÈS L'ONDÉE *Floral Oriental / Fleuri Oriental* 48 ●
APRIL FIELDS *Floral / Florale* 34 ●
APRIL VIOLETS *Floral / Florale* 31 ●●●●
AQUAFLORE *Water / Marine* 26 ●
AQUA DI AQUA *Mossy Woods / Chypre Boisé* 66 ●
AQUA RELAX *Aromatic / Fougère* 76 ●
ARABIE ⚥ *Woody Oriental / Oriental Boisé* 61 ●●●●
ARIA MISSONI *Floral / Florale* 32 ●●
ARMAND BASI FEMME *Citrus / Hespéridé* 16 ●
ARMANI *Mossy Woods / Chypre Boisé* 66 ●
AROMACALM *Woody Oriental / Oriental Boisé* 61 ●●●
AROMANTIC *Floral / Florale* 34 ●
AROMATICS ELIXIR *Dry Woods / Boisé Cuir* 72 ●
AROMATONIC *Citrus / Hespéridé* 16 ●
ARÔME 3 ⚥ *Floral / Florale* 31 ●●●
ARÔME 3 TRADITION ⚥ *Floral / Florale* 31 ●●●●
ARPÈGE *Soft Floral / Fleuri Aldéhydé* 43 ●●●●
ARROGANCE ME *Floral / Florale* 38 ●
ARROGANCE POUR FEMME *Floral / Florale* 32 ●●
ARTE DI GUCCI* – L' *Mossy Woods / Chypre Boisé* 67 ●●●
ASJA *Soft Oriental / Oriental Doux* 53 ●●●
ASMERA *Oriental / Oriental* 57 ●●●
ASPEN FOR WOMEN *Water / Marine* 27 ●●●
ASPEN SENSATION *Floral / Florale* 34 ●
ASPHALT FLOWER *Floral / Florale* 33 ●●●●
ATKINSON GOLD MEDAL ⚥ *Citrus / Hespéridé* 17 ●●●
ATREVIDA *Floral Oriental / Fleuri Oriental* 46 ●●
ATTAR *Oriental / Oriental* 57 ●●●●
AUBUSSON COULEURS *Floral / Florale* 32 ●
AURA FOR WOMEN *Floral / Florale* 32 ●●
AURA LOEWE *Floral Oriental / Fleuri Oriental* 46 ●
AUTHENTIC MAROUSSIA *Floral Oriental / Fleuri Oriental* 48 ●
AUTOUR DU THÉ CLASSIQUE *Floral / Florale* 34 ●
AUTOUR DU THÉ EXOTIQUE *Soft Floral / Fleuri Aldéhydé* 42 ●●
AUTOUR DU THÉ ROMANTIQUE *Floral / Florale* 34 ●●
AUTRE – L' ⚥ *Dry Woods / Boisé Cuir* 73 ●●●●
AV *Floral / Florale* 36 ●●
AYAKO *Oriental / Oriental* 56 ●
AZURÉE *Dry Woods / Boisé Cuir* 73 ●●●
AZZARO *Mossy Woods / Chypre Boisé* 67 ●●●
AZZARO 9 *Floral / Florale* 33 ●●●●
AZZURA *Floral / Florale* 32 ●●

B

BABY DOLL PARIS *Floral / Florale* 32 ●
BABY ROSE JEANS *Floral / Florale* 38 ●
BAÏMÉ ⚥ *Mossy Woods / Chypre Boisé* 66 ●
BAISER – LE *Floral / Florale* 32 ●●
BALAHÉ *Floral Oriental / Fleuri Oriental* 47 ●●●
BAL À VERSAILLES *Floral Oriental / Fleuri Oriental* 47 ●●●
BALMAIN *Mossy Woods / Chypre Boisé* 66 ●

BAMBOU   *Floral / Florale   32* ●●
BANDIT   *Dry Woods / Boisé Cuir   73* ●●●
BAROQUE   *Floral Oriental / Fleuri Oriental   46* ●●
BARYSHNIKOV POUR FEMME   *Floral / Florale   33* ●●●
BASE FOR HER – LA   *Floral / Florale   30* ●●
BASI FEMME   *Woody Oriental / Oriental Boisé   60* ●
BASILIC FLEUR D'ORANGER   *Floral / Florale   31* ●●●●
BASIL TONIC #7   *Citrus / Hespéridé   16* ●
BEAUTIFUL   *Floral / Florale   32* ●●
BE BOP   *Floral / Florale   32* ●●
BELLA FIRENZE   *Floral Oriental / Fleuri Oriental   46* ●
BELLE DE MINUIT   *Oriental / Oriental   56* ●●
BELLE DE RAUCH   *Floral / Florale   33* ●●●
BELLODGIA   *Floral / Florale   31* ●●●●
BENETTON SPORT WOMAN   *Floral / Florale   32* ●
BERNINI WOMEN   *Floral Oriental / Fleuri Oriental   46* ●
BEST LADY   *Floral / Florale   33* ●●●
BEST OF CHEVIGNON ♂   *Water / Marine   27* ●●●
BETTY BARCLAY WOMAN   *Floral / Florale   36* ●
BETTY BARCLAY WOMAN N° 2   *Floral Oriental / Fleuri Oriental   48* ●
BETTY BARCLAY WOMAN N° 3   *Floral / Florale   33* ●●●
BEVERLY HILLS   *Woody Oriental / Oriental Boisé   60* ●
BIJAN   *Woody Oriental / Oriental Boisé   61* ●●●
BIJAN WITH A TWIST   *Floral Oriental / Fleuri Oriental   46* ●
BILL BLASS   *Floral / Florale   33* ●●●●
BIRMANE   *Floral / Florale   32* ●●
BLACKBERRY & VANILLA MUSK #9   *Woody Oriental / Oriental Boisé   60* ●
BLACK JEANS FEMME Roccobarocco   *Floral / Florale   33* ●●●●
BLACK PEARLS*   *Floral Oriental / Fleuri Oriental   46* ●
BLACK SILVER ♂   *Aromatic / Fougère   76* ●●
BLACK TIE   *Woody Oriental / Oriental Boisé   60* ●
BLASÉ   *Soft Floral / Fleuri Aldéhydé   43* ●●●●
BLEU DE CHINE   *Soft Oriental / Oriental Doux   53* ●●●●
BLONDE   → VERSACE'S BLONDE
BLU BLUMARINE   *Floral / Florale   38* ●●
BLUE N° 655 HER   *Floral / Florale   32* ●
BLUEBELL / WOODLAND HYACINTH   *Floral / Florale   34* ●
BLUE GRASS   *Floral / Florale   33* ●●●●
BLUMARINE*   *Soft Floral / Fleuri Aldéhydé   42* ●●
BLUMARINE II   *Soft Floral / Fleuri Aldéhydé   42* ●
BOBBI   *Floral / Florale   34* ●
BOB MACKIE   → MACKIE
BODY POWER   *Green / Vert   23* ●●●
BOGNER WOMAN   *Floral Oriental / Fleuri Oriental   46* ●
BOHÈME   *Mossy Woods / Chypre Boisé   66* ●●
BOIS DE CÉDRAT ♂   *Citrus / Hespéridé   17* ●●●
BOIS DES ÎLES   *Woody Oriental / Oriental Boisé   61* ●●●
BOLERO   *Floral / Florale   32* ●●
BOND   *Oriental / Oriental   56* ●
BONFIRE ♂   *Dry Woods / Boisé Cuir   73* ●●●●
BONJOUR   *Floral Oriental / Fleuri Oriental   46* ●●
BORONIA   *Floral / Florale   31* ●●●
BORSALINO DONNA   → DONNA BORSALINO
BOSS WOMAN   *Floral / Florale   32* ●●
BOUCHERON   *Floral Oriental / Fleuri Oriental   47* ●●●
BOUDOIR   *Floral Oriental / Fleuri Oriental   47* ●●●
BOUQUET IMPÉRIAL ♂   *Citrus / Hespéridé   17* ●●●●
BOUTON D'OR*   *Floral / Florale   32* ●
BOUVARDIA*   *Floral Oriental / Fleuri Oriental   47* ●●●
BULGARI BLACK ♂   *Dry Woods / Boisé Cuir   72* ●●
BULGARI BLU   *Soft Floral / Fleuri Aldéhydé   43* ●●●●
BULGARI EAU PARFUMÉE ♂   *Citrus / Hespéridé   16* ●
BULGARI PETITS ET MAMANS   *Soft Oriental / Oriental Doux   53* ●●●
BULGARI POUR FEMME   *Floral / Florale   33* ●●●
BULLES DE FRAÎCHEUR   *Citrus / Hespéridé   16* ●
BURBERRY FOR WOMEN   *Floral Oriental / Fleuri Oriental   46* ●
BURBERRY TOUCH FOR WOMEN   *Floral Oriental / Fleuri Oriental   46* ●
BURBERRY WEEK END FOR WOMEN   *Floral / Florale   34* ●●
BUTTERFLY KISSES   *Floral / Florale   32* ●●
BYBLOS*   *Floral / Florale   32* ●●
BYBLOS BREEZA / BREEZE   *Floral Oriental / Fleuri Oriental   46* ●
BYBLOS CIELO / SKY   *Woody Oriental / Oriental Boisé   60* ●
BYBLOS FUOCO / FIRE   *Woody Oriental / Oriental Boisé   61* ●●●
BYBLOS GHIACCIA / ICE   *Citrus / Hespéridé   17* ●●●●
BYBLOS MARE / SEA   *Floral / Florale   34* ●
BYBLOS TERRA / EARTH   *Floral Oriental / Fleuri Oriental   46* ●●
BYBLOS URAGANO / HURRICANE   *Oriental / Oriental   56* ●●

BY WOMAN   *Woody Oriental / Oriental Boisé   61* ●●●
BYZANCE   *Floral Oriental / Fleuri Oriental   48* ●●
BYZANTINE*   *Floral Oriental / Fleuri Oriental   48* ●

C

CABOCHARD   *Dry Woods / Boisé Cuir   73* ●●●
CABOTINE DE GRÈS   *Floral / Florale   34* ●●
CACHET (Original)   *Dry Woods / Boisé Cuir   73* ●●●
CAESARS WOMAN   *Floral / Florale   33* ●●●●
CAFÉ   *Soft Oriental / Oriental Doux   53* ●●●
CAFÉ-CAFÉ   *Soft Floral / Fleuri Aldéhydé   42* ●●
CAFÉ-CAFÉ ADVENTURE POUR FEMME
   Mossy Woods / Chypre Boisé   66 ●●
CALANDRE   *Soft Floral / Fleuri Aldéhydé   42* ●●
CALÈCHE   *Mossy Woods / Chypre Boisé   67* ●●●
CALIFORNIA   *Soft Floral / Fleuri Aldéhydé   43* ●●●●
CÂLINE   *Soft Floral / Fleuri Aldéhydé   42* ●●
CALLA   *Soft Oriental / Oriental Doux   53* ●●●
CALVIN KLEIN*   *Soft Floral / Fleuri Aldéhydé   42* ●
CALYPSO JASMIN   *Floral / Florale   31* ●●●
CALYPSO MIMOSA   *Floral / Florale   30* ●●
CALYPSO VIOLETTE   *Floral / Florale   31* ●●●●
CALYX   *Floral / Florale   32* ●
CAMÉLIA CHINOIS   *Green / Vert   23* ●●●●
CAMÉLIA IRIS (BLEU)   *Soft Floral / Fleuri Aldéhydé   42* ●
CAMP BEVERLY HILLS*   *Soft Floral / Fleuri Aldéhydé   42* ●●
CANDIE'S   *Floral / Florale   33* ●●●
CANNELLE ORANGE ♂   *Citrus / Hespéridé   16* ●
CAPRICCI   *Floral / Florale   33* ●●●
CAPUCCI DE CAPUCCI   *Woody Oriental / Oriental Boisé   60* ●●
CARAMEL PAIN D'ÉPICE   *Soft Oriental / Oriental Doux   52* ●●
CARITA   *Water / Marine   26* ●●
CAROLINA HERRERA   *Floral / Florale   31* ●●●●
CARRIÈRE   *Citrus / Hespéridé   16* ●●
CASCAYA   *Floral Oriental / Fleuri Oriental   46* ●●
CASCAYA SUMMER   *Floral / Florale   34* ●
CASHMERE MIST   *Dry Woods / Boisé Cuir   72* ●
CASMIR   *Woody Oriental / Oriental Boisé   60* ●●
CASSINI   *Mossy Woods / Chypre Boisé   66* ●●
CASSISSIER   *Floral / Florale   34* ●
CASUAL   *Floral / Florale   38* ●
CATALYST   *Floral / Florale   34* ●
CÉDRAT POMELO ♂   *Citrus / Hespéridé   16* ●●
CELEBRATE   *Floral / Florale   32* ●●
CERRUTI 1881 POUR FEMME   *Floral / Florale   32* ●●
CERRUTI IMAGE WOMAN   *Green / Vert   22* ●●
CE SOIR OU JAMAIS   *Floral / Florale   30* ●●
C'EST LA VIE*   *Floral Oriental / Fleuri Oriental   46* ●
C'EST MAGIQUE   *Floral / Florale   32* ●●
CEYLON   *Citrus / Hespéridé   16* ●●
CHALDÉE   *Floral Oriental / Fleuri Oriental   47* ●●●
CHALEUR D'ANIMALE   *Floral / Florale   34* ●
CHAMADE   *Floral Oriental / Fleuri Oriental   46* ●●
CHAMPAGNE   → YVRESSE
CHAMPS-ÉLYSÉES   *Floral / Florale   30* ●●
CHAMPS-ÉLYSÉES TOO MUCH   *Floral / Florale   30* ●●
CHANEL N° 5   *Soft Floral / Fleuri Aldéhydé   43* ●●●
CHANEL N° 19   *Soft Floral / Fleuri Aldéhydé   42* ●
CHANEL N° 22   *Floral / Florale   33* ●●●
CHANSON D'AIR   *Floral / Florale   32* ●
CHANSON D'EAU   *Citrus / Hespéridé   17* ●●●
CHANSON DE VIE   *Citrus / Hespéridé   16* ●
CHANT D'ARÔMES   *Mossy Woods / Chypre Boisé   66* ●●
CHANTILLY   *Oriental / Oriental   57* ●●●
CHAOS*   *Woody Oriental / Oriental Boisé   60* ●●
CHAPEAU BLEU   *Mossy Woods / Chypre Boisé   66* ●●
CHARLIE   *Floral / Florale   34* ●●
CHARLIE GOLD   *Floral Oriental / Fleuri Oriental   46* ●
CHARLIE RED   *Floral / Florale   32* ●●
CHARLIE SILVER   *Floral / Florale   32* ●
CHARLIE SUNSHINE   *Floral / Florale   32* ●
CHARLIE WHITE   *Water / Marine   26* ●
CHARLIE WHITE MUSK   *Soft Floral / Fleuri Aldéhydé   42* ●
CHARTREUSE DE PARME   *Floral / Florale   31* ●●●●
CHASSE AUX PAPILLONS – LA   *Floral / Florale   38* ●●
CHAUMET   *Floral / Florale   34* ●

CHEAP & CHIC   *Floral / Florale   32* ●
CHELSEA DREAMS   *Floral / Florale   32* ●●
CHERISH*   *Floral / Florale   32* ●
CHERRY BLOSSOM   *Floral / Florale   32* ●
CHERRY MUSK   *Floral / Florale   32* ●●
CHEVIGNON 57 FOR HER   *Floral / Florale   32* ●●
CHÈVREFEUILLE Le Jardin Retrouvé   *Floral / Florale   30* ●●
CHÈVREFEUILLE Molinard*   *Floral / Florale   30* ●●
CHÈVREFEUILLE ORIGINAL Creed ♂   *Green / Vert   22* ●
CHIARA BONI   *Floral / Florale   31* ●●●●
CHIARA BONI LIGHT   *Soft Floral / Fleuri Aldéhydé   42* ●●
CHIC* – LE   *Soft Floral / Fleuri Aldéhydé   42* ●●
CHIEMSEE WOMAN   *Floral / Florale   36* ●
CHIEMSEE WOMAN TWO   *Floral / Florale   32* ●●
CHINA ROSE   *Floral Oriental / Fleuri Oriental   47* ●●●●
CHIQUE   *Mossy Woods / Chypre Boisé   67* ●●●●
CHIPIE   *Floral Oriental / Fleuri Oriental   46* ●
CHLOÉ   *Floral / Florale   31* ●●●●
CHLOÉ INNOCENCE*   *Floral / Florale   38* ●
CHLOÉ NARCISSE   *Floral Oriental / Fleuri Oriental   46* ●●
CHOC   *Mossy Woods / Chypre Boisé   66* ●
CHOCOLAT MENTHE   *Oriental / Oriental   56* ●●
CHRISTIAN BRETON POUR FEMME   *Floral / Florale   32* ●●
CHRISTIAN LACROIX   *Soft Floral / Fleuri Aldéhydé   42* ●●
CHYPRE DE COTY*   *Mossy Woods / Chypre Boisé   67* ●●●
CIALENGA   *Soft Floral / Fleuri Aldéhydé   42* ●
CIARA   *Oriental / Oriental   57* ●●●●
CIARA FEMME FATALE*   *Floral Oriental / Fleuri Oriental   46* ●●
CIELO   *Mossy Woods / Chypre Boisé   66* ●
CINNABAR   *Soft Oriental / Oriental Doux   53* ●●●
CIRQUE DE POPY MORENI – LE   *Soft Floral / Fleuri Aldéhydé   42* ●
CITRON VERT* ♂   *Citrus / Hespéridé   16* ●
CITRUS BIGARRADE ♂   *Citrus / Hespéridé   17* ●●●
CITRUS PETALS #8   *Citrus / Hespéridé   17* ●●●●
cK BE ♂   *Aromatic / Fougère   76* ●
cK ONE ♂   *Citrus / Hespéridé   16* ●
CLAIRE DE NILANG   *Floral / Florale   32* ●
CLANDESTINE*   *Floral Oriental / Fleuri Oriental   47* ●●●●
CLARTÉ   *Floral / Florale   32* ●●
CLASSIC Banana Republic ♂   *Citrus / Hespéridé   17* ●●●
CLASSIC GARDENIA   *Floral / Florale   30* ●●
CLEAR DAY   *Floral / Florale   32* ●●
CLEAR DAY LIGHT   *Floral / Florale   32* ●
CLÉMENTINE   *Citrus / Hespéridé   17* ●●●
CLIMAT   *Soft Floral / Fleuri Aldéhydé   43* ●●●●
CLOSE   *Soft Floral / Fleuri Aldéhydé   42* ●
CLUB COLOGNE ♂   *Citrus / Hespéridé   17* ●●●
COCKTAIL   *Mossy Woods / Chypre Boisé   66* ●
COCO   *Soft Oriental / Oriental Doux   53* ●●●
COEUR DE PARFUM*   *Dry Woods / Boisé Cuir   72* ●●
COEUR DE RAISIN   *Floral / Florale   32* ●
COEUR D'OR   *Woody Oriental / Oriental Boisé   60* ●
COEUR-JOIE   *Soft Floral / Fleuri Aldéhydé   43* ●●●
COLD ♂   *Citrus / Hespéridé   17* ●●●●
COLÈRE DE RODIER   *Woody Oriental / Oriental Boisé   60* ●
COLOGNE SOLOGNE ♂   *Citrus / Hespéridé   17* ●●●
COLONY   *Mossy Woods / Chypre Boisé   66* ●●
COLORS Alexander Julian   *Soft Floral / Fleuri Aldéhydé   42* ●
COLORS OF BENETTON   *Floral Oriental / Fleuri Oriental   46* ●
COMME DES GARÇONS ♂   *Mossy Woods / Chypre Boisé   67* ●●●●
COMME DES GARÇONS 2 ♂   *Mossy Woods / Chypre Boisé   66* ●
CONFIDENT / CONSIDERATIONS   *Mossy Woods / Chypre Boisé   66* ●
CONSIDERATIONS / CONFIDENT   *Mossy Woods / Chypre Boisé   66* ●
CONTRADICTION   *Floral Oriental / Fleuri Oriental   46* ●
CONVICTION   *Floral Oriental / Fleuri Oriental   46* ●
COOL WATER WOMAN   *Floral / Florale   36* ●●
COPAINS – LES   *Floral Oriental / Fleuri Oriental   46* ●
CORIANDRE   *Mossy Woods / Chypre Boisé   67* ●●●●
CORNUBIA   *Floral Oriental / Fleuri Oriental   47* ●●●
COTONNADE ♂   *Soft Oriental / Oriental Doux   52* ●●
COUNTRY ROAD WOMAN   *Soft Floral / Fleuri Aldéhydé   42* ●●
COUNTRY WEEKEND   → ESCADA COUNTRY WEEKEND
COUPE D'OR – LA   *Floral Oriental / Fleuri Oriental   46* ●●
COURRÈGES 2020   *Floral / Florale   32* ●●
COURRÈGES IN BLUE   *Floral / Florale   33* ●●●●
COUTURE POUR ELLE   *Woody Oriental / Oriental Boisé   60* ●
CRÉATION   *Mossy Woods / Chypre Boisé   66* ●

CRÊPE DE CHINE*   *Mossy Woods / Chypre Boisé   66* ●●
CRISTAL DE MUSC   *Soft Oriental / Oriental Doux   52* ●
CRISTALLE   *Citrus / Hespéridé   16* ●●
CRISTOBAL   *Woody Oriental / Oriental Boisé   60* ●
CROWN ALPINE LILY   *Floral / Florale   30* ●
CROWN BOUQUET   *Floral / Florale   34* ●●
CROWN COURT BOUQUET   *Aromatic / Fougère   77* ●●●
CROWN ESS BOUQUET   *Citrus / Hespéridé   16* ●
CROWN ESTERHAZY   *Citrus / Hespéridé   17* ●●●
CROWN HELIOTROPE   *Woody Oriental / Oriental Boisé   61* ●●●
CROWN OF GOLD   *Mossy Woods / Chypre Boisé   67* ●●●
CROWN ROSE   *Floral / Florale   31* ●●●
CROWN STEPHANOTIS   *Floral / Florale   33* ●●●
CRUISER FOR WOMEN   *Floral / Florale   33* ●●●●
CUIR DE RUSSIE Chanel   *Dry Woods / Boisé Cuir   73* ●●●
CUIR DE RUSSIE L.T.Piver ♂   *Dry Woods / Boisé Cuir   73* ●●●
CURVE FOR WOMEN   *Floral / Florale   32* ●
CYBERSP@CE ♂   *Water / Marine   26* ●

D

D&G FEMININE   *Soft Floral / Fleuri Aldéhydé   43* ●●●●
DALIFLOR   *Floral / Florale   32* ●
DALIMANIA   *Floral Oriental / Fleuri Oriental   46* ●●
DALIMIX ♂   *Citrus / Hespéridé   16* ●
DALIMIX GOLD ♂   *Green / Vert   22* ●
DALISSIME   *Floral / Florale   32* ●●
DAMASK ROSE   *Soft Floral / Fleuri Aldéhydé   42* ●●
DANDELION ♂   *Floral / Florale   34* ●●
DANIEL DE FASSON   *Floral Oriental / Fleuri Oriental   47* ●●●
DANIEL HECHTER SPORT POUR ELLE   *Floral / Florale   32* ●
DANS LA NUIT   *Woody Oriental / Oriental Boisé   61* ●●●
DARBY ROSE   *Floral / Florale   31* ●●●
DARK VANILLA   *Floral Oriental / Fleuri Oriental   47* ●●●●
DAY ♂   *Citrus / Hespéridé   17* ●●●●
DAZZLING GOLD   *Floral / Florale   32* ●●
DAZZLING SILVER   *Soft Floral / Fleuri Aldéhydé   42* ●●
DE – LE*   *Floral / Florale   33* ●●
DEAUVILLE   *Soft Floral / Fleuri Aldéhydé   42* ●●
DE BERCHELAI   *Floral / Florale   32* ●●
DÉCADENCE*   *Floral / Florale   38* ●●
DECI DELÀ   *Mossy Woods / Chypre Boisé   66* ●●
DÉLICE D'ÉPICES   *Floral Oriental / Fleuri Oriental   47* ●●●
"DELICIOUS"   *Soft Floral / Fleuri Aldéhydé   43* ●●●●
"DELICIOUS" FEELINGS   *Floral / Florale   36* ●
DÉLIRIUM DE NUIT   *Citrus / Hespéridé   17* ●●●●
DÉLIRIUM OCEANE   *Floral / Florale   32* ●
DÉLIRIUM ROSE   *Floral / Florale   32* ●
DÉLIRIUM TEA   *Floral / Florale   34* ●
DEMI-JOUR   *Soft Floral / Fleuri Aldéhydé   43* ●●●●
DENEUVE*   *Mossy Woods / Chypre Boisé   66* ●
DESIGN   *Soft Floral / Fleuri Aldéhydé   42* ●
DÉSIRADE   *Floral Oriental / Fleuri Oriental   46* ●●
DESNUDA   *Woody Oriental / Oriental Boisé   60* ●●
DESTINY Marilyn Miglin   *Floral / Florale   38* ●
DESTINY WOMAN   *Woody Oriental / Oriental Boisé   60* ●
DETCHÉMA   *Soft Floral / Fleuri Aldéhydé   43* ●●●●
DIAMANT D'OR*   *Floral Oriental / Fleuri Oriental   46* ●●
DIAMONDS & EMERALDS*   *Floral / Florale   38* ●●
DIAMONDS & RUBIES*   *Woody Oriental / Oriental Boisé   61* ●●●
DIAMONDS & SAPPHIRES*   *Floral / Florale   36* ●
DI BORGHESE*   *Green / Vert   23* ●●●
DIESEL ♂   *Woody Oriental / Oriental Boisé   61* ●●●
DIESEL PLUS PLUS FEMININE   *Floral Oriental / Fleuri Oriental   48* ●
DIESEL ZERO PLUS FEMININE   *Woody Oriental / Oriental Boisé   60* ●
DILYS   *Floral / Florale   33* ●●●●
DIONNE   *Oriental / Oriental   56* ●
DIORAMA   *Mossy Woods / Chypre Boisé   67* ●●●
DIORELLA   *Citrus / Hespéridé   16* ●●
DIORESSENCE   *Soft Oriental / Oriental Doux   53* ●●●
DIORISSIMO   *Floral / Florale   30* ●
DIORLING   *Dry Woods / Boisé Cuir   73* ●●●
DI ROMEO GIGLI   *Soft Floral / Fleuri Aldéhydé   43* ●●●●
DIRT ♂   *Mossy Woods / Chypre Boisé   66* ●●
DIVA   *Mossy Woods / Chypre Boisé   67* ●●●●
DIVINA   *Floral / Florale   34* ●●
DIVINE FOLIE   *Floral Oriental / Fleuri Oriental   47* ●●●

DIX – LE *Soft Floral / Fleuri Aldéhydé 43* ●●●●
DKNY WOMEN *Soft Floral / Fleuri Aldéhydé 42* ●
DNA* *Soft Floral / Fleuri Aldéhydé 43* ●●●●
DOLCE & GABBANA *Soft Floral / Fleuri Aldéhydé 43* ●●●●
DOLCE VITA *Woody Oriental / Oriental Boisé 60* ●●
DOLCE VITA – EAU DE *Floral / Florale 32* ●
DONNA Compagnia Delle Indie *Floral / Florale 36* ●
DONNA BORSALINO *Floral Oriental / Fleuri Oriental 46* ●●
DONNA KARAN *Dry Woods / Boisé Cuir 73* ●●●
DONNA NAUTILUS *Floral / Florale 32* ●●
DONNA TRUSSARDI *Mossy Woods / Chypre Boisé 67* ●●●
DOUBLE CLICK ♂ *Citrus / Hespéridé 16* ●
DOUBLE FRAÎCHEUR POUR ELLE *Citrus / Hespéridé 17* ●●●●
DOUCE AMÈRE ♂ *Woody Oriental / Oriental Boisé 60* ●●
DOULTON *Floral Oriental / Fleuri Oriental 46* ●●
DREAM *Floral / Florale 38* ●
DREAM ANGELS DIVINE *Soft Floral / Fleuri Aldéhydé 42* ●●
DREAM ANGELS HALO *Floral / Florale 31* ●●●●
DREAM ANGELS HEAVENLY *Floral Oriental / Fleuri Oriental 46* ●●
DREAMING PRINCESS *Floral Oriental / Fleuri Oriental 46* ●●
DREAMS BY TABU* *Floral / Florale 36* ●
DRÔLE DE ROSE *Soft Floral / Fleuri Aldéhydé 42* ●●
DUÉ DAY *Floral / Florale 32* ●
DUÉ NIGHT *Floral / Florale 32* ●●
DUENDE *Water / Marine 26* ●
DULCE VANILLA *Woody Oriental / Oriental Boisé 60* ●
DUNE *Woody Oriental / Oriental Boisé 60* ●
DUO POUR ELLE *Floral / Florale 32* ●
DZING! *Dry Woods / Boisé Cuir 73* ●●●●

E

EARL GREY TEA ♂ *Citrus / Hespéridé 16* ●
EARTH ♂ *Mossy Woods / Chypre Boisé 66* ●
EASY KRIZIA *Mossy Woods / Chypre Boisé 66* ●
EAU – L' Diptyque ♂ *Soft Oriental / Oriental Doux 52* ●●
EAU BELLE *Citrus / Hespéridé 16* ●
EAU BY LAURA – L' *Citrus / Hespéridé 16* ●●
EAU D'AMBRE – L' *Oriental / Oriental 57* ●●●
EAU DE BIARRITZ *Soft Floral / Fleuri Aldéhydé 42* ●●
EAU DE CAMILLE *Floral / Florale 34* ●
EAU DE CAMPAGNE ♂ *Green / Vert 23* ●●●
EAU DE CARON *Oriental / Oriental 56* ●●
EAU DE CARON FORTE ♂ *Citrus / Hespéridé 17* ●●●●
EAU DE CÈDRE ♂ *Dry Woods / Boisé Cuir 72* ●
EAU DE CHARLOTTE *Floral / Florale 32* ●
EAU DE CHEVERNY → VIE DE CHATEAU (CHEVERNY) ♂
EAU DE COLOGNE Penhaligon's ♂ *Citrus / Hespéridé 17* ●●●
EAU DE CORIANDRE *Floral / Florale 32* ●
EAU DE COURRÈGES *Citrus / Hespéridé 17* ●●●●
EAU DE COUTURE *Soft Floral / Fleuri Aldéhydé 43* ●●●●
EAU DE DALI *Floral / Florale 32* ●
EAU D'EDEN *Floral / Florale 36* ●
EAU DE DIOR COLORESSENCE ENERGISANTE *Citrus / Hespéridé 16* ●
EAU DE DIOR COLORESSENCE RELAXANTE *Citrus / Hespéridé 17* ●●●●
EAU DE DOLCE VITA *Floral / Florale 32* ●
EAU DE FATH *Floral / Florale 32* ●
EAU DE FLEURS DE CÉDRAT ♂ *Citrus / Hespéridé 17* ●●●
EAU DE GIVENCHY *Floral / Florale 32* ●
EAU DE GUCCI* *Floral / Florale 38* ●
EAU DE GUERLAIN ♂ *Citrus / Hespéridé 17* ●●●
EAU DE KOOKAÏ – L' *Citrus / Hespéridé 16* ●
EAU DE LANCASTER *Citrus / Hespéridé 17* ●●●
EAU DE L'ARTISAN – L' ♂ *Citrus / Hespéridé 17* ●●●
EAU DE LAVANDE Annick Goutal *Floral / Florale 31* ●●●
EAU D'ÉLIDE ♂ *Aromatic / Fougère 77* ●●●
EAU DE MER *Water / Marine 26* ●
EAU DE MONTEIL – L' *Floral / Florale 33* ●●●●
EAU DE MURANO *Floral / Florale 31* ●●●
EAU DE MÛRE *Citrus / Hespéridé 17* ●●●
EAU DE PATOU *Citrus / Hespéridé 17* ●●●
EAU DE PIVER *Woody Oriental / Oriental Boisé 61* ●●●
EAU DE PROVENCE ♂ *Floral / Florale 31* ●●●
EAU DE RÉVILLON *Floral / Florale 36* ●
EAU DE ROCHAS *Citrus / Hespéridé 17* ●●●
EAU DE SONIA RYKIEL – L' *Floral / Florale 32* ●
EAU DE SUCCÈS* – L' *Floral / Florale 32* ●●

EAU D'ÉTÉ *Citrus / Hespéridé 16* ●●
EAU DE THÉ VERT ♂ *Citrus / Hespéridé 16* ●
EAU DE TOUCH Tocca *Floral / Florale 30* ●●
EAU DE VARENS N° 2 ♂ *Citrus / Hespéridé 16* ●
EAU DE VARENS N° 3 ♂ *Citrus / Hespéridé 16* ●●
EAU DE VARENS N° 4 ♂ *Citrus / Hespéridé 17* ●●●●
EAU DE VERINO *Floral / Florale 36* ●
EAU DE VERVEINE Penhaligon's ♂ *Citrus / Hespéridé 17* ●●●●
EAU D'HADRIEN ♂ *Citrus / Hespéridé 17* ●●●
EAU D'HERMÈS ♂ *Dry Woods / Boisé Cuir 73* ●●●
EAU D'INFINITIF *Floral / Florale 32* ●
EAU D'ISSEY – L' *Water / Marine 26* ●●
EAU D'IVOIRE *Floral / Florale 34* ●
EAU D'ORANGE VERTE ♂ *Citrus / Hespéridé 17* ●●●●
EAU D'ORLANE *Citrus / Hespéridé 16* ●
EAU DU CIEL *Floral / Florale 34* ●●
EAU DU COQ ♂ *Citrus / Hespéridé 17* ●●●
EAU DU GANTIER ♂ *Citrus / Hespéridé 17* ●●●
EAU DU SOIR *Mossy Woods / Chypre Boisé 67* ●●●
EAU DU SUD ♂ *Citrus / Hespéridé 16* ●●
EAU DYNAMISANTE ♂ *Citrus / Hespéridé 17* ●●●
EAU FRAÎCHE Caron ♂ *Citrus / Hespéridé 17* ●●●
EAU FRAÎCHE Christian Dior *Mossy Woods / Chypre Boisé 67* ●●●
EAU FRAÎCHE Christian Tortu *Citrus / Hespéridé 17* ●●●
EAU FRAÎCHE Elizabeth Arden *Floral / Florale 30* ●
EAU FRAÎCHE Léonard *Citrus / Hespéridé 17* ●●●
EAU FRAÎCHE Molinard ♂ *Citrus / Hespéridé 16* ●●
EAU FRANCE ♂ *Citrus / Hespéridé 17* ●●●
EAU IMPÉRIALE ♂ *Citrus / Hespéridé 17* ●●●
EAU LENTE ♂ *Oriental / Oriental 57* ●●●
EAU LES COEURS* *Floral / Florale 32* ●●
EAU LILIAN – L' *Water / Marine 26* ●●
EAU MARINE *Floral / Florale 36* ●
EAU PAR KENZO – L' *Floral / Florale 38* ●
EAU POUR SOI *Floral / Florale 32* ●
EAU PURE ♂ *Water / Marine 26* ●
EAU ROSÉE *Soft Floral / Fleuri Aldéhydé 42* ●
EAU SANS PAREIL ♂ *Aromatic / Fougère 76* ●●
EAU SVELTE *Floral / Florale 32* ●
EAU TROIS – L' ♂ *Dry Woods / Boisé Cuir 72* ●●
EAU VITAMINÉE *Citrus / Hespéridé 16* ●●
EAU VIVE *Citrus / Hespéridé 16* ●●
ECLIX *Woody Oriental / Oriental Boisé 60* ●
ÉCOUTE-MOI *Floral / Florale 33* ●●●●
ÉCUSSON *Soft Floral / Fleuri Aldéhydé 43* ●●●
EDEN *Floral Oriental / Fleuri Oriental 48* ●
EDWARDIAN BOUQUET *Floral / Florale 38* ●
EFFLEUR – L' *Floral / Florale 34* ●●
ÉLÀ NONCHALANCE *Floral / Florale 38* ●●
ELISABETHAN ROSE *Floral / Florale 31* ●●●
ELLEN TRACY *Woody Oriental / Oriental Boisé 61* ●●●
ÉLUE – L' *Floral Oriental / Fleuri Oriental 46* ●●
ELYSIUM *Floral / Florale 32* ●
ÉMERAUDE *Oriental / Oriental 57* ●●●
EMOZIONI FOR WOMAN *Floral / Florale 38* ●
EMPORIO ARMANI SHE / ELLE *Floral Oriental / Fleuri Oriental 47* ●●●
EMPREINTE *Dry Woods / Boisé Cuir 73* ●●●
EN AVION *Floral Oriental / Fleuri Oriental 47* ●●●●
ENCHANTÉ *Woody Oriental / Oriental Boisé 60* ●
E.N.C.O.R.E *Woody Oriental / Oriental Boisé 60* ●
ENERGIZING FRAGRANCE *Soft Floral / Fleuri Aldéhydé 42* ●●
ENFANTS DU SOLEIL *Floral Oriental / Fleuri Oriental 46* ●●
ENGLISH FERN ♂ *Aromatic / Fougère 77* ●●●
ENGLISH FINE COLOGNE ♂ *Citrus / Hespéridé 17* ●●●
ENGLISH LAVENDER Atkinson ♂ *Floral / Florale 31* ●●●
ENGLISH LAVENDER Yardley *Floral / Florale 31* ●●●
ENGLISH ROSE Perfumers Guild *Floral / Florale 31* ●●●
ENGLISH ROSE Yardley *Floral / Florale 31* ●●●
ENIGMA *Woody Oriental / Oriental Boisé 61* ●●●
ENJOLI *Floral / Florale 31* ●●●●
ENJOLI MIDNIGHT *Soft Oriental / Oriental Doux 53* ●●●
ENRICO COVERI *Soft Oriental / Oriental Doux 53* ●●●
ENVY *Floral / Florale 38* ●
ERUPTION WOMAN *Floral Oriental / Fleuri Oriental 46* ●●
ESCADA *Floral Oriental / Fleuri Oriental 47* ●●●
ESCADA COLLECTION *Woody Oriental / Oriental Boisé 60* ●
ESCADA COUNTRY WEEKEND ♂ *Aromatic / Fougère 76* ●●

ESCADA EN FLEURS   *Floral / Florale   32* ●
ESCADA FEELING FREE   *Floral / Florale   34* ●
ESCADA SENTIMENT   → SENTIMENT
ESCADA SPORT SPIRIT ♂   *Citrus / Hespéridé   16* ●
ESCADA TENDER LIGHT   *Floral Oriental / Fleuri Oriental   48* ●
ESENCIA DE DUENDE   *Floral / Florale   36* ●
ESCAPE   *Water / Marine   27* ●●●●
ESPÍRITU DE MONTESINOS   *Floral / Florale   38* ●
ESPRIT DE LAVANDE ♂   *Aromatic / Fougère   76* ●
ESPRIT DU ROI ♂   *Citrus / Hespéridé   16* ●●
ESP STAYFAST   *Floral / Florale   33* ●●●●
ESSENTIALLY JAGUAR   *Floral Oriental / Fleuri Oriental   46* ●●
ESSENZA DI MEDITERRANEÒ DONNA   *Floral / Florale   32* ●
ESTÉE   *Floral / Florale   33* ●●●●
ESTIVALIA   *Citrus / Hespéridé   16* ●●
ÉTÉ DE VENTILO – L'   *Floral Oriental / Fleuri Oriental   46* ●
ETERNITY   *Floral / Florale   38* ●
ÉTHÉRÉ   *Floral / Florale   36* ●
ÉTIQUETTE BLEUE ♂   *Citrus / Hespéridé   16* ●●
ETRA ♂   *Soft Oriental / Oriental Doux   53* ●●●●
EUNECE   *Woody Oriental / Oriental Boisé   61* ●●●
EVELYN   *Floral / Florale   31* ●●●
EVENING IN PARIS   → SOIR DE PARIS ORIGINAL
EXCITING ARROGANCE   *Soft Floral / Fleuri Aldéhydé   42* ●
EX'CLA.MA'TION   *Floral Oriental / Fleuri Oriental   46* ●●
EX'CLA.MA'TION BLUSH   *Floral / Florale   32* ●
EX'CLA.MA'TION DARE   *Floral / Florale   38* ●
EX'CLA.MA'TION EAU   *Citrus / Hespéridé   16* ●
EX'CLA.MA'TION NOIR   *Mossy Woods / Chypre Boisé   67* ●●●
EXPERIENCES   *Floral / Florale   33* ●●●●
EXPLOSIVE*   *Mossy Woods / Chypre Boisé   66* ●●
EXTASE BODY TALK ♂   *Citrus / Hespéridé   16* ●
EXTASE DEVOTION WOMAN   *Woody Oriental / Oriental Boisé   60* ●
EXTASE EXOTIC NATURE WOMAN   *Floral / Florale   36* ●●
EXTASE MUSK WOMAN   *Oriental / Oriental   57* ●●●
EXTASE PURE PASSION WOMAN
   Woody Oriental / Oriental Boisé   61 ●●●
EXTRACT OF LIMES Penhaligon's ♂   *Citrus / Hespéridé   17* ●●●●
EXTRAVAGANCE D'AMARIGE   *Floral / Florale   36* ●

F

FABERGÉ IMPERIAL   *Floral / Florale   33* ●●●●
FABLE   *Woody Oriental / Oriental Boisé   61* ●●●
FABULEUSE   *Floral / Florale   32* ●
FABULOUS   *Floral Oriental / Fleuri Oriental   47* ●●●
FACE À FACE FEMME   *Floral / Florale   36* ●
FAÇONNABLE   *Floral / Florale   34* ●●
FANTASIA   *Floral / Florale   32* ●●
FANTASIA DE FLEURS   *Floral / Florale   33* ●●●●
FANTASME   *Floral Oriental / Fleuri Oriental   46* ●●
FARNESIANA   *Floral / Florale   30* ●●
FAROUCHE   *Soft Floral / Fleuri Aldéhydé   42* ●●
FASCINATION   *Floral / Florale   32* ●●
FASHION   *Floral Oriental / Fleuri Oriental   46* ●●
FASHION FAIR N° 1   *Floral / Florale   34* ●●
FAST FORWARD   → OBLIQUE FAST FORWARD
FATH DE FATH   *Oriental / Oriental   56* ●●
FEELING FREE   → ESCADA FEELING FREE
FEMINA*   *Floral / Florale   36* ●
FEMINITÉ DU BOIS   *Woody Oriental / Oriental Boisé   61* ●●●
FEMME   *Mossy Woods / Chypre Boisé   67* ●●●
FENDI   *Woody Oriental / Oriental Boisé   61* ●●●●
FERENTINA   *Floral Oriental / Fleuri Oriental   47* ●●●
FERRARI DONNA   *Floral / Florale   36* ●●
FERRÉ BY FERRÉ   *Soft Floral / Fleuri Aldéhydé   43* ●●●
FÉTICHE   *Floral Oriental / Fleuri Oriental   47* ●●●
FETISH   *Floral / Florale   36* ●
FEU D'ISSEY – LE   *Woody Oriental / Oriental Boisé   61* ●●●
FEU D'ISSEY LIGHT – LE   *Soft Floral / Fleuri Aldéhydé   43* ●●●●
FEUILLE D'HERBE FLORALE & FRUITÉE
   Mossy Woods / Chypre Boisé   66 ●
FEUILLE D'HERBE FRAÎCHE & EPICÉE
   Woody Oriental / Oriental Boisé   61 ●●●●
FEUILLE D'HERBE FRAÎCHE & HERBACÉE   *Green / Vert   22* ●●●●
FEUILLE DE VERVEINE ♂   *Citrus / Hespéridé   16* ●
FÍDJI   *Floral / Florale   36* ●

FIFTH AVENUE   *Floral / Florale   34* ●
FIG LEAF ♂   *Mossy Woods / Chypre Boisé   66* ●
FIG TEA   *Citrus / Hespéridé   17* ●●●●
FILLE D'EVE   *Mossy Woods / Chypre Boisé   67* ●●●
FIORI DI KRIZIA*   *Floral / Florale   32* ●
FIORILU EN FLEURS   *Floral / Florale   32* ●●
FIORUCCI   *Floral / Florale   32* ●●
FIRE & ICE   *Oriental / Oriental   56* ●●
FIRE & ICE COOL   *Citrus / Hespéridé   16* ●
FIRE & ICE SMOULDER FOR HER   *Woody Oriental / Oriental Boisé   60* ●
FIRENZE   *Soft Floral / Fleuri Aldéhydé   42* ●●
FIRST   *Soft Floral / Fleuri Aldéhydé   43* ●●●●
FLEUR Floris   *Floral / Florale   36* ●
FLEUR Lenthéric   *Floral / Florale   32* ●●
FLEURAGE   *Soft Floral / Fleuri Aldéhydé   42* ●●
FLEUR D'EAU   *Floral / Florale   36* ●
FLEUR DE CAROTTE ①   *Mossy Woods / Chypre Boisé   66* ●●
FLEUR DE DÉSIRADE   *Soft Floral / Fleuri Aldéhydé   42* ●●
FLEUR DE DIVA   *Floral / Florale   36* ●
FLEUR DE FIGUIER   *Mossy Woods / Chypre Boisé   66* ●
FLEUR DE FLEURS   *Soft Floral / Fleuri Aldéhydé   42* ●
FLEUR DE LOTUS   *Water / Marine   26* ●●
FLEUR DE ROCAILLE   *Floral / Florale   34* ●●
FLEUR DE WEIL*   *Floral / Florale   32* ●
FLEUR D'INTERDIT   *Floral / Florale   36* ●
FLEUR D'IRIS   *Soft Floral / Fleuri Aldéhydé   43* ●●●
FLEURISSIMO   *Floral / Florale   38* ●
FLEURS Morabito   *Floral / Florale   38* ●
FLEURS DE BULGARIE   *Floral / Florale   31* ●●●
FLEURS DE CHIARA BONI   *Floral / Florale   38* ●
FLEURS DE LA FORÊT   *Mossy Woods / Chypre Boisé   67* ●●●
FLEURS DE PÊCHER   *Soft Floral / Fleuri Aldéhydé   42* ●
FLEURS DE ROCAILLE   *Floral / Florale   33* ●●●
FLEURS DES COMORES   *Mossy Woods / Chypre Boisé   66* ●●
FLEURS D'ORLANE   *Floral / Florale   38* ●
FLIRT   *Floral / Florale   34* ●●
FLORAMYE   *Mossy Woods / Chypre Boisé   66* ●●
FLORA NEROLIA   *Floral / Florale   31* ●●●●
FLORE Carolina Herrera   *Floral / Florale   30* ●
FLORE AUBUSSON   *Floral / Florale   36* ●
FLORET   *Floral / Florale   30* ●●
FLORISSA   *Soft Floral / Fleuri Aldéhydé   42* ●●
FLOWER BY KENZO   *Floral Oriental / Fleuri Oriental   46* ●●
FLUID ICEBERG WOMAN   *Woody Oriental / Oriental Boisé   61* ●●●
FOLAVRIL   *Soft Floral / Fleuri Aldéhydé   42* ●●
FOLIE DOUCE   *Floral / Florale   32* ●●
FOREVER Alfred Sung   *Floral / Florale   36* ●
FOREVER KRYSTLE   *Floral Oriental / Fleuri Oriental   47* ●●●
FORGET-ME-NOT   *Soft Floral / Fleuri Aldéhydé   43* ●●●
FORMIDABLE   *Floral Oriental / Fleuri Oriental   47* ●●●
FORUM   *Oriental / Oriental   56* ●●
FOU D'ELLE   *Floral / Florale   32* ●●
FRACAS   *Floral / Florale   31* ●●●●
FRAGILE   *Floral / Florale   31* ●●●●
FRAÎCHE PASSIFLORE   *Citrus / Hespéridé   16* ●●
FRAÎCHEUR MUSKISSIME ♂   *Citrus / Hespéridé   17* ●●●●
FRANGIPANE   *Floral / Florale   31* ●●●●
FREEDOM FOR HER   *Floral / Florale   38* ●
FREESIA Crabtree & Evelyn   *Floral / Florale   30* ●●
FREESIA Woods of Windsor   *Floral / Florale   30* ●●
FREE WORLD WOMAN   *Floral / Florale   36* ●
FREEZIA D'OR   *Floral / Florale   33* ●●●●
FRENCH CANCAN   *Floral Oriental / Fleuri Oriental   48* ●●
FRENCH CONNECTION   *Citrus / Hespéridé   16* ●
FRENCH LIME BLOSSOM   *Floral / Florale   30* ●
FRENCH VANILLA   *Woody Oriental / Oriental Boisé   60* ●●
FRUITS & FLOWERS   *Floral / Florale   32* ●
FRUITS SAUVAGES   *Citrus / Hespéridé   17* ●●●●
FUJIYAMA ♂   *Citrus / Hespéridé   16* ●
FUNTASTIC GIRL   *Floral / Florale   32* ●
FUN WATER WOMAN   *Water / Marine   26* ●●

G

G   *Soft Floral / Fleuri Aldéhydé   42* ●
GABRIELA SABATINI   *Floral Oriental / Fleuri Oriental   48* ●●
GAI MATTIOLO   *Floral Oriental / Fleuri Oriental   46* ●

GALA DE DIA   *Floral / Florale   38* ●
GALA LOEWE   *Floral Oriental / Fleuri Oriental   46* ●●
GALANOS   *Soft Floral / Fleuri Aldéhydé   43* ●●●
GALANOS DE SERENE   *Soft Oriental / Oriental Doux   53* ●●●
GALICE   *Floral Oriental / Fleuri Oriental   46* ●●
GALORÉ   *Floral Oriental / Fleuri Oriental   47* ●●●
GARDÉNIA Chanel   *Floral / Florale   30* ●●
GARDENIA Crabtree & Evelyn   *Floral / Florale   30* ●●
GARDENIA Demeter   *Floral / Florale   30* ●●
GARDENIA Floris   *Floral / Florale   30* ●●
GARDENIA Jo Malone   *Floral / Florale   30* ●●
GARDENIA Penhaligon's   *Floral / Florale   30* ●●
GARDENIA MUSK #4   *Floral / Florale   30* ●●
GARDÉNIA PASSION   *Floral / Florale   31* ●●●●
GATTINONI À PORTER   *Floral / Florale   32* ●
GATTINONI COUTURE   *Woody Oriental / Oriental Boisé   60* ●
GAULOISE*   *Mossy Woods / Chypre Boisé   66* ●
GEM   *Woody Oriental / Oriental Boisé   61* ●●●●
GÉNÉRATION COURRÈGES   *Floral / Florale   32* ●
GENNY (Original)   *Dry Woods / Boisé Cuir   72* ●
GENNY (New)   *Floral / Florale   32* ●●
GENNY SHINE*   *Floral Oriental / Fleuri Oriental   46* ●●
GEOFFREY BEENE   *Floral / Florale   34* ●●
GERANI   *Woody Oriental / Oriental Boisé   60* ●
GFF F   *Floral / Florale   34* ●●
G GIGLI*   *Soft Floral / Fleuri Aldéhydé   42* ●
GHOST   *Floral Oriental / Fleuri Oriental   46* ●●
GHOST MYST   *Water / Marine   26* ●
GIANFRANCO FERRÉ   *Floral / Florale   38* ●
GIANFRANCO FERRÉ 20   *Floral / Florale   33* ●●●
GIANNI VERSACE   *Mossy Woods / Chypre Boisé   67* ●●●●
GIEFFEFFE ♂   *Citrus / Hespéridé   16* ●
GIN & TONIC ♂   *Citrus / Hespéridé   17* ●●●
GINGERALE ♂   *Citrus / Hespéridé   17* ●●●●
GINGERBREAD ♂   *Oriental / Oriental   57* ●●●●
GINGER ESSENCE   *Citrus / Hespéridé   17* ●●●●
GINGHAM   *Aromatic / Fougère   77* ●●●
GIÒ   *Floral / Florale   33* ●●●●
GIORGIO   *Floral / Florale   38* ●●
GIORGIO AIRE*   *Soft Floral / Fleuri Aldéhydé   42* ●
GIORGIO HOLIDAY* Ⓛ   *Floral / Florale   32* ●●
GIVENCHY III   *Mossy Woods / Chypre Boisé   66* ●
GIVRINE (SICILE) ♂   *Citrus / Hespéridé   17* ●●●
GLAMOUR   *Floral Oriental / Fleuri Oriental   47* ●●●
GMV DONNA   *Floral Oriental / Fleuri Oriental   46* ●●
GODDESS   *Floral Oriental / Fleuri Oriental   46* ●●
GOLD   *Woody Oriental / Oriental Boisé   60* ●
GOLDEN DELICIOUS ♂   *Citrus / Hespéridé   16* ●●
GOLDEN MOMENT   *Floral Oriental / Fleuri Oriental   46* ●
GOLD JEANS FEMME   *Citrus / Hespéridé   16* ●
GOMMA ♂   *Dry Woods / Boisé Cuir   73* ●●●●
GOODLIFE WOMAN   *Floral Oriental / Fleuri Oriental   46* ●
GOSSIP   *Woody Oriental / Oriental Boisé   60* ●
GOURMANDISE DE RODIER   *Citrus / Hespéridé   16* ●
GRAFFITI VANILLA   *Woody Oriental / Oriental Boisé   60* ●●
GRAIN DE FOLIE   *Green / Vert   22* ●●
GRAIN DE PLAISIR ♂   *Mossy Woods / Chypre Boisé   66* ●
GRAIN DE SOLEIL   *Woody Oriental / Oriental Boisé   61* ●●●
GRAND AMOUR   *Soft Floral / Fleuri Aldéhydé   43* ●●●●
GRAPEFRUIT ♂   *Citrus / Hespéridé   16* ●●
GRAPEFRUIT & YELLOW FREESIA #1   *Citrus / Hespéridé   17* ●●●●
GRASS Demeter ♂   *Green / Vert   23* ●●●
GRASS Gap ♂   *Green / Vert   23* ●●●
GREEN GENERATION ♂   *Aromatic / Fougère   76* ●●
GREEN GENERATION HER   *Floral / Florale   32* ●
GREENHOUSE ♂   *Green / Vert   22* ●
GREEN TEA Elizabeth Arden   *Citrus / Hespéridé   16* ●
GREEN VALLEY ♂   *Mossy Woods / Chypre Boisé   66* ●
GUCCI ACCENTI   → ACCENTI
GUCCI N° 1*   *Soft Floral / Fleuri Aldéhydé   42* ●●
GUCCI N° 3*   *Mossy Woods / Chypre Boisé   66* ●●
GUCCI RUSH   *Woody Oriental / Oriental Boisé   60* ●●
GUÉPARD   *Woody Oriental / Oriental Boisé   61* ●●●
GUESS (Original)*   *Woody Oriental / Oriental Boisé   60* ●●
GUESS (New)   *Floral / Florale   32* ●
GUET-APENS* Ⓛ   *Woody Oriental / Oriental Boisé   60* ●
GUIRLANDES*   *Soft Floral / Fleuri Aldéhydé   42* ●

H

HABANITA   *Woody Oriental / Oriental Boisé   61* ●●●●
HAIE FLEURIE DU HAMEAU – LA   *Floral / Florale   31* ●●●
HALLOWEEN   *Floral / Florale   36* ●●
HALSTON   *Mossy Woods / Chypre Boisé   66* ●
HALSTON COUTURE*   *Mossy Woods / Chypre Boisé   67* ●●●
HANAE MORI   *Woody Oriental / Oriental Boisé   60* ●●
HANAE MORI HAUTE COUTURE   *Soft Floral / Fleuri Aldéhydé   42* ●
HAPPY   *Floral / Florale   32* ●
HAUTE PROVENCE   → EAU DE PROVENCE ♂
HAVANA POUR ELLE   *Floral / Florale   36* ●●
HEAD OVER HEELS   *Floral / Florale   32* ●
HEART   *Floral / Florale   36* ●
HEAVEN   *Soft Floral / Fleuri Aldéhydé   42* ●
HEAVEN SENT   *Aromatic / Fougère   77* ●●●
HELIOTROPE ♂   *Floral Oriental / Fleuri Oriental   47* ●●●
HELMUT LANG WOMAN   *Woody Oriental / Oriental Boisé   61* ●●●
HÉRBA FRESCA ♂   *Green / Vert   22* ●●
HERITAGE ROSE   *Floral / Florale   30* ●●
HEURE ATTENDUE – L'   *Woody Oriental / Oriental Boisé   61* ●●●
HEURE BLEUE – L'   *Floral Oriental / Fleuri Oriental   47* ●●●
HEURE EXQUISE   *Soft Floral / Fleuri Aldéhydé   42* ●
HERVÉ LÉGER   *Floral Oriental / Fleuri Oriental   47* ●●●
HIGH... (Cerise)   *Citrus / Hespéridé   16* ●●
HIGH TECH WOMEN   *Floral / Florale   32* ●
HIRIS   *Soft Floral / Fleuri Aldéhydé   42* ●
HISTOIRE D'AMOUR   *Mossy Woods / Chypre Boisé   67* ●●●
HOLLYWOOD   *Woody Oriental / Oriental Boisé   60* ●●
HOLY WATER ♂   *Water / Marine   27* ●●●●
HONEYMOON   *Woody Oriental / Oriental Boisé   60* ●●
HONEYSUCKLE Demeter   *Floral / Florale   30* ●●
HONEYSUCKLE & JASMINE   *Floral / Florale   38* ●●
HOPE   *Soft Floral / Fleuri Aldéhydé   43* ●●●●
HOT   *Floral Oriental / Fleuri Oriental   46* ●
HOT COUTURE   *Woody Oriental / Oriental Boisé   60* ●●
HUGO WOMAN   *Floral / Florale   36* ●●
HYPERSOUK   *Soft Oriental / Oriental Doux   53* ●●●
HYPNOTIC POISON   *Woody Oriental / Oriental Boisé   61* ●●●●

I

I AM CLEAR   *Citrus / Hespéridé   16* ●●
I AM COOL   *Water / Marine   26* ●●
I AM ENERGY   *Citrus / Hespéridé   16* ●
I AM ETERNAL   *Woody Oriental / Oriental Boisé   61* ●●●
I AM LOVE   *Floral / Florale   32* ●
I AM PASSION   *Floral / Florale   36* ●
I AM POWER   *Floral Oriental / Fleuri Oriental   46* ●
I AM RICH   *Soft Floral / Fleuri Aldéhydé   42* ●
I AM SERENE   *Green / Vert   23* ●●●
I AM WILD   *Oriental / Oriental   56* ●
ICEBERG   *Floral / Florale   32* ●
ICEBERG TWICE   *Floral / Florale   38* ●
ICEBERG TWICE ICE   *Citrus / Hespéridé   16* ●
ICEBERG UNIVERSE FEMME   *Floral Oriental / Fleuri Oriental   47* ●●●
ICI   *Floral Oriental / Fleuri Oriental   46* ●●
I EX'CLA.MA'TION   *Floral Oriental / Fleuri Oriental   46* ●
IL BACIO   *Floral / Florale   32* ●
ÎLES D'OR   *Floral / Florale   32* ●
I LOVE YOU   *Floral / Florale   32* ●
IMAGE WOMAN   → CERRUTI IMAGE WOMAN
IMPERIAL VETYVER ♂   *Mossy Woods / Chypre Boisé   67* ●●●
IMPLICITE   *Soft Floral / Fleuri Aldéhydé   42* ●
IMPOSIBLE (sic) ♂   *Citrus / Hespéridé   16* ●
IMPRÉVU   *Dry Woods / Boisé Cuir   73* ●●●
INCLINATION   *Floral / Florale   32* ●
INCOGNITO   *Floral Oriental / Fleuri Oriental   46* ●●
INDÉCENCE   → ORGANZA INDÉCENCE
INDEX AMARYLLIS CASSIS ♂   *Floral / Florale   32* ●
INDEX BERGAMOT CITRUS ♂   *Citrus / Hespéridé   16* ●
INDEX CEDAR ARMOISE ♂   *Mossy Woods / Chypre Boisé   66* ●●
INDEX CHINA GREEN TEA ♂   *Green / Vert   22* ●●
INDEX CORIANDER LAVENDER ♂   *Aromatic / Fougère   76* ●●
INDEX CURRANT MARINE ♂   *Water / Marine   26* ●●
INDEX FIG APRICOT ♂   *Mossy Woods / Chypre Boisé   66* ●
INDEX GALBANUM PATCHOULI ♂   *Mossy Woods / Chypre Boisé   66* ●

INDEX GERANIUM PEPPER ♂ *Aromatic / Fougère* 77 ●●●●
INDEX GRAPEFRUIT MUSC ♂ *Citrus / Hespéridé* 17 ●●●●
INDEX HONEYSUCKLE GRAPEFRUIT ♂ *Citrus / Hespéridé* 16 ●●
INDEX JASMINE LYS ♂ *Floral / Florale* 38 ●
INDEX MANDARINE AMBER ♂ *Mossy Woods / Chypre Boisé* 67 ●●●●
INDEX MOROCCAN MINT TEA ♂ *Citrus / Hespéridé* 16 ●●
INDEX OLIVE MUSCADE ♂ *Mossy Woods / Chypre Boisé* 67 ●●●
INDEX ORANGE CHOCOLATE ♂ *Soft Oriental / Oriental Doux* 52 ●
INDEX PEAR CASSIS ♂ *Floral / Florale* 32 ●●
INDEX POMEGRANATE ANISE ♂ *Citrus / Hespéridé* 16 ●
INDEX RED CURRANT BASIL ♂ *Floral / Florale* 32 ●●
INDEX SANDALWOOD PETITGRAIN ♂ *Citrus / Hespéridé* 17 ●●●●
INDEX TOBACCO CARAMEL ♂ *Dry Woods / Boisé Cuir* 73 ●●●
INDEX VIOLET MOSS ♂ *Mossy Woods / Chypre Boisé* 66 ●●
INDEX YLANG-YLANG HIBISCUS ♂ *Floral / Florale* 31 ●●●
INDIANA / TUBÉREUSE INDIANA *Floral / Florale* 38 ●●
INDIAN NIGHTS → NUITS INDIENNES
INDIAN SUMMER *Floral Oriental / Fleuri Oriental* 46 ●
INDISCRET *Green / Vert* 22 ●●
INDIVIDUELLE *Floral / Florale* 38 ●
INÈS DE LA FRESSANGE *Soft Floral / Fleuri Aldéhydé* 42 ●
INFINI *Soft Floral / Fleuri Aldéhydé* 43 ●●●●
INFINITIF *Mossy Woods / Chypre Boisé* 67 ●●●
INIS ♂ *Water / Marine* 26 ●
INITIAL *Oriental / Oriental* 57 ●●●
INITIATION* *Floral Oriental / Fleuri Oriental* 47 ●●●
IN LOVE* *Floral / Florale* 30 ●
IN LOVE AGAIN* Ⓛ *Floral / Florale* 32 ●
INOUÏ *Green / Vert* 23 ●●●
INSAISISSABLE – L' *Floral / Florale* 32 ●●
INSOLENT – L'* *Woody Oriental / Oriental Boisé* 60 ●●
INSPIRATION *Floral Oriental / Fleuri Oriental* 46 ●
INSTANT JASMIN - L' *Floral / Florale* 31 ●●●
INSTINCT D'ANIMALE *Mossy Woods / Chypre Boisé* 67 ●●●
INTENSE DE SCAPA *Citrus / Hespéridé* 17 ●●●●
INTERDIT – L' *Soft Floral / Fleuri Aldéhydé* 43 ●●●
INTERLUDE *Oriental / Oriental* 57 ●●●
INTIMATE* *Mossy Woods / Chypre Boisé* 66 ●
INTOXICATION D'AMOUR *Woody Oriental / Oriental Boisé* 61 ●●●
INTRIGUE* *Soft Floral / Fleuri Aldéhydé* 42 ●●
INTUITION *Floral Oriental / Fleuri Oriental* 46 ●
IO *Mossy Woods / Chypre Boisé* 66 ●●
IQUITA* *Mossy Woods / Chypre Boisé* 66 ●●
IRENA GREGORI *Floral Oriental / Fleuri Oriental* 48 ●
ISSEY → L'EAU D'ISSEY
IVANA *Floral / Florale* 33 ●●●●
IVOIRE *Soft Floral / Fleuri Aldéhydé* 42 ●

J

JACINTHE ROSE (ROMANTICA) *Floral / Florale* 38 ●
JACQUELINE *Oriental / Oriental* 56 ●●
J'ADORE *Floral / Florale* 32 ●
J'AI OSÉ *Soft Oriental / Oriental Doux* 53 ●●●
JAÏPUR *Floral / Florale* 32 ●●
JAÏPUR SAPHIR *Oriental / Oriental* 56 ●●
JARDIN – LE *Floral / Florale* 38 ●
JARDIN BLANC *Floral / Florale* 38 ●●
JARDIN D'AMOUR – LE *Floral Oriental / Fleuri Oriental* 47 ●●●●
JARDINS DE BAGATELLE *Floral / Florale* 33 ●●●●
JARDIN SECRET *Mossy Woods / Chypre Boisé* 66 ●●
JASMAL *Floral / Florale* 31 ●●●
JASMIN Le Jardin Retrouvé *Floral / Florale* 31 ●●●
JASMIN Maître Parfumeur et Gantier *Floral / Florale* 31 ●●●
JASMIN Molinard *Floral / Florale* 31 ●●●
JASMIN DE PROVENCE* *Floral / Florale* 31 ●●●
JASMINE & ROSE HONEY #2 *Green / Vert* 22 ●
JASMIN IMPÉRATRICE EUGÉNIE *Floral / Florale* 33 ●●●
JASMIN MANDARINE *Soft Floral / Fleuri Aldéhydé* 43 ●●●
JEAN LOUIS SCHERRER *Green / Vert* 23 ●●●●
JEAN LUC AMSLER FEMME *Floral / Florale* 36 ●●
JEAN LUC AMSLER PRIVÉ FEMME
  Woody Oriental / Oriental Boisé 61 ●●●
JEAN MARIE FARINA ♂ *Citrus / Hespéridé* 17 ●●●
JEAN NATÉ *Aromatic / Fougère* 77 ●●●
JEAN PAUL GAULTIER *Floral Oriental / Fleuri Oriental* 46 ●●
JE REVIENS *Soft Floral / Fleuri Aldéhydé* 43 ●●●●

JESS *Floral / Florale* 33 ●●●●
JESSICA McCLINTOCK *Floral / Florale* 30 ●
JE T'AIME *Floral Oriental / Fleuri Oriental* 47 ●●●
JICKY ♂ *Aromatic / Fougère* 77 ●●●
JIL *Woody Oriental / Oriental Boisé* 60 ●
JIL SANDER BATH & BEAUTY *Mossy Woods / Chypre Boisé* 67 ●●●
JIL SANDER N° 4 *Floral Oriental / Fleuri Oriental* 46 ●
JIL SANDER SUN *Floral Oriental / Fleuri Oriental* 47 ●●●
JIL SANDER WOMAN PURE* *Soft Floral / Fleuri Aldéhydé* 42 ●
JIL SANDER WOMAN II* *Mossy Woods / Chypre Boisé* 66 ●●
JIL SANDER WOMAN III *Dry Woods / Boisé Cuir* 72 ●●
JIN ABE *Floral Oriental / Fleuri Oriental* 46 ●
JITROIS *Dry Woods / Boisé Cuir* 72 ●●
JIVAGO 7 NOTES *Floral Oriental / Fleuri Oriental* 46 ●●
JIVAGO 24k WOMEN *Floral / Florale* 33 ●●●●
JOLIE MADAME *Woody Oriental / Oriental Boisé* 60 ●●
JONES NEW YORK *Green / Vert* 22 ●●
JONTUE *Floral / Florale* 31 ●●●●
JONTUE MOONLIGHT* *Floral / Florale* 38 ●
JOOP! *Woody Oriental / Oriental Boisé* 61 ●●●●
JOOP! BERLIN *Soft Floral / Fleuri Aldéhydé* 42 ●
JOOP! LE BAIN *Floral Oriental / Fleuri Oriental* 47 ●●●●
JOOP! NUIT D'ÉTÉ* *Woody Oriental / Oriental Boisé* 61 ●●●
JOSEPH DE JOUR *Soft Floral / Fleuri Aldéhydé* 42 ●
JOVAN FRESH MUSK *Floral / Florale* 32 ●
JOVAN MUSK *Soft Floral / Fleuri Aldéhydé* 43 ●●●●
JOVAN WHITE MUSK *Soft Oriental / Oriental Doux* 52 ●
JOY *Floral / Florale* 33 ●●●
JUNGLE GARDENIA *Floral / Florale* 30 ●●
JUNGLE: L'ÉLÉPHANT *Soft Oriental / Oriental Doux* 53 ●●●
JUNGLE: LE TIGRE *Floral Oriental / Fleuri Oriental* 46 ●
JUSTE UN RÊVE *Woody Oriental / Oriental Boisé* 60 ●●
JUST ME *Woody Oriental / Oriental Boisé* 60 ●●
JUST MUSK *Oriental / Oriental* 57 ●●●●

 **K**

K de KRIZIA *Soft Floral / Fleuri Aldéhydé* 42 ●●
KASHÂYA *Floral Oriental / Fleuri Oriental* 46 ●
KENZO *Floral / Florale* 32 ●●
KÉORA *Oriental / Oriental* 57 ●●●●
KIRI *Woody Oriental / Oriental Boisé* 61 ●●●
KISS & TELL *Floral / Florale* 38 ●
KITON DONNA *Floral / Florale* 32 ●●
KL *Soft Oriental / Oriental Doux* 52 ●
KNOWING *Mossy Woods / Chypre Boisé* 67 ●●●
KOOKAÏ OUI-NON *Floral / Florale* 32 ●●
KRAZY KRIZIA* *Oriental / Oriental* 56 ●●
KUMQUAT ♂ *Citrus / Hespéridé* 16 ●●

 **L**

L de LOEWE *Floral / Florale* 32 ●●
LA BASE FOR HER *Floral / Florale* 30 ●●
LACE *Mossy Woods / Chypre Boisé* 66 ●
LA CHASSE AUX PAPILLONS *Floral / Florale* 38 ●●
LACOSTE FOR WOMEN *Floral / Florale* 36 ●
LA COUPE D'OR *Floral Oriental / Fleuri Oriental* 46 ●●
LADY CARON *Mossy Woods / Chypre Boisé* 66 ●●
LADY STETSON *Soft Floral / Fleuri Aldéhydé* 43 ●●●●
LAGERFELD FEMME *Citrus / Hespéridé* 17 ●●●●
LAGUNA *Floral Oriental / Fleuri Oriental* 46 ●
LA HAIE FLEURIE DU HAMEAU *Floral / Florale* 31 ●●●
LAILA *Floral / Florale* 38 ●
L'AIMANT *Soft Floral / Fleuri Aldéhydé* 43 ●●●
L'AIR DU TEMPS *Floral / Florale* 33 ●●●
LAIT SUCRÉ *Floral / Florale* 32 ●●
LALIQUE *Floral Oriental / Fleuri Oriental* 48 ●●
LAMBORGHINI POUR FEMME *Floral / Florale* 32 ●
LANCASTER BODY & BATH *Oriental / Oriental* 56 ●
LANCETTI *Soft Floral / Fleuri Aldéhydé* 43 ●●●
LANCETTI EAU DE JOIE *Floral / Florale* 34 ●●
LANCETTI MADAME *Mossy Woods / Chypre Boisé* 67 ●●●
LA NUIT *Dry Woods / Boisé Cuir* 73 ●●●●
LA PARISIENNE *Soft Floral / Fleuri Aldéhydé* 42 ●●
LA PERLA *Dry Woods / Boisé Cuir* 73 ●●●
LA PLAGE *Woody Oriental / Oriental Boisé* 60 ●

LAPIS *Woody Oriental / Oriental Boisé 60* ●●
LA PRAIRIE *Floral / Florale 33* ●●●●
LA ROSE DE ROSINE *Soft Floral / Fleuri Aldéhydé 43* ●●●●
LASTING *Floral / Florale 32* ●
LATA *Floral Oriental / Fleuri Oriental 47* ●●●
LAUNDROMAT ♂ *Water / Marine 26* ●●
LAURA *Floral / Florale 38* ●
LAURA ASHLEY N° 1 *Soft Floral / Fleuri Aldéhydé 42* ●
LAUREN *Floral / Florale 32* ●●
L'AUTRE ♂ *Dry Woods / Boisé Cuir 73* ●●●●
LAVANDA Myrurgia ♂ *Floral / Florale 31* ●●●
LAVANDE Molinard ♂ *Floral / Florale 31* ●●●●
LAVANDE L'Occitane ♂ *Aromatic / Fougère 77* ●●●●
LAVANDE ROYALE *Floral / Florale 31* ●●●
LAVANDE VELOURS ♂ *Floral / Florale 31* ●●●
LAVENDER Crabtree & Evelyn ♂ *Floral / Florale 31* ●●●
LAVENDER Demeter ♂ *Floral / Florale 31* ●●●
LAVENDER Floris ♂ *Floral / Florale 31* ●●●
LAVENDER Woods of Windsor *Floral / Florale 31* ●●●
LAVENDER INSPIRATIONS: GINGER & LIME *Citrus / Hespéridé 16* ●●
LAVENDER INSPIRATIONS: JUNIPER & ROSE *Floral / Florale 31* ●●●●
LAVENDER INSPIRATIONS: SEAWEED & ALOE *Water / Marine 26* ●●
LAVENDER SPICE #10 *Aromatic / Fougère 76* ●●
L'EAU Diptyque ♂ *Soft Oriental / Oriental Doux 52* ●●
L'EAU BY LAURA *Citrus / Hespéridé 16* ●●
L'EAU D'AMBRE *Oriental / Oriental 57* ●●●
L'EAU DE KOOKAÏ *Citrus / Hespéridé 16* ●
L'EAU DE L'ARTISAN ♂ *Citrus / Hespéridé 17* ●●●
L'EAU DE MONTEIL *Floral / Florale 33* ●●●●
L'EAU DE SONIA RYKIEL *Floral / Florale 32* ●
L'EAU DE SUCCÈS* *Floral / Florale 32* ●●
L'EAU D'ISSEY *Water / Marine 26* ●●
L'EAU LILIAN *Water / Marine 26* ●●
L'EAU PAR KENZO *Floral / Florale 38* ●
L'EAU TROIS ♂ *Dry Woods / Boisé Cuir 72* ●●
LE BAISER *Floral / Florale 32* ●●
LE CHIC* *Soft Floral / Fleuri Aldéhydé 42* ●●
LE CIRQUE DE POPY MORENI *Soft Floral / Fleuri Aldéhydé 42* ●
LE DE* *Floral / Florale 33* ●●●
LE DIX *Soft Floral / Fleuri Aldéhydé 43* ●●●●
LE FEU D'ISSEY *Woody Oriental / Oriental Boisé 61* ●●●
LE FEU D'ISSEY LIGHT *Soft Floral / Fleuri Aldéhydé 43* ●●●●
L'EFFLEUR *Floral / Florale 34* ●●
LE JARDIN *Floral / Florale 38* ●
LE JARDIN D'AMOUR *Floral Oriental / Fleuri Oriental 47* ●●●●
LELONG POUR FEMME *Woody Oriental / Oriental Boisé 61* ●●●
L'ÉLUE *Floral Oriental / Fleuri Oriental 46* ●●
LE MONDE EST BEAU *Floral / Florale 36* ●
LEMON SORBET ♂ *Aromatic / Fougère 76* ●
LE MUGUET DE ROSINE *Floral / Florale 30* ●
LÉONARD DE LÉONARD* *Soft Floral / Fleuri Aldéhydé 42* ●
LE PARFUM *Woody Oriental / Oriental Boisé 60* ●●
LE ROY SOLEIL *Soft Oriental / Oriental Doux 52* ●●
LES BELLES DE RICCI → LIBERTÉ ACIDULÉE
LES COPAINS *Floral Oriental / Fleuri Oriental 46* ●
LES FLORALIES GREEN TEA *Citrus / Hespéridé 17* ●●●●
LES FLORALIES WHITE GINGER *Citrus / Hespéridé 16* ●
L'ÉTÉ DE VENTILO' *Floral Oriental / Fleuri Oriental 46* ●
LE TEMPS D'AIMER *Mossy Woods / Chypre Boisé 67* ●●●
LE TEMPS D'UNE FÊTE *Floral / Florale 36* ●
LETTUCE ♂ *Green / Vert 22* ●●
L'HEURE ATTENDUE *Woody Oriental / Oriental Boisé 61* ●●●
L'HEURE BLEUE *Floral Oriental / Fleuri Oriental 47* ●●●
LIBERTÉ ACIDULÉE *Floral / Florale 32* ●
LIBERTINE *Mossy Woods / Chypre Boisé 66* ●
LIGHT HER *Floral / Florale 32* ●●
LILAC Demeter *Floral / Florale 30* ●●
LILIAN *Floral / Florale 32* ●
LILY Christian Dior* Ⓛ *Floral / Florale 30* ●
LILY CHIC* Ⓛ *Floral / Florale 32* ●●
LILY OF THE VALLEY Crabtree & Evelyn *Floral / Florale 30* ●
LILY OF THE VALLEY Floris *Floral / Florale 30* ●
LILY OF THE VALLEY Penhaligon's *Floral / Florale 30* ●
LILY OF THE VALLEY Perfumers Guild *Floral / Florale 30* ●
LILY OF THE VALLEY Woods of Windsor *Floral / Florale 30* ●
LILY OF THE VALLEY Yardley *Floral / Florale 30* ●

LIME, BASIL & MANDARIN ♂ *Citrus / Hespéridé 17* ●●●●
LIMES Floris ♂ *Citrus / Hespéridé 17* ●●●●
L'INSAISISSABLE *Floral / Florale 32* ●●
L'INSOLENT* *Woody Oriental / Oriental Boisé 60* ●●
L'INSTANT JASMIN *Floral / Florale 31* ●●●
L'INTERDIT *Soft Floral / Fleuri Aldéhydé 43* ●●●
LIÙ *Soft Floral / Fleuri Aldéhydé 43* ●●●
LIZ CLAIBORNE *Floral / Florale 32* ●
LIZSPORT *Floral / Florale 36* ●
LOLITA LEMPICKA *Woody Oriental / Oriental Boisé 60* ●
L'OMBRE DANS L'EAU *Floral / Florale 34* ●●
LONG AGO / WISTFUL *Floral / Florale 36* ●
LONGING *Floral Oriental / Fleuri Oriental 46* ●
L'OR DES BOURBON *Woody Oriental / Oriental Boisé 60* ●
L'ORIGAN* *Floral Oriental / Fleuri Oriental 47* ●●●
LOULOU *Soft Oriental / Oriental Doux 53* ●●●●
LOULOU BLUE* *Floral Oriental / Fleuri Oriental 48* ●●
LOVE'S BABY SOFT *Soft Floral / Fleuri Aldéhydé 43* ●●●
LOVE STORY *Floral Oriental / Fleuri Oriental 47* ●●●●
LOVING BOUQUET* Ⓛ *Floral / Florale 36* ●
LOVIN' GIRL *Citrus / Hespéridé 16* ●●
LP N° 9 *Floral Oriental / Fleuri Oriental 46* ●
LUCE ♂ *Floral / Florale 31* ●●●
LUCKY BRAND WOMEN'S* *Floral / Florale 38* ●
LUCKY YOU FOR WOMEN *Floral / Florale 32* ●
LUMIÈRE (Original)* *Floral / Florale 38* ●
LUMIÈRE (New) *Soft Floral / Fleuri Aldéhydé 42* ●●
LUNE D'ÉTÉ *Woody Oriental / Oriental Boisé 60* ●
LUSCIOUS *Floral Oriental / Fleuri Oriental 47* ●●●
LUTÈCE *Floral Oriental / Fleuri Oriental 47* ●●●●
LYRA *Oriental / Oriental 57* ●●●
LYRA 2 *Woody Oriental / Oriental Boisé 60* ●●
LYRA 3 *Floral / Florale 32* ●
LYS *Floral / Florale 30* ●●

Ⓜ

MA GRIFFE *Mossy Woods / Chypre Boisé 66* ●●
MA LIBERTÉ* *Aromatic / Fougère 77* ●●●
MACKIE *Floral Oriental / Fleuri Oriental 46* ●●
MADAME CARVEN* *Floral / Florale 33* ●●●●
MADAME ROCHAS *Soft Floral / Fleuri Aldéhydé 43* ●●●●
MADELEINE DE MADELEINE *Floral / Florale 31* ●●●●
MADELEINE VIONNET *Floral Oriental / Fleuri Oriental 47* ●●●
MADLY *Floral / Florale 32* ●●
MAGIC *Mossy Woods / Chypre Boisé 66* ●
MAGIE NOIRE *Woody Oriental / Oriental Boisé 60* ●●
MAGNETIC *Floral Oriental / Fleuri Oriental 46* ●
MAGOT ♂ *Oriental / Oriental 56* ●
MAHORA *Floral Oriental / Fleuri Oriental 47* ●●●●
MAJA *Soft Oriental / Oriental Doux 53* ●●●
MALABAR *Oriental / Oriental 57* ●●●
MALMAISON *Floral / Florale 31* ●●●●
MANDARIN *Floral / Florale 31* ●●●●
MANDARIN & GINGER LILY #6 *Floral / Florale 32* ●
MANDARINE ♂ *Citrus / Hespéridé 16* ●●
MANIA *Woody Oriental / Oriental Boisé 61* ●●●
MANIFESTO *Floral / Florale 36* ●
MARBERT WOMAN *Oriental / Oriental 57* ●●●
MARBERT WOMAN RED *Floral / Florale 34* ●
MARE *Water / Marine 26* ●●
MARÉCHALE 90 *Mossy Woods / Chypre Boisé 67* ●●●
MARÉCHALE ORIGINAL *Floral / Florale 31* ●●●
MARIELLA *Soft Oriental / Oriental Doux 52* ●
MARIELLA BURANI *Soft Floral / Fleuri Aldéhydé 42* ●●
MARIELLA BURANI EAU ROSÉE → EAU ROSÉE
MARINA DE BOURBON *Woody Oriental / Oriental Boisé 60* ●
MARJOLAINE *Floral / Florale 34* ●
MAROC* *Mossy Woods / Chypre Boisé 67* ●●●●
MAROUSSIA *Floral Oriental / Fleuri Oriental 47* ●●●
MARQUIS POUR FEMME *Woody Oriental / Oriental Boisé 60* ●
MASQUERADE *Woody Oriental / Oriental Boisé 60* ●
MAT; *Floral / Florale 36* ●
MATIN D'ÉTÉ – UN *Floral / Florale 30* ●●
MATSUKITA *Floral Oriental / Fleuri Oriental 48* ●●
MAUBOUSSIN *Woody Oriental / Oriental Boisé 60* ●●
MAXIM'S DE PARIS* *Floral Oriental / Fleuri Oriental 46* ●

MCM   *Floral / Florale*   32 ●●
MCM 1900   *Floral Oriental / Fleuri Oriental*   47 ●●●
MCM BLUE PARADISE   *Floral / Florale*   32 ●●
MCM OBELISK   *Oriental / Oriental*   56 ●
MCM ROUGE   *Floral Oriental / Fleuri Oriental*   46 ●
MEA CULPA   *Floral / Florale*   38 ●●
MELODIE D'AMOUR   *Floral / Florale*   34 ●
MENTHE FROISSÉE   *Green / Vert*   22 ●
MERGE ♂   *Aromatic / Fougère*   76 ●
MESSE DE MINUIT ♂   *Oriental / Oriental*   57 ●●●●
MÉTAL   *Soft Floral / Fleuri Aldéhydé*   42 ●
METAL JEANS WOMEN   *Floral Oriental / Fleuri Oriental*   48 ●
METALLICA ⓛ   *Floral Oriental / Fleuri Oriental*   47 ●●●
MÉTÉORITES   *Floral / Florale*   31 ●●●●
MEXX WOMAN   *Floral / Florale*   34 ●
MICHAEL   *Floral / Florale*   31 ●●●●
MICHEL JORDI   → THE SPIRIT OF SWITZERLAND
MICHELLE   *Floral / Florale*   31 ●●●●
MICK MICHEYL   *Floral / Florale*   34 ●●
MIEL ORANGE   *Citrus / Hespéridé*   17 ●●●●
MILA SCHÖN   *Mossy Woods / Chypre Boisé*   67 ●●●
MILLENNIUM HOPE WOMAN   *Floral / Florale*   32 ●●
MILLENNIUM ROSE   *Soft Floral / Fleuri Aldéhydé*   43 ●●●●
MILLÉSIME IMPÉRIAL ♂   *Water / Marine*   27 ●●●●
MIMOSA Molinard   *Floral / Florale*   30 ●●
MIMOSA Woods of Windsor   *Floral / Florale*   30 ●●
MIMOSAÏQUE   *Floral / Florale*   30 ●●
MIMOSA POUR MOI   *Floral / Florale*   30 ●●
MIRA BAÏ   *Woody Oriental / Oriental Boisé*   60 ●●
MIRACLE   *Floral / Florale*   32 ●●
MISHA   *Mossy Woods / Chypre Boisé*   67 ●●●●
MISS ARPELS   *Floral / Florale*   34 ●
MISS BALAHÉ   *Floral / Florale*   34 ●●
MISS BALMAIN   *Dry Woods / Boisé Cuir*   73 ●●●
MISS BE BOP   *Floral / Florale*   33 ●●●●
MISS DIOR   *Mossy Woods / Chypre Boisé*   66 ●
MISS HABANITA   *Floral / Florale*   34 ●
MISS JAGUAR   *Floral / Florale*   36 ●●
MISS MORABITO   *Floral / Florale*   38 ●
MISSONI   *Mossy Woods / Chypre Boisé*   67 ●●●●
MISS WORTH   *Floral / Florale*   33 ●●●●
MISUKI   *Oriental / Oriental*   57 ●●●
MITSOUKO   *Mossy Woods / Chypre Boisé*   67 ●●●
MODERN   *Floral / Florale*   34 ●●
MODERN QUARTZ   *Floral / Florale*   34 ●
MOLINARD DE MOLINARD   *Floral / Florale*   34 ●●
MOLTO MISSONI   *Oriental / Oriental*   57 ●●●●
MOMENTS   *Woody Oriental / Oriental Boisé*   61 ●●●
MOMENT SUPRÊME   *Floral / Florale*   33 ●●●●
MON BOUQUET   *Floral / Florale*   34 ●
MON CLASSIQUE   *Floral / Florale*   38 ●●
MONDE EST BEAU – LE   *Floral / Florale*   36 ●
MON PARFUM Bourjois   *Floral / Florale*   34 ●●
MONSOON   *Floral / Florale*   34 ●●
MONSOON EAU   *Water / Marine*   26 ●●
MONTAIGNE   *Floral / Florale*   34 ●●
MONTANA BLU   *Floral / Florale*   36 ●
MONTANA PARFUM D'ELLE*   *Mossy Woods / Chypre Boisé*   66 ●
MONTANA PARFUM DE PEAU   *Dry Woods / Boisé Cuir*   73 ●●●●
MONTE CARLO   *Oriental / Oriental*   56 ●●
MOODS*   *Floral / Florale*   36 ●●
MOONDROPS   *Floral / Florale*   33 ●●●●
MORGANE LE FAY   *Floral / Florale*   36 ●
MORGANE LE FAY BLUE   *Woody Oriental / Oriental Boisé*   61 ●●●
MOSCHINO   *Oriental / Oriental*   57 ●●●
MOTU   *Water / Marine*   26 ●
MUGUET / LILY OF THE VALLEY Molinard   *Floral / Florale*   30 ●
MUGUET DE ROSINE – LE   *Floral / Florale*   30 ●
MUGUET DES BOIS   *Floral / Florale*   30 ●
MUGUET DU BONHEUR   *Floral / Florale*   30 ●
MUKKI ♂   *Soft Floral / Fleuri Aldéhydé*   42 ●●
MULBERRY   *Soft Oriental / Oriental Doux*   53 ●●●
MURASAKI   *Soft Floral / Fleuri Aldéhydé*   42 ●
MÛRE / BLACKBERRY   *Citrus / Hespéridé*   17 ●●●●
MÛRE ET MUSC   *Citrus / Hespéridé*   17 ●●●●
MÛRE ET MUSC EXTRÊME   *Citrus / Hespéridé*   17 ●●●●
MUSC   *Woody Oriental / Oriental Boisé*   61 ●●●

MUST DE CARTIER   *Oriental / Oriental*   56 ●
MUST DE CARTIER (JOUR)*   *Floral / Florale*   34 ●
MUST DE CARTIER II   *Water / Marine*   26 ●
MV   *Floral / Florale*   36 ●
MYSTÈRE   *Woody Oriental / Oriental Boisé*   60 ●●
MYSTIC   *Floral / Florale*   34 ●●

NAF NAF   → UNE TOUCHE DE NAF NAF
NAHÉMA   *Floral Oriental / Fleuri Oriental*   47 ●●●●
N'AIMEZ QUE MOI   *Floral / Florale*   33 ●●●
NAJ-OLEARI   *Soft Floral / Fleuri Aldéhydé*   43 ●●●●
NANTUCKET BRIAR   *Floral Oriental / Fleuri Oriental*   46 ●●
NAOMAGIC   *Floral Oriental / Fleuri Oriental*   46 ●
NAOMI CAMPBELL   *Woody Oriental / Oriental Boisé*   61 ●●●●
NARCISSE BLANC   *Floral / Florale*   31 ●●●●
NARCISSE NOIR   *Floral / Florale*   31 ●●●●
NARCISSUS Yardley   *Floral / Florale*   38 ●
NATURE SYSTEM ♂   *Citrus / Hespéridé*   16 ●●
NAUTICA WOMAN   *Floral / Florale*   38 ●
NAVY   *Floral Oriental / Fleuri Oriental*   47 ●●●●
NAZARENO GABRIELLI POUR FEMME
   Floral Oriental / Fleuri Oriental   46 ●●
NAZARENO POUR FEMME   *Floral / Florale*   34 ●●
NEIGES   *Floral / Florale*   38 ●
NETWORK ♂   *Citrus / Hespéridé*   16 ●
NEW WEST FOR HER*   *Water / Marine*   27 ●●●
NICOLE   *Floral / Florale*   38 ●
NICOLE MILLER   *Floral Oriental / Fleuri Oriental*   46 ●●
NIGHT SCENTED STOCK   *Floral / Florale*   31 ●●●●
NIKE WOMAN   *Woody Oriental / Oriental Boisé*   60 ●
NIKI DE SAINT PHALLE   *Mossy Woods / Chypre Boisé*   66 ●
NILANG   *Floral Oriental / Fleuri Oriental*   48 ●
NINA   *Soft Floral / Fleuri Aldéhydé*   42 ●●
NIRMALA   *Woody Oriental / Oriental Boisé*   60 ●
NOA   *Soft Floral / Fleuri Aldéhydé*   43 ●●●●
NOCTURNES   *Soft Floral / Fleuri Aldéhydé*   43 ●●●●
NOHIBA (TULIPE NOIRE)   *Soft Oriental / Oriental Doux*   53 ●●●
NOI DONNA   *Floral Oriental / Fleuri Oriental*   46 ●●
NOI MISSONI   *Citrus / Hespéridé*   16 ●●
NOKOMIS   *Floral Oriental / Fleuri Oriental*   46 ●●
NONCHALANCE   *Soft Floral / Fleuri Aldéhydé*   43 ●●●
NO REGRETS   *Floral / Florale*   38 ●●
NORELL   *Floral / Florale*   36 ●●
NORMANDIE   *Soft Oriental / Oriental Doux*   53 ●●●
NUAGE D'OR   *Soft Floral / Fleuri Aldéhydé*   43 ●●●●
NUAGES D'EAU   *Floral / Florale*   31 ●●●
NUBIADE*   *Woody Oriental / Oriental Boisé*   61 ●●●
NUDE   *Soft Floral / Fleuri Aldéhydé*   42 ●
NUIT – LA   *Dry Woods / Boisé Cuir*   73 ●●●●
NUIT DE NOËL   *Woody Oriental / Oriental Boisé*   61 ●●●
NUITS INDIENNES   *Oriental / Oriental*   57 ●●●
N° 5   → CHANEL N° 5
N° 19   → CHANEL N° 19
N° 22   → CHANEL N° 22
NUMBER ONE   *Floral / Florale*   38 ●●
NUTMEG & GINGER ♂   *Woody Oriental / Oriental Boisé*   60 ●●

Ô de LANCÔME   *Citrus / Hespéridé*   17 ●●●
OBLIQUE FAST FORWARD   *Floral / Florale*   36 ●
OBLIQUE PLAY   *Citrus / Hespéridé*   17 ●●●●
OBLIQUE REWIND   *Woody Oriental / Oriental Boisé*   60 ●●
OBSESSION   *Oriental / Oriental*   56 ●
OCEAN DREAM   *Floral / Florale*   38 ●
ODALISQUE   *Floral / Florale*   38 ●
ODEUR 53 ♂   *Water / Marine*   26 ●●
ODEUR 71 ♂   *Dry Woods / Boisé Cuir*   72 ●
OEILLET*   *Floral / Florale*   31 ●●●●
OFRÉSIA   *Floral / Florale*   36 ●
OH! DE MOSCHINO   *Soft Floral / Fleuri Aldéhydé*   42 ●
OH LÀ LÀ   *Soft Oriental / Oriental Doux*   52 ●●
OH! MY DOG   *Floral / Florale*   36 ●●
OLÈNE   *Floral / Florale*   38 ●●
OLIVIER STRELLI   *Soft Oriental / Oriental Doux*   52 ●●

OM ♂ *Woody Oriental / Oriental Boisé* 61 ●●●
OMAR SHARIF* *Floral / Florale* 33 ●●●
OMBRE BLEUE* *Floral / Florale* 33 ●●●●
OMBRE DANS L'EAU – L' *Floral / Florale* 34 ●●
OMBRE D'OR* *Soft Floral / Fleuri Aldéhydé* 42 ●
OMBRE ROSE *Floral Oriental / Fleuri Oriental* 47 ●●●●
OMBRE ROSE FRAÎCHE *Floral / Florale* 34 ●
ON AIR FEMME *Floral / Florale* 34 ●●
ONLY *Woody Oriental / Oriental Boisé* 61 ●●●
Ô OUI *Floral / Florale* 34 ●
OPERA III *Woody Oriental / Oriental Boisé* 60 ●
OPHÉLIE *Soft Floral / Fleuri Aldéhydé* 43 ●●●
OPIUM *Soft Oriental / Oriental Doux* 53 ●●●
OPÔNÉ ♂ *Mossy Woods / Chypre Boisé* 67 ●●●
OPOPONAX *Aromatic / Fougère* 77 ●●●
ORANGE BLOSSOM Penhaligon's *Floral / Florale* 31 ●●●●
ORANGE CAFÉ *Citrus / Hespéridé* 17 ●●●●
ORANGE-CANNELLE *Soft Oriental / Oriental Doux* 52 ●●
ORANGE SPICE ♂ *Aromatic / Fougère* 76 ●●
OR DES BOURBON – L' *Woody Oriental / Oriental Boisé* 60 ●
OR DES INDES *Oriental / Oriental* 57 ●●●
OR ET NOIR *Floral Oriental / Fleuri Oriental* 47 ●●●
ORGANZA *Woody Oriental / Oriental Boisé* 60 ●●
ORGANZA INDÉCENCE *Woody Oriental / Oriental Boisé* 61 ●●●●
ORGUEIL DE RODIER *Floral Oriental / Fleuri Oriental* 46 ●
ORIENT *Soft Oriental / Oriental Doux* 53 ●●●
ORIGAN – L'* *Floral Oriental / Fleuri Oriental* 47 ●●●
ORMOLU *Woody Oriental / Oriental Boisé* 60 ●●
ORO POUR FEMME *Mossy Woods/ Chypre Boisé* 66 ●●
ORPHÉE ♂ *Aromatic / Fougère* 76 ●●
ORVAL *Floral / Florale* 33 ●●●
OSCAR *Floral Oriental / Fleuri Oriental* 47 ●●●
OUI-NON → KOOKAÏ OUI-NON
OXYGÈNE *Soft Floral / Fleuri Aldéhydé* 42 ●
O₂XYGEN WOMAN *Citrus / Hespéridé* 16 ●
OYÉDO ♂ *Citrus / Hespéridé* 17 ●●●●
OZBEK *Floral / Florale* 31 ●●●
OZBEK 1001 *Oriental / Oriental* 56 ●
O•ZONE WOMAN *Citrus / Hespéridé* 17 ●●●●

P

PACO ♂ *Citrus / Hespéridé* 16 ●
PACO ENERGY ♂ *Citrus / Hespéridé* 16 ●●
PAGAN *Mossy Woods / Chypre Boisé* 67 ●●●
PAIN D'ÉPICES *Woody Oriental / Oriental Boisé* 61 ●●●
PALACE *Soft Floral / Fleuri Aldéhydé* 42 ●●
PALAIS JAMAIS ♂ *Dry Woods / Boisé Cuir* 73 ●●●●
PALOMA PICASSO *Mossy Woods / Chypre Boisé* 67 ●●●
PAMPLELUNE ♂ *Citrus / Hespéridé* 17 ●●●●
PAMPLEMOUSSE ♂ *Citrus / Hespéridé* 16 ●●
PANACHE *Soft Floral / Fleuri Aldéhydé* 42 ●●
PANTHÈRE *Floral Oriental / Fleuri Oriental* 46 ●●
PAPERWHITES *Floral / Florale* 38 ●
PARADOX *Floral Oriental / Fleuri Oriental* 48 ●
PARAH *Floral / Florale* 33 ●●●●
PARCE QUE!* *Soft Floral / Fleuri Aldéhydé* 43 ●●●
PARESSE DE RODIER *Soft Floral / Fleuri Aldéhydé* 42 ●
PARFUM – LE *Woody Oriental / Oriental Boisé* 60 ●●
PARFUM ALLIÉ BEATS 14 *Green / Vert* 22 ●●
PARFUM ALLIÉ CRYSTAL 32 *Floral / Florale* 36 ●
PARFUM ALLIÉ DELICIOUS 62 *Woody Oriental / Oriental Boisé* 61 ●●●
PARFUM ALLIÉ DREAM 45 *Soft Floral / Fleuri Aldéhydé* 42 ●●
PARFUM ALLIÉ FOREST 02 *Aromatic / Fougère* 76 ●●
PARFUM ALLIÉ MARIA 66 *Floral Oriental / Fleuri Oriental* 48 ●
PARFUM ALLIÉ MELLOW 51 *Floral / Florale* 34 ●●
PARFUM ALLIÉ PASTEL 43 *Floral / Florale* 38 ●●
PARFUM ALLIÉ SPLASH 24 *Citrus / Hespéridé* 16 ●●
PARFUM ALLIÉ SWING 36 *Floral / Florale* 36 ●●
PARFUM D'ELLE → MONTANA PARFUM D'ELLE
PARFUM D'ÉTÉ *Floral / Florale* 36 ●
PARFUM D'HERMÈS *Floral Oriental / Fleuri Oriental* 46 ●●
PARFUM D'OR *Mossy Woods / Chypre Boisé* 66 ●●
PARFUM PRIVÉ* *Mossy Woods / Chypre Boisé* 67 ●●●
PARFUM SACRÉ *Floral Oriental / Fleuri Oriental* 47 ●●●
PARIS *Floral / Florale* 31 ●●●
PARISIENNE – LA *Soft Floral / Fleuri Aldéhydé* 42 ●●

PARURE *Mossy Woods / Chypre Boisé* 67 ●●●
PASSAGE D'ENFER *Dry Woods / Boisé Cuir* 72 ●●
PASSION Annick Goutal *Floral / Florale* 38 ●●
PASSION Elizabeth Taylor *Woody Oriental / Oriental Boisé* 61 ●●●
PASSION DE FEMME *Dry Woods / Boisé Cuir* 72 ●
PASSION FLOWER* *Floral / Florale* 34 ●
PASTEL DE CABOTINE *Floral / Florale* 34 ●
PATCHOULI L'Artisan Parfumeur ♂ *Citrus / Hespéridé* 17 ●●●●
PATCHOULI Molinard ♂ *Mossy Woods / Chypre Boisé* 67 ●●●
PATCHOULY Etro ♂ *Woody Oriental / Oriental Boisé* 61 ●●●
PATOU FOR EVER *Floral / Florale* 34 ●●
PATTI LaBELLE *Floral Oriental / Fleuri Oriental* 46 ●
PAUL SMITH WOMEN *Floral / Florale* 34 ●
PAVAROTTI DONNA *Mossy Woods / Chypre Boisé* 66 ●●
PAVLOVA *Floral / Florale* 31 ●●●●
PENHALIGON'S CASTILE ♂ *Citrus / Hespéridé* 17 ●●●
PENNY BLACK WOMAN *Floral / Florale* 34 ●
PEOPLE DONNA *Floral / Florale* 36 ●
PERHAPS *Floral Oriental / Fleuri Oriental* 46 ●
PERLA – LA *Dry Woods / Boisé Cuir* 73 ●●●
PERLE D'AUBUSSON *Floral Oriental / Fleuri Oriental* 46 ●
PERLE DE SILENCES *Soft Oriental / Oriental Doux* 52 ●
PERRY ELLIS FOR WOMEN *Soft Floral / Fleuri Aldéhydé* 42 ●●
PERRY ELLIS PORTFOLIO *Floral / Florale* 38 ●
PETITE CHÉRIE *Floral / Florale* 34 ●
PETIT GUERLAIN ♂ *Citrus / Hespéridé* 17 ●●●
PHANTOM OF THE OPERA* *Floral Oriental / Fleuri Oriental* 48 ●●
PHEROMONE *Green / Vert* 23 ●●●●
PHILOSYKOS ♂ *Mossy Woods / Chypre Boisé* 66 ●
PIAZZA DI SPAGNA *Floral / Florale* 36 ●
PLAGE – LA *Woody Oriental / Oriental Boisé* 60 ●
PLAY → OBLIQUE PLAY
PLEASURES *Floral / Florale* 36 ●
PLEINE LUNE *Woody Oriental / Oriental Boisé* 60 ●
PLUMES *Floral / Florale* 34 ●
POÊME *Floral Oriental / Fleuri Oriental* 47 ●●●
POIS DE SENTEUR *Soft Oriental / Oriental Doux* 53 ●●●
POISON *Floral Oriental / Fleuri Oriental* 47 ●●●●
POIVRE *Soft Oriental / Oriental Doux* 53 ●●●●
POLEMIC! *Floral Oriental / Fleuri Oriental* 46 ●
POLO SPORT WOMAN *Water / Marine* 26 ●●
POMME CANNELLE *Mossy Woods / Chypre Boisé* 66 ●●
POMPEÏA *Dry Woods / Boisé Cuir* 73 ●●●
POPY MORENI *Woody Oriental / Oriental Boisé* 60 ●
POPY MORENI DE FÊTE *Floral / Florale* 36 ●●
PORTFOLIO → PERRY ELLIS PORTFOLIO
POTION → PRESCRIPTIVES POTION
POUR UNE FEMME *Floral / Florale* 38 ●
PRAIRIE – LA *Floral / Florale* 33 ●●●●
PRÉLUDE *Soft Oriental / Oriental Doux* 53 ●●●
PREMIER FIGUIER *Mossy Woods / Chypre Boisé* 66 ●
PREMIER JOUR *Floral Oriental / Fleuri Oriental* 46 ●
PRESCRIPTIVES POTION *Floral / Florale* 36 ●●
PRIMROSE Penhaligon's *Floral / Florale* 31 ●●●
PRINCESSE CHIPIE *Woody Oriental / Oriental Boisé* 60 ●
PRINCESS GRACE DE MONACO *Floral / Florale* 36 ●
PRIORITÉ *Citrus / Hespéridé* 16 ●
PRIORITÉ EAU BLEU *Floral / Florale* 36 ●
PRIVATE COLLECTION *Green / Vert* 23 ●●●●
PRIVATE NUMBER FOR WOMEN* *Floral / Florale* 34 ●●
PROFUMO DI MONTECATINI ♂ *Water / Marine* 27 ●●●
PROVENCE LAVENDER Perfumers Guild *Floral / Florale* 31 ●●●
PRUNING SHEARS ♂ *Floral / Florale* 36 ●
PURE *Floral / Florale* 34 ●
PURE MOMENT *Floral Oriental / Fleuri Oriental* 46 ●
PURE SILK *Mossy Woods / Chypre Boisé* 67 ●●●
PURE WISH *Floral Oriental / Fleuri Oriental* 46 ●
PURPLE FANTASY � *Floral / Florale* 34 ●●
PYTHON *Woody Oriental / Oriental Boisé* 61 ●●●

Q

QUADRILLE *Mossy Woods / Chypre Boisé* 67 ●●●
QUARTZ *Floral / Florale* 34 ●
QUELQUES FLEURS *Floral / Florale* 33 ●●●
QUELQUES ROSES *Floral / Florale* 31 ●●●
QUELQUES VIOLETTES *Floral / Florale* 31 ●●●●

QUERCUS ♂ *Citrus / Hespéridé* 16 ●
QUE SAIS-JE? *Mossy Woods / Chypre Boisé* 67 ●●●

R

RACINE ♂ *Mossy Woods / Chypre Boisé* 66 ●●
RAFFINÉE *Floral Oriental / Fleuri Oriental* 47 ●●●
RALPH *Floral / Florale* 34 ●
RAVELLO *Floral Oriental / Fleuri Oriental* 47 ●●●
REALITIES* *Floral / Florale* 34 ●●
REALLY PARAH *Soft Floral / Fleuri Aldéhydé* 42 ●●
REALM WOMEN *Soft Oriental / Oriental Doux* 52 ●
REBEL WOMEN *Soft Floral / Fleuri Aldéhydé* 43 ●●●●
RECTOVERSO LOLLIPOP TOFFEE *Woody Oriental / Oriental Boisé* 60 ●●
RECTOVERSO MANDARIN MUSK *Citrus / Hespéridé* 16 ●●
RECTOVERSO SUN SEA *Floral / Florale* 38 ●
RECTOVERSO SWEETY FRUITY *Floral / Florale* 34 ●
RED *Mossy Woods / Chypre Boisé* 66 ●●
RED 2* *Floral Oriental / Fleuri Oriental* 46 ●
RED DOOR *Floral / Florale* 33 ●●●●
RED JEANS *Floral / Florale* 34 ●●
RED PEARL *Floral Oriental / Fleuri Oriental* 46 ●●
RED ROSES *Floral / Florale* 31 ●●●
RÉGINE'S *Woody Oriental / Oriental Boisé* 61 ●●●
RELAXING FRAGRANCE *Floral / Florale* 36 ●
RÉMY FOR WOMAN *Floral / Florale* 34 ●●
RÉPLIQUE* *Mossy Woods / Chypre Boisé* 67 ●●●
RÊVE D'OR *Soft Floral / Fleuri Aldéhydé* 43 ●●●●
RÊVERIE *Floral Oriental / Fleuri Oriental* 47 ●●●
RÊVERIE PURE *Floral / Florale* 36 ●
REVOLUTION À VERSAILLES* *Floral Oriental / Fleuri Oriental* 46 ●●
REWIND → OBLIQUE REWIND
REYNALD KATZ ♂ *Citrus / Hespéridé* 16 ●
RICHARDSON BAY ♂ *Green / Vert* 22 ●
RIVE GAUCHE *Soft Floral / Fleuri Aldéhydé* 42 ●●
RIVIERA PALACE *Mossy Woods / Chypre Boisé* 66 ●●
RIZIÈRES ♂ *Mossy Woods / Chypre Boisé* 67 ●●●
ROBERTA DI CAMERINO *Floral Oriental / Fleuri Oriental* 46 ●
ROCCOBAROCCO TRE *Floral / Florale* 34 ●●
ROCOCO *Woody Oriental / Oriental Boisé* 61 ●●
RODIER *Woody Oriental / Oriental Boisé* 60 ●
ROGER & GALLET EXTRA-VIEILLE ♂ *Citrus / Hespéridé* 17 ●●●
ROMA *Oriental / Oriental* 56 ●●
ROMANCE Ralph Lauren *Floral / Florale* 33 ●●●
ROMANCE Royal Secret *Floral / Florale* 33 ●●●●
ROMEO *Floral / Florale* 34 ●●
ROOTS FOR HER *Floral / Florale* 36 ●
ROOTS UNISCENT ♂ *Water / Marine* 26 ●
ROSA MAGNIFICA *Floral / Florale* 30 ●●
ROSE Caron *Floral / Florale* 31 ●●●
ROSE Molinard *Floral / Florale* 31 ●●●
ROSE ABSOLUE *Floral / Florale* 31 ●●●
ROSEBERRY *Soft Floral / Fleuri Aldéhydé* 42 ●●
ROSE CARDIN *Mossy Woods / Chypre Boisé* 67 ●●●
ROSE D'ARGENT *Floral / Florale* 31 ●●●
ROSE DE ROSINE – LA *Soft Floral / Fleuri Aldéhydé* 43 ●●●●
ROSE D'ÉTÉ *Floral / Florale* 36 ●
ROSE MUSKISSIME *Floral / Florale* 34 ●
ROSE NÉROLI *Floral / Florale* 31 ●●●
ROSE OPULENTE *Floral / Florale* 31 ●●●
ROSE-PIVOINE *Floral / Florale* 31 ●●●
ROSES AND MORE *Floral / Florale* 31 ●●●
ROSE SANTAL *Floral / Florale* 31 ●●●
ROSE THÉ *Floral / Florale* 31 ●●●
ROSE VANILLE *Floral / Florale* 33 ●●●
ROUGE *Woody Oriental / Oriental Boisé* 60 ●
ROUGE DE REVLON *Floral Oriental / Fleuri Oriental* 46 ●●
ROUGE FORMIDABLE *Soft Floral / Fleuri Aldéhydé* 42 ●●
ROUGE HERMÈS *Floral Oriental / Fleuri Oriental* 47 ●●●
ROUTE DU THÉ ♂ *Citrus / Hespéridé* 16 ●
ROYAL BAIN DE CHAMPAGNE ♂ *Soft Oriental / Oriental Doux* 52 ●
ROYAL DELIGHT ♂ *Soft Oriental / Oriental Doux* 53 ●●●●
ROYALISSIME *Soft Floral / Fleuri Aldéhydé* 42 ●●
ROYAL PAVILLON ♂ *Floral / Florale* 36 ●●
ROYAL SECRET *Oriental / Oriental* 57 ●●●
ROYAL SECRET II *Woody Oriental / Oriental Boisé* 60 ●●
ROY SOLEIL – LE ♂ *Soft Oriental / Oriental Doux* 52 ●●

RUBIS D'OR* *Floral Oriental / Fleuri Oriental* 46 ●
RUE PEROGLÈSE *Mossy Woods / Chypre Boisé* 66 ●●
RUFFLES* *Floral Oriental / Fleuri Oriental* 48 ●●
RUMBA *Dry Woods / Boisé Cuir* 72 ●●
RUSH → GUCCI RUSH
RYKIEL ROSE *Floral / Florale* 34 ●●

S

S pour FEMME *Floral / Florale* 34 ●●
SABI *Green / Vert* 23 ●●●●
SACREBLEU! *Floral Oriental / Fleuri Oriental* 47 ●●●
SAFARI *Soft Floral / Fleuri Aldéhydé* 42 ●
SALVADOR DALI *Soft Oriental / Oriental Doux* 53 ●●●
SALVATORE FERRAGAMO *Floral / Florale* 34 ●●
SA MAJESTÉ LA ROSE *Floral / Florale* 30 ●●
SAMBA *Floral / Florale* 34 ●●
SAMBA HEAT WOMAN *Woody Oriental / Oriental Boisé* 61 ●●●
SAMBA NATURAL *Water / Marine* 26 ●●
SAMBA NOVA *Mossy Woods / Chypre Boisé* 66 ●
SAMBA RED WOMAN *Soft Floral / Fleuri Aldéhydé* 42 ●●
SAMOURAÏ WOMAN *Floral / Florale* 34 ●●
SAMSARA *Woody Oriental / Oriental Boisé* 61 ●●●
SAMSARA – UN AIR DE *Woody Oriental / Oriental Boisé* 60 ●
SAND & SABLE *Floral / Florale* 33 ●●●●
SANDALO ♂ *Woody Oriental / Oriental Boisé* 61 ●●●●
SANDALWOOD Yardley ♂ *Woody Oriental / Oriental Boisé* 61 ●●●
SANGUINE MUSKISSIME ♂ *Citrus / Hespéridé* 16 ●
SANS ADIEU *Water / Marine* 26 ●●
SANTAL IMPÉRIAL ♂ *Woody Oriental / Oriental Boisé* 61 ●●●
SARCANTHUS *Floral / Florale* 36 ●●
SAVAGE VANILLA *Woody Oriental / Oriental Boisé* 60 ●●
SAVANNA *Floral / Florale* 36 ●●
SAVANNAH GARDENS *Oriental / Oriental* 57 ●●●
SAWDUST ♂ *Mossy Woods / Chypre Boisé* 67 ●●●
SCAASI *Floral / Florale* 34 ●●
SCAPA *Citrus / Hespéridé* 16 ●●
SCARF *Woody Oriental / Oriental Boisé* 60 ●●
SCARF TAORMINA *Floral / Florale* 34 ●●
SCENT OF FLOWERS *Floral / Florale* 38 ●
SCENT OF ROMANCE ORIGINAL *Soft Oriental / Oriental Doux* 53 ●●●
SCENT OF ROMANCE ST VALENTINE *Soft Floral / Fleuri Aldéhydé* 43 ●●●
SCENT OF ROMANCE UNFORGETTABLE *Floral / Florale* 33 ●●●
SCENT OF ROMANCE WITH LOVE *Floral / Florale* 36 ●●
SCHERRER → JEAN-LOUIS SCHERRER
SCHERRER 2 *Floral Oriental / Fleuri Oriental* 48 ●●
SCHÖN *Floral / Florale* 34 ●●
SCULPTURE *Floral Oriental / Fleuri Oriental* 48 ●
SECRET DE VÉNUS *Woody Oriental / Oriental Boisé* 61 ●●●
SECRÈTE DATURA *Oriental / Oriental* 57 ●●●
SECRET INTENTION Ⓛ *Floral / Florale* 34 ●●
SENSATIONS *Floral Oriental / Fleuri Oriental* 46 ●
SENSES *Floral / Florale* 33 ●●●●
SENSO *Floral / Florale* 34 ●●
SENTIMENT *Floral / Florale* 33 ●●●●
SERGIO TACCHINI DONNA *Water / Marine* 26 ●●
SERINGA *Floral / Florale* 36 ●
SÉXUAL *Floral Oriental / Fleuri Oriental* 46 ●
SHAAL NUR ♂ *Woody Oriental / Oriental Boisé* 61 ●●●●
SHADES BY NAVY* *Floral / Florale* 34 ●●
SHAHI *Woody Oriental / Oriental Boisé* 61 ●●●●
SHAHI AQUA *Floral / Florale* 34 ●
SHAHI GOLDEN SUN *Floral Oriental / Fleuri Oriental* 47 ●●●
SHALIMAR *Oriental / Oriental* 57 ●●●
SHE* *Floral / Florale* 34 ●●
SHEER HALSTON *Floral Oriental / Fleuri Oriental* 48 ●
SHEER TIFFANY *Floral / Florale* 38 ●
SHI *Floral / Florale* 34 ●
SHIMÓ *Floral Oriental / Fleuri Oriental* 46 ●●
SHOCKING *Oriental / Oriental* 57 ●●●
SHU UEMURA *Mossy Woods / Chypre Boisé* 66 ●●
SHU UEMURA 029 ♂ *Aromatic / Fougère* 76 ●
SI FLEURI *Floral / Florale* 36 ●●
SIGNATURE POUR FEMME *Floral Oriental / Fleuri Oriental* 46 ●●
SILENCES *Green / Vert* 23 ●●●●
SILVER JEANS FEMME *Floral / Florale* 34 ●
SINAÏ *Floral Oriental / Fleuri Oriental* 46 ●

SIRÈNE *Floral Oriental / Fleuri Oriental 46* ●●
SIROCCO DONNA *Woody Oriental / Oriental Boisé 60* ●
SISSI *Floral / Florale 33* ●●●
SI TENDRE *Soft Floral / Fleuri Aldéhydé 42* ●
SKINLIGHTS *Citrus / Hespéridé 16* ●
SMALTO DONNA* *Woody Oriental / Oriental Boisé 61* ●●●
SNOW ♂ *Mossy Woods / Chypre Boisé 66* ●●
SNOWDROP & CRYSTAL FLOWERS #3 *Floral / Florale 36* ●
SO...? *Woody Oriental / Oriental Boisé 61* ●●●
SO...? INSPIRED *Floral / Florale 34* ●
SO...? WILD *Floral / Florale 34* ●
SOCIETY Burberry* *Soft Floral / Fleuri Aldéhydé 42* ●●
SOCIETY Perfumers Guild *Floral / Florale 33* ●●●●
SO DE LA RENTA *Floral / Florale 34* ●
SOIE ROUGE *Dry Woods / Boisé Cuir 72* ●●
SOIR DE PARIS (Original) *Soft Floral / Fleuri Aldéhydé 43* ●●●●
SOIR DE PARIS (New) *Floral / Florale 31* ●●
SOIR D'ÉTÉ *Mossy Woods / Chypre Boisé 67* ●●●
SOLEIL *Floral / Florale 36* ●●
SOLEIL LEVANT *Woody Oriental / Oriental Boisé 61* ●●●
SOLILOQUY *Soft Floral / Fleuri Aldéhydé 43* ●●●●
SOLO SOPRANI ♂ *Citrus / Hespéridé 16* ●
SOLO SOPRANI BLU ♂ *Aromatic / Fougère 76* ●
SOLYTIS *Floral Oriental / Fleuri Oriental 46* ●●
SONG DE CHINE* *Floral / Florale 38* ●
SONIA RYKIEL *Woody Oriental / Oriental Boisé 60* ●
SONOMA VALLEY *Green / Vert 22* ●
SOPHIA* *Soft Oriental / Oriental Doux 53* ●●●
SOPRANI 2 *Woody Oriental / Oriental Boisé 60* ●
SO PRETTY *Soft Floral / Fleuri Aldéhydé 42* ●
SO PRETTY EAU FRUITÉE *Soft Floral / Fleuri Aldéhydé 42* ●
SORENZA *Floral / Florale 33* ●●●
SORTILÈGE* *Soft Floral / Fleuri Aldéhydé 43* ●●●●
SOTTO VOCE* *Woody Oriental / Oriental Boisé 61* ●●●
SOUTHERN EXPOSURE *Citrus / Hespéridé 16* ●●
SPARKLING WHITE DIAMONDS *Soft Floral / Fleuri Aldéhydé 42* ●
SPAZIO KRIZIA DONNA *Floral Oriental / Fleuri Oriental 47* ●●●
SPECIAL N° 127 ♂ *Citrus / Hespéridé 17* ●●●
SPELLBOUND *Floral Oriental / Fleuri Oriental 47* ●●●
SPIRIT OF SWITZERLAND – THE *Floral / Florale 36* ●
SPIRIT OF ZEN *Floral / Florale 38* ●●
SPLENDOR *Floral / Florale 38* ●
SPORT SPIRIT → ESCADA SPORT SPIRIT
SPRING FEVER *Floral / Florale 34* ●●
SPRING FLOWER *Floral / Florale 34* ●
SPRING RAIN *Floral / Florale 36* ●
STARDUST *Floral Oriental / Fleuri Oriental 46* ●●
S.T.DUPONT FEMME *Floral / Florale 34* ●
STETSON FOR WOMEN: AMERICAN ORIGINAL *Floral / Florale 32* ●●
ST JOHN *Floral Oriental / Fleuri Oriental 47* ●●●●
STÉPHANIE *Woody Oriental / Oriental Boisé 61* ●●●
STEPHANOTIS *Floral / Florale 31* ●●●●
STYLE *Floral Oriental / Fleuri Oriental 46* ●
SUBLIME *Soft Oriental / Oriental Doux 53* ●●●
SUGAR ♂ *Citrus / Hespéridé 16* ●●
SUGAR COOKIE ♂ *Soft Oriental / Oriental Doux 52* ●●
SUGGESTION EAU CUIVRÉE* *Floral Oriental / Fleuri Oriental 47* ●●●
SUGGESTION EAU D'ARGENT* *Floral / Florale 36* ●●
SUGGESTION EAU D'OR* *Floral / Florale 34* ●●
SUI DREAMS *Oriental / Oriental 56* ●●
SULTRY/ANTICIPATE *Floral Oriental / Fleuri Oriental 48* ●●
SUMATRA RAIN WOMAN *Floral Oriental / Fleuri Oriental 46* ●
SUMMER *Floral / Florale 34* ●
SUMMER HILL *Floral / Florale 38* ●
SUMMER SPLASH *Citrus / Hespéridé 16* ●
SUNFLOWERS *Water / Marine 27* ●●●
SUNG *Floral / Florale 38* ●
SUNG SPA *Green / Vert 22* ●
SUN MOON STARS *Floral Oriental / Fleuri Oriental 46* ●
SUNSET BOULEVARD *Floral Oriental / Fleuri Oriental 48* ●●
SUNSHINE Chiara Boni *Floral / Florale 34* ●
SUNSHINE My Very Own *Floral / Florale 36* ●
SUN SPIRIT* *Floral / Florale 34* ●●
SUNWATER *Floral / Florale 36* ●
SWEET COURRÈGES *Soft Floral / Fleuri Aldéhydé 42* ●●
SWEETPEA Demeter *Floral / Florale 30* ●●
SYNTHETIC NIRVANA *Woody Oriental / Oriental Boisé 60* ●●

T

TABAC BLOND *Dry Woods / Boisé Cuir 73* ●●●
TABU *Oriental / Oriental 57* ●●●●
TALISMAN *Mossy Woods / Chypre Boisé 66* ●●
TALISMAN EAU TRANSPARENTE *Floral / Florale 34* ●
TAMANGO *Soft Floral / Fleuri Aldéhydé 42* ●●
TANGLEWOOD BOUQUET *Floral Oriental / Fleuri Oriental 47* ●●●
TATIANA *Floral / Florale 33* ●●●●
TÉ ♂ *Citrus / Hespéridé 16* ●
TEA FOR TWO *Woody Oriental / Oriental Boisé 61* ●●●●
TEA ROSE *Floral / Florale 31* ●●●
TEATRO ALLA SCALA* *Soft Oriental / Oriental Doux 53* ●●●
TED BAKER WOMAN *Soft Floral / Fleuri Aldéhydé 42* ●
TEMPORE DONNA *Woody Oriental / Oriental Boisé 60* ●●
TEMPS D'AIMER – LE *Mossy Woods / Chypre Boisé 67* ●●●
TEMPS D'UNE FÊTE – LE *Floral / Florale 36* ●
TENDRE POISON *Floral / Florale 36* ●●
TENTATIONS* *Woody Oriental / Oriental Boisé 61* ●●●
THAÏS *Floral / Florale 38* ●
THAT'S AMORE! LEI *Floral Oriental / Fleuri Oriental 46* ●
THÉ ♂ *Woody Oriental / Oriental Boisé 61* ●●●
THEOREMA *Soft Oriental / Oriental Doux 53* ●●●
THEOREMA ESPRIT D'ÉTÉ *Soft Oriental / Oriental Doux 52* ●●
THÉ POUR UN ÉTÉ ♂ *Citrus / Hespéridé 16* ●
THÉ VERT ♂ *Citrus / Hespéridé 16* ●●
THIARA *Floral Oriental / Fleuri Oriental 47* ●●●
THIS IS NOT A PIPE ♂ *Dry Woods / Boisé Cuir 73* ●●●
TIARÉ Chantecaille *Floral / Florale 30* ●●
TIARÉ Comptoir Sud Pacifique *Floral / Florale 30* ●●
TIEMPE PASSATE *Mossy Woods / Chypre Boisé 67* ●●●
TIFFANY *Floral / Florale 33* ●●●●
TIGRESS* *Floral Oriental / Fleuri Oriental 47* ●●●
TILLEUL ♂ *Floral / Florale 30* ●
TILLEUL CHÈVREFEUILLE *Soft Floral / Fleuri Aldéhydé 42* ●
TOCADE *Floral Oriental / Fleuri Oriental 47* ●●●
TOCADILLY* *Floral / Florale 34* ●●
TODD OLDHAM* *Woody Oriental / Oriental Boisé 60* ●
TOMATO ♂ *Green / Vert 22* ●●
TOMMY GIRL *Floral / Florale 36* ●
TOSCA *Soft Floral / Fleuri Aldéhydé 43* ●●●●
TOUCH Fred Hayman *Floral / Florale 36* ●●
TOUCHE DE NAF NAF – UNE *Floral / Florale 34* ●
TOUCH FOR WOMEN → BURBERRY TOUCH FOR WOMEN
TOUJOURS L'AIMANT *Soft Floral / Fleuri Aldéhydé 42* ●●
TOUJOURS MOI *Woody Oriental / Oriental Boisé 61* ●●●●
TOVA *Soft Floral / Fleuri Aldéhydé 43* ●●●●
TRAMP *Floral / Florale 33* ●●●
TRÈS CHIC *Soft Oriental / Oriental Doux 52* ●
TRÈS JOURDAN* *Floral / Florale 34* ●●
TRÉSOR *Floral Oriental / Fleuri Oriental 46* ●●
TRIANGLE *Floral / Florale 34* ●●
TRIBÙ *Floral / Florale 34* ●●
TRIBÙ ACQUA FRESCA *Floral / Florale 38* ●
TRIGÈRE *Soft Floral / Fleuri Aldéhydé 42* ●●
TROPICAL PUNCH ⓛ *Floral / Florale 34* ●
TRUE LOVE* *Soft Floral / Fleuri Aldéhydé 42* ●
TRUESTE *Soft Floral / Fleuri Aldéhydé 42* ●
TRULY LACE *Floral Oriental / Fleuri Oriental 47* ●●●
TRUSSARDI *Dry Woods / Boisé Cuir 73* ●●●
TRUTH CALVIN KLEIN *Woody Oriental / Oriental Boisé 60* ●
TUBÉREUSE Annick Goutal *Floral / Florale 31* ●●●●
TUBÉREUSE L'Artisan Parfumeur *Floral / Florale 31* ●●●●
TUBÉREUSE Le Jardin Retrouvé *Floral / Florale 31* ●●●●
TUBÉREUSE Maître Parfumeur et Gantier *Floral / Florale 31* ●●●●
TUBÉREUSE INDIANA / INDIANA *Floral / Florale 38* ●●
TUBEROSE Floris *Floral / Florale 31* ●●●●
TUBEROSE Jo Malone *Floral / Florale 31* ●●●●
TURBULENCES *Mossy Woods / Chypre Boisé 67* ●●●●
TURQUOISE Comptoir Sud Pacifique
   Soft Floral / Fleuri Aldéhydé 43 ●●●
TURQUOISE Morabito *Citrus / Hespéridé 17* ●●●●
TUSCANY PER DONNA *Woody Oriental / Oriental Boisé 60* ●
TUXEDO* *Mossy Woods / Chypre Boisé 67* ●●●
TWEED *Floral / Florale 33* ●●●●
TWENTY ONE ♂ *Citrus / Hespéridé 17* ●●●●
TWICE ICEBERG → ICEBERG TWICE

U

U   *Floral / Florale   34* ●
U II SHEER SCENT   *Mossy Woods / Chypre Boisé   66* ●
U de V POUR ELLE   *Floral / Florale   34* ●●
UBAR   *Mossy Woods / Chypre Boisé   67* ●●●
ULTRAVIOLET   *Floral Oriental / Fleuri Oriental   46* ●
UN AIR DE SAMSARA   *Woody Oriental / Oriental Boisé   60* ●
UN AIR D'HABANITA   *Floral Oriental / Fleuri Oriental   46* ●
UN AMOUR DE PATOU   *Floral / Florale   36* ●
UNE TOUCHE DE NAF NAF   *Floral / Florale   34* ●
UNFORGETTABLE   *Woody Oriental / Oriental Boisé   61* ●●●●
UNFORGETTABLE TOO   *Floral Oriental / Fleuri Oriental   46* ●●
UNGARO   *Woody Oriental / Oriental Boisé   61* ●●●●
UNINHIBITED*   *Floral Oriental / Fleuri Oriental   47* ●●●●
UN MATIN D'ÉTÉ   *Floral / Florale   30* ●●
UNTAMED MUSK   *Oriental / Oriental   57* ●●●●
UNZIPPED   *Woody Oriental / Oriental Boisé   60* ●
UNZIPPED SPORT   *Floral / Florale   34* ●
UNZIPPED UNIVERSE   *Floral Oriental / Fleuri Oriental   46* ●
URBAN ENERGY   *Floral / Florale   34* ●
URVÂSHI   *Floral Oriental / Fleuri Oriental   46* ●●

V

V   *Soft Floral / Fleuri Aldéhydé   42* ●●
VACANCES   *Green / Vert   23* ●●●
VALENTIN YUDASHKIN   *Floral Oriental / Fleuri Oriental   46* ●
VALENTINO   *Floral / Florale   34* ●●
VALERIA   *Floral / Florale   36* ●●
VALLÉE DES ROIS   *Floral Oriental / Fleuri Oriental   47* ●●●
VAN CLEEF   *Floral Oriental / Fleuri Oriental   46* ●●
VANDERBILT   *Floral Oriental / Fleuri Oriental   47* ●●●
VANILIA L'Artisan Parfumeur   *Oriental / Oriental   57* ●●●
VANILLA Crabtree & Evelyn   *Floral Oriental / Fleuri Oriental   48* ●
VANILLA FIELDS   *Woody Oriental / Oriental Boisé   60* ●●
VANILLA MUSK   *Woody Oriental / Oriental Boisé   61* ●●●
VANILLE Comptoir Sud Pacifique ♀   *Oriental / Oriental   56* ●●
VANILLE E.Coudray   *Oriental / Oriental   57* ●●●
VANILLE L'Occitane ♀   *Soft Oriental / Oriental Doux   53* ●●●
VANILLE Molinard   *Oriental / Oriental   57* ●●●
VANILLE ABRICOT   *Oriental / Oriental   56* ●
VANILLE AMANDE   *Oriental / Oriental   56* ●
VANILLE AMBRE   *Oriental / Oriental   57* ●●●
VANILLE CAFÉ ♀   *Oriental / Oriental   57* ●●●
VANILLE CANNELLE   *Oriental / Oriental   57* ●●●
VANILLE CERISE   *Oriental / Oriental   56* ●
VANILLE COCO   *Woody Oriental / Oriental Boisé   60* ●
VANILLE FLEURIE   *Floral / Florale   31* ●●●●
VANILLE FRAÎCHEUR   *Oriental / Oriental   56* ●●
VANILLE FRUITÉE   *Oriental / Oriental   56* ●●
VANILLE MARINE   *Water / Marine   27* ●●●●
VANILLE PATCHOULI   *Woody Oriental / Oriental Boisé   61* ●●●
VANILLE TIARÉ   *Oriental / Oriental   56* ●
VANILLE-TONKA   *Oriental / Oriental   57* ●●●
VANISIA   *Oriental / Oriental   57* ●●●
VARENSIA   *Mossy Woods / Chypre Boisé   66* ●●
VARIATIONS   *Floral / Florale   34* ●●
VENDETTA*   *Woody Oriental / Oriental Boisé   60* ●
VENET   *Floral Oriental / Fleuri Oriental   47* ●●●
VENEZIA*   *Woody Oriental / Oriental Boisé   61* ●●●
VENEZIA PASTELLO*   *Soft Floral / Fleuri Aldéhydé   42* ●
VENT VERT   *Green / Vert   23* ●●●
VENTILO   *Floral Oriental / Fleuri Oriental   46* ●●
VÉNUS DE L'AMOUR   *Floral Oriental / Fleuri Oriental   47* ●●●
VERANDA   *Floral Oriental / Fleuri Oriental   46* ●
VERBENAS OF PROVENCE ♀   *Citrus / Hespéridé   17* ●●●
VERINO   *Floral Oriental / Fleuri Oriental   46* ●●
VERSACE   → GIANNI VERSACE
VERSACE ESSENCE EMOTIONAL   *Soft Floral / Fleuri Aldéhydé   42* ●●
VERSACE ESSENCE ETHEREAL   *Floral / Florale   36* ●
VERSACE ESSENCE EXCITING   *Floral / Florale   30* ●●
VERSACE WOMAN   *Mossy Woods / Chypre Boisé   66* ●●
VERSACE'S BLONDE   *Floral / Florale   31* ●●●●
VERS LE JOUR   *Floral / Florale   34* ●
VERS TOI   *Soft Floral / Fleuri Aldéhydé   43* ●●●●
VERSUS DONNA*   *Floral Oriental / Fleuri Oriental   46* ●●

VERVEINE Le Jardin Retrouvé ♀   *Citrus / Hespéridé   17* ●●●
VERY M.C. ♀   *Citrus / Hespéridé   16* ●
VERY VALENTINO   *Oriental / Oriental   56* ●
VETIVER Etro ♀   *Dry Woods / Boisé Cuir   73* ●●●
VETYVER Jo Malone ♀   *Mossy Woods / Chypre Boisé   66* ●●
VETYVER HAITI ♀   *Mossy Woods / Chypre Boisé   66* ●●
V'E VERSACE*   *Mossy Woods / Chypre Boisé   66* ●●
VICE VERSA* ⓛ   *Floral / Florale   34* ●●
VICKY TIEL ORIGINALÉ   *Floral / Florale   33* ●●●●
VICOLO FIORI ♀   *Floral Oriental / Fleuri Oriental   48* ●
VICTORIAN POSY   *Floral / Florale   33* ●●●●
VIE DE CHATEAU (CHEVERNY) ♀   *Mossy Woods / Chypre Boisé   67* ●●●
VIOLET Woods of Windsor   *Floral / Florale   31* ●●●●
VIOLETTA Penhaligon's   *Floral / Florale   31* ●●●●
VIOLETTA DI PARMA   *Floral / Florale   31* ●●●●
VIOLETTE Molinard   *Floral / Florale   31* ●●●●
VIOLETTE PRÉCIEUSE   *Floral / Florale   31* ●●●●
VIRGILIO ♀   *Green / Vert   22* ●●
VIVA DI TOSCA   *Floral Oriental / Fleuri Oriental   47* ●●●
VIVID   *Floral / Florale   33* ●●●●
VIVRE   *Soft Floral / Fleuri Aldéhydé   42* ●●
VOCALISE Maître Parfumeur et Gantier   *Citrus / Hespéridé   16* ●●
VOCALISE Shiseido   *Floral Oriental / Fleuri Oriental   46* ●
VOICE BY BETTY BARCLAY   *Floral Oriental / Fleuri Oriental   47* ●●●
VOILE D'ÉTÉ   *Floral Oriental / Fleuri Oriental   47* ●●●
VOL DE NUIT   *Woody Oriental / Oriental Boisé   60* ●●
VOLEUR DE ROSES ♀   *Dry Woods / Boisé Cuir   72* ●
VOLUPTÉ   *Floral Oriental / Fleuri Oriental   46* ●●
VÔTRE*   *Floral / Florale   36* ●
V/S WOMAN   *Floral / Florale   34* ●

W

W   *Floral / Florale   36* ●
WATERPERRY   *Floral Oriental / Fleuri Oriental   47* ●●●
WATT PINK   *Floral / Florale   38* ●
WATT RED   *Woody Oriental / Oriental Boisé   60* ●●
WATT YELLOW   *Floral / Florale   34* ●●
WEEK END FOR WOMEN   → BURBERRY WEEK END FOR WOMEN
WEIL DE WEIL   *Green / Vert   23* ●●●
WEIL EAU DE FRAÎCHEUR ♀   *Citrus / Hespéridé   16* ●
WHITE CAMELLIA   *Floral / Florale   38* ●
WHITE CHANTILLY   *Floral / Florale   34* ●
WHITE DIAMONDS   *Soft Floral / Fleuri Aldéhydé   42* ●●
WHITE JEANS*   *Mossy Woods / Chypre Boisé   67* ●●●
WHITE LAVENDER   *Floral / Florale   34* ●●
WHITE LINEN   *Soft Floral / Fleuri Aldéhydé   42* ●●
WHITE LINEN BREEZE   *Soft Floral / Fleuri Aldéhydé   42* ●
WHITE SATIN   *Soft Floral / Fleuri Aldéhydé   42* ●●
WHITE SHOULDERS   *Floral / Florale   33* ●●●
WHITE SPELL   *Floral / Florale   38* ●
WILD MUGUET   *Floral / Florale   30* ●
WILD MUSK Coty   *Oriental / Oriental   57* ●●●●
WILD ROSE Woods of Windsor   *Floral / Florale   31* ●●●
WILD WIND   *Water / Marine   26* ●●
WILKES SAN FRANCISCO ♀   *Aromatic / Fougère   76* ●
WIND SONG   *Floral / Florale   33* ●●●
WINGS*   *Floral / Florale   33* ●●●●
WINTER DELICE ⓛ   *Woody Oriental / Oriental Boisé   61* ●●●●
WISH   *Woody Oriental / Oriental Boisé   60* ●
WISTERIA   *Floral / Florale   30* ●●
WISTFUL / LONG AGO   *Floral / Florale   36* ●
WITH LOVE*   *Woody Oriental / Oriental Boisé   60* ●
WITH PLEASURE   *Green / Vert   23* ●●●●
WOMAN Herbalife   *Floral / Florale   34* ●
WOMAN RED   → MARBERT WOMAN RED
WOMENSWEAR   *Soft Floral / Fleuri Aldéhydé   42* ●●
WOODHUE*   *Woody Oriental / Oriental Boisé   61* ●●●
WOODLAND HYACINTH / BLUEBELL   *Floral / Florale   34* ●
WRAPPINGS   *Water / Marine   26* ●

X

X LIMITED ♀   *Citrus / Hespéridé   16* ●
XI'A XI'ANG*   *Floral Oriental / Fleuri Oriental   46* ●●
XS POUR ELLE   *Floral / Florale   38* ●

Y   *Mossy Woods / Chypre Boisé*   66 ●
YELLOW JEANS*   *Floral / Florale*   34 ●
YENDI*   *Soft Floral / Fleuri Aldéhydé*   43 ●●●●
YES FOR WOMEN   *Floral Oriental / Fleuri Oriental*   46 ●
YIN   *Floral / Florale*   34 ●●
YLANG & VANILLE   *Floral / Florale*   31 ●●●
YOHJI   *Oriental / Oriental*   56 ●●
YOHJI ESSENTIAL   *Mossy Woods / Chypre Boisé*   66 ●●
YOU'RE THE FIRE FOR WOMEN   *Soft Oriental / Oriental Doux*   53 ●●●
YOUTH-DEW   *Soft Oriental / Oriental Doux*   53 ●●●
YSATIS   *Woody Oriental / Oriental Boisé*   60 ●
YSEULT   *Citrus / Hespéridé*   17 ●●●●
YVRESSE (CHAMPAGNE)   *Mossy Woods / Chypre Boisé*   66 ●

ZAHAROFF   *Floral Oriental / Fleuri Oriental*   46 ●
ZAHRA   *Floral Oriental / Fleuri Oriental*   46 ●●
ZARA WOMAN   *Floral / Florale*   34 ●●
ZEN (Original)   *Floral / Florale*   33 ●●●
ZEN (New)   *Mossy Woods / Chypre Boisé*   66 ●
ZESTE MANDARINE PAMPLEMOUSSE ♂   *Citrus / Hespéridé*   17 ●●●●
ZIBELINE   *Mossy Woods / Chypre Boisé*   67 ●●●
ZIGZAG   *Citrus / Hespéridé*   17 ●●●●
ZILLION   *Floral Oriental / Fleuri Oriental*   46 ●●
ZINNIA   *Floral / Florale*   38 ●
ZOA   *Floral / Florale*   34 ●●
ZUT   *Woody Oriental / Oriental Boisé*   60 ●

π *Woody Oriental / Oriental Boisé* 63 ●●●
1-12 → HALSTON 1-12
3ᵉ HOMME / THIRD MAN / Nº 3 *Aromatic / Fougère* 77 ●●●●
57 FOR HIM → CHEVIGNON 57 FOR HIM
212 MEN *Mossy Woods / Chypre Boisé* 68 ●
273 RODEO DRIVE FOR MEN *Dry Woods / Boisé Cuir* 72 ●●
360° FOR MEN *Aromatic / Fougère* 80 ●
4711 ORIGINAL ♂ *Citrus / Hespéridé* 19 ●●●

A

ACIER ALUMINIUM *Mossy Woods / Chypre Boisé* 69 ●●●●
ACQUA CLASSICA DI BORSARI ♂ *Citrus / Hespéridé* 19 ●●●
ACQUA DI GIÒ HOMME *Water / Marine* 26 ●●
ACQUA DI MIELE ♂ *Floral / Florale* 38 ●
ACQUA DI PARMA COLONIA ♂ *Citrus / Hespéridé* 19 ●●●
ACQUA DI PARMA LAVANDA TONICA ♂ *Floral / Florale* 39 ●●●
ACQUA DI SELVA *Mossy Woods / Chypre Boisé* 69 ●●●
ACTEUR *Dry Woods / Boisé Cuir* 72 ●●
ACTION SPORT *Citrus / Hespéridé* 19 ●●●●
ACTION UOMO* *Aromatic / Fougère* 80 ●
ADIDAS ACTION *Aromatic / Fougère* 80 ●
ADIDAS ACTIVE BODIES *Aromatic / Fougère* 76 ●●
ADIDAS ADVENTURE *Aromatic / Fougère* 82 ●●
ADIDAS CLASSIC *Dry Woods / Boisé Cuir* 72 ●●
ADIDAS DYNAMIC *Aromatic / Fougère* 82 ●
ADIDAS MOVES *Aromatic / Fougère* 80 ●
ADIDAS SPORT *Citrus / Hespéridé* 18 ●●
ADIDAS TEAM *Aromatic / Fougère* 80 ●
ADOLFO DOMINGUEZ* *Aromatic / Fougère* 80 ●
ADVENTURE QUASAR *Aromatic / Fougère* 76 ●
AGUA BRAVA *Mossy Woods / Chypre Boisé* 69 ●●●
AGUA DE LOEWE ♂ *Citrus / Hespéridé* 18 ●
AGUA FRESCA *Mossy Woods / Chypre Boisé* 69 ●●●
AGUA LAVANDA ♂ *Floral / Florale* 39 ●●●
AIGNER Nº 1 → ETIENNE AIGNER Nº 1*
AIGNER Nº 2 → ETIENNE AIGNER Nº 2
AIGNER POUR HOMME *Dry Woods / Boisé Cuir* 72 ●●
AIR DE JAVA – UN *Mossy Woods / Chypre Boisé* 68 ●●
ALAIN DELON POUR HOMME *Aromatic / Fougère* 76 ●
ALEGRIA HOMBRE *Water / Marine* 26 ●●
ALLURE HOMME *Woody Oriental / Oriental Boisé* 62 ●
ALVIERO MARTINI UOMO *Aromatic / Fougère* 80 ●
AMAZING FOR MEN *Aromatic / Fougère* 76 ●
AMBER & LAVENDER ♂ *Woody Oriental / Oriental Boisé* 63 ●●●
AMBRA ♂ *Oriental / Oriental* 57 ●●●
AMBRE PRECIEUX ♂ *Oriental / Oriental* 57 ●●●●
AMBRE SULTAN ♂ *Soft Oriental / Oriental Doux* 53 ●●●●
AMBRO DE JACOMO *Woody Oriental / Oriental Boisé* 63 ●●●
A*MEN / ANGEL MEN *Woody Oriental / Oriental Boisé* 60 ●●
AMERICA FOR MEN *Aromatic / Fougère* 80 ●
AMOUAGE GENTLEMEN *Soft Floral / Fleuri Aldéhydé* 43 ●●●●
ANARCHISTE – L' ♂ *Aromatic / Fougère* 77 ●●●●
ANDY WARHOL FOR MEN *Aromatic / Fougère* 76 ●
ANGEL FOOD ♂ *Soft Oriental / Oriental Doux* 53 ●●●
ANGEL MEN / A*MEN *Woody Oriental / Oriental Boisé* 60 ●●
ANIMALE ANIMALE FOR MEN *Woody Oriental / Oriental Boisé* 62 ●
ANIMALE FOR MEN *Aromatic / Fougère* 80 ●
ANNAYAKÉ POUR LUI *Aromatic / Fougère* 80 ●
ANTAEUS *Dry Woods / Boisé Cuir* 73 ●●●●
ANTHRACITE POUR L'HOMME *Aromatic / Fougère* 82 ●●
AQUA QUORUM *Aromatic / Fougère* 82 ●
AQUA-FITNESS *Citrus / Hespéridé* 18 ●
AQUA VELVA ICE BLUE *Mossy Woods / Chypre Boisé* 68 ●●
ARABIE ♂ *Woody Oriental / Oriental Boisé* 63 ●●●●
ARAMIS *Dry Woods / Boisé Cuir* 73 ●●●
ARAMIS 900 *Dry Woods / Boisé Cuir* 72 ●
ARAMIS GOLD *Dry Woods / Boisé Cuir* 73 ●●●
ARGENTO POUR HOMME *Mossy Woods / Chypre Boisé* 69 ●●●
ARMAND BASI HOMME *Woody Oriental / Oriental Boisé* 60 ●●
ARMANI POUR HOMME *Citrus / Hespéridé* 19 ●●●●
ARÒME 3 ♂ *Floral / Florale* 39 ●●●
ARÒME 3 TRADITION ♂ *Floral / Florale* 39 ●●●●
ARROGANCE POUR HOMME *Aromatic / Fougère* 76 ●
ARROGANCE UOMO *Aromatic / Fougère* 76 ●●
ARROGANCE YOU *Aromatic / Fougère* 82 ●●

ASPEN DISCOVERY *Aromatic / Fougère* 76 ●
ASPEN FOR MEN *Aromatic / Fougère* 78 ●
ATKINSON GOLD MEDAL ♂ *Citrus / Hespéridé* 19 ●●●
ATMAN *Dry Woods / Boisé Cuir* 73 ●●●
AUBUSSON HOMME *Mossy Woods / Chypre Boisé* 68 ●●
AURA FOR MEN *Mossy Woods / Chypre Boisé* 69 ●●●
AUTRE – L' ♂ *Dry Woods / Boisé Cuir* 73 ●●●●
AVATAR *Aromatic / Fougère* 76 ●
AZZARO POUR HOMME *Aromatic / Fougère* 76 ●

B

BABY BLUE JEANS *Citrus / Hespéridé* 19 ●●●
BACKGROUND* *Woody Oriental / Oriental Boisé* 60 ●●
BAIE DE GENIÈVRE *Woody Oriental / Oriental Boisé* 63 ●●●
BAÏMÉ ♂ *Mossy Woods / Chypre Boisé* 68 ●
BALADIN *Dry Woods / Boisé Cuir* 73 ●●●
BALENCIAGA POUR HOMME* *Woody Oriental / Oriental Boisé* 63 ●●●●
BARBIER DES ISLES *Dry Woods / Boisé Cuir* 73 ●●●
BARON – THE *Aromatic / Fougère* 77 ●●●
BARYSHNIKOV *Aromatic / Fougère* 76 ●●
BARYSHNIKOV SPORT *Aromatic / Fougère* 80 ●
BASALA *Aromatic / Fougère* 77 ●●●●
BASE FOR HIM – LA *Dry Woods / Boisé Cuir* 73 ●●●●
BASI HOMME *Mossy Woods / Chypre Boisé* 68 ●●
BASILE UOMO *Dry Woods / Boisé Cuir* 72 ●●
BE BOP MAN *Dry Woods / Boisé Cuir* 72 ●
BE BOP POUR HOMME *Aromatic / Fougère* 76 ●●
BEL AMI *Dry Woods / Boisé Cuir* 73 ●●●●
BENETTON SPORT MAN *Aromatic / Fougère* 78 ●
BERNINI MEN *Aromatic / Fougère* 82 ●●
BERNINI SPORT *Aromatic / Fougère* 78 ●
BERNINI VODA *Water / Marine* 26 ●●
BEST MAN *Woody Oriental / Oriental Boisé* 62 ●
BEST OF CHEVIGNON ♂ *Water / Marine* 27 ●●●
BETWEEN SHEETS *Aromatic / Fougère* 78 ●
BIJAN FOR MEN *Aromatic / Fougère* 76 ●●
BLACK JEANS Roccobarocco *Woody Oriental / Oriental Boisé* 60 ●●
BLACK JEANS Versace* *Aromatic / Fougère* 76 ●●
BLACK LABEL *Aromatic / Fougère* 77 ●●●
BLACK SILVER ♂ *Aromatic / Fougère* 76 ●●
BLENHEIM BOUQUET *Citrus / Hespéridé* 19 ●●●
BLEU – LE *Aromatic / Fougère* 78 ●●
BLEU FORMIDABLE *Aromatic / Fougère* 82 ●
BLEU MARINE *Woody Oriental / Oriental Boisé* 62 ●
BLUE *Aromatic / Fougère* 82 ●
BLUE JEANS *Woody Oriental / Oriental Boisé* 60 ●●
BLUE Nº 655 HIM *Aromatic / Fougère* 80 ●
BLUE SILVER MEN *Aromatic / Fougère* 82 ●
BLUE STRATOS *Aromatic / Fougère* 80 ●
BODY KOUROS *Woody Oriental / Oriental Boisé* 62 ●
BOGART *Aromatic / Fougère* 78 ●●
BOGNER MAN *Aromatic / Fougère* 80 ●
BOGNER MAN II* *Aromatic / Fougère* 76 ●●
BOGNER SNOW *Aromatic / Fougère* 78 ●
BOIS DE CÉDRAT ♂ *Citrus / Hespéridé* 19 ●●●
BOIS DU PORTUGAL *Woody Oriental / Oriental Boisé* 63 ●●●●
BOIS PRÉCIEUX *Mossy Woods / Chypre Boisé* 69 ●●●●
BONFIRE ♂ *Dry Woods / Boisé Cuir* 73 ●●●●
BOOSTER *Citrus / Hespéridé* 18 ●●
BORSALINO *Aromatic / Fougère* 82 ●●
BOSS *Woody Oriental / Oriental Boisé* 60 ●●
BOSS NUMBER ONE *Aromatic / Fougère* 76 ●●
BOSS SPIRIT* *Dry Woods / Boisé Cuir* 72 ●●
BOSS SPORT* *Aromatic / Fougère* 80 ●●
BOSTON MAN *Aromatic / Fougère* 82 ●●
BOUCHERON POUR HOMME *Citrus / Hespéridé* 19 ●●●●
BOUQUET IMPÉRIAL ♂ *Citrus / Hespéridé* 19 ●●●●
BOURBON HOMME *Mossy Woods / Chypre Boisé* 69 ●●●●
BOWLING GREEN *Aromatic / Fougère* 78 ●●
BRISTOL BLUE *Aromatic / Fougère* 76 ●●
BRITISH STERLING *Aromatic / Fougère* 77 ●●●
BROOKS BROTHERS *Aromatic / Fougère* 80 ●
BROOKSFIELD FOR MEN *Aromatic / Fougère* 80 ●●
BROOKSFIELD ROYAL BLUE *Aromatic / Fougère* 78 ●
BRUNO BANANI *Woody Oriental / Oriental Boisé* 62 ●
BRUT *Aromatic / Fougère* 77 ●●●

BRUT ACTIF BLUE   *Aromatic / Fougère   82* ●
BRUT INSTINCT   *Aromatic / Fougère   76* ●●
BUCKINGHAM   *Aromatic / Fougère   76* ●●
BUGATTI   *Aromatic / Fougère   78* ●
BULGARI BLACK ♂   *Dry Woods / Boisé Cuir   72* ●●
BULGARI EAU PARFUMÉE ♂   *Citrus / Hespéridé   18* ●
BULGARI POUR HOMME   *Aromatic / Fougère   78* ●
BURBERRY FOR MEN (New)   *Aromatic / Fougère   76* ●●
BURBERRYS FOR MEN (Original)*   *Woody Oriental / Oriental Boisé   62* ●●
BURBERRY TOUCH FOR MEN   *Mossy Woods / Chypre Boisé   68* ●
BURBERRY WEEK END FOR MEN   *Mossy Woods / Chypre Boisé   68* ●●
BURL   *Woody Oriental / Oriental Boisé   63* ●●●●
BYBLOS UOMO*   *Aromatic / Fougère   78* ●●
BY MAN   *Woody Oriental / Oriental Boisé   62* ●●

C

CACHAREL POUR L'HOMME   *Aromatic / Fougère   82* ●●
CAESARS MAN   *Aromatic / Fougère   76* ●●
CAFÉ-CAFÉ ADVENTURE POUR HOMME   *Aromatic / Fougère   76* ●●
CAFÉ-CAFÉ POUR HOMME   *Aromatic / Fougère   80* ●
CALIFORNIA FOR MEN   *Aromatic / Fougère   76* ●●
CALVIN   *Aromatic / Fougère   76* ●●
CAMP BEVERLY HILLS FOR MEN*   *Citrus / Hespéridé   19* ●●●●
CANDIE'S MEN   *Aromatic / Fougère   78* ●
CANNELLE ORANGE ♂   *Citrus / Hespéridé   18* ●
CANOÉ   *Aromatic / Fougère   77* ●●●
CAPTAIN*   *Aromatic / Fougère   76* ●●
CAPUCCI POUR HOMME   *Citrus / Hespéridé   18* ●●
CARACTÈRE   *Dry Woods / Boisé Cuir   72* ●●
CARLO CORINTO   *Dry Woods / Boisé Cuir   72* ●●
CARRÉ D'AS   *Aromatic / Fougère   80* ●
CARVEN HOMME   *Dry Woods / Boisé Cuir   72* ●●
CASRAN   *Woody Oriental / Oriental Boisé   62* ●
CASSINI FOR MEN   *Aromatic / Fougère   76* ●
CASUAL FRIDAY   *Woody Oriental / Oriental Boisé   62* ●
CATALYST FOR MEN   *Woody Oriental / Oriental Boisé   62* ●●
CÉDRAT POMELO ♂   *Citrus / Hespéridé   18* ●●
CENTAURE   *Aromatic / Fougère   77* ●●●
CENTAURE CUIR AMBRE   *Woody Oriental / Oriental Boisé   62* ●●
CENTAURE CUIR BLANC   *Mossy Woods / Chypre Boisé   68* ●●
CENTAURE CUIR CASAQUE   *Aromatic / Fougère   80* ●●
CENTAURE CUIR ÉTALON   *Dry Woods / Boisé Cuir   73* ●●●
CENTAURE CUIR FOUGÈRE   *Aromatic / Fougère   76* ●
CENTAURE DIAMANT NOIR   *Aromatic / Fougère   76* ●
CENTAURE TÊTE D'OR   *Aromatic / Fougère   76* ●●
CERRUTI 1881 POUR HOMME   *Citrus / Hespéridé   18* ●●
CERRUTI IMAGE POUR HOMME   *Aromatic / Fougère   80* ●
C'EST MAGIQUE HOMME   *Aromatic / Fougère   76* ●●
CHALEUR D'ANIMALE POUR HOMME   *Aromatic / Fougère   82* ●
CHALLENGE   → PUMA CHALLENGE
CHAMADE POUR HOMME* ⓛ   *Mossy Woods / Chypre Boisé   68* ●
CHANEL POUR MONSIEUR   *Mossy Woods / Chypre Boisé   69* ●●●
CHAPEAU   *Aromatic / Fougère   76* ●
CHAPS   *Woody Oriental / Oriental Boisé   63* ●●●
CHAPS MUSK   *Woody Oriental / Oriental Boisé   63* ●●●
CHAUMET HOMME   *Mossy Woods / Chypre Boisé   68* ●
CHEMISTRY   *Aromatic / Fougère   80* ●
CHEVALIER D'ORSAY   *Citrus / Hespéridé   19* ●●●●
CHEVIGNON   *Mossy Woods / Chypre Boisé   68* ●●
CHEVIGNON 57 FOR HIM   *Woody Oriental / Oriental Boisé   62* ●
CHÈVREFEUILLE ORIGINAL ♂   *Green / Vert   22* ●
CHIARA BONI UOMO   *Aromatic / Fougère   80* ●
CHIEMSEE MAN   *Aromatic / Fougère   80* ●
CHIEMSEE MAN TWO   *Woody Oriental / Oriental Boisé   62* ●
CHROME   *Citrus / Hespéridé   18* ●●
CIGAR   *Woody Oriental / Oriental Boisé   62* ●●
CIGAR AFICIONADO   *Aromatic / Fougère   77* ●●●●
CIGARILLO   *Dry Woods / Boisé Cuir   73* ●●●●
CITRON VERT* ♂   *Citrus / Hespéridé   18* ●
CITRUS BIGARRADE ♂   *Citrus / Hespéridé   19* ●●●
cK BE ♂   *Aromatic / Fougère   78* ●
cK ONE ♂   *Citrus / Hespéridé   18* ●
CLAIBORNE FOR MEN*   *Citrus / Hespéridé   18* ●
CLAIBORNE SPORT   *Aromatic / Fougère   82* ●
CLARTÉ FOR MEN   *Aromatic / Fougère   76* ●
CLASSIC Banana Republic ♂   *Citrus / Hespéridé   19* ●●●

CLASSIC Parfums Bleu   *Mossy Woods / Chypre Boisé   69* ●●●
CLEAR DAY FOR MEN   *Aromatic / Fougère   78* ●
CLUB COLOGNE ♂   *Citrus / Hespéridé   19* ●●●
ᶜN   *Dry Woods / Boisé Cuir   73* ●●●
COLD ♂   *Citrus / Hespéridé   19* ●●●●
COLOGNE SOLOGNE ♂   *Citrus / Hespéridé   19* ●●●
COLORS FOR MEN   *Woody Oriental / Oriental Boisé   62* ●
COMME DES GARÇONS ♂   *Mossy Woods / Chypre Boisé   69* ●●●●
COMME DES GARÇONS 2 ♂   *Mossy Woods / Chypre Boisé   68* ●
CONTRADICTION FOR MEN   *Woody Oriental / Oriental Boisé   62* ●
CONVICTION MEN   *Woody Oriental / Oriental Boisé   62* ●●
COOL WATER   *Aromatic / Fougère   80* ●
COPAINS L'HOMME – LES   *Mossy Woods / Chypre Boisé   68* ●●
CORIOLAN   *Mossy Woods / Chypre Boisé   68* ●●
COTONNADE ♂   *Soft Oriental / Oriental Doux   52* ●●
COTY MUSK FOR MEN   *Woody Oriental / Oriental Boisé   63* ●●●
COUNTRY ROAD MAN   *Aromatic / Fougère   80* ●
COUNTRY WEEKEND   → ESCADA COUNTRY WEEKEND
COUTURE POUR LUI   *Woody Oriental / Oriental Boisé   62* ●
CRABTREE & EVELYN FOR MEN*   *Dry Woods / Boisé Cuir   73* ●●●
CRISTOBAL POUR HOMME   *Woody Oriental / Oriental Boisé   63* ●●●
CROSSROADS   *Aromatic / Fougère   80* ●
CROWN FOUGÈRE   *Aromatic / Fougère   77* ●●●
CROWN IMPERIAL   *Citrus / Hespéridé   19* ●●●●
CROWN PARK ROYAL   *Dry Woods / Boisé Cuir   72* ●●
CROWN SPICED LIMES   *Citrus / Hespéridé   19* ●●●●
CRUISER FOR MEN   *Aromatic / Fougère   76* ●
CUIR DE RUSSIE Le Jardin Retrouvé   → EAU DE CUIR DE RUSSIE
CUIR DE RUSSIE L.T. Piver ♂   *Dry Woods / Boisé Cuir   73* ●●●
CULTURE by TABAC   *Aromatic / Fougère   82* ●●
CULTURE by TABAC BLUE   *Aromatic / Fougère   82* ●
CURVE FOR MEN   *Aromatic / Fougère   76* ●
CYBERSP@CE ♂   *Water / Marine   26* ●

D

D Dunhill   *Aromatic / Fougère   80* ●
D & G MASCULINE   *Citrus / Hespéridé   19* ●●●●
DAKS   *Woody Oriental / Oriental Boisé   62* ●●
DALIMIX ♂   *Citrus / Hespéridé   18* ●
DALIMIX GOLD ♂   *Green / Vert   22* ●
DANDELION ♂   *Floral / Florale   38* ●●
DANDY – LE   *Dry Woods / Boisé Cuir   72* ●
DANIEL HECHTER SPORT   *Aromatic / Fougère   76* ●
DAVIDOFF   *Dry Woods / Boisé Cuir   73* ●●●●
DAVINCI UOMO   *Dry Woods / Boisé Cuir   73* ●●●●
DAY ♂   *Citrus / Hespéridé   19* ●●●●
DEAUVILLE POUR HOMME   *Aromatic / Fougère   76* ●
DÉCLARATION   *Dry Woods / Boisé Cuir   72* ●
DEEP BLUE   *Aromatic / Fougère   80* ●
DEEP FOREST*   *Dry Woods / Boisé Cuir   73* ●●●●
DERBY   *Dry Woods / Boisé Cuir   73* ●●●●
DERRICK   *Woody Oriental / Oriental Boisé   63* ●●●
DESIGN FOR MEN   *Aromatic / Fougère   80* ●
DESIRE   *Woody Oriental / Oriental Boisé   62* ●
DESTINY   *Mossy Woods / Chypre Boisé   69* ●●●
DEVIN   *Green / Vert   23* ●●●●
DIESEL ♂   *Woody Oriental / Oriental Boisé   63* ●●●
DIESEL PLUS PLUS MASCULINE   *Woody Oriental / Oriental Boisé   62* ●
DIESEL ZERO PLUS MASCULINE   *Woody Oriental / Oriental Boisé   63* ●●●
DIRT ♂   *Mossy Woods / Chypre Boisé   68* ●●
DISCOVER   *Aromatic / Fougère   76* ●●
DK MEN*   *Dry Woods / Boisé Cuir   72* ●●
DK MEN UNLEADED*   *Dry Woods / Boisé Cuir   72* ●
DKNY MEN   *Aromatic / Fougère   78* ●
DNA FOR MEN*   *Woody Oriental / Oriental Boisé   62* ●●
DOLCE & GABBANA POUR HOMME   *Aromatic / Fougère   77* ●●●
DOUBLE CLICK ♂   *Citrus / Hespéridé   18* ●
DOUBLE FRAÎCHEUR POUR LUI   *Citrus / Hespéridé   19* ●●●●
DOUCE AMÈRE ♂   *Woody Oriental / Oriental Boisé   62* ●●
DRAKKAR DYNAMIK   *Aromatic / Fougère   80* ●
DRAKKAR NOIR   *Aromatic / Fougère   76* ●●
DREAMER – THE   *Woody Oriental / Oriental Boisé   62* ●●
DUC DE VERVINS   *Aromatic / Fougère   76* ●
DUÉ CLASSIC   *Aromatic / Fougère   76* ●
DUÉ WILD   *Woody Oriental / Oriental Boisé   62* ●●
DUNE POUR HOMME   *Woody Oriental / Oriental Boisé   62* ●

DUNHILL *Dry Woods / Boisé Cuir* 73 ●●●
DUNHILL D → D
DUNHILL EDITION *Aromatic / Fougère* 82 ●●
DUO POUR HOMME *Mossy Woods / Chypre Boisé* 68 ●●

E

EARL GREY TEA ♂ *Citrus / Hespéridé* 18 ●
EARTH ♂ *Mossy Woods / Chypre Boisé* 68 ●
EAU – L' Diptyque ♂ *Soft Oriental / Oriental Doux* 52 ●●
EAU DE CAMPAGNE ♂ *Green / Vert* 23 ●●●
EAU DE CARON FORTE ♂ *Citrus / Hespéridé* 19 ●●●●
EAU DE CÈDRE ♂ *Dry Woods / Boisé Cuir* 72 ●
EAU DE CHEVERNY → VIE DE CHATEAU (CHEVERNY) ♂
EAU DE COLOGNE Penhaligon's ♂ *Citrus / Hespéridé* 19 ●●●
EAU DE COLOGNE EXTRA FINE L'Occitane *Citrus / Hespéridé* 19 ●●●●
EAU DE CUIR DE RUSSIE *Dry Woods / Boisé Cuir* 72 ●●
EAU DE FLEURS DE CÉDRAT ♂ *Citrus / Hespéridé* 19 ●●●
EAU DE GREY FLANNEL *Mossy Woods / Chypre Boisé* 68 ●
EAU DE GUERLAIN ♂ *Citrus / Hespéridé* 19 ●●●
EAU DE L'ARTISAN – L' ♂ *Citrus / Hespéridé* 19 ●●●
EAU DE LAVANDE Annick Goutal ♂ *Floral / Florale* 39 ●●●
EAU D'ÉLIDE ♂ *Aromatic / Fougère* 77 ●●●
EAU DE MONSIEUR *Mossy Woods / Chypre Boisé* 69 ●●●
EAU DE PROVENCE ♂ *Floral / Florale* 39 ●●●
EAU DE QUININE *Citrus / Hespéridé* 19 ●●●
EAU DE ROCHAS HOMME *Citrus / Hespéridé* 19 ●●●●
EAU DE RUSSE Crown *Oriental / Oriental* 56 ●●
EAU DES 4 VOLEURS *Aromatic / Fougère* 78 ●
EAU DES ÎLES *Dry Woods / Boisé Cuir* 73 ●●●●
EAU DES PRINCES *Citrus / Hespéridé* 19 ●●●
EAU DE SANDALWOOD *Woody Oriental / Oriental Boisé* 63 ●●●
EAU DE SPORT Alain Delon* *Aromatic / Fougère* 78 ●●
EAU DES TROPIQUES *Citrus / Hespéridé* 19 ●●●
EAU DE THÉ VERT ♂ *Citrus / Hespéridé* 18 ●
EAU DE VARENS N° 2 ♂ *Citrus / Hespéridé* 18 ●
EAU DE VARENS N° 3 ♂ *Citrus / Hespéridé* 18 ●
EAU DE VARENS N° 4 ♂ *Citrus / Hespéridé* 19 ●●●●
EAU DE VERVEINE Penhaligon's ♂ *Citrus / Hespéridé* 19 ●●●●
EAU DE VÉTYVER *Mossy Woods / Chypre Boisé* 68 ●●
EAU D'HADRIEN ♂ *Citrus / Hespéridé* 19 ●●●
EAU D'HERMÈS ♂ *Dry Woods / Boisé Cuir* 73 ●●●
EAU D'ISSEY POUR HOMME – L' *Water / Marine* 27 ●●●
EAU D'ORANGE VERTE ♂ *Citrus / Hespéridé* 19 ●●●●
EAU DU BADIAN *Citrus / Hespéridé* 18 ●●
EAU DU CAPORAL – L' *Aromatic / Fougère* 77 ●●●●
EAU DU CONTADOUR *Aromatic / Fougère* 77 ●●●
EAU DU COQ ♂ *Citrus / Hespéridé* 19 ●●
EAU DU FIER *Dry Woods / Boisé Cuir* 73 ●●●●
EAU DU GANTIER ♂ *Citrus / Hespéridé* 19 ●●●
EAU DU NAVIGATEUR – L' *Dry Woods / Boisé Cuir* 73 ●●●●
EAU DU SUD ♂ *Citrus / Hespéridé* 18 ●●
EAU DU TSAR *Aromatic / Fougère* 80 ●
EAU DYNAMISANTE ♂ *Citrus / Hespéridé* 19 ●●●
EAU FRAÎCHE Caron ♂ *Citrus / Hespéridé* 19 ●●●
EAU FRAÎCHE Molinard ♂ *Citrus / Hespéridé* 18 ●●
EAU FRANCE ♂ *Citrus / Hespéridé* 19 ●●●
EAU FRESH Jacques Bogart *Aromatic / Fougère* 78 ●●
EAU GRISE *Mossy Woods / Chypre Boisé* 68 ●
EAU IMPÉRIALE ♂ *Citrus / Hespéridé* 19 ●●●
EAU LENTE ♂ *Oriental / Oriental* 57 ●●●
EAU PAR KENZO POUR HOMME – L' *Citrus / Hespéridé* 18 ●●
EAU POUR HOMME L.T. Piver *Citrus / Hespéridé* 19 ●●●●
EAU POUR LE JEUNE HOMME *Citrus / Hespéridé* 18 ●
EAU PURE ♂ *Water / Marine* 26 ●
EAU SANS PAREIL ♂ *Aromatic / Fougère* 76 ●●
EAU SAUVAGE *Citrus / Hespéridé* 19 ●●●
EAU SAUVAGE EXTRÊME *Citrus / Hespéridé* 19 ●●●●
EAU SPORT MEN – L' *Water / Marine* 26 ●
EAU TROIS – L' ♂ *Dry Woods / Boisé Cuir* 72 ●●
ÉBÈNE *Aromatic / Fougère* 78 ●●
ÉGOÏSTE / L'ÉGOÏSTE *Woody Oriental / Oriental Boisé* 63 ●●●
ÉGOÏSTE PLATINUM *Aromatic / Fougère* 78 ●
ELEMENTS *Aromatic / Fougère* 76 ●
ELEMENTS AQUA *Aromatic / Fougère* 82 ●●
ELITE *Citrus / Hespéridé* 19 ●●●●
EL PASO *Aromatic / Fougère* 76 ●●

EMOZIONI FOR MAN *Aromatic / Fougère* 82 ●
EMPORIO ARMANI HE / LUI *Mossy Woods / Chypre Boisé* 68 ●●
ENDURANCE *Aromatic / Fougère* 76 ●
ENGLISH BLAZER *Aromatic / Fougère* 76 ●●
ENGLISH FERN ♂ *Aromatic / Fougère* 77 ●●●
ENGLISH FINE COLOGNE ♂ *Citrus / Hespéridé* 19 ●●●
ENGLISH LAVENDER Atkinson ♂ *Floral / Florale* 39 ●●●
ENGLISH LEATHER *Dry Woods / Boisé Cuir* 72 ●●
ENIGME *Aromatic / Fougère* 82 ●●
ENVY FOR MEN *Woody Oriental / Oriental Boisé* 62 ●
EPICÉA *Aromatic / Fougère* 82 ●●
ÉQUIPAGE *Aromatic / Fougère* 77 ●●●●
EROLFA *Water / Marine* 26 ●
ERUPTION MAN *Woody Oriental / Oriental Boisé* 62 ●●
ESCADA COUNTRY WEEKEND ♂ *Aromatic / Fougère* 80 ●●
ESCADA POUR HOMME *Woody Oriental / Oriental Boisé* 62 ●●
ESCADA SPORT SPIRIT ♂ *Citrus / Hespéridé* 18 ●
ESCAPE FOR MEN *Aromatic / Fougère* 82 ●
ESENCIA LOEWE *Dry Woods / Boisé Cuir* 72 ●●
ESPRIT DE LAVANDE ♂ *Aromatic / Fougère* 76 ●
ESPRIT DU ROI ♂ *Citrus / Hespéridé* 18 ●●
ESSENZA DI MEDITERRANEÒ UOMO *Dry Woods / Boisé Cuir* 72 ●
ETERNITY FOR MEN *Aromatic / Fougère* 80 ●
ETIENNE AIGNER N° 1* *Dry Woods / Boisé Cuir* 73 ●●●
ETIENNE AIGNER N° 2 *Aromatic / Fougère* 77 ●●●●
ÉTIQUETTE BLEUE ♂ *Citrus / Hespéridé* 18 ●●
ETRA ♂ *Soft Oriental / Oriental Doux* 53 ●●●●
EXTASE BODY TALK ♂ *Citrus / Hespéridé* 18 ●
EXTASE EXOTIC NATURE MAN *Aromatic / Fougère* 76 ●●
EXTASE MAGMA MAN *Woody Oriental / Oriental Boisé* 63 ●●●
EXTASE MUSK MAN *Oriental / Oriental* 57 ●●●●
EXTASE PURE PASSION MAN *Woody Oriental / Oriental Boisé* 62 ●●
EXTRACT OF LIMES Penhaligon's ♂ *Citrus / Hespéridé* 19 ●●●●

 **F**

FACE À FACE HOMME *Aromatic / Fougère* 82 ●
FAÇONNABLE *Aromatic / Fougère* 82 ●
FAHRENHEIT *Mossy Woods / Chypre Boisé* 68 ●
FEELING MAN → JIL SANDER FEELING MAN
FENDI UOMO *Dry Woods / Boisé Cuir* 73 ●●●●
FERRARI RED *Woody Oriental / Oriental Boisé* 62 ●
FERRARI BLACK *Mossy Woods / Chypre Boisé* 68 ●●
FERRARI YELLOW COLOGNE WATER *Citrus / Hespéridé* 19 ●●●
FERRARI YELLOW EAU DE TOILETTE *Aromatic / Fougère* 78 ●
FERRÉ FOR MAN *Woody Oriental / Oriental Boisé* 63 ●●●
FEUILLE DE VERVEINE ♂ *Citrus / Hespéridé* 18 ●
FIG LEAF ♂ *Mossy Woods / Chypre Boisé* 68 ●
FIRE & ICE FOR MEN *Aromatic / Fougère* 80 ●
FIRE & ICE SMOULDER FOR HIM *Mossy Woods / Chypre Boisé* 68 ●●
FLUID ICEBERG MAN *Dry Woods / Boisé Cuir* 72 ●
FORCE MAJEURE *Woody Oriental / Oriental Boisé* 62 ●●
FOR GENTLEMEN Woods of Windsor
  Mossy Woods / Chypre Boisé 69 ●●●
FORMIDABLE HOMME *Aromatic / Fougère* 78 ●●
FOUGÈRE ROYALE* *Aromatic / Fougère* 77 ●●●
FRAÎCHE BADIANE *Mossy Woods / Chypre Boisé* 68 ●●
FRAÎCHEUR MUSKISSIME ♂ *Citrus / Hespéridé* 19 ●●●●
FREEDOM FOR HIM *Aromatic / Fougère* 78 ●●
FREE WORLD MAN *Aromatic / Fougère* 78 ●
FRENCH LINE* *Dry Woods / Boisé Cuir* 73 ●●●●
FUJIYAMA ♂ *Citrus / Hespéridé* 18 ●
FUNTASTIC BOY *Citrus / Hespéridé* 18 ●
FUN WATER FOR MEN *Aromatic / Fougère* 78 ●
FURYO* *Woody Oriental / Oriental Boisé* 63 ●●●●

 **G**

G2 *Woody Oriental / Oriental Boisé* 63 ●●●
GAI MATTIOLO UOMO *Citrus / Hespéridé* 18 ●
GALE HAYMAN MAN *Aromatic / Fougère* 82 ●●
GALILEO 21st CENTURY *Aromatic / Fougère* 82 ●
GALILEO DE VIENTO *Aromatic / Fougère* 78 ●●
GANT CLASSIC *Aromatic / Fougère* 76 ●
GARRIGUE *Aromatic / Fougère* 76 ●●
GENDARME *Citrus / Hespéridé* 19 ●●●●
GENGIS KHAN *Woody Oriental / Oriental Boisé* 62 ●

GENTLEMAN GUÉPARD *Mossy Woods / Chypre Boisé* 68 ●
GENTRY *Aromatic / Fougère* 82 ●
GERANI UOMO *Woody Oriental / Oriental Boisé* 62 ●
GFF M *Aromatic / Fougère* 78 ●
GIEFFEFFE ♂ *Citrus / Hespéridé* 18 ●
GIGLI PER UOMO *Woody Oriental / Oriental Boisé* 62 ●●
GIN & TONIC ♂ *Citrus / Hespéridé* 19 ●●●
GINGERALE ♂ *Citrus / Hespéridé* 19 ●●●●
GINGERBREAD ♂ *Oriental / Oriental* 57 ●●●●
GINSENG N.R.G *Woody Oriental / Oriental Boisé* 62 ●●
GIORGIO MEN* *Mossy Woods / Chypre Boisé* 69 ●●●●
GIVENCHY GENTLEMAN *Mossy Woods / Chypre Boisé* 69 ●●●●
GIVRINE (SICILE) ♂ *Citrus / Hespéridé* 19 ●●●
GLOBE* *Aromatic / Fougère* 80 ●●
GMV ENERGY *Aromatic / Fougère* 82 ●
GMV HOT *Woody Oriental / Oriental Boisé* 62 ●●
GMV UOMO *Aromatic / Fougère* 80 ●
GOAL *Water / Marine* 26 ●●
GOLD *Aromatic / Fougère* 76 ●
GOLDEN DELICIOUS ♂ *Citrus / Hespéridé* 18 ●●
GOLD JEANS HOMME *Aromatic / Fougère* 82 ●●
GOMMA ♂ *Dry Woods / Boisé Cuir* 73 ●●●●
GOODLIFE *Aromatic / Fougère* 80 ●●
GRABAZZI *Soft Oriental / Oriental Doux* 53 ●●●
GRAIN DE PLAISIR ♂ *Mossy Woods / Chypre Boisé* 68 ●
GRAND SLAM *Citrus / Hespéridé* 18 ●
GRANITE BLUE *Aromatic / Fougère* 80 ●
GRANITE ORIGINAL *Aromatic / Fougère* 82 ●
GRAPEFRUIT ♂ *Citrus / Hespéridé* 18 ●●
GRASS Demeter ♂ *Green / Vert* 23 ●●●
GRASS Gap ♂ *Green / Vert* 23 ●●●
GRAVITY *Woody Oriental / Oriental Boisé* 62 ●●
GREENERGY *Mossy Woods / Chypre Boisé* 68 ●●
GREEN GENERATION ♂ *Aromatic / Fougère* 78 ●●
GREEN GENERATION HIM *Aromatic / Fougère* 76 ●
GREENHOUSE ♂ *Green / Vert* 22 ●
GREEN IRISH TWEED *Green / Vert* 23 ●●●
GREEN JEANS* *Aromatic / Fougère* 78 ●
GREEN VALLEY ♂ *Mossy Woods / Chypre Boisé* 68 ●
GREEN WATER *Citrus / Hespéridé* 18 ●●
GREY FLANNEL *Mossy Woods / Chypre Boisé* 68 ●
GREY FLANNEL – EAU DE *Mossy Woods / Chypre Boisé* 68 ●
GRIGIOPERLA *Aromatic / Fougère* 82 ●
GUCCI NOBILE* *Aromatic / Fougère* 80 ●●
GUCCI RUSH FOR MEN *Mossy Woods / Chypre Boisé* 68 ●●
GUÉPARD HOMME *Mossy Woods / Chypre Boisé* 68 ●●
GUESS FOR MEN* *Aromatic / Fougère* 77 ●●●●

H

HABIT ROUGE *Oriental / Oriental* 56 ●●
HALSTON 1-12 *Green / Vert* 23 ●●●
HALSTON Z *Mossy Woods / Chypre Boisé* 68 ●●
HALSTON Z-14 *Mossy Woods / Chypre Boisé* 68 ●●
HAMMAM BOUQUET *Woody Oriental / Oriental Boisé* 63 ●●●
HAPPY FOR MEN *Citrus / Hespéridé* 18 ●
HAUTE PROVENCE → EAU DE PROVENCE ♂
HAVANA *Aromatic / Fougère* 77 ●●●●
HEAVEN *Aromatic / Fougère* 78 ●
HELIOTROPE ♂ *Floral Oriental / Fleuri Oriental* 49 ●●●
HELMUT LANG MAN *Aromatic / Fougère* 77 ●●●
HERBA FRESCA ♂ *Green / Vert* 22 ●●
HERBISSIMO CEDRO *Citrus / Hespéridé* 19 ●●●
HERBISSIMO ENEBRO *Green / Vert* 23 ●●●
HERBISSIMO MEJORANA *Aromatic / Fougère* 76 ●●
HERBISSIMO TÉ VERDE *Citrus / Hespéridé* 18 ●
HÉRITAGE *Woody Oriental / Oriental Boisé* 62 ●●
HÉROS *Woody Oriental / Oriental Boisé* 62 ●●
HÉROS SPORT *Aromatic / Fougère* 78 ●
HERRERA FOR MEN *Woody Oriental / Oriental Boisé* 62 ●●
HIGH... (Turquoise) *Aromatic / Fougère* 78 ●
HIGH TECH MEN *Mossy Woods / Chypre Boisé* 68 ●●
HILFIGER ATHLETICS *Citrus / Hespéridé* 18 ●
H.M. *Woody Oriental / Oriental Boisé* 62 ●
HO HANG *Aromatic / Fougère* 82 ●●
HO HANG CLUB* *Dry Woods / Boisé Cuir* 73 ●●●●
HOLLYWOOD FOR MEN *Aromatic / Fougère* 76 ●●

HOLY WATER ♂ *Water / Marine* 27 ●●●●
HOMBRE DE FLORES JASMINUM *Mossy Woods / Chypre Boisé* 68 ●●
HOMBRE DE FLORES NARCISSUS
   Woody Oriental / Oriental Boisé 63 ●●●●
HOMBRE DE FLORES POLIANTHES TUBEROSE *Floral / Florale* 39 ●●●●
HOMME – L' Comptoir Sud Pacifique *Dry Woods / Boisé Cuir* 72 ●●
HOMME – L' Roger & Gallet *Aromatic / Fougère* 76 ●●
HOMME I → MOLINARD HOMME I
HOMME II → MOLINARD HOMME II
HOMME III → MOLINARD HOMME III
HOMME DE GRÈS *Dry Woods / Boisé Cuir* 73 ●●●●
HOMME DE VENTILO – L' *Dry Woods / Boisé Cuir* 73 ●●●●
HORIZON* *Aromatic / Fougère* 78 ●
HUGO *Aromatic / Fougère* 80 ●
HUGO DARK BLUE *Mossy Woods / Chypre Boisé* 68 ●
HUNGARY WATER *Citrus / Hespéridé* 19 ●●●
HUNTSMAN *Mossy Woods / Chypre Boisé* 68 ●

I

ICEBERG HOMME *Citrus / Hespéridé* 19 ●●●●
ICEBERG TWICE HOMME *Aromatic / Fougère* 80 ●
ICEBERG UNIVERSE HOMME *Woody Oriental / Oriental Boisé* 62 ●
ICE WATER* *Aromatic / Fougère* 82 ●
IGNIS* *Dry Woods / Boisé Cuir* 73 ●●●
IMAGE → CERRUTI IMAGE POUR HOMME
IMPERIAL VETYVER ♂ *Mossy Woods / Chypre Boisé* 69 ●●●
IMPLICITE HOMME *Mossy Woods / Chypre Boisé* 68 ●●
IMPOSIBLE ♂ *Citrus / Hespéridé* 18 ●
IMPROV *Woody Oriental / Oriental Boisé* 62 ●
INDEPENDENCE → PUMA INDEPENDENCE
INDEX AMARYLLIS CASSIS ♂ *Floral / Florale* 38 ●
INDEX BERGAMOT CITRUS ♂ *Citrus / Hespéridé* 18 ●
INDEX CEDAR ARMOISE ♂ *Mossy Woods / Chypre Boisé* 68 ●●
INDEX CHINA GREEN TEA ♂ *Green / Vert* 22 ●●
INDEX CORIANDER LAVENDER ♂ *Aromatic / Fougère* 78 ●●
INDEX CURRANT MARINE ♂ *Water / Marine* 26 ●●
INDEX FIG APRICOT ♂ *Mossy Woods / Chypre Boisé* 68 ●
INDEX GALBANUM PATCHOULI ♂ *Mossy Woods / Chypre Boisé* 68 ●
INDEX GERANIUM PEPPER ♂ *Aromatic / Fougère* 77 ●●●●
INDEX GRAPEFRUIT MUSC ♂ *Citrus / Hespéridé* 19 ●●●●
INDEX HONEYSUCKLE GRAPEFRUIT ♂ *Citrus / Hespéridé* 18 ●●
INDEX JASMINE LYS ♂ *Floral / Florale* 38 ●
INDEX MANDARINE AMBER ♂ *Mossy Woods / Chypre Boisé* 69 ●●●●
INDEX MOROCCAN MINT TEA ♂ *Citrus / Hespéridé* 18 ●●
INDEX OLIVE MUSCADE ♂ *Mossy Woods / Chypre Boisé* 69 ●●●
INDEX ORANGE CHOCOLATE ♂ *Soft Oriental / Oriental Doux* 52 ●
INDEX PEAR CASSIS ♂ *Floral / Florale* 38 ●
INDEX POMEGRANATE ANISE ♂ *Citrus / Hespéridé* 18 ●
INDEX RED CURRANT BASIL ♂ *Floral / Florale* 38 ●●
INDEX SANDALWOOD PETITGRAIN ♂ *Citrus / Hespéridé* 19 ●●●●
INDEX TOBACCO CARAMEL ♂ *Dry Woods / Boisé Cuir* 73 ●●●
INDEX VIOLET MOSS ♂ *Mossy Woods / Chypre Boisé* 68 ●●
INDEX YLANG-YLANG HIBISCUS ♂ *Floral / Florale* 39 ●●●
INDIGO *Citrus / Hespéridé* 19 ●●●
INIS ♂ *Water / Marine* 26 ●
INSATIABLE* *Aromatic / Fougère* 76 ●
INSENSÉ *Floral / Florale* 38 ●●
INSENSÉ ULTRAMARINE *Aromatic / Fougère* 82 ●
INSTINCT *Aromatic / Fougère* 76 ●●
IQUITOS* *Mossy Woods / Chypre Boisé* 69 ●●●●
IRIS BLEU GRIS *Mossy Woods / Chypre Boisé* 68 ●
IRISCH MOOS / IRISH MOSS *Mossy Woods / Chypre Boisé* 68 ●●

J

JACOMO DE JACOMO *Woody Oriental / Oriental Boisé* 62 ●●
JACQUES FATH → POUR L'HOMME
JADE EAST *Aromatic / Fougère* 77 ●●●
JAGUAR *Aromatic / Fougère* 77 ●●●
JAGUAR MARK II *Woody Oriental / Oriental Boisé* 62 ●●
JAGUAR SPECIAL EDITION *Aromatic / Fougère* 82 ●
JAÏPUR HOMME *Woody Oriental / Oriental Boisé* 62 ●●
JAKO *Woody Oriental / Oriental Boisé* 62 ●●
JARDIN DU NIL *Floral / Florale* 38 ●●
JAZZ *Aromatic / Fougère* 76 ●
JB BLEND *Aromatic / Fougère* 76 ●

JEAN LUC AMSLER HOMME *Water / Marine* 27 ●●●
JEAN LUC AMSLER PRIVÉ HOMME *Dry Woods / Boisé Cuir* 72 ●●
JEAN-MARIE FARINA ♂ *Citrus / Hespéridé* 19 ●●●
J.F. *Aromatic / Fougère* 80 ●
J.H.L.* *Soft Oriental / Oriental Doux* 53 ●●●
JICKY ♂ *Aromatic / Fougère* 77 ●●●
JIL SANDER FEELING MAN *Soft Oriental / Oriental Doux* 52 ●
JIL SANDER MAN III* *Aromatic / Fougère* 82 ●●
JIL SANDER MAN PURE* *Dry Woods / Boisé Cuir* 73 ●●●●
JIMMY'Z *Woody Oriental / Oriental Boisé* 62 ●●
JIVAGO 7 ELEMENTS *Woody Oriental / Oriental Boisé* 62 ●●
JIVAGO 24k MEN *Aromatic / Fougère* 76 ●
JOHNNY LAMBS *Woody Oriental / Oriental Boisé* 62 ●●
JOOP! HOMME *Woody Oriental / Oriental Boisé* 63 ●●●
JORDAN BY MICHAEL *Woody Oriental / Oriental Boisé* 62 ●
JOSEPH ABBOUD *Aromatic / Fougère* 80 ●●
JOVAN MUSK FOR MEN *Soft Floral / Fleuri Aldéhydé* 43 ●●●●
JOVAN WHITE MUSK FOR MEN *Woody Oriental / Oriental Boisé* 62 ●
JULES *Aromatic / Fougère* 77 ●●●●
JUNGLE POUR HOMME *Woody Oriental / Oriental Boisé* 62 ●●

K

KANØN *Woody Oriental / Oriental Boisé* 63 ●●●
KENZO POUR HOMME *Water / Marine* 26 ●
KIPLING *Woody Oriental / Oriental Boisé* 62 ●●
KITON MEN *Mossy Woods / Chypre Boisé* 68 ●
KITON NAPOLI *Woody Oriental / Oriental Boisé* 62 ●
KL HOMME* *Oriental / Oriental* 57 ●●●
KNIZE TEN *Dry Woods / Boisé Cuir* 73 ●●●
KOUROS *Aromatic / Fougère* 77 ●●●●
KOUROS FRAÎCHEUR *Aromatic / Fougère* 78 ●●
KRIZIA UOMO *Dry Woods / Boisé Cuir* 73 ●●●●
KUMQUAT ♂ *Citrus / Hespéridé* 18 ●●
KYRIAZ *Aromatic / Fougère* 80 ●

L

LA BASE FOR HIM *Dry Woods / Boisé Cuir* 73 ●●●●
LACOSTE *Aromatic / Fougère* 78 ●●
LACOSTE 2000 *Aromatic / Fougère* 78 ●
LAGERFELD *Woody Oriental / Oriental Boisé* 63 ●●●
LALIQUE POUR HOMME *Woody Oriental / Oriental Boisé* 62 ●●
LALIQUE POUR HOMME BLEU *Woody Oriental / Oriental Boisé* 62 ●
LAMBORGHINI POUR HOMME *Aromatic / Fougère* 78 ●●
LAMBROSIO *Woody Oriental / Oriental Boisé* 63 ●●●
L'ANARCHISTE *Aromatic / Fougère* 77 ●●●●
LANCETTI MONSIEUR *Dry Woods / Boisé Cuir* 73 ●●●
LANCETTI POUR HOMME *Aromatic / Fougère* 78 ●●
LAND *Woody Oriental / Oriental Boisé* 62 ●
LANVIN L'HOMME *Aromatic / Fougère* 78 ●
LAPIDUS POUR HOMME *Aromatic / Fougère* 77 ●●●●
LATITUDE *Aromatic / Fougère* 76 ●●
LATITUDE LONGTITUDE *Aromatic / Fougère* 76 ●
LATITUDE SPORT *Water / Marine* 27 ●●●
LAUDER FOR MEN *Aromatic / Fougère* 78 ●●
LAUNDROMAT ♂ *Water / Marine* 26 ●
L'AUTRE ♂ *Dry Woods / Boisé Cuir* 73 ●●●●
LAVANDA Myrurgia ♂ *Floral / Florale* 39 ●●●
LAVANDE L'Occitane ♂ *Aromatic / Fougère* 77 ●●●●
LAVANDE Molinard ♂ *Floral / Florale* 39 ●●●●
LAVANDE DES PRINCES L.T. Piver *Floral / Florale* 39 ●●●●
LAVENDER Crabtree & Evelyn ♂ *Floral / Florale* 39 ●●●
LAVENDER Demeter ♂ *Floral / Florale* 39 ●●●
LAVENDER Floris ♂ *Floral / Florale* 39 ●●●
LAVANDE VELOURS Guerlain ♂ *Floral / Florale* 39 ●●●
L'EAU Diptyque ♂ *Soft Oriental / Oriental Doux* 52 ●●
L'EAU DE L'ARTISAN ♂ *Citrus / Hespéridé* 19 ●●●
L'EAU D'ISSEY POUR HOMME *Water / Marine* 27 ●●●
L'EAU DU CAPORAL *Aromatic / Fougère* 77 ●●●●
L'EAU DU NAVAGATEUR *Dry Woods / Boisé Cuir* 73 ●●●●
L'EAU PAR KENZO POUR HOMME *Citrus / Hespéridé* 18 ●●
L'EAU SPORT MEN *Water / Marine* 26 ●●
L'EAU TROIS ♂ *Dry Woods / Boisé Cuir* 72 ●●
LE BLEU *Aromatic / Fougère* 78 ●●
LE DANDY *Dry Woods / Boisé Cuir* 72 ●
LEGENDARY *Dry Woods / Boisé Cuir* 72 ●●

L'ÉGOÏSTE → ÉGOÏSTE
L'ÉGOÏSTE PLATINUM → ÉGOÏSTE PLATINUM
LE MÂLE *Woody Oriental / Oriental Boisé* 62 ●●
LEMON SORBET ♂ *Aromatic / Fougère* 78 ●
LÉONARD POUR HOMME* *Dry Woods / Boisé Cuir* 73 ●●●●
LE PETIT PRINCE *Citrus / Hespéridé* 19 ●●●
LE ROY SOLEIL HOMME *Mossy Woods / Chypre Boisé* 68 ●●
LES COPAINS L'HOMME *Mossy Woods / Chypre Boisé* 68 ●●
LETTUCE ♂ *Green / Vert* 22 ●●
L'HOMME Comptoir Sud Pacifique *Dry Woods / Boisé Cuir* 72 ●●
L'HOMME Roger & Gallet *Aromatic / Fougère* 76 ●●
L'HOMME DE VENTILO *Dry Woods / Boisé Cuir* 73 ●●●●
LIFE ESSENCE *Mossy Woods / Chypre Boisé* 68 ●●
LIGHT HIM *Woody Oriental / Oriental Boisé* 62 ●
LIME, BASIL & MANDARIN ♂ *Citrus / Hespéridé* 19 ●●●●
LIMES Floris ♂ *Citrus / Hespéridé* 19 ●●●●
LIVE JAZZ *Aromatic / Fougère* 82 ●
LOEWE POUR HOMME *Aromatic / Fougère* 82 ●●
LOLITA LEMPICKA AU MASCULIN *Woody Oriental / Oriental Boisé* 62 ●●
LOMANI *Aromatic / Fougère* 76 ●●
LORD MOLYNEUX* *Dry Woods / Boisé Cuir* 72 ●●
LORDS Penhaligon's *Citrus / Hespéridé* 19 ●●●●
L'ORIGINAL *Aromatic / Fougère* 82 ●
LP N° 9 FOR MEN *Woody Oriental / Oriental Boisé* 63 ●●●
LUCE ♂ *Floral / Florale* 39 ●●●
LUCIANO *Aromatic / Fougère* 80 ●
LUCIANO PAVAROTTI *Dry Woods / Boisé Cuir* 73 ●●●
LUCKY BRAND MEN'S* *Aromatic / Fougère* 80 ●
LUCKY YOU FOR MEN *Mossy Woods / Chypre Boisé* 68 ●●
L'UOMO TRUSSARDI *Aromatic / Fougère* 82 ●

M

M *Citrus / Hespéridé* 18 ●●
M de BOURBON *Aromatic / Fougère* 82 ●●
M de M *Soft Oriental / Oriental Doux* 52 ●●
M de MORABITO *Woody Oriental / Oriental Boisé* 63 ●●●●
M pour MONSIEUR *Aromatic / Fougère* 78 ●
MACASSAR *Dry Woods / Boisé Cuir* 73 ●●●●
MACKIE FOR MEN *Aromatic / Fougère* 80 ●
MADRIGAL *Mossy Woods / Chypre Boisé* 68 ●●
MAGOT ♂ *Oriental / Oriental* 56 ●
MÂLE – LE *Woody Oriental / Oriental Boisé* 62 ●●
MAN Herbalife *Aromatic / Fougère* 78 ●
MAN.AUBUSSON *Woody Oriental / Oriental Boisé* 62 ●●
MAN DE RAUCH *Woody Oriental / Oriental Boisé* 63 ●●●●
MANDARINE ♂ *Citrus / Hespéridé* 18 ●●
MANDATE *Aromatic / Fougère* 76 ●●
MANÈS *Woody Oriental / Oriental Boisé* 62 ●●
MANÈS ICE *Aromatic / Fougère* 78 ●
MARBERT GENTLEMAN *Mossy Woods / Chypre Boisé* 68 ●●
MARBERT HOMME *Dry Woods / Boisé Cuir* 72 ●●
MARBERT MAN *Aromatic / Fougère* 82 ●●
MARBERT MAN PURE *Mossy Woods / Chypre Boisé* 68 ●●
MARBERT MAN TOO *Aromatic / Fougère* 80 ●
MARE ♂ *Water / Marine* 26 ●●
MARK II → JAGUAR MARK II
MARK BIRLEY FOR MEN *Dry Woods / Boisé Cuir* 72 ●●
MARQUIS Crown *Aromatic / Fougère* 80 ●
MARQUIS Rémy Marquis *Aromatic / Fougère* 80 ●
MASCULIN ACIER *Aromatic / Fougère* 80 ●●
MASCULIN EQUATEUR *Aromatic / Fougère* 77 ●●●
MASCULIN EVASION *Citrus / Hespéridé* 18 ●●
MASCULIN EXTRÊME *Citrus / Hespéridé* 19 ●●●●
MASCULIN OURAGAN *Woody Oriental / Oriental Boisé* 62 ●●
MASERATI *Aromatic / Fougère* 76 ●●
MAXIM'S POUR HOMME* *Woody Oriental / Oriental Boisé* 63 ●●●●
MCM SUCCESS* *Mossy Woods / Chypre Boisé* 69 ●●●●
MCM 24 EVENING* *Woody Oriental / Oriental Boisé* 63 ●●●
MCM 24 MORNING* *Aromatic / Fougère* 80 ●
MÉCHANT LOUP *Dry Woods / Boisé Cuir* 73 ●●●●
MENNEN SKIN BRACER *Aromatic / Fougère* 77 ●●●
MERGE ♂ *Aromatic / Fougère* 78 ●
MESSE DE MINUIT ♂ *Oriental / Oriental* 57 ●●●●
MESSIRE *Citrus / Hespéridé* 19 ●●●
METAL JEANS MEN *Water / Marine* 26 ●
METROPOLIS *Mossy Woods / Chypre Boisé* 68 ●●

MEXX MAN *Aromatic / Fougère* 76 ●●
MICHAEL JORDAN *Aromatic / Fougère* 76 ●
MILA SCHÖN UOMO *Green / Vert* 23 ●●●●
MILLENNIUM HOPE MAN *Aromatic / Fougère* 82 ●
MILLÉSIME IMPÉRIAL ♂ *Water / Marine* 27 ●●●●
MINOTAURE* *Woody Oriental / Oriental Boisé* 62 ●●
MISSONI SPORT *Citrus / Hespéridé* 19 ●●●●
MISSONI UOMO *Dry Woods / Boisé Cuir* 73 ●●●
MODERN FOR HIM *Aromatic / Fougère* 78 ●●
MOLINARD HOMME I *Aromatic / Fougère* 80 ●●
MOLINARD HOMME II *Woody Oriental / Oriental Boisé* 62 ●
MOLINARD HOMME III *Water / Marine* 27 ●●●
MOLTO SMALTO* *Aromatic / Fougère* 76 ●
MONSIEUR BALMAIN *Citrus / Hespéridé* 19 ●●●●
MONSIEUR CARVEN* *Soft Oriental / Oriental Doux* 52 ●●
MONSIEUR DE GIVENCHY *Citrus / Hespéridé* 19 ●●●
MONSIEUR LÉONARD *Aromatic / Fougère* 77 ●●●●
MONSIEUR MORABITO *Aromatic / Fougère* 82 ●
MONSIEUR MUSK *Oriental / Oriental* 57 ●●●●
MONSIEUR ROCHAS *Aromatic / Fougère* 77 ●●●
MONTANA POUR HOMME *Woody Oriental / Oriental Boisé* 62 ●●
MONTECRISTO *Dry Woods / Boisé Cuir* 72 ●●
MOODS UOMO* *Woody Oriental / Oriental Boisé* 63 ●●●
MOSCHINO POUR HOMME *Dry Woods / Boisé Cuir* 72 ●●
MOUCHOIR DE MONSIEUR *Aromatic / Fougère* 77 ●●●
MOUSTACHE *Mossy Woods / Chypre Boisé* 68 ●●
MOVES → ADIDAS MOVES
MR J *Aromatic / Fougère* 78 ●●
MUKKI ♂ *Soft Floral / Fleuri Aldéhydé* 42 ●●
MULBERRY FOR MEN *Dry Woods / Boisé Cuir* 72 ●●
MUSK FOR MEN Coty → COTY MUSK FOR MEN
MUSK FOR MEN Jovan → JOVAN MUSK FOR MEN
MUST DE CARTIER POUR HOMME
  Woody Oriental / Oriental Boisé 63 ●●●

N

NATURE SYSTEM ♂ *Citrus / Hespéridé* 18 ●●
NAUTICA *Water / Marine* 26 ●
NAUTICA COMPETITION *Woody Oriental / Oriental Boisé* 62 ●●
NAUTILUS AQUA *Water / Marine* 27 ●●●●
NAVEGAR *Citrus / Hespéridé* 19 ●●●●
NAVIGATOR *Aromatic / Fougère* 78 ●
NAVY FOR MEN *Aromatic / Fougère* 80 ●
NAZARENO GABRIELLI POUR HOMME *Aromatic / Fougère* 78 ●
NAZARENO POUR HOMME *Aromatic / Fougère* 80 ●●
NEIGES POUR HOMME *Citrus / Hespéridé* 18 ●●
NEMO *Woody Oriental / Oriental Boisé* 62 ●●
NÉROLI SAUVAGE *Citrus / Hespéridé* 19 ●●●●
NETWORK ♂ *Citrus / Hespéridé* 18 ●
NEW WEST FOR HIM* *Water / Marine* 27 ●●●●
NEW YORK *Woody Oriental / Oriental Boisé* 62 ●●
NIAGARA *Dry Woods / Boisé Cuir* 72 ●●
NICKI LAUDA *Aromatic / Fougère* 78 ●●
NICOLE MILLER FOR MEN *Woody Oriental / Oriental Boisé* 62 ●●
NIGHTFLIGHT *Aromatic / Fougère* 80 ●
NIKE *Aromatic / Fougère* 80 ●
NINO CERRUTI *Green / Vert* 23 ●●●●
NK *Aromatic / Fougère* 82 ●
NOIR *Dry Woods / Boisé Cuir* 73 ●●●
NOI UOMINI *Citrus / Hespéridé* 18 ●
NOMAD *Aromatic / Fougère* 80 ●
N° 89 *Aromatic / Fougère* 77 ●●●
NUTMEG & GINGER ♂ *Woody Oriental / Oriental Boisé* 62 ●●

O

Ô pour HOMME *Green / Vert* 22 ●●
OBSESSION FOR MEN *Woody Oriental / Oriental Boisé* 62 ●
ODEUR 53 ♂ *Water / Marine* 26 ●●
ODEUR 71 ♂ *Dry Woods / Boisé Cuir* 72 ●
OLD SPICE *Soft Oriental / Oriental Doux* 53 ●●●
OLD SPICE WHITEWATER *Aromatic / Fougère* 80 ●●
OLYMPIOS *Aromatic / Fougère* 78 ●
OM ♂ *Woody Oriental / Oriental Boisé* 63 ●●●
OMAR SHARIF POUR HOMME* *Aromatic / Fougère* 80 ●●
ON AIR HOMME *Aromatic / Fougère* 76 ●

ONE MAN SHOW *Dry Woods / Boisé Cuir* 73 ●●●●
ONLY FOR MEN *Aromatic / Fougère* 77 ●●●
OPEN *Aromatic / Fougère* 82 ●●
OPERA IV *Mossy Woods / Chypre Boisé* 68 ●●
OPIUM POUR HOMME *Woody Oriental / Oriental Boisé* 62 ●●
OPÔNÉ ♂ *Mossy Woods / Chypre Boisé* 69 ●●●
OPPORTUNE / PERIPHERY *Woody Oriental / Oriental Boisé* 62 ●
ORANGE SPICE ♂ *Aromatic / Fougère* 82 ●●
ORIGINAL – L' *Aromatic / Fougère* 82 ●
ORPHÉE ♂ *Aromatic / Fougère* 80 ●●
OSCAR DE LA RENTA POUR LUI *Dry Woods / Boisé Cuir* 72 ●●
OSCAR FOR MEN *Dry Woods / Boisé Cuir* 72 ●●
O₂XYGEN *Citrus / Hespéridé* 18 ●
OYÉDO ♂ *Citrus / Hespéridé* 19 ●●●●
O•ZONE MAN *Citrus / Hespéridé* 19 ●●●●

P

π *Woody Oriental / Oriental Boisé* 63 ●●●
PACO ♂ *Citrus / Hespéridé* 18 ●
PACO ENERGY ♂ *Citrus / Hespéridé* 18 ●●
PACO RABANNE POUR HOMME *Aromatic / Fougère* 78 ●●
PALAIS JAMAIS ♂ *Dry Woods / Boisé Cuir* 73 ●●●●
PAMPLELUNE ♂ *Citrus / Hespéridé* 19 ●●●●
PAMPLEMOUSSE ♂ *Citrus / Hespéridé* 18 ●●
PARADOX FOR MEN *Woody Oriental / Oriental Boisé* 62 ●
PARFUM D'HABIT *Dry Woods / Boisé Cuir* 73 ●●●●
PARFUM D'HOMME *Aromatic / Fougère* 78 ●●
PASHA *Aromatic / Fougère* 78 ●●
PASSION D'HOMME *Woody Oriental / Oriental Boisé* 62 ●●
PASSION FOR MEN *Woody Oriental / Oriental Boisé* 63 ●●●
PATCHOULI Crabtree *Woody Oriental / Oriental Boisé* 62 ●●
PATCHOULI L'Artisan Parfumeur ♂ *Citrus / Hespéridé* 19 ●●●●
PATCHOULI Molinard ♂ *Mossy Woods / Chypre Boisé* 69 ●●●
PATCHOULY Etro ♂ *Woody Oriental / Oriental Boisé* 63 ●●●
PATOU POUR HOMME *Woody Oriental / Oriental Boisé* 63 ●●●
PATOU POUR HOMME PRIVÉ *Aromatic / Fougère* 77 ●●●
PAUL SMITH MEN *Aromatic / Fougère* 80 ●●
PEN DUICK *Aromatic / Fougère* 82 ●
PENHALIGON'S CASTILE ♂ *Citrus / Hespéridé* 19 ●●●
PENNY BLACK *Aromatic / Fougère* 80 ●●
PEOPLE UOMO *Woody Oriental / Oriental Boisé* 62 ●
PERIPHERY / OPPORTUNE *Woody Oriental / Oriental Boisé* 62 ●
PERRY ELLIS FOR MEN *Dry Woods / Boisé Cuir* 73 ●●●
PERRY ELLIS PORTFOLIO FOR MEN *Aromatic / Fougère* 76 ●
PERRY ELLIS RESERVE *Aromatic / Fougère* 80 ●
PERSONALITY *Aromatic / Fougère* 77 ●●●●
PETIT GUERLAIN ♂ *Citrus / Hespéridé* 19 ●●●
PETIT PRINCE – LE *Citrus / Hespéridé* 19 ●●●
PHAROS *Aromatic / Fougère* 80 ●
PHEROMONE FOR MEN *Dry Woods / Boisé Cuir* 72 ●●
PHILOSYKOS ♂ *Mossy Woods / Chypre Boisé* 68 ●
PHOTO *Aromatic / Fougère* 78 ●●
PIAZZA DI SPAGNA UOMO *Aromatic / Fougère* 82 ●
PIERRE CARDIN POUR MONSIEUR *Soft Oriental / Oriental Doux* 52 ●
PIERRE CARDIN MUSK* *Aromatic / Fougère* 77 ●●●●
PINO SILVESTRE EXTREME *Citrus / Hespéridé* 19 ●●●●
PINO SILVESTRE ORIGINAL *Mossy Woods / Chypre Boisé* 69 ●●●
PINSTRIPE *Aromatic / Fougère* 76 ●
PIROGUIER *Dry Woods / Boisé Cuir* 73 ●●●
PLEASURES FOR MEN *Aromatic / Fougère* 80 ●
POLICE *Aromatic / Fougère* 77 ●●●
POLO *Dry Woods / Boisé Cuir* 72 ●●
POLO CREST *Dry Woods / Boisé Cuir* 72 ●●
POLO SPORT *Aromatic / Fougère* 82 ●
POLO SPORT EXTREME *Dry Woods / Boisé Cuir* 72 ●●
PONTACCIO 21 *Dry Woods / Boisé Cuir* 72 ●●
POUR L'HOMME Jacques Fath *Woody Oriental / Oriental Boisé* 62 ●●
POUR L'HOMME Roger & Gallet *Citrus / Hespéridé* 18 ●●
POUR MONSIEUR → CHANEL POUR MONSIEUR
POUR UN HOMME Caron *Floral / Florale* 39 ●●●●
PREFERRED STOCK *Aromatic / Fougère* 76 ●
PRESSURE *Aromatic / Fougère* 82 ●●
PRIVATE NUMBER FOR MEN* *Mossy Woods / Chypre Boisé* 68 ●●
PROFUMO DI MONTECATINI ♂ *Water / Marine* 27 ●●●
PRUNING SHEARS ♂ *Floral / Florale* 38 ●
PS *Soft Oriental / Oriental Doux* 53 ●●●

PUB   *Aromatic / Fougère*   77 ●●●
PUMA CHALLENGE   *Aromatic / Fougère*   80 ●●
PUMA INDEPENDENCE   *Aromatic / Fougère*   82 ●
PURE VÉTIVER   *Mossy Woods / Chypre Boisé*   68 ●●

Q

QUARTZ POUR HOMME   *Citrus / Hespéridé*   18 ●●
QUASAR   *Aromatic / Fougère*   82 ●
QUERCUS ♂   *Citrus / Hespéridé*   18 ●
QUORUM   *Dry Woods / Boisé Cuir*   72 ●●

R

R Révillon   *Mossy Woods / Chypre Boisé*   68 ●
R de CAPUCCI*   *Aromatic / Fougère*   78 ●
RACINE ♂   *Mossy Woods / Chypre Boisé*   68 ●●
RACQUETS FORMULA   *Aromatic / Fougère*   77 ●●●
RAFALE   *Aromatic / Fougère*   78 ●●
RÄKS   *Aromatic / Fougère*   78 ●●
RAPPORT   *Aromatic / Fougère*   78 ●●
RAW VANILLA   *Woody Oriental / Oriental Boisé*   62 ●
REALM MEN   *Woody Oriental / Oriental Boisé*   62 ●●
REBEL ... JAMES DEAN   *Aromatic / Fougère*   80 ●
REBEL MEN   *Aromatic / Fougère*   78 ●●
RED FOR MEN   *Aromatic / Fougère*   78 ●●
RÉGINE'S FOR MEN   *Woody Oriental / Oriental Boisé*   62 ●
RELAX   *Woody Oriental / Oriental Boisé*   62 ●●
RÉMY   *Woody Oriental / Oriental Boisé*   62 ●●
REPLAY   *Woody Oriental / Oriental Boisé*   62 ●
REYNALD KATZ ♂   *Citrus / Hespéridé*   18 ●
RICCI-CLUB   *Woody Oriental / Oriental Boisé*   62 ●●
RICHARDSON BAY ♂   *Green / Vert*   22 ●
RIZIÈRES ♂   *Mossy Woods / Chypre Boisé*   69 ●●●
ROBERTA DI CAMERINO POUR HOMME   *Aromatic / Fougère*   76 ●
ROCABAR   *Dry Woods / Boisé Cuir*   73 ●●●●
ROCCOBAROCCO*   *Aromatic / Fougère*   77 ●●●●
ROCHAS MAN   *Woody Oriental / Oriental Boisé*   62 ●●
ROGER & GALLET   ➙ POUR L'HOMME
ROGER & GALLET EXTRA-VIEILLE ♂   *Citrus / Hespéridé*   19 ●●●
ROI SANTAL   *Woody Oriental / Oriental Boisé*   63 ●●●
ROLAND GARROS   *Aromatic / Fougère*   78 ●
ROMANCE MEN   *Aromatic / Fougère*   80 ●
ROMA UOMO   *Woody Oriental / Oriental Boisé*   62 ●●
ROMEO GIGLI PER UOMO   ➙ GIGLI PER UOMO
ROOTS FOR HIM   *Water / Marine*   26 ●●
ROOTS UNISCENT ♂   *Water / Marine*   26 ●
ROUTE 66   *Aromatic / Fougère*   78 ●●
ROUTE 66 COLORADO RAIN   *Aromatic / Fougère*   76 ●
ROUTE DU THÉ ♂   *Citrus / Hespéridé*   18 ●
ROUTE DU VÉTIVER   *Mossy Woods / Chypre Boisé*   69 ●●●
ROYAL BAIN DE CHAMPAGNE ♂   *Soft Oriental / Oriental Doux*   52 ●
ROYAL COPENHAGEN   *Woody Oriental / Oriental Boisé*   63 ●●●
ROYAL COPENHAGEN MUSK   *Soft Oriental / Oriental Doux*   53 ●●●●
ROYAL COPENHAGEN SPORT*   *Aromatic / Fougère*   82 ●
ROYAL DELIGHT ♂   *Soft Oriental / Oriental Doux*   53 ●●●●
ROYAL ENGLISH LEATHER   *Dry Woods / Boisé Cuir*   73 ●●●
ROYAL GREEN   *Aromatic / Fougère*   80 ●
ROYAL PAVILLON ♂   *Floral / Florale*   38 ●●
ROYAL SCOTTISH LAVENDER   *Floral / Florale*   39 ●●●
ROYAL SECRET FOR MEN*   *Woody Oriental / Oriental Boisé*   62 ●●
ROYAL WATER   *Aromatic / Fougère*   77 ●●●●
ROY SOLEIL HOMME – LE   *Mossy Woods / Chypre Boisé*   68 ●●
RYKIEL HOMME   *Aromatic / Fougère*   82 ●

S

S pour HOMME   *Woody Oriental / Oriental Boisé*   62 ●
SABLES   *Woody Oriental / Oriental Boisé*   62 ●●
SAFARI FOR MEN   *Aromatic / Fougère*   76 ●
SAFRANIER   *Woody Oriental / Oriental Boisé*   62 ●●
SALVADOR   *Aromatic / Fougère*   82 ●●
SALVADOR DALI POUR HOMME   *Woody Oriental / Oriental Boisé*   62 ●●
SALVATORE FERRAGAMO POUR HOMME
   Mossy Woods / Chypre Boisé   68 ●
SAMBA FOR MEN   *Citrus / Hespéridé*   19 ●●●●
SAMBA HEAT MAN   *Woody Oriental / Oriental Boisé*   62 ●

SAMBA NATURAL MAN   *Aromatic / Fougère*   82 ●
SAMBA NOVA HOMME   *Woody Oriental / Oriental Boisé*   62 ●●
SAMBA RED MAN   *Mossy Woods / Chypre Boisé*   68 ●●
SAMOURAÏ   *Soft Oriental / Oriental Doux*   52 ●
SANDALO ♂   *Woody Oriental / Oriental Boisé*   63 ●●●●
SANDALWOOD Crabtree & Evelyn   63 ●●●
   Woody Oriental / Oriental Boisé   63 ●●●
SANDALWOOD Yardley ♂   *Woody Oriental / Oriental Boisé*   63 ●●●
SANDER FOR MEN   *Aromatic / Fougère*   78 ●●
SANDRINGHAM   *Woody Oriental / Oriental Boisé*   63 ●●●
SANGUINE MUSKISSIME ♂   *Citrus / Hespéridé*   18 ●
SANTA FE FOR MEN   *Woody Oriental / Oriental Boisé*   62 ●
SANTAL L'Artisan Parfumeur   *Dry Woods / Boisé Cuir*   73 ●●●
SANTAL IMPÉRIAL ♂   *Woody Oriental / Oriental Boisé*   63 ●●●
SANTAL NOBLE   *Mossy Woods / Chypre Boisé*   69 ●●●●
SANTOS   *Aromatic / Fougère*   78 ●●
SANTOS EAU DE SPORT   *Citrus / Hespéridé*   19 ●●●●
SAWDUST ♂   *Mossy Woods / Chypre Boisé*   69 ●●●
SCAPA POUR HOMME*   *Aromatic / Fougère*   78 ●●
SCOTT McCLINTOCK   *Soft Oriental / Oriental Doux*   52 ●
SCULPTURE HOMME   *Woody Oriental / Oriental Boisé*   62 ●●
SEAWARD   *Dry Woods / Boisé Cuir*   72 ●●
SECRET MÉLANGE   *Aromatic / Fougère*   76 ●
SÉLECTION VERTE   *Citrus / Hespéridé*   18 ●●
SERGIO TACCHINI   *Aromatic / Fougère*   76 ●
SERGIO TACCHINI SPORT EXTREME*   *Aromatic / Fougère*   82 ●
SERGIO TACCHINI UOMO   *Aromatic / Fougère*   78 ●●
SÉXUAL POUR HOMME   *Woody Oriental / Oriental Boisé*   62 ●●
SHAAL NUR ♂   *Woody Oriental / Oriental Boisé*   63 ●●●●
SHU UEMURA 029 ♂   *Aromatic / Fougère*   82 ●
SIENNA   *Mossy Woods / Chypre Boisé*   68 ●●
SIESTE   *Dry Woods / Boisé Cuir*   73 ●●●
SIGNATURE POUR HOMME   *Woody Oriental / Oriental Boisé*   62 ●
SIGNORICCI   *Citrus / Hespéridé*   19 ●●●
SILVER*   *Aromatic / Fougère*   77 ●●●
SILVER JEANS HOMME   *Aromatic / Fougère*   76 ●
SILVER LIGHT   *Citrus / Hespéridé*   18 ●
SILVER MOUNTAIN WATER   *Water / Marine*   26 ●●
SILVESTRE   *Mossy Woods / Chypre Boisé*   69 ●●●
SIROCCO UOMO   *Woody Oriental / Oriental Boisé*   62 ●●
SMALTO   *Mossy Woods / Chypre Boisé*   68 ●●
SNOW ♂   *Mossy Woods / Chypre Boisé*   68 ●●
SOCIETY GENTLEMEN   *Aromatic / Fougère*   78 ●
SO HIM   *Aromatic / Fougère*   82 ●
SOLO SOPRANI ♂   *Citrus / Hespéridé*   18 ●
SOLO SOPRANI BLU ♂   *Aromatic / Fougère*   76 ●
SO MAX   *Aromatic / Fougère*   78 ●
SOPRANI ACTIVE MAN   *Aromatic / Fougère*   80 ●●
SOUL   *Aromatic / Fougère*   80 ●
SPAZIO KRIZIA UOMO   *Dry Woods / Boisé Cuir*   72 ●●
SPECIAL N° 127 ♂   *Citrus / Hespéridé*   19 ●●●
SPORT 2000   *Aromatic / Fougère*   76 ●
SPORT DE PACO RABANNE   *Citrus / Hespéridé*   18 ●●
SPORTIF   *Aromatic / Fougère*   80 ●
SPORT SPIRIT   ➙ ESCADA SPORT SPIRIT
SPRINGFIELD   *Dry Woods / Boisé Cuir*   72 ●
STATEMENT FOR MEN*   *Aromatic / Fougère*   78 ●
S.T.DUPONT HOMME   *Dry Woods / Boisé Cuir*   73 ●●●●
STETSON   *Woody Oriental / Oriental Boisé*   63 ●●●
STETSON COUNTRY   *Mossy Woods / Chypre Boisé*   68 ●●
STETSON SIERRA   *Aromatic / Fougère*   78 ●
SUD EST   *Aromatic / Fougère*   82 ●
SUGAR ♂   *Citrus / Hespéridé*   18 ●●
SUGAR COOKIE ♂   *Soft Oriental / Oriental Doux*   52 ●●
SUMARE   *Citrus / Hespéridé*   19 ●●●●
SUMATRA RAIN MEN   *Aromatic / Fougère*   80 ●●
SUMATRA RAIN FRESH   *Aromatic / Fougère*   78 ●
SUMATRA RAIN WOOD   *Woody Oriental / Oriental Boisé*   62 ●●
SUNG HOMME   *Aromatic / Fougère*   78 ●●
SWISH   *Aromatic / Fougère*   78 ●
SWISS ARMY   *Aromatic / Fougère*   80 ●
SYBARIS   *Woody Oriental / Oriental Boisé*   62 ●●

T

TABAC ORIGINAL (Aftershave)   *Aromatic / Fougère*   78 ●●
TABAC ORIGINAL (EdC)   *Soft Floral / Fleuri Aldéhydé*   42 ●●

TABAC EXTREME *Aromatic / Fougère* 78 ●
TABAC MAN *Aromatic / Fougère* 77 ●●●●
TABAROME *Dry Woods / Boisé Cuir* 73 ●●●●
TACTICS *Green / Vert* 23 ●●●●
TÉ ♂ *Citrus / Hespéridé* 18 ●
TECK *Dry Woods / Boisé Cuir* 73 ●●●
TED *Woody Oriental / Oriental Boisé* 62 ●●
TED BAKER SKINWEAR *Citrus / Hespéridé* 19 ●●●●
TEMPORE UOMO *Woody Oriental / Oriental Boisé* 62 ●
TENAZ *Aromatic / Fougère* 77 ●●●●
TÉNÉRÉ *Floral / Florale* 39 ●●●●
THAT MAN *Citrus / Hespéridé* 19 ●●●●
THAT'S AMORE! LUI *Woody Oriental / Oriental Boisé* 62 ●
THÉ ♂ *Woody Oriental / Oriental Boisé* 63 ●●●
THEOREMA UOMO *Mossy Woods / Chypre Boisé* 68 ●●
THÉ POUR UN ÉTÉ ♂ *Citrus / Hespéridé* 18 ●
THÉ VERT ♂ *Citrus / Hespéridé* 18 ●●
THIRD MAN / 3ᵉ HOMME / N° 3 *Aromatic / Fougère* 77 ●●●●
THIS IS NOT A PIPE ♂ *Dry Woods / Boisé Cuir* 73 ●●●
TIFFANY FOR MEN *Woody Oriental / Oriental Boisé* 63 ●●●
TIFFANY FOR MEN SPORT *Green / Vert* 22 ●
TILLEUL ♂ *Floral / Florale* 38 ●
TIMBERLINE *Mossy Woods / Chypre Boisé* 69 ●●●
TOMATO ♂ *Green / Vert* 22 ●●
TOMMY *Aromatic / Fougère* 78 ●
TOUCHDOWN Mäurer & Wirtz *Dry Woods / Boisé Cuir* 72 ●●
TOUCH DOWN My Very Own *Aromatic / Fougère* 82 ●
TOUCH FOR MEN → BURBERRY TOUCH FOR MEN
TOUCH FOR MEN Fred Hayman* *Aromatic / Fougère* 77 ●●●
TOUCH GRIGIOPERLA *Woody Oriental / Oriental Boisé* 62 ●
TOWN & COUNTRY *Mossy Woods / Chypre Boisé* 68 ●●
TRISTAN *Dry Woods / Boisé Cuir* 73 ●●●●
TROPHÉE LANCÔME* *Citrus / Hespéridé* 19 ●●●●
TRUSSARDI UOMO FRESH *Dry Woods / Boisé Cuir* 72 ●●
TSAR *Aromatic / Fougère* 78 ●
TUSCANY PER UOMO *Aromatic / Fougère* 78 ●
TWENTY ONE ♂ *Citrus / Hespéridé* 19 ●●●●
TYCOON *Woody Oriental / Oriental Boisé* 62 ●●

 **U**

U de V Ulric de Varens *Aromatic / Fougère* 78 ●
U de V FUN *Aromatic / Fougère* 80 ●
U de V N° 2 *Woody Oriental / Oriental Boisé* 62 ●●
ULYSSE *Woody Oriental / Oriental Boisé* 62 ●
UN AIR DE JAVA *Mossy Woods / Chypre Boisé* 68 ●●
UNGARO POUR L'HOMME III *Aromatic / Fougère* 78 ●
UNIVERSO *Aromatic / Fougère* 78 ●
UOMO Compagnia Delle Indie *Mossy Woods / Chypre Boisé* 68 ●
UOMO? MOSCHINO *Woody Oriental / Oriental Boisé* 62 ●
UOMO TRUSSARDI – L' *Aromatic / Fougère* 82 ●

V

VAN CLEEF & ARPELS POUR HOMME
    Dry Woods / Boisé Cuir 73 ●●●●
VANDERBILT FOR MEN *Woody Oriental / Oriental Boisé* 62 ●
VAN GILS *Aromatic / Fougère* 77 ●●●●
VANILLE L'Occitane ♂ *Soft Oriental / Oriental Doux* 53 ●●●
VANILLE CAFÉ ♂ *Oriental / Oriental* 57 ●●●
VANITECK *Dry Woods / Boisé Cuir* 73 ●●●●
VENDETTA POUR HOMME* *Dry Woods / Boisé Cuir* 72 ●●
VENEZIA UOMO* *Woody Oriental / Oriental Boisé* 62 ●●
VERBENAS OF PROVENCE ♂ *Citrus / Hespéridé* 19 ●●●
VERDI 800 *Woody Oriental / Oriental Boisé* 63 ●●●
VERINO POUR HOMME *Aromatic / Fougère* 78 ●●
VERSACE L'HOMME *Woody Oriental / Oriental Boisé* 63 ●●●
VERSAILLES *Oriental / Oriental* 56 ●●
VERSION HOMME* *Mossy Woods / Chypre Boisé* 68 ●●
VERSUS UOMO* *Woody Oriental / Oriental Boisé* 62 ●
VERVEINE Le Jardin Retrouvé ♂ *Citrus / Hespéridé* 19 ●●●
VERVEINE Molinard *Citrus / Hespéridé* 19 ●●●
VERY M.C. ♂ *Citrus / Hespéridé* 18 ●
VERY VALENTINO POUR HOMME *Woody Oriental / Oriental Boisé* 62 ●●
VÉTIVER Annick Goutal *Dry Woods / Boisé Cuir* 73 ●●●
VÉTIVER Carven *Mossy Woods / Chypre Boisé* 69 ●●●
VETIVER Creed *Mossy Woods / Chypre Boisé* 69 ●●●

VETIVER Etro ♂ *Dry Woods / Boisé Cuir* 73 ●●●
VETIVER Floris *Mossy Woods / Chypre Boisé* 69 ●●●
VETIVER Guerlain *Mossy Woods / Chypre Boisé* 69 ●●●
VETIVER L'Artisan Parfumeur *Dry Woods / Boisé Cuir* 72 ●
VÉTIVER DRY Carven* *Aromatic / Fougère* 80 ●●
VETIVER HOMBRE *Mossy Woods / Chypre Boisé* 68 ●●
VETYVER Jo Malone ♂ *Mossy Woods / Chypre Boisé* 68 ●●
VÉTYVER Le Jardin Retrouvé → EAU DE VÉTYVER
VÉTYVER L.T. Piver *Mossy Woods / Chypre Boisé* 69 ●●●
VETYVER Molinard *Mossy Woods / Chypre Boisé* 69 ●●●
VÉTYVER Roger & Gallet *Mossy Woods / Chypre Boisé* 69 ●●●
VETYVER HAITI ♂ *Mossy Woods / Chypre Boisé* 68 ●●
VICOLO FIORI ♂ *Floral Oriental / Fleuri Oriental* 48 ●
VIE DE CHATEAU (CHEVERNY) ♂ *Mossy Woods / Chypre Boisé* 69 ●●●
VIKING *Aromatic / Fougère* 80 ●
VIRGILIO ♂ *Green / Vert* 22 ●●
VOLCANO HOMME *Aromatic / Fougère* 82 ●
VOLEUR DE ROSES ♂ *Dry Woods / Boisé Cuir* 72 ●
VORAGO *Aromatic / Fougère* 78 ●●
VORAGO ACTION *Citrus / Hespéridé* 19 ●●●
VOYAGEUR *Mossy Woods / Chypre Boisé* 68 ●
VUARNET *Aromatic / Fougère* 78 ●
V/S MAN *Woody Oriental / Oriental Boisé* 62 ●

 **W**

WATERPERRY GENTLEMEN *Aromatic / Fougère* 78 ●
WATT FOR MEN BLUE *Aromatic / Fougère* 78 ●●
WATT FOR MEN GREEN *Woody Oriental / Oriental Boisé* 62 ●●
WEEK END FOR MEN → BURBERRY WEEK END FOR MEN
WEIL EAU DE FRAÎCHEUR ♂ *Citrus / Hespéridé* 18 ●
WEIL POUR HOMME *Aromatic / Fougère* 82 ●●
WHAT ABOUT ADAM *Aromatic / Fougère* 80 ●
WILD WIND FOR MEN *Aromatic / Fougère* 78 ●
WILKES SAN FRANCISCO ♂ *Aromatic / Fougère* 78 ●
WINGS FOR MEN *Aromatic / Fougère* 80 ●
WORTH POUR HOMME *Aromatic / Fougère* 78 ●●

 **X**

X *Woody Oriental / Oriental Boisé* 62 ●
X LIMITED ♂ *Citrus / Hespéridé* 18 ●
XERYUS *Aromatic / Fougère* 78 ●●
XERYUS ROUGE *Woody Oriental / Oriental Boisé* 62 ●●
XS POUR HOMME *Aromatic / Fougère* 78 ●
XXL Hechter *Woody Oriental / Oriental Boisé* 62 ●

 **Y**

YANG *Woody Oriental / Oriental Boisé* 62 ●
YARDLEY ORIGINAL *Aromatic / Fougère* 80 ●
YATAGAN *Dry Woods / Boisé Cuir* 73 ●●●●
YES FOR MEN *Oriental / Oriental* 56 ●●
YOHJI HOMME *Aromatic / Fougère* 77 ●●●●
YOU'RE THE FIRE FOR MEN *Dry Woods / Boisé Cuir* 73 ●●●
YSL POUR HOMME *Citrus / Hespéridé* 19 ●●●●

 **Z**

Z-14 → HALSTON Z-14
ZAHAROFF POUR HOMME *Woody Oriental / Oriental Boisé* 63 ●●●●
ZEGNA *Aromatic / Fougère* 78 ●●
ZESTE MANDARINE PAMPLEMOUSSE ♂ *Citrus / Hespéridé* 19 ●●●●
ZINO DAVIDOFF *Woody Oriental / Oriental Boisé* 63 ●●●●
ZIPPED *Citrus / Hespéridé* 18 ●●
ZIPPED SPORTS *Aromatic / Fougère* 80 ●
ZIPPED UNIVERSE *Woody Oriental / Oriental Boisé* 62 ●●
ZIZANIE *Woody Oriental / Oriental Boisé* 63 ●●●

ACQUA DI PARMA
1916 ACQUA DI PARMA COLONIA ♂ *Citrus / Hespéridé* 17 ●●●
1999 ACQUA DI PARMA LAVANDA TONICA ♂ *Floral / Florale* 31 ●●●
2000 ACQUA DI PARMA PROFUMO *Mossy Woods / Chypre Boisé* 67 ●●●

ADIDAS
1988/97 ADIDAS WOMAN *Floral / Florale* 34 ●
1997 ADIDAS WOMAN SPORT *Floral / Florale* 32 ●
2000 ADIDAS MOVES FOR HER *Aromatic / Fougère* 76 ●
2000 ADIDAS WOMAN ACTIVE *Floral / Florale* 32 ●
2000 ADIDAS WOMAN ENERGY *Floral / Florale* 36 ●
2000 ADIDAS WOMAN FITNESS *Floral / Florale* 34 ●
1986 ADIDAS CLASSIC *Dry Woods / Boisé Cuir* 72 ●●
1990 ADIDAS ACTIVE BODIES *Aromatic / Fougère* 76 ●●
1992 ADIDAS ADVENTURE *Aromatic / Fougère* 82 ●●
1994 ADIDAS SPORT *Citrus / Hespéridé* 18 ●●
1997 ADIDAS DYNAMIC *Aromatic / Fougère* 82 ●
1998 ADIDAS ACTION *Aromatic / Fougère* 80 ●
1999 ADIDAS MOVES *Aromatic / Fougère* 80 ●
2000 ADIDAS TEAM *Aromatic / Fougère* 80 ●

ADOLFO DOMINGUEZ
1995 AGUA FRESCA DE ROSAS *Floral / Florale* 30 ●●
1999 ALEGRIA *Floral / Florale* 32 ●●
1991 ADOLFO DOMINGUEZ* *Aromatic / Fougère* 80 ●
1996 AGUA FRESCA *Mossy Woods / Chypre Boisé* 69 ●●●
1998 VETIVER HOMBRE *Mossy Woods / Chypre Boisé* 68 ●●
2000 ALEGRIA HOMBRE *Water / Marine* 26 ●●

ADRIENNE VITTADINI
1994 AV *Floral / Florale* 36 ●●
1999 ADRIENNE VITTADINI *Oriental / Oriental* 56 ●

AGENT PROVOCATEUR
2000 AGENT PROVOCATEUR *Mossy Woods / Chypre Boisé* 67 ●●●

AIGNER → ETIENNE AIGNER

ALAIN DELON
1981 LE TEMPS D'AIMER *Mossy Woods / Chypre Boisé* 67 ●●●
1993 LYRA *Oriental / Oriental* 57 ●●●
1995 LYRA 2 *Woody Oriental / Oriental Boisé* 60 ●●
1996 IQUITA* *Mossy Woods / Chypre Boisé* 66 ●●
1998 LYRA 3 *Floral / Florale* 32 ●
2001 SAMOURAÏ WOMAN *Floral / Florale* 34 ●●
1987 IQUITOS* *Mossy Woods / Chypre Boisé* 69 ●●●●
1995 SAMOURAÏ *Soft Oriental / Oriental Doux* 52 ●●
1997 EAU DE SPORT* *Aromatic / Fougère* 78 ●●
1997 PHAROS *Aromatic / Fougère* 80 ●
2000 ALAIN DELON POUR HOMME *Aromatic / Fougère* 76 ●

ALBERTA FERRETTI
1993 FEMINA* *Floral / Florale* 36 ●

ALEXANDER JULIAN
1992 WOMENSWEAR *Soft Floral / Fleuri Aldéhydé* 42 ●●
1993 COLORS *Soft Floral / Fleuri Aldéhydé* 42 ●

ALEXANDRA DE MARKOFF
1972 ENIGMA *Woody Oriental / Oriental Boisé* 61 ●●●
1979 ALEXANDRA *Soft Oriental / Oriental Doux* 53 ●●●
1994 NO REGRETS *Floral / Florale* 38 ●●

ALFRED DUNHILL
1934 DUNHILL *Dry Woods / Boisé Cuir* 73 ●●●
1985 DUNHILL EDITION *Aromatic / Fougère* 82 ●●
1996 D *Aromatic / Fougère* 80 ●
2000 DESIRE *Woody Oriental / Oriental Boisé* 62 ●

ALFRED SUNG
1986 SUNG *Floral / Florale* 38 ●
1990 E.N.C.O.R.E *Woody Oriental / Oriental Boisé* 60 ●
1992 SUNG SPA *Green / Vert* 22 ●
1995 FOREVER *Floral / Florale* 36 ●
1997 PURE *Floral / Florale* 34 ●
2000 PURE MOMENT *Floral Oriental / Fleuri Oriental* 46 ●
2000 SHI *Floral / Florale* 34 ●

1988 SUNG HOMME *Aromatic / Fougère* 78 ●●

ALVIERO MARTINI
1997 ALVIERO MARTINI DONNA *Floral Oriental / Fleuri Oriental* 46 ●
1997 ALVIERO MARTINI UOMO *Aromatic / Fougère* 80 ●

ALYSSA ASHLEY (a selection *un choix*)
1992 ALYSSA ASHLEY MUSK *Soft Floral / Fleuri Aldéhydé* 43 ●●●●
1996 ALYSSA ASHLEY VANILLA *Woody Oriental / Oriental Boisé* 60 ●

AMOUAGE
1983 AMOUAGE *Soft Floral / Fleuri Aldéhydé* 43 ●●●●
1995 UBAR *Mossy Woods / Chypre Boisé* 67 ●●●
1983 AMOUAGE GENTLEMEN *Soft Floral / Fleuri Aldéhydé* 43 ●●●●

AMWAY
1997 LONG AGO / WISTFUL *Floral / Florale* 36 ●
1997 SOLILOQUY *Soft Floral / Fleuri Aldéhydé* 43 ●●●●
1998 ANTICIPATE / SULTRY *Floral Oriental / Fleuri Oriental* 48 ●●
1998 CONSIDERATIONS / CONFIDENT *Mossy Woods / Chypre Boisé* 66 ●
1997 CROSSROADS *Aromatic / Fougère* 80 ●
1998 PERIPHERY / OPPORTUNE *Woody Oriental / Oriental Boisé* 62 ●

ANDRÉ BARNWELL
1998 RÄKS *Aromatic / Fougère* 78 ●●

ANDY WARHOL
1999 ANDY WARHOL FOR WOMEN *Floral / Florale* 32 ●
1999 ANDY WARHOL FOR MEN *Aromatic / Fougère* 76 ●

ANNABELLA
1997 ANNABELLA *Green / Vert* 22 ●
1999 ROUGE *Woody Oriental / Oriental Boisé* 60 ●

ANNA SUI
1999 ANNA SUI *Soft Floral / Fleuri Aldéhydé* 42 ●●
2000 SUI DREAMS *Oriental / Oriental* 56 ●●

ANNAYAKÉ
2000 ANNAYAKÉ POUR ELLE *Floral / Florale* 34 ●
2000 ANNAYAKÉ POUR LUI *Aromatic / Fougère* 80 ●

ANNÉ PLISKA
1987 ANNÉ PLISKA *Soft Oriental / Oriental Doux* 53 ●●●

ANNICK GOUTAL
1981 EAU D'HADRIEN ♂ *Citrus / Hespéridé* 17 ●●●
1981 EAU DE LAVANDE ♂ *Floral / Florale* 31 ●●●
1981 FOLAVRIL *Soft Floral / Fleuri Aldéhydé* 42 ●●
1982 EAU DE CHARLOTTE *Floral / Florale* 32 ●
1983 EAU DE CAMILLE *Floral / Florale* 34 ●
1983 PASSION *Floral / Florale* 38 ●●
1984 HEURE EXQUISE *Soft Floral / Fleuri Aldéhydé* 42 ●
1984 ROSE ABSOLUE *Floral / Florale* 31 ●●●
1984 TUBÉREUSE *Floral / Florale* 31 ●●●●
1985 EAU DU CIEL *Floral / Florale* 34 ●●
1989 GARDÉNIA PASSION *Floral / Florale* 31 ●●●●
1995 EAU DU SUD ♂ *Citrus / Hespéridé* 16 ●●
1996 GRAND AMOUR *Soft Floral / Fleuri Aldéhydé* 43 ●●●●
1998 PETITE CHÉRIE *Floral / Florale* 34 ●
1999 CE SOIR OU JAMAIS *Floral / Florale* 30 ●●
1981 EAU DE MONSIEUR *Mossy Woods / Chypre Boisé* 69 ●●●
1985 SABLES *Woody Oriental / Oriental Boisé* 62 ●●
1985 VÉTIVER *Dry Woods / Boisé Cuir* 73 ●●●
2000 EAU DU FIER *Dry Woods / Boisé Cuir* 73 ●●●●

ANTOINE DE SAINT-EXUPÉRY
1998 LE PETIT PRINCE *Citrus / Hespéridé* 19 ●●●

ANTONIA'S FLOWERS
1984 ANTONIA'S FLOWERS *Floral / Florale* 30 ●●
1995 FLORET *Floral / Florale* 30 ●●
1999 TIEMPE PASSATE *Mossy Woods / Chypre Boisé* 67 ●●●

ANTONIO PUIG (a selection *un choix*)
1940 AGUA LAVANDA ♂ *Floral / Florale* 31 ●●●
1975 ESTIVALIA *Citrus / Hespéridé* 16 ●●

1989 ANOUCK *Floral / Florale 34* ●
1996 THAÏS *Floral / Florale 38* ●
1999 ZARA WOMAN *Floral / Florale 34* ●●
1968 AGUA BRAVA *Mossy Woods / Chypre Boisé 69* ●●●
1982 QUORUM *Dry Woods / Boisé Cuir 72* ●●
1988 SYBARIS *Woody Oriental / Oriental Boisé 62* ●●
1989 BOSTON MAN *Aromatic / Fougère 82* ●●
1993 SPRINGFIELD *Dry Woods / Boisé Cuir 72* ●
1994 AQUA QUORUM *Aromatic / Fougère 82* ●

APPLEWOODS
1996 BRISTOL BLUE *Aromatic / Fougère 76* ●●

ARAMIS
1990 NEW WEST FOR HER* *Water / Marine 27* ●●●
1992 TUSCANY PER DONNA *Woody Oriental / Oriental Boisé 60* ●
1995 HAVANA POUR ELLE *Floral / Florale 36* ●●
1965 ARAMIS *Dry Woods / Boisé Cuir 73* ●●●
1973 ARAMIS 900 *Dry Woods / Boisé Cuir 72* ●
1978 DEVIN *Green / Vert 23* ●●●●
1982 J.H.L.* *Soft Oriental / Oriental Doux 53* ●●●
1984 TUSCANY PER UOMO *Aromatic / Fougère 78* ●
1988 NEW WEST FOR HIM* *Water / Marine 27* ●●●●
1994 HAVANA *Aromatic / Fougère 77* ●●●●
1998 ARAMIS GOLD *Dry Woods / Boisé Cuir 73* ●●●

ARDEN → ELIZABETH ARDEN

ARMAND BASI → IDESA
ARMANI → GIORGIO ARMANI

ARROGANCE
1982 ARROGANCE POUR FEMME *Floral / Florale 32* ●●
1997 ARROGANCE ME *Floral / Florale 38* ●
1999 EXCITING ARROGANCE *Soft Floral / Fleuri Aldéhydé 42* ●
1987 ARROGANCE UOMO *Aromatic / Fougère 76* ●●
1997 ARROGANCE YOU *Aromatic / Fougère 82* ●●
2000 ARROGANCE POUR HOMME *Aromatic / Fougère 76* ●

ARTISAN PARFUMEUR → L'ARTISAN PARFUMEUR

ASHLEY → LAURA ASHLEY

ATKINSON (a selection *un choix*)
1799 ATKINSON GOLD MEDAL ♂ *Citrus / Hespéridé 17* ●●●
1910 ENGLISH LAVENDER ♂ *Floral / Florale 31* ●●●

ATMAN
1998 ATMAN *Dry Woods / Boisé Cuir 73* ●●●

AUBUSSON
1984 HISTOIRE D'AMOUR *Mossy Woods / Chypre Boisé 67* ●●●
1990 DÉSIRADE *Floral Oriental / Fleuri Oriental 46* ●●
1994 25 *Woody Oriental / Oriental Boisé 60* ●
1995 FLEUR DE DÉSIRADE *Soft Floral / Fleuri Aldéhydé 42* ●●
1997 AUBUSSON COULEURS *Floral / Florale 32* ●
1998 FLORE AUBUSSON *Floral / Florale 36* ●
2000 PERLE D'AUBUSSON *Floral Oriental / Fleuri Oriental 46* ●
1992 AUBUSSON HOMME *Mossy Woods / Chypre Boisé 68* ●●
2000 MAN.AUBUSSON *Woody Oriental / Oriental Boisé 62* ●●

AZZARO
1975 AZZARO *Mossy Woods / Chypre Boisé 67* ●●●
1984 AZZARO 9 *Floral / Florale 33* ●●●●
1993 OH LÀ LÀ *Soft Oriental / Oriental Doux 52* ●●
1995 EAU BELLE *Citrus / Hespéridé 16* ●
1999 AZZURA *Floral / Florale 32* ●●
1978 AZZARO POUR HOMME *Aromatic / Fougère 76* ●
1989 ACTEUR *Dry Woods / Boisé Cuir 72* ●●
1996 CHROME *Citrus / Hespéridé 18* ●●
2000 PURE VÉTIVER *Mossy Woods / Chypre Boisé 68* ●●

BALENCIAGA
1947 LE DIX *Soft Floral / Fleuri Aldéhydé 43* ●●●●
1955 QUADRILLE *Mossy Woods / Chypre Boisé 67* ●●●
1973 CIALENGA *Soft Floral / Fleuri Aldéhydé 42* ●
1979 MICHELLE *Floral / Florale 31* ●●●●

1982 PRÉLUDE *Soft Oriental / Oriental Doux 53* ●●●
1988 RUMBA *Dry Woods / Boisé Cuir 72* ●●
1994 TALISMAN *Mossy Woods / Chypre Boisé 66* ●●
1996 TALISMAN EAU TRANSPARENTE *Floral / Florale 34* ●
1998 CRISTOBAL *Woody Oriental / Oriental Boisé 60* ●
1971 HO HANG *Aromatic / Fougère 82* ●●
1986 HO HANG CLUB* *Dry Woods / Boisé Cuir 73* ●●●●
1990 BALENCIAGA POUR HOMME* *Woody Oriental / Oriental Boisé 63* ●●●●
2000 CRISTOBAL POUR HOMME *Woody Oriental / Oriental Boisé 63* ●●●

BALMAIN → PIERRE BALMAIN

BANANA REPUBLIC
1995 CLASSIC ♂ *Citrus / Hespéridé 17* ●●●
1995 W *Floral / Florale 36* ●
1997 MODERN *Floral / Florale 34* ●●
1995 M *Citrus / Hespéridé 18* ●●
1997 MODERN FOR HIM *Aromatic / Fougère 78* ●●

BARNEYS NEW YORK
1986 ROUTE DU THÉ ♂ *Citrus / Hespéridé 16* ●

BARONY → LILIAN BARONY
BARYSHNIKOV → MIKHAIL BARYSHNIKOV

BASILE
1987 BASILE UOMO *Dry Woods / Boisé Cuir 72* ●●

BEENE → GEOFFREY BEENE

BENETTON
1987/93 COLORS OF BENETTON *Floral Oriental / Fleuri Oriental 46* ●
1993 TRIBÙ *Floral / Florale 34* ●●
1995 TRIBÙ ACQUA FRESCA *Floral / Florale 38* ●
1997 COLD ♂ *Citrus / Hespéridé 17* ●●●●
1997 HOT *Floral Oriental / Fleuri Oriental 46* ●
1999 BENETTON SPORT WOMAN *Floral / Florale 32* ●
2000 FUNTASTIC GIRL *Floral / Florale 32* ●
1988 COLORS FOR MEN *Woody Oriental / Oriental Boisé 62* ●
1999 BENETTON SPORT MAN *Aromatic / Fougère 78* ●
2000 FUNTASTIC BOY *Citrus / Hespéridé 18* ●

BERNINI
1996 BERNINI WOMEN *Floral Oriental / Fleuri Oriental 46* ●
1994 BERNINI MEN *Aromatic / Fougère 82* ●●
1999 BERNINI SPORT *Aromatic / Fougère 78* ●
2000 BERNINI VODA *Water / Marine 26* ●●

BIAGIOTTI → LAURA BIAGIOTTI

BIJAN
1987 BIJAN *Woody Oriental / Oriental Boisé 61* ●●●
1993 DNA* *Soft Floral / Fleuri Aldéhydé 43* ●●●●
2001 BIJAN WITH A TWIST *Floral Oriental / Fleuri Oriental 46* ●
1981 BIJAN FOR MEN *Aromatic / Fougère 76* ●●
1993 DNA FOR MEN* *Woody Oriental / Oriental Boisé 62* ●●
1996 MICHAEL JORDAN *Aromatic / Fougère 76* ●
1999 JORDAN BY MICHAEL *Woody Oriental / Oriental Boisé 62* ●

BILL BLASS
1978 BILL BLASS *Floral / Florale 33* ●●●●
1990 NUDE *Soft Floral / Fleuri Aldéhydé 42* ●
1999 AMAZING *Soft Floral / Fleuri Aldéhydé 42* ●●
2000 AMAZING FOR MEN *Aromatic / Fougère 76* ●●

BIOTHERM
1997 EAU VITAMINÉE *Citrus / Hespéridé 16* ●●
1999 AQUA RELAX *Aromatic / Fougère 76* ●
1999 AQUA-FITNESS *Citrus / Hespéridé 18* ●

BLUMARINE
1988 BLUMARINE* *Soft Floral / Fleuri Aldéhydé 42* ●●
1995 BLU BLUMARINE *Floral / Florale 38* ●●
2000 BLUMARINE II *Soft Floral / Fleuri Aldéhydé 42* ●

BOB MACKIE
1985/91 MACKIE *Floral Oriental / Fleuri Oriental 46* ●●

1997 PERHAPS *Floral Oriental / Fleuri Oriental* 46 ●
2000 MASQUERADE *Woody Oriental / Oriental Boisé* 60 ●
1992 MACKIE FOR MEN *Aromatic / Fougère* 80 ●

BOBBI BROWN
1998 BOBBI *Floral / Florale* 34 ●

BOGART → JACQUES BOGART

BOGNER
1999 BOGNER WOMAN *Floral Oriental / Fleuri Oriental* 46 ●
1985/90/99 BOGNER MAN *Aromatic / Fougère* 80 ●
1988 BOGNER MAN II* *Aromatic / Fougère* 76 ●●
1995 DEEP FOREST* *Dry Woods / Boisé Cuir* 73 ●●●●
2000 BOGNER SNOW *Aromatic / Fougère* 78 ●

BOND → JAMES BOND
BOND STREET → YARDLEY / BOND STREET

BONJOUR
1994 BONJOUR *Floral Oriental / Fleuri Oriental* 46 ●●

BORGHESE
1978 DI BORGHESE* *Green / Vert* 23 ●●●
1993 IL BACIO *Floral / Florale* 32 ●
1993 PROFUMO DI MONTECATINI ♂ *Water / Marine* 27 ●●●

BORSALINO
1995 DONNA BORSALINO *Floral Oriental / Fleuri Oriental* 46 ●●
1984 BORSALINO *Aromatic / Fougère* 82 ●●
1997 CHAPEAU *Aromatic / Fougère* 76 ●

BORSARI
1870 VIOLETTA DI PARMA *Floral / Florale* 31 ●●●●
1880 ACQUA CLASSICA DI BORSARI ♂ *Citrus / Hespéridé* 17 ●●●

BOSS → HUGO BOSS

BOUCHERON
1988 BOUCHERON *Floral Oriental / Fleuri Oriental* 47 ●●●
1994 JAÏPUR *Floral / Florale* 32 ●●
1999 JAÏPUR SAPHIR *Oriental / Oriental* 56 ●●
2000 INITIAL *Oriental / Oriental* 57 ●●●
1991 BOUCHERON POUR HOMME *Citrus / Hespéridé* 19 ●●●●
1997 JAÏPUR HOMME *Woody Oriental / Oriental Boisé* 62 ●●

BOURJOIS
1925/95 MON PARFUM *Floral / Florale* 34 ●●
1928 SOIR DE PARIS (Original) *Soft Floral / Aldéhydé* 43 ●●●●
1928/91 SOIR DE PARIS (New) *Floral / Florale* 31 ●●●
1988 MASCULIN ACIER *Aromatic / Fougère* 80 ●●
1993 MASCULIN EQUATEUR *Aromatic / Fougère* 77 ●●●
1996 MASCULIN EVASION *Citrus / Hespéridé* 18 ●●
1997 MASCULIN OURAGAN *Woody Oriental / Oriental Boisé* 62 ●
2000 MASCULIN EXTRÊME *Citrus / Hespéridé* 19 ●●●●

BROOKS BROTHERS
1998 BROOKS BROTHERS *Aromatic / Fougère* 80 ●

BROOKSFIELD
1993 BROOKSFIELD FOR MEN *Aromatic / Fougère* 80 ●●
1998 BROOKSFIELD ROYAL BLUE *Aromatic / Fougère* 78 ●

BROSSEAU → JEAN-CHARLES BROSSEAU

BRUNO BANANI
2000 BRUNO BANANI *Woody Oriental / Oriental Boisé* 62 ●

BUGATTI → ETTORE BUGATTI

BULGARI
1993 BULGARI EAU PARFUMÉE ♂ *Citrus / Hespéridé* 16 ●
1994 BULGARI POUR FEMME *Floral / Florale* 33 ●●●
1998 BULGARI BLACK ♂ *Dry Woods / Boisé Cuir* 72 ●●
1998 BULGARI PETITS ET MAMANS *Soft Oriental / Oriental Doux* 53 ●●●
2000 BULGARI BLU *Soft Floral / Fleuri Aldéhydé* 43 ●●●●
1995 BULGARI POUR HOMME *Aromatic / Fougère* 78 ●

BURANI → MARIELLA BURANI

BURBERRY
1991 SOCIETY* *Soft Floral / Fleuri Aldéhydé* 42 ●●
1995 BURBERRY FOR WOMEN *Floral Oriental / Fleuri Oriental* 46 ●
1997 BURBERRY WEEK END FOR WOMEN *Floral / Florale* 34 ●●
2000 BURBERRY TOUCH FOR WOMEN *Floral Oriental / Fleuri Oriental* 46 ●
1992 BURBERRYS FOR MEN (Original)* *Woody Oriental / Oriental Boisé* 62 ●●
1992/95 BURBERRY FOR MEN (New) *Aromatic / Fougère* 76 ●●
1997 BURBERRY WEEK END FOR MEN *Mossy Woods / Chypre Boisé* 68 ●●
2000 BURBERRY TOUCH FOR MEN *Mossy Woods / Chypre Boisé* 68 ●

BYBLOS
1990 BYBLOS* *Floral / Florale* 32 ●●
1997 BYBLOS CIELO / SKY *Woody Oriental / Oriental Boisé* 60 ●
1997 BYBLOS MARE / SEA *Floral / Florale* 34 ●
1997 BYBLOS TERRA / EARTH *Floral Oriental / Fleuri Oriental* 46 ●●
1998 BYBLOS FUOCO / FIRE *Woody Oriental / Oriental Boisé* 61 ●●●
1998 BYBLOS GHIACCIA / ICE *Citrus / Hespéridé* 17 ●●●●
2000 BYBLOS BREEZA / BREEZE *Floral Oriental / Fleuri Oriental* 46 ●
2000 BYBLOS URAGANO / HURRICANE *Oriental / Oriental* 56 ●●
1993 BYBLOS UOMO* *Aromatic / Fougère* 78 ●●

CACHAREL
1978 ANAÏS ANAÏS *Floral / Florale* 38 ●
1987 LOULOU *Soft Oriental / Oriental Doux* 53 ●●●●
1994 EDEN *Floral Oriental / Fleuri Oriental* 48 ●
1995 LOULOU BLUE* *Floral Oriental / Fleuri Oriental* 48 ●●
1996 EAU D'EDEN *Floral / Florale* 36 ●
1998 NOA *Soft Floral / Fleuri Aldéhydé* 43 ●●●●
1981 CACHAREL POUR L'HOMME *Aromatic / Fougère* 82 ●●
1999 NEMO *Woody Oriental / Oriental Boisé* 62 ●●

CAESARS WORLD
1988 CAESARS WOMAN *Floral / Florale* 33 ●●●●
1994 FERENTINA *Floral Oriental / Fleuri Oriental* 47 ●●●
1988 CAESARS MAN *Aromatic / Fougère* 76 ●●

CALIFORNIA FRAGRANCES
1987 VORAGO *Aromatic / Fougère* 78 ●●
1992 VORAGO ACTION *Citrus / Hespéridé* 19 ●●●

CALIFORNIA NORTH
1991 RICHARDSON BAY ♂ *Green / Vert* 22 ●
1996 O₂XYGEN WOMAN *Citrus / Hespéridé* 16 ●
1994 O₂XYGEN *Citrus / Hespéridé* 18 ●
1995 'N *Dry Woods / Boisé Cuir* 73 ●●●

CALVIN KLEIN
1978 CALVIN KLEIN * *Soft Floral / Fleuri Aldéhydé* 42 ●
1985 OBSESSION *Oriental / Oriental* 56 ●
1988 ETERNITY *Floral / Florale* 38 ●
1991 ESCAPE *Water / Marine* 27 ●●●●
1994 cK ONE ♂ *Citrus / Hespéridé* 16 ●
1996 cK BE ♂ *Aromatic / Fougère* 76 ●
1997 CONTRADICTION *Floral Oriental / Fleuri Oriental* 46 ●
2000 TRUTH CALVIN KLEIN *Woody Oriental / Oriental Boisé* 60 ●
1981 CALVIN *Aromatic / Fougère* 76 ●●
1986 OBSESSION FOR MEN *Woody Oriental / Oriental Boisé* 62 ●
1989 ETERNITY FOR MEN *Aromatic / Fougère* 80 ●
1993 ESCAPE FOR MEN *Aromatic / Fougère* 82 ●
1998 CONTRADICTION FOR MEN *Woody Oriental / Oriental Boisé* 62 ●

CALYPSO ST BARTH
1998 CALYPSO MIMOSA *Floral / Florale* 30 ●●
1999 CALYPSO JASMIN *Floral / Florale* 31 ●●●
1999 CALYPSO VIOLETTE *Floral / Florale* 31 ●●●●

CAPUCCI → ROBERTO CAPUCCI
CARDIN → PIERRE CARDIN

CARITA
1996 CARITA *Water / Marine* 26 ●●

CARLO CORINTO
1984 CARLO CORINTO *Dry Woods / Boisé Cuir* 72 ●●

CAROLINA HERRERA

1988 CAROLINA HERRERA *Floral / Florale* 31 ●●●●
1994 FLORE *Floral / Florale* 30 ●
1996 AQUAFLORE *Water / Marine* 26 ●
1997 212 *Soft Floral / Fleuri Aldéhydé* 42 ●
1991 HERRERA FOR MEN *Woody Oriental / Oriental Boisé* 62 ●●
1999 212 MEN *Mossy Woods / Chypre Boisé* 68 ●

CARON

1911 NARCISSE NOIR *Floral / Florale* 31 ●●●●
1912/70 INFINI *Soft Floral / Fleuri Aldéhydé* 43 ●●●●
1916 N'AIMEZ QUE MOI *Floral / Florale* 33 ●●●
1918 VIOLETTE PRÉCIEUSE *Floral / Florale* 31 ●●●●
1919 TABAC BLOND *Dry Woods / Boisé Cuir* 73 ●●●
1922 NUIT DE NOËL *Woody Oriental / Oriental Boisé* 61 ●●●
1923 NARCISSE BLANC *Floral / Florale* 31 ●●●●
1924 ACACIOSA *Floral / Florale* 38 ●
1927 BELLODGIA *Floral / Florale* 31 ●●●●
1927 POIS DE SENTEUR *Soft Oriental / Oriental Doux* 53 ●●●
1930 EN AVION *Floral Oriental / Fleuri Oriental* 47 ●●●●
1933 FLEURS DE ROCAILLE *Floral / Florale* 33 ●●●
1936 FRENCH CANCAN *Floral Oriental / Fleuri Oriental* 48 ●●
1939 ALPONA *Citrus / Hespéridé* 17 ●●●●
1941 ROYAL BAIN DE CHAMPAGNE ♂ *Soft Oriental / Oriental Doux* 52 ●
1947 FARNESIANA *Floral / Florale* 30 ●●
1949 OR ET NOIR *Floral Oriental / Fleuri Oriental* 47 ●●●
1949 ROSE *Floral / Florale* 31 ●●●
1949 WITH PLEASURE *Green / Vert* 23 ●●●●
1952 MUGUET DU BONHEUR *Floral / Florale* 30 ●
1954 POIVRE *Soft Oriental / Oriental Doux* 53 ●●●●
1980 EAU DE CARON *Oriental / Oriental* 56 ●●
1981 NOCTURNES *Soft Floral / Fleuri Aldéhydé* 43 ●●●●
1986 MONTAIGNE *Floral / Florale* 34 ●●
1990 PARFUM SACRÉ *Floral Oriental / Fleuri Oriental* 47 ●●●
1993 FLEUR DE ROCAILLE *Floral / Florale* 34 ●●
1996 AIMEZ-MOI *Soft Floral / Fleuri Aldéhydé* 43 ●●●●
1996 EAU PURE ♂ *Water / Marine* 26 ●
1997 EAU FRAÎCHE ♂ *Citrus / Hespéridé* 17 ●●●
1999 EAU DE CARON FORTE ♂ *Citrus / Hespéridé* 17 ●●●●
2000 LADY CARON *Mossy Woods / Chypre Boisé* 66 ●●
1934 POUR UN HOMME *Floral / Florale* 39 ●●●●
1976 YATAGAN *Dry Woods / Boisé Cuir* 73 ●●●●
1998 THIRD MAN / 3ᵉ HOMME / N° 3 *Aromatic / Fougère* 77 ●●●●
2000 L'ANARCHISTE *Aromatic / Fougère* 77 ●●●●

CARTIER

1981 MUST DE CARTIER *Oriental / Oriental* 56 ●
1981 MUST DE CARTIER (JOUR)* *Floral / Florale* 34 ●
1987 PANTHÈRE *Floral Oriental / Fleuri Oriental* 46 ●●
1993 MUST DE CARTIER II *Water / Marine* 26 ●
1995 SO PRETTY *Soft Floral / Fleuri Aldéhydé* 42 ●
2000 SO PRETTY EAU FRUITÉE *Soft Floral / Fleuri Aldéhydé* 42 ●
1981 SANTOS *Aromatic / Fougère* 78 ●●
1989 SANTOS EAU DE SPORT *Citrus / Hespéridé* 19 ●●●●
1992 PASHA *Aromatic / Fougère* 78 ●●
1998 DÉCLARATION *Dry Woods / Boisé Cuir* 72 ●
2000 MUST DE CARTIER POUR HOMME
       Woody Oriental / Oriental Boisé 63 ●●●

CARVEN

1946 MA GRIFFE *Mossy Woods / Chypre Boisé* 66 ●●
1966/95 EAU VIVE *Citrus / Hespéridé* 16 ●●
1979 MADAME CARVEN* *Floral / Florale* 33 ●●●●
1982 GUIRLANDES* *Soft Floral / Fleuri Aldéhydé* 42 ●
1986 INTRIGUE* *Soft Floral / Fleuri Aldéhydé* 42 ●●
2000 VARIATIONS *Floral / Florale* 34 ●●
1957 VÉTIVER *Mossy Woods / Chypre Boisé* 69 ●●●
1978 MONSIEUR CARVEN* *Soft Oriental / Oriental Doux* 52 ●●
1988 VÉTIVER DRY* *Aromatic / Fougère* 80 ●●
1999 CARVEN HOMME *Dry Woods / Boisé Cuir* 72 ●●

CASSINI → OLEG CASSINI

CATHERINE DENEUVE

1986 DENEUVE* *Mossy Woods / Chypre Boisé* 66 ●

CBH

1986 CAMP BEVERLY HILLS* *Soft Floral / Fleuri Aldéhydé* 42 ●●
1988 CAMP BEVERLY HILLS FOR MEN* *Citrus / Hespéridé* 19 ●●●●

CÉLINE

1996 MAGIC *Mossy Woods / Chypre Boisé* 66 ●

CERRUTI

1995 CERRUTI 1881 POUR FEMME *Floral / Florale* 32 ●●
2000 CERRUTI IMAGE WOMAN *Green / Vert* 22 ●●
1979 NINO CERRUTI *Green / Vert* 23 ●●●●
1990 CERRUTI 1881 POUR HOMME *Citrus / Hespéridé* 18 ●●
1998 CERRUTI IMAGE POUR HOMME *Aromatic / Fougère* 80 ●

CHANEL

1921 CHANEL N° 5 *Soft Floral / Fleuri Aldéhydé* 43 ●●●
1922 CHANEL N° 22 *Floral / Florale* 33 ●●●
1924 CUIR DE RUSSIE *Dry Woods / Boisé Cuir* 73 ●●●
1925 GARDÉNIA *Floral / Florale* 30 ●
1926 BOIS DES ÎLES *Woody Oriental / Oriental Boisé* 61 ●●●
1971 CHANEL N° 19 *Soft Floral / Fleuri Aldéhydé* 42 ●
1974 CRISTALLE *Citrus / Hespéridé* 16 ●●
1984 COCO *Soft Oriental / Oriental Doux* 53 ●●●
1996 ALLURE *Floral Oriental / Fleuri Oriental* 46 ●
1955 CHANEL POUR MONSIEUR *Mossy Woods / Chypre Boisé* 69 ●●●
1981 ANTAEUS *Dry Woods / Boisé Cuir* 73 ●●●●
1990 ÉGOÏSTE / L'ÉGOÏSTE *Woody Oriental / Oriental Boisé* 63 ●●●
1993 ÉGOÏSTE PLATINUM *Aromatic / Fougère* 78 ●
1998 ALLURE HOMME *Woody Oriental / Oriental Boisé* 62 ●

CHANTECAILLE

1997 FRANGIPANE *Floral / Florale* 31 ●●●●
1997 TIARÉ *Floral / Florale* 30 ●●
1997 WISTERIA *Floral / Florale* 30 ●●
1999 DARBY ROSE *Floral / Florale* 31 ●●●

CHARLES JOURDAN

1978 VÔTRE* *Floral / Florale* 36 ●
1992 TRÈS JOURDAN* *Floral / Florale* 34 ●●
1995 L'INSOLENT* *Woody Oriental / Oriental Boisé* 60 ●●
1996 INDIVIDUELLE *Floral / Florale* 38 ●
1998 INSPIRATION *Floral Oriental / Fleuri Oriental* 46 ●

CHAUMET

1999 CHAUMET *Floral / Florale* 34 ●
2001 CHAUMET HOMME *Mossy Woods / Chypre Boisé* 68 ●

CHER

1989 UNINHIBITED* *Floral Oriental / Fleuri Oriental* 47 ●●●●

CHEVIGNON

1996 BEST OF CHEVIGNON ♂ *Water / Marine* 27 ●●●
1999 CHEVIGNON 57 FOR HER *Floral / Florale* 32 ●●
1992 CHEVIGNON *Mossy Woods / Chypre Boisé* 68 ●●
1999 CHEVIGNON 57 FOR HIM *Woody Oriental / Oriental Boisé* 62 ●

CHIARA BONI

1990 CHIARA BONI *Floral / Florale* 31 ●●●●
1997 CHIARA BONI LIGHT *Soft Floral / Fleuri Aldéhydé* 42 ●●
1998 SUNSHINE *Floral / Florale* 34 ●
1999 FLEURS DE CHIARA BONI *Floral / Florale* 38 ●
1997 CHIARA BONI UOMO *Aromatic / Fougère* 80 ●

CHIEMSEE

1999 CHIEMSEE WOMAN *Floral / Florale* 36 ●
2000 CHIEMSEE WOMAN TWO *Floral / Florale* 32 ●●
1999 CHIEMSEE MAN *Aromatic / Fougère* 80 ●
2000 CHIEMSEE MAN TWO *Woody Oriental / Oriental Boisé* 62 ●

CHLOÉ

1975 CHLOÉ *Floral / Florale* 31 ●●●●
1992 CHLOÉ NARCISSE *Floral Oriental / Fleuri Oriental* 46 ●●
1996 CHLOÉ INNOCENCE* *Floral / Florale* 38 ●

CHOPARD

1991 CASMIR *Woody Oriental / Oriental Boisé* 60 ●●
1997 WISH *Woody Oriental / Oriental Boisé* 60 ●

1998 MIRA BAÏ   *Woody Oriental / Oriental Boisé   60* ●●
2000 PURE WISH   *Floral Oriental / Fleuri Oriental   46* ●
1994 HEAVEN   *Aromatic / Fougère   78* ●●
1999 CASRAN   *Woody Oriental / Oriental Boisé   62* ●

CHRISTIAN BRETON
2000 CHRISTIAN BRETON POUR FEMME   *Floral / Florale   32* ●●

CHRISTIAN DIOR
1947 MISS DIOR   *Mossy Woods / Chypre Boisé   66* ●
1949 DIORAMA   *Mossy Woods / Chypre Boisé   67* ●●●
1953 EAU FRAÎCHE   *Mossy Woods / Chypre Boisé   67* ●●●
1956 DIORISSIMO   *Floral / Florale   30* ●
1963 DIORLING   *Dry Woods / Boisé Cuir   73* ●●●
1969/79 DIORESSENCE   *Soft Oriental / Oriental Doux   53* ●●●
1972 DIORELLA   *Citrus / Hespéridé   16* ●●
1985 POISON   *Floral Oriental / Fleuri Oriental   47* ●●●●
1991 DUNE   *Woody Oriental / Oriental Boisé   60* ●
1994 TENDRE POISON   *Floral / Florale   36* ●●
1995 DOLCE VITA   *Woody Oriental / Oriental Boisé   60* ●●
1995 EAU SVELTE   *Floral / Florale   32* ●
1998 EAU DE DOLCE VITA   *Floral / Florale   32* ●
1998 HYPNOTIC POISON   *Woody Oriental / Oriental Boisé   61* ●●●●
1999 J'ADORE   *Floral / Florale   32* ●
1999 LILY* Ⓛ   *Floral / Florale   30* ●
2000 EAU DE DIOR COLORESSENCE ENERGISANTE   *Citrus / Hespéridé   16* ●
2000 EAU DE DIOR COLORESSENCE RELAXANTE   *Citrus / Hespéridé   17* ●●●●
1966 EAU SAUVAGE   *Citrus / Hespéridé   19* ●●●
1980 JULES   *Aromatic / Fougère   77* ●●●●
1984 EAU SAUVAGE EXTRÊME   *Citrus / Hespéridé   19* ●●●●
1988 FAHRENHEIT   *Mossy Woods / Chypre Boisé   68* ●
1997 DUNE POUR HOMME   *Woody Oriental / Oriental Boisé   62* ●

CHRISTIAN LACROIX
1990 C'EST LA VIE*   *Floral Oriental / Fleuri Oriental   46* ●
1999 CHRISTIAN LACROIX   *Soft Floral / Fleuri Aldéhydé   42* ●●

CHRISTIAN TORTU
1997 EAU FRAÎCHE   *Citrus / Hespéridé   17* ●●●

CHYPRON
1995 SHAHI   *Woody Oriental / Oriental Boisé   61* ●●●●
1997 SHAHI GOLDEN SUN   *Floral Oriental / Fleuri Oriental   47* ●●●
1998 SHAHI AQUA   *Floral / Florale   34* ●

CIGAR AFICIONADO
1997 CIGAR AFICIONADO   *Aromatic / Fougère   77* ●●●●

CINDY ADAMS
1997 GOSSIP   *Woody Oriental / Oriental Boisé   60* ●

CLAIBORNE → LIZ CLAIBORNE
CLAIRE → HOUBIGANT: CLAIRE

CLARINS
1987 EAU DYNAMISANTE ♂   *Citrus / Hespéridé   17* ●●●
1993 ELYSIUM   *Floral / Florale   32* ●

CLINIQUE
1971 AROMATICS ELIXIR   *Dry Woods / Boisé Cuir   72* ●
1990 WRAPPINGS   *Water / Marine   26* ●
1997 HAPPY   *Floral / Florale   32* ●
1995 CHEMISTRY   *Aromatic / Fougère   80* ●
1999 HAPPY FOR MEN   *Citrus / Hespéridé   18* ●

COFINLUXE
1978 CAFÉ   *Soft Oriental / Oriental Doux   53* ●●●
1993 WATT PINK   *Floral / Florale   38* ●
1996 CAFÉ-CAFÉ   *Soft Floral / Fleuri Aldéhydé   42* ●●
2000 CAFÉ-CAFÉ ADVENTURE POUR FEMME
       Mossy Woods / Chypre Boisé   66 ●●
2000 WATT RED   *Woody Oriental / Oriental Boisé   60* ●●
2000 WATT YELLOW   *Floral / Florale   34* ●●
1991 WATT FOR MEN BLUE   *Aromatic / Fougère   78* ●●
1996 CAFÉ-CAFÉ POUR HOMME   *Aromatic / Fougère   80* ●
2000 CAFÉ-CAFÉ ADVENTURE POUR HOMME   *Aromatic / Fougère   76* ●●
2000 WATT FOR MEN GREEN   *Woody Oriental / Oriental Boisé   62* ●●

COMME DES GARÇONS
1994 COMME DES GARÇONS ♂   *Mossy Woods / Chypre Boisé   67* ●●●●
1998 ODEUR 53 ♂   *Water / Marine   26* ●●
1999 COMME DES GARÇONS 2 ♂   *Mossy Woods / Chypre Boisé   66* ●
2000 ODEUR 71 ♂   *Dry Woods / Boisé Cuir   72* ●

COMPAGNIA DELLE INDIE
2000 DONNA   *Floral / Florale   36* ●
2000 UOMO   *Mossy Woods / Chypre Boisé   68* ●

COMPTOIR SUD PACIFIQUE
1975 EAU DE CÈDRE ♂   *Dry Woods / Boisé Cuir   72* ●
1975 SOLEIL LEVANT   *Woody Oriental / Oriental Boisé   61* ●●●
1976 FLEURS DE PÊCHER   *Soft Floral / Fleuri Aldéhydé   42* ●
1976 MANDARINE ♂   *Citrus / Hespéridé   16* ●●
1977 VETYVER HAITI ♂   *Mossy Woods / Chypre Boisé   66* ●●
1978 VANILLE   *Oriental / Oriental   56* ●●
1984 TIARÉ   *Floral / Florale   30* ●●
1985 PAMPLEMOUSSE ♂   *Citrus / Hespéridé   16* ●●
1986 CRISTAL DE MUSC   *Soft Oriental / Oriental Doux   52* ●
1986 PAIN D'ÉPICES   *Woody Oriental / Oriental Boisé   61* ●●●
1987 FRUITS SAUVAGES   *Citrus / Hespéridé   17* ●●●●
1987 VANILLE CAFÉ ♂   *Oriental / Oriental   57* ●●●
1988 COTONNADE ♂   *Soft Oriental / Oriental Doux   52* ●●
1989 ROSE VANILLE   *Floral / Florale   33* ●●●
1989 VANILLE TIARÉ   *Oriental / Oriental   56* ●
1991 TURQUOISE   *Soft Floral / Fleuri Aldéhydé   43* ●●●
1992 MOTU   *Water / Marine   26* ●
1992 OPOPONAX   *Aromatic / Fougère   77* ●●●
1993 AMOUR DE CACAO   *Oriental / Oriental   56* ●●
1994 VANILLE ABRICOT   *Oriental / Oriental   56* ●
1994 VANILLE AMANDE   *Oriental / Oriental   56* ●
1995 EAU DE BIARRITZ   *Soft Floral / Fleuri Aldéhydé   42* ●●
1997 THÉ ♂   *Woody Oriental / Oriental Boisé   61* ●●●
1997 VANILLE CERISE   *Oriental / Oriental   56* ●
1998 KUMQUAT ♂   *Citrus / Hespéridé   16* ●●
1999 ENFANTS DU SOLEIL   *Floral Oriental / Fleuri Oriental   46* ●●
1999 LAIT SUCRÉ   *Floral / Florale   32* ●
2000 COEUR DE RAISIN   *Floral / Florale   32* ●
2001 RIZIÈRES ♂   *Mossy Woods / Chypre Boisé   67* ●●●
1976 EAU GRISE   *Mossy Woods / Chypre Boisé   68* ●
1978 BARBIER DES ISLES   *Dry Woods / Boisé Cuir   73* ●●●
1988 EAU DES TROPIQUES   *Citrus / Hespéridé   19* ●●●
1988 ROI SANTAL   *Woody Oriental / Oriental Boisé   63* ●●●
1990 PIROGUIER   *Dry Woods / Boisé Cuir   73* ●●●
1993 L'HOMME   *Dry Woods / Boisé Cuir   72* ●●
1996 SAFRANIER   *Woody Oriental / Oriental Boisé   62* ●●

COPAINS → LES COPAINS
CORDAY / DANA → DANA

COTY
1905 L'ORIGAN*   *Floral Oriental / Fleuri Oriental   47* ●●●
1917 CHYPRE DE COTY*   *Mossy Woods / Chypre Boisé   67* ●●●
1921 ÉMERAUDE   *Oriental / Oriental   57* ●●●
1927 L'AIMANT   *Soft Floral / Fleuri Aldéhydé   43* ●●●
1942 MUGUET DES BOIS   *Floral / Florale   30* ●
1950/95 JUNGLE GARDENIA   *Floral / Florale   30* ●●
1966 IMPRÉVU   *Dry Woods / Boisé Cuir   73* ●●●
1973 WILD MUSK   *Oriental / Oriental   57* ●●●●
1980 SOPHIA*   *Soft Oriental / Oriental Doux   53* ●●●
1983 SAND & SABLE   *Floral / Florale   33* ●●●●
1986 LADY STETSON   *Soft Floral / Fleuri Aldéhydé   43* ●●●●
1988 EX'CLA.MA'TION   *Floral Oriental / Fleuri Oriental   46* ●●
1990 ASPEN FOR WOMEN   *Water / Marine   27* ●●●
1990 L'EFFLEUR   *Floral / Florale   34* ●●
1992 TRULY LACE   *Floral Oriental / Fleuri Oriental   47* ●●●
1993 VANILLA FIELDS   *Woody Oriental / Oriental Boisé   60* ●●
1994 LONGING   *Floral Oriental / Fleuri Oriental   46* ●
1994 VANILLA MUSK   *Woody Oriental / Oriental Boisé   61* ●●●
1995 CHANSON D'EAU   *Citrus / Hespéridé   17* ●●●
1995 CHIPIE   *Floral Oriental / Fleuri Oriental   46* ●
1995 GHOST MYST   *Water / Marine   26* ●
1995 ICI   *Floral Oriental / Fleuri Oriental   46* ●●
1996 CELEBRATE   *Floral / Florale   32* ●●
1996 EX'CLA.MA'TION BLUSH   *Floral / Florale   32* ●
1996 EX'CLA.MA'TION DARE   *Floral / Florale   38* ●

110

1996 EX'CLA.MA'TION EAU *Citrus / Hespéridé 16* ●
1996 ROOTS UNISCENT ♂ *Water / Marine 26* ●
1997 CHANSON D'AIR *Floral / Florale 32* ●
1997 NOKOMIS *Floral Oriental / Fleuri Oriental 46* ●●
1997 PRINCESSE CHIPIE *Woody Oriental / Oriental Boisé 60* ●
1998 100% PURE CHIPIE GREEN *Floral / Florale 32* ●
1998 100% PURE CHIPIE PURPLE *Woody Oriental / Oriental Boisé 60* ●
1998 ASPEN SENSATION *Floral / Florale 34* ●
1998 DARK VANILLA *Floral Oriental / Fleuri Oriental 47* ●●●●
1998 EXC'LA.MA'TION NOIR *Mossy Woods / Chypre Boisé 67* ●●●
1998 I EX'CLA.MA'TION *Floral Oriental / Fleuri Oriental 46* ●
1998 ROOTS FOR HER *Floral / Florale 36* ●
1999 APRIL FIELDS *Floral / Florale 34* ●
1999 CHANSON DE VIE *Citrus / Hespéridé 16* ●
1999 DULCE VANILLA *Woody Oriental / Oriental Boisé 60* ●
2000 TOUJOURS L'AIMANT *Soft Floral / Fleuri Aldéhydé 42* ●●
2001 AMERICAN ORIGINAL: STETSON FOR WOMEN *Floral / Florale 32* ●●
1974 COTY MUSK FOR MEN *Woody Oriental / Oriental Boisé 63* ●●●
1981 STETSON *Woody Oriental / Oriental Boisé 63* ●●●
1989 ASPEN FOR MEN *Aromatic / Fougère 78* ●
1990 PREFERRED STOCK *Aromatic / Fougère 76* ●
1992 GRAVITY *Woody Oriental / Oriental Boisé 62* ●●
1992 ROLAND GARROS *Aromatic / Fougère 78* ●
1993 STETSON SIERRA *Aromatic / Fougère 78* ●
1994 UNIVERSO *Aromatic / Fougère 78* ●
1995 ROUTE 66 *Aromatic / Fougère 78* ●●
1996 RAW VANILLA *Woody Oriental / Oriental Boisé 62* ●
1997 AVATAR *Aromatic / Fougère 76* ●
1997 ROUTE 66 COLORADO RAIN *Aromatic / Fougère 76* ●
1998 STETSON COUNTRY *Mossy Woods / Chypre Boisé 68* ●●
2000 ASPEN DISCOVERY *Aromatic / Fougère 76* ●
2001 ROOTS FOR HIM *Water / Marine 26* ●●

COUDRAY → E.COUDRAY

COUNTRY ROAD WOMAN
1999 COUNTRY ROAD WOMAN *Soft Floral / Fleuri Aldéhydé 42* ●●
1999 COUNTRY ROAD MAN *Aromatic / Fougère 80* ●

COURRÈGES
1971/92 EMPREINTE *Dry Woods / Boisé Cuir 73* ●●●
1977 EAU DE COURRÈGES *Citrus / Hespéridé 17* ●●●●
1983 COURRÈGES IN BLUE *Floral / Florale 33* ●●●●
1993 SWEET COURRÈGES *Soft Floral / Fleuri Aldéhydé 42* ●●
1996 GÉNÉRATION COURRÈGES *Floral / Florale 32* ●
1997 COURRÈGES 2020 *Floral / Florale 32* ●●
1995 NIAGARA *Dry Woods / Boisé Cuir 72* ●●

COUTURIER → JEAN COUTURIER
COVER GIRL / DANA → DANA
COVERI → ENRICO COVERI

CRABTREE & EVELYN
1970 JASMIN DE PROVENCE* *Floral / Florale 31* ●●●
1970 LAVENDER ♂ *Floral / Florale 31* ●●●
1970 LILY OF THE VALLEY *Floral / Florale 30* ●
1974 GARDENIA *Floral / Florale 30* ●●
1976/91 DAMASK ROSE *Soft Floral / Fleuri Aldéhydé 42* ●●
1979 SPRING RAIN *Floral / Florale 36* ●
1984 SAVANNAH GARDENS *Oriental / Oriental 57* ●●●
1985 NANTUCKET BRIAR *Floral Oriental / Fleuri Oriental 46* ●●
1988 SUMMER HILL *Floral / Florale 38* ●
1990 VERANDA *Floral Oriental / Fleuri Oriental 46* ●
1993 EVELYN *Floral / Florale 31* ●●●
1993 FREESIA *Floral / Florale 30* ●●
1994 VANILLA *Floral Oriental / Fleuri Oriental 48* ●
1996 PASSION FLOWER* *Floral / Florale 34* ●
1997 SONG DE CHINE* *Floral / Florale 38* ●
1999 SONOMA VALLEY *Green / Vert 22* ●
1970 PATCHOULI *Woody Oriental / Oriental Boisé 62* ●●
1970 SANDALWOOD *Woody Oriental / Oriental Boisé 63* ●●●
1975 HUNGARY WATER* *Citrus / Hespéridé 19* ●●●
1984 CRABTREE & EVELYN FOR MEN* *Dry Woods / Boisé Cuir 73* ●●●
1990 SIENNA *Mossy Woods / Chypre Boisé 68* ●●
1999 NOMAD *Aromatic / Fougère 80* ●

CREATIVE UNIVERSE
1996 TÉ ♂ *Citrus / Hespéridé 16* ●
1999 MARE ♂ *Water / Marine 26* ●●
2000 LUCE ♂ *Floral / Florale 31* ●●●

CREED
1845/1980 FLEURS DE BULGARIE *Floral / Florale 31* ●●●
1850 SANTAL IMPÉRIAL ♂ *Woody Oriental / Oriental Boisé 61* ●●●
1862/1983 FANTASIA DE FLEURS *Floral / Florale 33* ●●●●
1870/1989 JASMIN IMPÉRATRICE EUGÉNIE *Floral / Florale 33* ●●●
1875 BOIS DE CÉDRAT ♂ *Citrus / Hespéridé 17* ●●●
1901 CITRUS BIGARRADE ♂ *Citrus / Hespéridé 17* ●●●
1933 ANGÉLIQUE ENCENS *Oriental / Oriental 57* ●●●
1949 AMBRE CANNELLE *Soft Oriental / Oriental Doux 53* ●●●
1950 ORANGE SPICE ♂ *Aromatic / Fougère 76* ●●
1959 JASMAL *Floral / Florale 31* ●●●
1972 FLEURISSIMO *Floral / Florale 38* ●
1975 ZESTE MANDARINE PAMPLEMOUSSE ♂ *Citrus / Hespéridé 17* ●●●●
1980 INDIANA / TUBÉREUSE INDIANA *Floral / Florale 38* ●●
1982 CHÈVREFEUILLE ORIGINAL ♂ *Green / Vert 22* ●
1987 VANISIA *Oriental / Oriental 57* ●●●
1993 ROYAL DELIGHT ♂ *Soft Oriental / Oriental Doux 53* ●●●●
1995 MILLÉSIME IMPÉRIAL ♂ *Water / Marine 27* ●●●●
1996 SPRING FLOWER *Floral / Florale 34* ●
1999 GREEN VALLEY ♂ *Mossy Woods / Chypre Boisé 66* ●
2000 2000 FLEURS *Floral / Florale 34* ●
1781 ROYAL ENGLISH LEATHER *Dry Woods / Boisé Cuir 73* ●●●
1856 ROYAL SCOTTISH LAVENDER *Floral / Florale 39* ●●●
1875/1999 TABAROME *Dry Woods / Boisé Cuir 73* ●●●●
1948 VETIVER *Mossy Woods / Chypre Boisé 69* ●●●
1965 EPICÉA *Aromatic / Fougère 82* ●●
1970 SÉLECTION VERTE *Citrus / Hespéridé 18* ●●
1973 ACIER ALUMINIUM *Mossy Woods / Chypre Boisé 69* ●●●●
1982 BAIE DE GENIÈVRE *Woody Oriental / Oriental Boisé 63* ●●●
1985 GREEN IRISH TWEED *Green / Vert 23* ●●●
1987 BOIS DU PORTUGAL *Woody Oriental / Oriental Boisé 63* ●●●●
1992 EROLFA *Water / Marine 26* ●
1994 NÉROLI SAUVAGE *Citrus / Hespéridé 19* ●●●●
1995 SILVER MOUNTAIN WATER *Water / Marine 26* ●●
1997 ROYAL WATER *Aromatic / Fougère 77* ●●●●

THE CROSS
1996 FRUITS & FLOWERS *Floral / Florale 32* ●

CROWN
1669/1994 MARÉCHALE ORIGINAL *Floral / Florale 31* ●●●
1872 CROWN ESS BOUQUET *Citrus / Hespéridé 16* ●
1873 CROWN ROSE *Floral / Florale 31* ●●●
1874 CROWN ESTERHAZY *Citrus / Hespéridé 17* ●●●
1879 CROWN ALPINE LILY *Floral / Florale 30* ●
1882 CROWN COURT BOUQUET *Aromatic / Fougère 77* ●●●
1910 CROWN OF GOLD *Mossy Woods / Chypre Boisé 67* ●●●
1919 MALABAR *Oriental / Oriental 57* ●●●
1921 CROWN STEPHANOTIS *Floral / Florale 33* ●●●
1929 MATSUKITA *Floral Oriental / Fleuri Oriental 48* ●●
1931 SARCANTHUS *Floral / Florale 36* ●●
1932 TANGLEWOOD BOUQUET *Floral Oriental / Fleuri Oriental 47* ●●●
1936 CROWN BOUQUET *Floral / Florale 34* ●●
1939 CROWN HELIOTROPE *Woody Oriental / Oriental Boisé 61* ●●●
1994 MARÉCHALE 90 *Mossy Woods / Chypre Boisé 67* ●●●
1873 SANDRINGHAM *Woody Oriental / Oriental Boisé 63* ●●●
1880 BUCKINGHAM *Aromatic / Fougère 76* ●●
1885 CROWN FOUGÈRE *Aromatic / Fougère 77* ●●●
1890 EAU DE QUININE *Citrus / Hespéridé 19* ●●●
1905 CROWN IMPERIAL *Citrus / Hespéridé 19* ●●●●
1911 EAU DE RUSSE *Oriental / Oriental 56* ●●
1921 CROWN SPICED LIMES *Citrus / Hespéridé 19* ●●●●
1925 SUMARE *Citrus / Hespéridé 19* ●●●●
1925 TOWN & COUNTRY *Mossy Woods / Chypre Boisé 68* ●●
1928 MARQUIS *Aromatic / Fougère 80* ●
1929 CROWN PARK ROYAL *Dry Woods / Boisé Cuir 72* ●●

DAKS
2001 DAKS *Woody Oriental / Oriental Boisé 62* ●●

D'ALBRET → JEAN D'ALBRET
DALI → SALVADOR DALI

DANA

1921 TOUJOURS MOI *Woody Oriental / Oriental Boisé   61* ●●●●
1932 TABU *Oriental / Oriental   57* ●●●●
1941 CHANTILLY *Oriental / Oriental   57* ●●●
1941 HEAVEN SENT *Aromatic / Fougère   77* ●●●
1942/2000 SIROCCO DONNA *Woody Oriental / Oriental Boisé   60* ●
1949/98 PRIORITÉ *Citrus / Hespéridé   16* ●●
1949/99 ZIGZAG *Citrus / Hespéridé   17* ●●●●
1950/99 IMPOSIBLE ♂ *Citrus / Hespéridé   16* ●
1955/97 AMBUSH *Woody Oriental / Oriental Boisé   60* ●●
1974 LOVE'S BABY SOFT *Soft Floral / Fleuri Aldéhydé   43* ●●●
1982 RAFFINÉE *Floral Oriental / Fleuri Oriental   47* ●●●
1984 LUTÈCE *Floral Oriental / Fleuri Oriental   47* ●●●●
1988 DEMI-JOUR *Soft Floral / Fleuri Aldéhydé   43* ●●●●
1989 CALIFORNIA *Soft Floral / Fleuri Aldéhydé   43* ●●●●
1990 NAVY *Floral Oriental / Fleuri Oriental   47* ●●●●
1992 INCOGNITO *Floral Oriental / Fleuri Oriental   46* ●●
1994 FRENCH VANILLA *Woody Oriental / Oriental Boisé   60* ●●
1995 CLASSIC GARDENIA *Floral / Florale   30* ●●
1995 WHITE CHANTILLY *Floral / Florale   34* ●
1996 DREAMS BY TABU* *Floral / Florale   36* ●
1997 FETISH *Floral / Florale   36* ●
1998 SHADES BY NAVY* *Floral / Florale   34* ●●
2000 ESPÍRITU DE MONTESINOS *Floral / Florale   38* ●
2000 PRIORITÉ EAU BLEU *Floral / Florale   36* ●
1935 CANOÉ *Aromatic / Fougère   77* ●●●
1949 ENGLISH LEATHER *Dry Woods / Boisé Cuir   72* ●●
1965 BRITISH STERLING *Aromatic / Fougère   77* ●●●
1968 TIMBERLINE *Mossy Woods / Chypre Boisé   69* ●●●
1971/99 GENTRY *Aromatic / Fougère   82* ●
1973 MONSIEUR MUSK *Oriental / Oriental   57* ●●●●
1978 HERBISSIMO CEDRO *Citrus / Hespéridé   19* ●●●
1978 HERBISSIMO ENEBRO *Green / Vert   23* ●●●
1978 HERBISSIMO MEJORANA *Aromatic / Fougère   76* ●●
1989 SILVER* *Aromatic / Fougère   77* ●●●
1990 CALIFORNIA FOR MEN *Aromatic / Fougère   76* ●●
1996 HERBISSIMO TÉ VERDE *Citrus / Hespéridé   18* ●
1996 NAVIGATOR *Aromatic / Fougère   78* ●
1996 NAVY FOR MEN *Aromatic / Fougère   80* ●
2000 SIROCCO UOMO *Woody Oriental / Oriental Boisé   62* ●●

DANICA AROMATICS

1999 I AM ENERGY *Citrus / Hespéridé   16* ●
1999 I AM ETERNAL *Woody Oriental / Oriental Boisé   61* ●●●
1999 I AM PASSION *Floral / Florale   36* ●
1999 I AM SERENE *Green / Vert   23* ●●●
1999 I AM WILD *Oriental / Oriental   56* ●
2000 I AM CLEAR *Citrus / Hespéridé   16* ●●
2000 I AM COOL *Water / Marine   26* ●●
2000 I AM LOVE *Floral / Florale   32* ●
2000 I AM POWER *Floral Oriental / Fleuri Oriental   46* ●
2000 I AM RICH *Soft Floral / Fleuri Aldéhydé   42* ●

DANIEL DE FASSON

1990 DANIEL DE FASSON *Floral Oriental / Fleuri Oriental   47* ●●●
1994 TENAZ *Aromatic / Fougère   77* ●●●●

DANIEL HECHTER

2000 DANIEL HECHTER SPORT POUR ELLE *Floral / Florale   32* ●
1989 CARACTÈRE *Dry Woods / Boisé Cuir   72* ●●
1997 XXL *Woody Oriental / Oriental Boisé   62* ●
1999 DANIEL HECHTER SPORT *Aromatic / Fougère   76* ●

DAVIDOFF

1996 COOL WATER WOMAN *Floral / Florale   36* ●●
1999 GOODLIFE WOMAN *Floral Oriental / Fleuri Oriental   46* ●
1984 DAVIDOFF *Dry Woods / Boisé Cuir   73* ●●●●
1986 ZINO DAVIDOFF *Woody Oriental / Oriental Boisé   63* ●●●●
1988 COOL WATER *Aromatic / Fougère   80* ●
1990 RELAX *Woody Oriental / Oriental Boisé   62* ●●
1998 GOODLIFE *Aromatic / Fougère   80* ●●

DAVINCI

1991 DAVINCI UOMO *Dry Woods / Boisé Cuir   73* ●●●●
1997 SPORT 2000 *Aromatic / Fougère   76* ●

DC DESIGN

1994 CHAPEAU BLEU *Mossy Woods / Chypre Boisé   66* ●●

DECLÉOR

1999 AROMANTIC *Floral / Florale   34* ●
2000 L'ORIGINAL *Aromatic / Fougère   82* ●
2000 UN AIR DE JAVA *Mossy Woods / Chypre Boisé   68* ●●

DÉCO

1976 BORONIA *Floral / Florale   31* ●●●
1981 ORIENT *Soft Oriental / Oriental Doux   53* ●●●
1987 ENCHANTÉ *Woody Oriental / Oriental Boisé   60* ●
1994 UNTAMED MUSK *Oriental / Oriental   57* ●●●●

DE LA MORANDIÈRE
→ MARC DE LA MORANDIÈRE
DELON → ALAIN DELON
DEL POZO → J. DEL POZO

DEMETER FRAGRANCE LIBRARY
(a selection *un choix*)

1995 LAVENDER ♂ *Floral / Florale   31* ●●●
1996 DIRT ♂ *Mossy Woods / Chypre Boisé   66* ●●
1996 EARL GREY TEA ♂ *Citrus / Hespéridé   16* ●
1996 FIG LEAF ♂ *Mossy Woods / Chypre Boisé   66* ●
1996 GRASS ♂ *Green / Vert   23* ●●●
1996 SUGAR COOKIE ♂ *Soft Oriental / Oriental Doux   52* ●●
1996 TOMATO ♂ *Green / Vert   22* ●●
1997 ANGEL FOOD ♂ *Soft Oriental / Oriental Doux   53* ●●●
1997 GARDENIA *Floral / Florale   30* ●●
1997 GIN & TONIC ♂ *Citrus / Hespéridé   17* ●●●
1997 GINGERALE ♂ *Citrus / Hespéridé   17* ●●●●
1997 GREENHOUSE ♂ *Green / Vert   22* ●
1998 DANDELION ♂ *Floral / Florale   34* ●●
1998 GINGERBREAD ♂ *Oriental / Oriental   57* ●●●●
1998 HONEYSUCKLE *Floral / Florale   30* ●●
1998 LETTUCE ♂ *Green / Vert   22* ●●
1998 LILAC *Floral / Florale   30* ●●
1998 PRUNING SHEARS ♂ *Floral / Florale   36* ●
1998 SWEETPEA *Floral / Florale   30* ●●
1998 THIS IS NOT A PIPE ♂ *Dry Woods / Boisé Cuir   73* ●●●
1999 GOLDEN DELICIOUS ♂ *Citrus / Hespéridé   16* ●●
1999 HOLY WATER ♂ *Water / Marine   27* ●●●●
1999 SAWDUST ♂ *Mossy Woods / Chypre Boisé   67* ●●●
1999 SNOW ♂ *Mossy Woods / Chypre Boisé   66* ●●
2000 BONFIRE ♂ *Dry Woods / Boisé Cuir   73* ●●●●
2000 LAUNDROMAT ♂ *Water / Marine   26* ●●

DE NICOLAÏ → PATRICIA DE NICOLAÏ

DE RUY

1998 ATREVIDA *Floral Oriental / Fleuri Oriental   46* ●●
1998 FUN WATER WOMAN *Water / Marine   26* ●●
1999 ACQUA DI FIORI *Floral / Florale   36* ●
1996 FUN WATER FOR MEN *Aromatic / Fougère   78* ●

DE VARENS → ULRIC DE VARENS

DIANA DE SILVA

1996 DIVINA *Floral / Florale   34* ●●

DIANA VON FURSTENBERG

1975 TATIANA *Floral / Florale   33* ●●●●

DIDIER CALVO-UOMO

1995 HÉROS *Woody Oriental / Oriental Boisé   62* ●●
1997 HÉROS SPORT *Aromatic / Fougère   78* ●

DIESEL

1996 DIESEL ♂ *Woody Oriental / Oriental Boisé   61* ●●●
1997 DIESEL PLUS PLUS FEMININE *Floral Oriental / Fleuri Oriental   48* ●
1999 DIESEL ZERO PLUS FEMININE *Woody Oriental / Oriental Boisé   60* ●
1997 DIESEL PLUS PLUS MASCULINE *Woody Oriental / Oriental Boisé   62* ●
1999 DIESEL ZERO PLUS MASCULINE *Woody Oriental / Oriental Boisé   63* ●●●

DIONNE WARWICK

1986 DIONNE *Oriental / Oriental   56* ●

DIOR → CHRISTIAN DIOR

DIPTYQUE
1968 L'EAU ♂ *Soft Oriental / Oriental Doux 52* ●●
1973 L'AUTRE ♂ *Dry Woods / Boisé Cuir 73* ●●●●
1975 L'EAU TROIS ♂ *Dry Woods / Boisé Cuir 72* ●●
1983 L'OMBRE DANS L'EAU *Floral / Florale 34* ●●
1986 EAU LENTE ♂ *Oriental / Oriental 57* ●●●
1988 EAU D'ÉLIDE ♂ *Aromatic / Fougère 77* ●●●
1988 OLÈNE *Floral / Florale 38* ●●
1990 VIRGILIO ♂ *Green / Vert 22* ●●
1996 PHILOSYKOS ♂ *Mossy Woods / Chypre Boisé 66* ●
1999 OFRÉSIA *Floral / Florale 36* ●
2000 OYÉDO ♂ *Citrus / Hespéridé 17* ●●●●
2001 OPÔNÉ ♂ *Mossy Woods / Chypre Boisé 67* ●●●

DOG GENERATION
2000 OH! MY DOG *Floral / Florale 36* ●●

DOLCE & GABBANA
1992 DOLCE & GABBANA *Soft Floral / Fleuri Aldéhydé 43* ●●●●
1997 BY WOMAN *Woody Oriental / Oriental Boisé 61* ●●●
1999 D&G FEMININE *Soft Floral / Fleuri Aldéhydé 43* ●●●●
1994 DOLCE & GABBANA POUR HOMME *Aromatic / Fougère 77* ●●●
1998 BY MAN *Woody Oriental / Oriental Boisé 62* ●●
1999 D&G MASCULINE *Citrus / Hespéridé 19* ●●●●

DOMINGUEZ → ADOLFO DOMINGUEZ

DONNA KARAN
1992 DONNA KARAN *Dry Woods / Boisé Cuir 73* ●●●
1994 CASHMERE MIST *Dry Woods / Boisé Cuir 72* ●
1996 CHAOS* *Woody Oriental / Oriental Boisé 60* ●●
1999 DKNY WOMEN *Soft Floral / Fleuri Aldéhydé 42* ●
1994 DK MEN* *Dry Woods / Boisé Cuir 72* ●●
1995 DK MEN UNLEADED* *Dry Woods / Boisé Cuir 72* ●
2000 DKNY MEN *Aromatic / Fougère 78* ●

D'ORSAY
1908 ÉTIQUETTE BLEUE ♂ *Citrus / Hespéridé 16* ●●
1943 ARÔME 3 ♂ *Floral / Florale 31* ●●●
1955/95 TILLEUL ♂ *Floral / Florale 30* ●
1942/97 INTOXICATION D'AMOUR *Woody Oriental / Oriental Boisé 61* ●●●
1998 ARÔME 3 TRADITION ♂ *Floral / Florale 31* ●●●●
1914 CHEVALIER D'ORSAY *Citrus / Hespéridé 19* ●●●●
1925/98 LE DANDY *Dry Woods / Boisé Cuir 72* ●

DUNHILL → ALFRED DUNHILL

E.COUDRAY
1922 NOHIBA (TULIPE NOIRE) *Soft Oriental / Oriental Doux 53* ●●●
1935 VANILLE CANNELLE *Oriental / Oriental 57* ●●●
1946 CAMÉLIA IRIS (BLEU) *Soft Floral / Fleuri Aldéhydé 42* ●
1950 GIVRINE (SICILE) ♂ *Citrus / Hespéridé 17* ●●●
1983 JACINTHE ROSE (ROMANTICA) *Floral / Florale 38* ●
1986 VANILLE *Oriental / Oriental 57* ●●●
1989 VANILLE COCO *Woody Oriental / Oriental Boisé 60* ●
1995 MIEL ORANGE *Citrus / Hespéridé 17* ●●●●
1998 FÉTICHE *Floral Oriental / Fleuri Oriental 47* ●●●

EDGAR DE BERCHELAI
1997 DE BERCHELAI *Floral / Florale 32* ●●

ELIZABETH ARDEN
1934/89 BLUE GRASS *Floral / Florale 33* ●●●●
1986 EAU FRAÎCHE *Floral / Florale 30* ●
1989 RED DOOR *Floral / Florale 33* ●●●●
1993 SUNFLOWERS *Water / Marine 27* ●●●
1994 TRUE LOVE* *Soft Floral / Fleuri Aldéhydé 42* ●
1996 5th AVENUE *Floral / Florale 34* ●
1998 SPLENDOR *Floral / Florale 38* ●
1999 GREEN TEA *Citrus / Hespéridé 16* ●

ELIZABETH TAYLOR
1987 PASSION *Woody Oriental / Oriental Boisé 61* ●●●
1991 WHITE DIAMONDS *Soft Floral / Fleuri Aldéhydé 42* ●●
1993 DIAMONDS & EMERALDS* *Floral / Florale 38* ●●
1993 DIAMONDS & RUBIES* *Woody Oriental / Oriental Boisé 61* ●●●
1993 DIAMONDS & SAPPHIRES* *Floral / Florale 36* ●
1996 BLACK PEARLS* *Floral Oriental / Fleuri Oriental 46* ●
1999 SPARKLING WHITE DIAMONDS *Soft Floral / Fleuri Aldéhydé 42* ●
1989 PASSION FOR MEN *Woody Oriental / Oriental Boisé 63* ●●●

ELLEN TRACY
1992/2000 ELLEN TRACY *Woody Oriental / Oriental Boisé 61* ●●●

ENRICO COVERI
1987 ENRICO COVERI *Soft Oriental / Oriental Doux 53* ●●●
1993 FIRENZE *Soft Floral / Fleuri Aldéhydé 42* ●●

ERIC TABARLY
1998 PEN DUICK *Aromatic / Fougère 82* ●

ERMENEGILDO ZEGNA
1992 ZEGNA *Aromatic / Fougère 78* ●●

ESCADA-MARGARETHA LEY
1990 ESCADA *Floral Oriental / Fleuri Oriental 47* ●●●
1995 ACTE 2 *Soft Floral / Fleuri Aldéhydé 42* ●●
1996 ESCADA COUNTRY WEEKEND ♂ *Aromatic / Fougère 76* ●●
1996 ESCADA FEELING FREE *Floral / Florale 34* ●
1996 ESCADA SPORT SPIRIT ♂ *Citrus / Hespéridé 16* ●
1997 ESCADA COLLECTION *Woody Oriental / Oriental Boisé 60* ●
1997 ESCADA EN FLEURS *Floral / Florale 32* ●
1999 ESCADA TENDER LIGHT *Floral Oriental / Fleuri Oriental 48* ●
1999 LOVING BOUQUET* Ⓛ *Floral / Florale 36* ●
2000 LILY CHIC* Ⓛ *Floral / Florale 32* ●●
2000 SENTIMENT *Floral / Florale 33* ●●●●
2001 TROPICAL PUNCH Ⓛ *Floral / Florale 34* ●
1993 ESCADA POUR HOMME *Woody Oriental / Oriental Boisé 62* ●●
1997 SILVER LIGHT *Citrus / Hespéridé 18* ●●
1999 CASUAL FRIDAY *Woody Oriental / Oriental Boisé 62* ●

ESTÉE LAUDER
1953 YOUTH-DEW *Soft Oriental / Oriental Doux 53* ●●●
1968 ESTÉE *Floral / Florale 33* ●●●●
1969 AZURÉE *Dry Woods / Boisé Cuir 73* ●●●
1972 ALIAGE / ALLIAGE *Green / Vert 23* ●●●
1973 PRIVATE COLLECTION *Green / Vert 23* ●●●●
1978 CINNABAR *Soft Oriental / Oriental Doux 53* ●●●
1978 WHITE LINEN *Soft Floral / Fleuri Aldéhydé 42* ●●
1985 BEAUTIFUL *Floral / Florale 32* ●●
1988 KNOWING *Mossy Woods / Chypre Boisé 67* ●●●
1991 SPELLBOUND *Floral Oriental / Fleuri Oriental 47* ●●●
1992 TUSCANY PER DONNA *Woody Oriental / Oriental Boisé 60* ●
1995 PLEASURES *Floral / Florale 36* ●
1996 WHITE LINEN BREEZE *Soft Floral / Fleuri Aldéhydé 42* ●
1998 DAZZLING GOLD *Floral / Florale 32* ●●
1998 DAZZLING SILVER *Soft Floral / Fleuri Aldéhydé 42* ●●
2000 BODY POWER *Green / Vert 23* ●●●
2000 INTUITION *Floral Oriental / Fleuri Oriental 46* ●
1987 LAUDER FOR MEN *Aromatic / Fougère 78* ●●
1987 METROPOLIS *Mossy Woods / Chypre Boisé 68* ●●
1997 PLEASURES FOR MEN *Aromatic / Fougère 80* ●

ETIENNE AIGNER
1986 EXPLOSIVE* *Mossy Woods / Chypre Boisé 66* ●●
1991 PRIVATE NUMBER FOR WOMEN* *Floral / Florale 34* ●●
1997 CLEAR DAY *Floral / Florale 32* ●●
1997 X LIMITED ♂ *Citrus / Hespéridé 16* ●
1999 CLEAR DAY LIGHT *Floral / Florale 32* ●
1975 ETIENNE AIGNER Nº 1* *Dry Woods / Boisé Cuir 73* ●●●
1976 ETIENNE AIGNER Nº 2 *Aromatic / Fougère 77* ●●●●
1992 PRIVATE NUMBER FOR MEN* *Mossy Woods / Chypre Boisé 68* ●●
1994 STATEMENT FOR MEN* *Aromatic / Fougère 78* ●
1998 CLEAR DAY FOR MEN *Aromatic / Fougère 78* ●
2000 AIGNER POUR HOMME *Dry Woods / Boisé Cuir 72* ●●

ETRO
1989 AMBRA ♂ *Oriental / Oriental 57* ●●●
1989 GOMMA ♂ *Dry Woods / Boisé Cuir 73* ●●●●
1989 HELIOTROPE ♂ *Floral Oriental / Fleuri Oriental 47* ●●●
1989 LEMON SORBET ♂ *Aromatic / Fougère 76* ●
1989 PALAIS JAMAIS ♂ *Dry Woods / Boisé Cuir 73* ●●●●

1989 PATCHOULY ♂ *Woody Oriental / Oriental Boisé* 61 ●●●
1989 ROYAL PAVILLON ♂ *Floral / Florale* 36 ●●
1989 SANDALO ♂ *Woody Oriental / Oriental Boisé* 61 ●●●●
1989 VETIVER ♂ *Dry Woods / Boisé Cuir* 73 ●●●
1994 MESSE DE MINUIT ♂ *Oriental / Oriental* 57 ●●●●
1996 MAGOT ♂ *Oriental / Oriental* 56 ●
1996 VICOLO FIORI ♀ *Floral Oriental / Fleuri Oriental* 48 ●
1997 SHAAL NUR ♂ *Woody Oriental / Oriental Boisé* 61 ●●●●
1999 ETRA ♂ *Soft Oriental / Oriental Doux* 53 ●●●●

ETTORE BUGATTI
1992/99 BUGATTI *Aromatic / Fougère* 78 ●

EUROITALIA
1993 JOSEPH ABBOUD *Aromatic / Fougère* 80 ●●

EVYAN
1945 WHITE SHOULDERS *Floral / Florale* 33 ●●●

EVYAN / LTL
1961/96 THE BARON *Aromatic / Fougère* 77 ●●●

FABERGÉ (Selection)
1938 APHRODISIA* *Mossy Woods / Chypre Boisé* 66 ●●
1938 TIGRESS* *Floral Oriental / Fleuri Oriental* 47 ●●●
1944 WOODHUE* *Woody Oriental / Oriental Boisé* 61 ●●●
1996 FABERGÉ IMPERIAL *Floral / Florale* 33 ●●●●
1998 PRINCESS GRACE DE MONACO *Floral / Florale* 36 ●
1964 BRUT *Aromatic / Fougère* 77 ●●●
1994 BRUT ACTIF BLUE *Aromatic / Fougère* 82 ●
1997 BRUT INSTINCT *Aromatic / Fougère* 76 ●●

FAÇONNABLE
1996 FACE À FACE FEMME *Floral / Florale* 36 ●
2000 FAÇONNABLE *Floral / Florale* 34 ●●
1994 FAÇONNABLE *Aromatic / Fougère* 82 ●
1996 FACE À FACE HOMME *Aromatic / Fougère* 82 ●

FASHION FAIR
1977 FASHION FAIR N° 1 *Floral / Florale* 34 ●●
1985 EUNECE *Woody Oriental / Oriental Boisé* 61 ●●●
1993 ZAHRA *Floral Oriental / Fleuri Oriental* 46 ●●
1975 MR J *Aromatic / Fougère* 78 ●●

FATH → JACQUES FATH

FENDI
1985 FENDI *Woody Oriental / Oriental Boisé* 61 ●●●●
1992 ASJA *Soft Oriental / Oriental Doux* 53 ●●●
1996 FANTASIA *Floral / Florale* 32 ●●
1998 THEOREMA *Soft Oriental / Oriental Doux* 53 ●●●
1999 THEOREMA ESPRIT D'ÉTÉ *Soft Oriental / Oriental Doux* 52 ●●
1988 FENDI UOMO *Dry Woods / Boisé Cuir* 73 ●●●●
1996 LIFE ESSENCE *Mossy Woods / Chypre Boisé* 68 ●●
2001 THEOREMA UOMO *Mossy Woods / Chypre Boisé* 68 ●●

FERRAGAMO → SALVATORE FERRAGAMO

FERRARI
1995 FERRARI DONNA *Floral / Florale* 36 ●●
1996 FERRARI RED *Woody Oriental / Oriental Boisé* 62 ●
1998 FERRARI YELLOW COLOGNE WATER *Citrus / Hespéridé* 19 ●●●
1999 FERRARI BLACK *Mossy Woods / Chypre Boisé* 68 ●●
2000 FERRARI YELLOW EAU DE TOILETTE *Aromatic / Fougère* 78 ●

FERRÉ → GIANFRANCO FERRÉ

FFC - FINE FRAGRANCES & COSMETICS
1924/92 TWEED *Floral / Florale* 33 ●●●●
1976 CHIQUE *Mossy Woods / Chypre Boisé* 67 ●●●●
1979 PANACHE *Soft Floral / Fleuri Aldéhydé* 42 ●●
1984 LACE *Mossy Woods / Chypre Boisé* 66 ●
1985 WHITE SATIN *Soft Floral / Fleuri Aldéhydé* 42 ●●

FILA
1997 EMOZIONI FOR WOMAN *Floral / Florale* 38 ●
1997 EMOZIONI FOR MAN *Aromatic / Fougère* 82 ●

FIORUCCI
1978/99 FIORUCCI *Floral / Florale* 32 ●●

FLORALIES → LES FLORALIES

FLORBATH
1978 NICKI LAUDA *Aromatic / Fougère* 78 ●●

FLORI ROBERTS (a selection *un choix*)
1996 PATTI LaBELLE *Floral Oriental / Fleuri Oriental* 46 ●

FLORIS
1786 STEPHANOTIS *Floral / Florale* 31 ●●●●
1828 LAVENDER ♂ *Floral / Florale* 31 ●●●
1830/1999 MALMAISON *Floral / Florale* 31 ●●●●
1832 LIMES ♂ *Citrus / Hespéridé* 17 ●●●●
1847 LILY OF THE VALLEY *Floral / Florale* 30 ●
1870/2000 TUBEROSE *Floral / Florale* 31 ●●●●
1901/84 EDWARDIAN BOUQUET *Floral / Florale* 38 ●
1910 SPECIAL N° 127 ♂ *Citrus / Hespéridé* 17 ●●●
1978 FLORISSA *Soft Floral / Fleuri Aldéhydé* 42 ●●
1990 ZINNIA *Floral / Florale* 38 ●
1993 SERINGA *Floral / Florale* 36 ●
1996 BOUVARDIA* *Floral Oriental / Fleuri Oriental* 47 ●●●
1997 GARDENIA *Floral / Florale* 30 ●●
2000 CHINA ROSE *Floral Oriental / Fleuri Oriental* 47 ●●●●
2000 FLEUR *Floral / Florale* 36 ●
1950 N° 89 *Aromatic / Fougère* 77 ●●●
1870/2000 VETIVER *Mossy Woods / Chypre Boisé* 69 ●●●
1980 ELITE *Citrus / Hespéridé* 19 ●●●●
1993 J.F. *Aromatic / Fougère* 80 ●

FRAGONARD
1995 SOLEIL *Floral / Florale* 36 ●●
1996 SORENZA *Floral / Florale* 33 ●●●
1999 GRAIN DE SOLEIL *Woody Oriental / Oriental Boisé* 61 ●●●
1932 ZIZANIE *Woody Oriental / Oriental Boisé* 63 ●●●
1999 SIESTE *Dry Woods / Boisé Cuir* 73 ●●●

FRAGRANCE INTERNATIONAL
1999 KISS & TELL *Floral / Florale* 38 ●

FRAGRANCES OF IRELAND (a selection *un choix*)
1998 INIS ♂ *Water / Marine* 26 ●

FRANCESCO SMALTO
1993 SMALTO DONNA* *Woody Oriental / Oriental Boisé* 61 ●●●
2001 S pour FEMME *Floral / Florale* 34 ●●
1987/98 SMALTO *Mossy Woods / Chypre Boisé* 68 ●●
1992 MOLTO SMALTO* *Aromatic / Fougère* 76 ●
2001 S pour HOMME *Woody Oriental / Oriental Boisé* 62 ●

FRANCES DENNEY
1952 HOPE *Soft Floral / Fleuri Aldéhydé* 43 ●●●●
1965 INTERLUDE *Oriental / Oriental* 57 ●●●

FRED HAYMAN
1989 273 RODEO DRIVE *Floral / Florale* 33 ●●●
1991 WITH LOVE* *Woody Oriental / Oriental Boisé* 60 ●
1993 TOUCH *Floral / Florale* 36 ●●
1998 HOLLYWOOD *Woody Oriental / Oriental Boisé* 60 ●●
1990 273 RODEO DRIVE FOR MEN *Dry Woods / Boisé Cuir* 72 ●●
1995 TOUCH FOR MEN* *Aromatic / Fougère* 77 ●●●
1998 HOLLYWOOD FOR MEN *Aromatic / Fougère* 76 ●●

FRENCH CONNECTION
1997 FRENCH CONNECTION *Citrus / Hesperide* 16 ●

FRESH (a selection *un choix*)
1996 INDEX BERGAMOT CITRUS ♂ *Citrus / Hespéridé* 16 ●
1996 INDEX CURRANT MARINE ♂ *Water / Marine* 26 ●●
1996 MUKKI ♂ *Soft Floral / Fleuri Aldéhydé* 42 ●●
1997 ACQUA DI MIELE ♂ *Floral / Florale* 38 ●
1997 INDEX CHINA GREEN TEA ♂ *Green / Vert* 22 ●●
1997 INDEX CORIANDER LAVENDER ♂ *Aromatic / Fougère* 76 ●●
1997 INDEX FIG APRICOT ♂ *Mossy Woods / Chypre Boisé* 66 ●
1997 INDEX MOROCCAN MINT TEA ♂ *Citrus / Hespéridé* 16 ●●

1997 INDEX ORANGE CHOCOLATE ♂ *Soft Oriental / Oriental Doux* 52 ●
1997 INDEX POMEGRANATE ANISE ♂ *Citrus / Hespéridé* 16 ●
1997 INDEX SANDALWOOD PETITGRAIN ♂ *Citrus / Hespéridé* 17 ●●●●
1997 INDEX VIOLET MOSS ♂ *Mossy Woods / Chypre Boisé* 66 ●●
1998 INDEX AMARYLLIS CASSIS ♂ *Floral / Florale* 32 ●
1998 INDEX GERANIUM PEPPER ♂ *Aromatic / Fougère* 77 ●●●●
1998 INDEX RED CURRANT BASIL ♂ *Floral / Florale* 32 ●●
1999 INDEX CEDAR ARMOISE ♂ *Mossy Woods / Chypre Boisé* 66 ●●
1999 INDEX GALBANUM PATCHOULI ♂ *Mossy Woods / Chypre Boisé* 66 ●
1999 INDEX HONEYSUCKLE GRAPEFRUIT ♂ *Citrus / Hespéridé* 16 ●●
1999 INDEX MANDARINE AMBER ♂ *Mossy Woods / Chypre Boisé* 67 ●●●●
1999 INDEX OLIVE MUSCADE ♂ *Mossy Woods / Chypre Boisé* 67 ●●●
1999 INDEX PEAR CASSIS ♂ *Floral / Florale* 32 ●●
1999 INDEX TOBACCO CARAMEL ♂ *Dry Woods / Boisé Cuir* 73 ●●●
1999 INDEX YLANG-YLANG HIBISCUS ♂ *Floral / Florale* 31 ●●●
1999 SUGAR ♂ *Citrus / Hespéridé* 16 ●●
2000 INDEX GRAPEFRUIT MUSC ♂ *Citrus / Hespéridé* 17 ●●●●
2000 INDEX JASMINE LYS ♂ *Floral / Florale* 38 ●
1999 HOMBRE DE FLORES JASMINUM *Mossy Woods / Chypre Boisé* 68 ●●
1999 HOMBRE DE FLORES NARCISSUS
　　　Woody Oriental / Oriental Boisé 63 ●●●●
1999 HOMBRE DE FLORES POLIANTHES TUBEROSE *Floral / Florale* 39 ●●●●

GABRIELA SABATINI

1989 GABRIELA SABATINI *Floral Oriental / Fleuri Oriental* 48 ●●
1992 MAGNETIC *Floral Oriental / Fleuri Oriental* 46 ●
1994 CASCAYA *Floral Oriental / Fleuri Oriental* 46 ●●
1997 BOLERO *Floral / Florale* 32 ●●
1998 CASCAYA SUMMER *Floral / Florale* 34 ●
1999 WILD WIND *Water / Marine* 26 ●●
2000 SUMMER *Floral / Florale* 34 ●
1999 WILD WIND FOR MEN *Aromatic / Fougère* 78 ●

GAI MATTIOLO

1997 GAI MATTIOLO *Floral Oriental / Fleuri Oriental* 46 ●
2000 THAT'S AMORE! LEI *Floral Oriental / Fleuri Oriental* 46 ●
1998 GAI MATTIOLO UOMO *Citrus / Hespéridé* 18 ●
2000 THAT'S AMORE! LUI *Woody Oriental / Oriental Boisé* 62 ●

GALANOS

1979 GALANOS DE SERENE *Soft Oriental / Oriental Doux* 53 ●●●
1979/96 GALANOS *Soft Floral / Fleuri Aldéhydé* 43 ●●●

GALE HAYMAN

1990 BEVERLY HILLS *Woody Oriental / Oriental Boisé* 60 ●
1993 "DELICIOUS" *Soft Floral / Fleuri Aldéhydé* 43 ●●●●
1996 "DELICIOUS" FEELINGS *Floral / Florale* 36 ●
1998 SUNSET BOULEVARD *Floral Oriental / Fleuri Oriental* 48 ●●
1999 GLAMOUR *Floral Oriental / Fleuri Oriental* 47 ●●●
1999 STYLE *Floral Oriental / Fleuri Oriental* 46 ●
1997 GALE HAYMAN MAN *Aromatic / Fougère* 82 ●●

GANDH SUGANDH

1999 LATA *Floral Oriental / Fleuri Oriental* 47 ●●●
1999 URVÂSHI *Floral Oriental / Fleuri Oriental* 46 ●●

GANT

1997 GANT CLASSIC *Aromatic / Fougère* 76 ●
1999 G2 *Woody Oriental / Oriental Boisé* 63 ●●●
2001 INDIGO *Citrus / Hespéridé* 19 ●●●

GAP

1994 DAY ♂ *Citrus / Hespéridé* 17 ●●●●
1994 GRASS ♂ *Green / Vert* 23 ●●●
1994 EARTH ♂ *Mossy Woods / Chypre Boisé* 66 ●
1994 HEAVEN *Soft Floral / Fleuri Aldéhydé* 42 ●
1995 DREAM *Floral / Florale* 38 ●
1996 OM ♂ *Woody Oriental / Oriental Boisé* 61 ●●●
1997 BLUE N° 655 HER *Floral / Florale* 32 ●
2000 CLOSE *Soft Floral / Fleuri Aldéhydé* 42 ●
1997 BLUE N° 655 HIM *Aromatic / Fougère* 80 ●

GATTINONI

1998 GATTINONI COUTURE *Woody Oriental / Oriental Boisé* 60 ●
1999 GATTINONI À PORTER *Floral / Florale* 32 ●●

GAULTIER → JEAN PAUL GAULTIER

GEIR NESS

1995 LAILA *Floral / Florale* 38 ●

GENDARME

1996 CARRIÈRE *Citrus / Hespéridé* 16 ●●
1991 GENDARME *Citrus / Hespéridé* 19 ●●●●
1995 GRABAZZI *Soft Oriental / Oriental Doux* 53 ●●●

GENNY

1987 GENNY (Original) *Dry Woods / Boisé Cuir* 72 ●
1987/98 GENNY (New) *Floral / Florale* 32 ●●
1993 GENNY SHINE* *Floral Oriental / Fleuri Oriental* 46 ●●

GEOFFREY BEENE

1998 GEOFFREY BEENE *Floral / Florale* 34 ●●
1976 GREY FLANNEL *Mossy Woods / Chypre Boisé* 68 ●
1987 BOWLING GREEN *Aromatic / Fougère* 78 ●●
1996 EAU DE GREY FLANNEL *Mossy Woods / Chypre Boisé* 68 ●

GERANI

1998 GERANI *Woody Oriental / Oriental Boisé* 60 ●
1999 GERANI UOMO *Woody Oriental / Oriental Boisé* 62 ●

GERMAINE MONTEIL → MONTEIL
GERMAINE MONTEIL / ROYAL SECRET
→ ROYAL SECRET

GHOST

2000 GHOST *Floral Oriental / Fleuri Oriental* 46 ●●

GIANFRANCO FERRÉ

1984 GIANFRANCO FERRÉ *Floral / Florale* 38 ●
1991 FERRÉ BY FERRÉ *Soft Floral / Fleuri Aldéhydé* 43 ●●●
1995 GIEFFEFFE ♂ *Citrus / Hespéridé* 16 ●
1997 GFF F *Floral / Florale* 34 ●●
1998 GIANFRANCO FERRÉ 20 *Floral / Florale* 33 ●●●
1986 FERRÉ FOR MAN *Woody Oriental / Oriental Boisé* 63 ●●●
1997 GFF M *Aromatic / Fougère* 78 ●
2000 PONTACCIO 21 *Dry Woods / Boisé Cuir* 72 ●●

GIAN MARCO VENTURI

1999 GMV DONNA *Floral Oriental / Fleuri Oriental* 46 ●●
1997 GMV UOMO *Aromatic / Fougère* 80 ●
1998 GMV ENERGY *Aromatic / Fougère* 82 ●
2000 GMV HOT *Woody Oriental / Oriental Boisé* 62 ●●

GIANNI VERSACE → VERSACE
GIGLI → ROMEO GIGLI

GIORGIO ARMANI

1982 ARMANI *Mossy Woods / Chypre Boisé* 66 ●
1992 GIÒ *Floral / Florale* 33 ●●●●
1995 ACQUA DI GIÒ *Floral / Florale* 36 ●
1998 EMPORIO ARMANI SHE / ELLE *Floral Oriental / Fleuri Oriental* 47 ●●●
1999 MANIA *Woody Oriental / Oriental Boisé* 61 ●●●
1984 ARMANI POUR HOMME *Citrus / Hespéridé* 19 ●●●●
1996 ACQUA DI GIÒ POUR HOMME *Water / Marine* 26 ●●
1998 EMPORIO ARMANI HE / LUI *Mossy Woods / Chypre Boisé* 68 ●●

GIORGIO BEVERLY HILLS

1981 GIORGIO *Floral / Florale* 38 ●●
1989 RED *Mossy Woods / Chypre Boisé* 66 ●●
1992 WINGS* *Floral / Florale* 33 ●●●●
1996 GIORGIO AIRE* *Soft Floral / Fleuri Aldéhydé* 42 ●
1996 OCEAN DREAM *Floral / Florale* 38 ●
1996 RED 2* *Floral Oriental / Fleuri Oriental* 46 ●
1998 GIORGIO HOLIDAY* ⓛ *Floral / Florale* 32 ●●
1999 G *Soft Floral / Fleuri Aldéhydé* 42 ●
1984 GIORGIO MEN* *Mossy Woods / Chypre Boisé* 69 ●●●●
1990 RED FOR MEN *Aromatic / Fougère* 78 ●●
1994 WINGS FOR MEN *Aromatic / Fougère* 80 ●

GIVENCHY

1957 LE DE* *Floral / Florale* 33 ●●●
1957 L'INTERDIT *Soft Floral / Fleuri Aldéhydé* 43 ●●●
1970 GIVENCHY III *Mossy Woods / Chypre Boisé* 66 ●
1980 EAU DE GIVENCHY *Floral / Florale* 32 ●

115

1984 YSATIS *Woody Oriental / Oriental Boisé 60* ●
1991 AMARIGE *Floral Oriental / Fleuri Oriental 48* ●●
1994 FLEUR D'INTERDIT *Floral / Florale 36* ●
1996 ORGANZA *Woody Oriental / Oriental Boisé 60* ●●
1998 EXTRAVAGANCE D'AMARIGE *Floral / Florale 36* ●
1999 ORGANZA INDÉCENCE *Woody Oriental / Oriental Boisé 61* ●●●●
2000 HOT COUTURE *Woody Oriental / Oriental Boisé 60* ●●
2000 OBLIQUE FAST FORWARD *Floral / Florale 36* ●
2000 OBLIQUE PLAY *Citrus / Hespéridé 17* ●●●●
2000 OBLIQUE REWIND *Woody Oriental / Oriental Boisé 60* ●●
1959 MONSIEUR DE GIVENCHY *Citrus / Hespéridé 19* ●●●
1974 GIVENCHY GENTLEMAN *Mossy Woods / Chypre Boisé 69* ●●●●
1986 XERYUS *Aromatic / Fougère 78* ●●
1993 INSENSÉ *Floral / Florale 38* ●●
1994 INSENSÉ ULTRAMARINE *Aromatic / Fougère 82* ●
1995 XERYUS ROUGE *Woody Oriental / Oriental Boisé 62* ●●
1998 π *Woody Oriental / Oriental Boisé 63* ●●●
1999 GREENERGY *Mossy Woods / Chypre Boisé 68* ●●

GLORIA VANDERBILT

1982 VANDERBILT *Floral Oriental / Fleuri Oriental 47* ●●●
1994 V *Soft Floral / Fleuri Aldéhydé 42* ●●
1996 HONEYMOON *Woody Oriental / Oriental Boisé 60* ●●
1999 RÊVERIE *Floral Oriental / Fleuri Oriental 47* ●●●
2000 RÊVERIE PURE *Floral / Florale 36* ●
2000 VANDERBILT FOR MEN *Woody Oriental / Oriental Boisé 62* ●

GOUTAL → ANNICK GOUTAL

GRANITE

1992 GRANITE ORIGINAL *Aromatic / Fougère 82* ●
1996 GRANITE BLUE *Aromatic / Fougère 80* ●

GRÈS

1959 CABOCHARD *Dry Woods / Boisé Cuir 73* ●●●
1990 CABOTINE DE GRÈS *Floral / Florale 34* ●●
1996 PASTEL DE CABOTINE *Floral / Florale 34* ●
1997 FOLIE DOUCE *Floral / Florale 32* ●●
1999 GRAIN DE FOLIE *Green / Vert 22* ●●
2000 AIR DE... CABOCHARD *Dry Woods / Boisé Cuir 72* ●
1996 HOMME DE GRÈS *Dry Woods / Boisé Cuir 73* ●●●●

GUCCI

1974 GUCCI N° 1* *Soft Floral / Fleuri Aldéhydé 42* ●●
1982/93 EAU DE GUCCI* *Floral / Florale 38* ●
1985 GUCCI N° 3* *Mossy Woods / Chypre Boisé 66* ●●
1991 L'ARTE DI GUCCI* *Mossy Woods / Chypre Boisé 67* ●●●
1995 ACCENTI *Floral Oriental / Fleuri Oriental 48* ●
1997 ENVY *Floral / Florale 38* ●
1999 GUCCI RUSH *Woody Oriental / Oriental Boisé 60* ●●
1988 GUCCI NOBILE* *Aromatic / Fougère 80* ●●
1998 ENVY FOR MEN *Woody Oriental / Oriental Boisé 62* ●
2000 GUCCI RUSH FOR MEN *Mossy Woods / Chypre Boisé 68* ●●

GUÉPARD

1997 GUÉPARD *Woody Oriental / Oriental Boisé 61* ●●●
2000 DÉLIRIUM DE NUIT *Citrus / Hespéridé 17* ●●●●
2000 DÉLIRIUM OCEANE *Floral / Florale 32* ●
2000 DÉLIRIUM ROSE *Floral / Florale 32* ●●
2000 DÉLIRIUM TEA *Floral / Florale 34* ●
1998 GUÉPARD HOMME *Mossy Woods / Chypre Boisé 68* ●●
2000 GENTLEMAN GUÉPARD *Mossy Woods / Chypre Boisé 68* ●

GUERLAIN

1853 EAU IMPÉRIALE ♂ *Citrus / Hespéridé 17* ●●●
1889 JICKY ♂ *Aromatic / Fougère 77* ●●●
1894 EAU DU COQ ♂ *Citrus / Hespéridé 17* ●●●
1904/96 CHAMPS-ÉLYSÉES *Floral / Florale 30* ●●
1906 APRÈS L'ONDÉE *Floral Oriental / Fleuri Oriental 48* ●
1912 L'HEURE BLEUE *Floral Oriental / Fleuri Oriental 47* ●●●
1919 MITSOUKO *Mossy Woods / Chypre Boisé 67* ●●●
1920 EAU DE FLEURS DE CÉDRAT ♂ *Citrus / Hespéridé 17* ●●●
1925 SHALIMAR *Oriental / Oriental 57* ●●●
1929 LIÙ *Soft Floral / Fleuri Aldéhydé 43* ●●●
1933 VOL DE NUIT *Woody Oriental / Oriental Boisé 60* ●●
1962 CHANT D'ARÔMES *Mossy Woods / Chypre Boisé 66* ●●
1969 CHAMADE *Floral Oriental / Fleuri Oriental 46* ●●

1974 EAU DE GUERLAIN ♂ *Citrus / Hespéridé 17* ●●●
1975 PARURE *Mossy Woods / Chypre Boisé 67* ●●●
1979 NAHÉMA *Floral Oriental / Fleuri Oriental 47* ●●●●
1983 JARDINS DE BAGATELLE *Floral / Florale 33* ●●●●
1989 SAMSARA *Woody Oriental / Oriental Boisé 61* ●●●
1994 PETIT GUERLAIN ♂ *Citrus / Hespéridé 17* ●●●
1995 UN AIR DE SAMSARA *Woody Oriental / Oriental Boisé 60* ●
1999 GUET-APENS* Ⓛ *Woody Oriental / Oriental Boisé 60* ●
1999 HERBA FRESCA ♂ *Green / Vert 22* ●●
1999 LAVANDE VELOURS ♂ *Floral / Florale 31* ●●●
1999 PAMPLELUNE ♂ *Citrus / Hespéridé 17* ●●●●
1999 ROSA MAGNIFICA *Floral / Florale 30* ●●
1999 YLANG & VANILLE *Floral / Florale 31* ●●●
1999 CHERRY BLOSSOM *Floral / Florale 32* ●
1999 VOILE D'ÉTÉ *Floral Oriental / Fleuri Oriental 47* ●●●
2000 CHAMPS-ÉLYSÉES TOO MUCH *Floral / Florale 30* ●●
2000 FLORA NEROLIA *Floral / Florale 31* ●●●●
2000 MÉTÉORITES *Floral / Florale 31* ●●●●
2000 MAHORA *Floral Oriental / Fleuri Oriental 47* ●●●●
2000 METALLICA Ⓛ *Floral Oriental / Fleuri Oriental 47* ●●●
2000 PURPLE FANTASY Ⓛ *Floral / Florale 34* ●●
2000 WINTER DELICE Ⓛ *Woody Oriental / Oriental Boisé 61* ●●●●
2001 SECRET INTENTION Ⓛ *Floral / Florale 34* ●●
1904 MOUCHOIR DE MONSIEUR *Aromatic / Fougère 77* ●●●
1959 VETIVER *Mossy Woods / Chypre Boisé 69* ●●●
1965 HABIT ROUGE *Oriental / Oriental 56* ●●
1985 DERBY *Dry Woods / Boisé Cuir 73* ●●●●
1992 HÉRITAGE *Woody Oriental / Oriental Boisé 62* ●●
1998 CORIOLAN *Mossy Woods / Chypre Boisé 68* ●●
1999 CHAMADE POUR HOMME* Ⓛ *Mossy Woods / Chypre Boisé 68* ●

GUESS

1990 GUESS (Original)* *Woody Oriental / Oriental Boisé 60* ●●
1990/2000 GUESS (New) *Floral / Florale 32* ●
1991 GUESS FOR MEN* *Aromatic / Fougère 77* ●●●●

GUY LAROCHE

1966 FIDJI *Floral / Florale 36* ●
1986 CLANDESTINE* *Floral Oriental / Fleuri Oriental 47* ●●●●
1982 DRAKKAR NOIR *Aromatic / Fougère 76* ●●
1993 HORIZON* *Aromatic / Fougère 78* ●
1999 DRAKKAR DYNAMIK *Aromatic / Fougère 80* ●

GUY LAROCHE / J'AI OSÉ

1977 J'AI OSÉ *Soft Oriental / Oriental Doux 53* ●●●

HALSTON

1975 HALSTON *Mossy Woods / Chypre Boisé 66* ●
1988 HALSTON COUTURE* *Mossy Woods / Chypre Boisé 67* ●●●
1993 CATALYST *Floral / Florale 34* ●
1998 SHEER HALSTON *Floral Oriental / Fleuri Oriental 48* ●
1976 HALSTON 1-12 *Green / Vert 23* ●●●
1976 HALSTON Z-14 *Mossy Woods / Chypre Boisé 68* ●●
1994 CATALYST FOR MEN *Woody Oriental / Oriental Boisé 62* ●●
1998 HALSTON Z *Mossy Woods / Chypre Boisé 68* ●●

HANAE MORI

1968/95 HANAE MORI *Woody Oriental / Oriental Boisé 60* ●●
1998 HANAE MORI HAUTE COUTURE *Soft Floral / Fleuri Aldéhydé 42* ●
1997 H.M. *Woody Oriental / Oriental Boisé 62* ●

HARLEY-DAVIDSON

1999 DESTINY WOMAN *Woody Oriental / Oriental Boisé 60* ●
1994 LEGENDARY *Dry Woods / Boisé Cuir 72* ●●
1999 DESTINY *Mossy Woods / Chypre Boisé 69* ●●●

HARTNELL

1946 IN LOVE* *Floral / Florale 30* ●●

H&BF - HEALTH & BEAUTY FOCUS

1975 BLASÉ *Soft Floral / Fleuri Aldéhydé 43* ●●●●
1983 LE JARDIN *Floral / Florale 38* ●
1987 LE JARDIN D'AMOUR *Floral Oriental / Fleuri Oriental 47* ●●●●
1976 MANDATE *Aromatic / Fougère 76* ●●
1988 RAPPORT *Aromatic / Fougère 78* ●●

HECHTER → DANIEL HECHTER

HELMUT LANG

2000 HELMUT LANG WOMAN *Woody Oriental / Oriental Boisé* 61 ●●●
2000 HELMUT LANG MAN *Aromatic / Fougère* 77 ●●●

HENRI D'ORLÉANS

1997 ROYALISSIME *Soft Floral / Fleuri Aldéhydé* 42 ●●

HENRY DUNAY

1998 SABI *Green / Vert* 23 ●●●●

HERBALIFE: PARFUMS VITESSENCE

1995 ASMERA *Oriental / Oriental* 57 ●●●
1995 LUSCIOUS *Floral Oriental / Fleuri Oriental* 47 ●●●
1995 ZILLION *Floral Oriental / Fleuri Oriental* 46 ●●
1996 WOMAN *Floral / Florale* 34 ●
2000 HEART *Floral / Florale* 36 ●
1995 IMPROV *Woody Oriental / Oriental Boisé* 62 ●
1995 PINSTRIPE *Aromatic / Fougère* 76 ●
1995 SEAWARD *Dry Woods / Boisé Cuir* 72 ●●
1996 MAN *Aromatic / Fougère* 78 ●
2000 SOUL *Aromatic / Fougère* 80 ●

HERMÈS

1951 EAU D'HERMÈS ♂ *Dry Woods / Boisé Cuir* 73 ●●●
1961/92 CALÈCHE *Mossy Woods / Chypre Boisé* 67 ●●●
1974/89 AMAZONE *Floral / Florale* 32 ●●
1979 EAU D'ORANGE VERTE ♂ *Citrus / Hespéridé* 17 ●●●●
1984 PARFUM D'HERMÈS *Floral Oriental / Fleuri Oriental* 46 ●●
1995 24, FAUBOURG *Floral / Florale* 38 ●●
1999 HIRIS *Soft Floral / Fleuri Aldéhydé* 42 ●
2000 ROUGE HERMÈS *Floral Oriental / Fleuri Oriental* 47 ●●●
1970 ÉQUIPAGE *Aromatic / Fougère* 77 ●●●●
1986 BEL AMI *Dry Woods / Boisé Cuir* 73 ●●●●
1998 ROCABAR *Dry Woods / Boisé Cuir* 73 ●●●●

HERRERA → CAROLINA HERRERA

HERVÉ LÉGER

1999 HERVÉ LÉGER *Floral Oriental / Fleuri Oriental* 47 ●●●

HILFIGER → TOMMY HILFIGER

HOLZMAN & STEPHANIE

1987 JE T'AIME *Floral Oriental / Fleuri Oriental* 47 ●●●
1987 MISUKI *Oriental / Oriental* 57 ●●●
1989 LA PARISIENNE *Soft Floral / Fleuri Aldéhydé* 42 ●●
1990 FASCINATION *Floral / Florale* 32 ●●
2000 TRÈS CHIC *Soft Oriental / Oriental Doux* 52 ●

HOPE DIAMOND COLLECTION

1999 FABLE *Woody Oriental / Oriental Boisé* 61 ●●●

HOUBIGANT: CLAIRE

1912/87 QUELQUES FLEURS *Floral / Florale* 33 ●●●
1996 QUELQUES VIOLETTES *Floral / Florale* 31 ●●●●
1997 QUELQUES ROSES *Floral / Florale* 31 ●●●
2000 APERÇU *Mossy Woods / Chypre Boisé* 67 ●●●
1882 FOUGÈRE ROYALE* *Aromatic / Fougère* 77 ●●●
1991 DUC DE VERVINS *Aromatic / Fougère* 76 ●●

HOUBIGANT / DANA → DANA

HUGO BOSS

1997 HUGO WOMAN *Floral / Florale* 36 ●●
2000 BOSS WOMAN *Floral / Florale* 32 ●●
1985 BOSS NUMBER ONE *Aromatic / Fougère* 76 ●●
1987 BOSS SPORT* *Aromatic / Fougère* 80 ●●
1989 BOSS SPIRIT* *Dry Woods / Boisé Cuir* 72 ●●
1993 ELEMENTS *Aromatic / Fougère* 76 ●
1995 HUGO *Aromatic / Fougère* 80 ●
1996 ELEMENTS AQUA *Aromatic / Fougère* 82 ●●
1998 BOSS *Woody Oriental / Oriental Boisé* 60 ●●
1999 HUGO DARK BLUE *Mossy Woods / Chypre Boisé* 68 ●

HUMAN PHEROMONE SCIENCES

1993 REALM WOMEN *Soft Oriental / Oriental Doux* 52 ●
1993 REALM MEN *Woody Oriental / Oriental Boisé* 62 ●●

ICEBERG

1989 ICEBERG *Floral / Florale* 32 ●
1994 ICEBERG TWICE *Floral / Florale* 38 ●
1997 ICEBERG UNIVERSE FEMME *Floral Oriental / Fleuri Oriental* 47 ●●●
1998 ICEBERG TWICE ICE *Citrus / Hespéridé* 16 ●
2000 FLUID ICEBERG WOMAN *Woody Oriental / Oriental Boisé* 61 ●●●
1991 ICEBERG HOMME *Citrus / Hespéridé* 19 ●●●●
1995 ICEBERG TWICE HOMME *Aromatic / Fougère* 80 ●
1997 ICEBERG UNIVERSE HOMME *Woody Oriental / Oriental Boisé* 62 ●
2000 FLUID ICEBERG MAN *Dry Woods / Boisé Cuir* 72 ●

IDESA

2000 ANGEL SCHLESSER FEMME *Mossy Woods / Chypre Boisé* 66 ●●
2000 ARMAND BASI FEMME *Citrus / Hespéridé* 16 ●
2000 BASI FEMME *Woody Oriental / Oriental Boisé* 60 ●
2000 ARMAND BASI HOMME *Woody Oriental / Oriental Boisé* 60 ●●
2000 BASI HOMME *Mossy Woods / Chypre Boisé* 68 ●●

INÈS DE LA FRESSANGE

1999 INÈS DE LA FRESSANGE *Soft Floral / Fleuri Aldéhydé* 42 ●

INFINITIF

1994 INFINITIF *Mossy Woods / Chypre Boisé* 67 ●●●
1996 EAU D'INFINITIF *Floral / Florale* 32 ●●

INNOXA

1970 GINGHAM *Aromatic / Fougère* 77 ●●●

ISABELL

1996 ATTAR *Oriental / Oriental* 57 ●●●●
1996 CALLA *Soft Oriental / Oriental Doux* 53 ●●●
1996 CEYLON *Citrus / Hespéridé* 16 ●●
1996 MANDARIN *Floral / Florale* 31 ●●●●
1996 SAVANNA *Floral / Florale* 36 ●●
1998 PAPERWHITES *Floral / Florale* 38 ●

ISABELLA ROSSELLINI

2000 MANIFESTO *Floral / Florale* 36 ●

ISSEY MIYAKE

1992 L'EAU D'ISSEY *Water / Marine* 26 ●●
1998 LE FEU D'ISSEY *Woody Oriental / Oriental Boisé* 61 ●●●
2000 LE FEU D'ISSEY LIGHT *Soft Floral / Fleuri Aldéhydé* 43 ●●●●
1994 L'EAU D'ISSEY POUR HOMME *Water / Marine* 27 ●●●

ITALART

1989 MASERATI *Aromatic / Fougère* 76 ●●

IVANA TRUMP

1995 IVANA *Floral / Florale* 33 ●●●●

JACLYN SMITH / DANA → DANA

JACOMO

1978 SILENCES *Green / Vert* 23 ●●●●
1987 COEUR DE PARFUM* *Dry Woods / Boisé Cuir* 72 ●●
1991 ANTHRACITE *Floral Oriental / Fleuri Oriental* 46 ●
1996 PERLE DE SILENCES *Soft Oriental / Oriental Doux* 52 ●
1998 PARADOX *Floral Oriental / Fleuri Oriental* 48 ●
2000 AURA FOR WOMEN *Floral / Florale* 32 ●●
1980 JACOMO DE JACOMO *Woody Oriental / Oriental Boisé* 62 ●●
1991 ANTHRACITE POUR L'HOMME *Aromatic / Fougère* 82 ●●
1996 AMBRO DE JACOMO *Woody Oriental / Oriental Boisé* 63 ●●●
1999 PARADOX FOR MEN *Woody Oriental / Oriental Boisé* 62 ●
2000 AURA FOR MEN *Mossy Woods / Chypre Boisé* 69 ●●●

JACQUES BOGART

1975 BOGART *Aromatic / Fougère* 78 ●●
1980 ONE MAN SHOW *Dry Woods / Boisé Cuir* 73 ●●●●
1988 FURYO* *Woody Oriental / Oriental Boisé* 63 ●●●●
1993 EAU FRESH *Aromatic / Fougère* 78 ●
1998 FORCE MAJEURE *Woody Oriental / Oriental Boisé* 62 ●●

Index des Maisons

JACQUES FATH
1953/93 FATH DE FATH *Oriental / Oriental* 56 ●●
1996 EAU DE FATH *Floral / Florale* 32 ●
1999 YIN *Floral / Florale* 34 ●●
1947/67/93 GREEN WATER *Citrus / Hespéridé* 18 ●●
1998 POUR L'HOMME *Woody Oriental / Oriental Boisé* 62 ●●
1999 YANG *Woody Oriental / Oriental Boisé* 62 ●

JAGUAR
1993 MISS JAGUAR *Floral / Florale* 36 ●●
1998 ESSENTIALLY JAGUAR *Floral Oriental / Fleuri Oriental* 46 ●●
1988 JAGUAR *Aromatic / Fougère* 77 ●●●●
1995 JAGUAR MARK II *Woody Oriental / Oriental Boisé* 62 ●●
1998 JAGUAR SPECIAL EDITION *Aromatic / Fougère* 82 ●

JAMES BOND
1997 BOND *Oriental / Oriental* 56 ●

JAN MORAN
1996 FABULOUS *Floral Oriental / Fleuri Oriental* 47 ●●●

JARDIN RETROUVÉ → LE JARDIN RETROUVÉ

J. DEL POZO
1992 DUENDE *Water / Marine* 26 ●
1995 ESENCIA DE DUENDE *Floral / Florale* 36 ●
1997 HALLOWEEN *Floral / Florale* 36 ●●
1994 QUASAR *Aromatic / Fougère* 82 ●
1999 ADVENTURE QUASAR *Aromatic / Fougère* 76 ●

JEAN-CHARLES BROSSEAU
1981 OMBRE ROSE *Floral Oriental / Fleuri Oriental* 47 ●●●●
1987 OMBRE BLEUE* *Floral / Florale* 33 ●●●●
1994 OMBRE D'OR* *Soft Floral / Fleuri Aldéhydé* 42 ●
1997 OMBRE ROSE FRAÎCHE *Floral / Florale* 34 ●

JEAN-CLAUDE JITROIS
1989 JITROIS *Dry Woods / Boisé Cuir* 72 ●●

JEAN COUTURIER
1973 CORIANDRE *Mossy Woods / Chypre Boisé* 67 ●●●●
1983 KÉORA *Oriental / Oriental* 57 ●●●●
1996 EAU DE CORIANDRE *Floral / Florale* 32 ●
1997 MARJOLAINE *Floral / Florale* 34 ●●

JEAN D'ALBRET
1947 ÉCUSSON *Soft Floral / Fleuri Aldéhydé* 43 ●●●
1961/96 MESSIRE *Citrus / Hespéridé* 19 ●●●

JEAN DESPREZ
1962/95 BAL À VERSAILLES *Floral Oriental / Fleuri Oriental* 47 ●●●
1989 REVOLUTION À VERSAILLES* *Floral Oriental / Fleuri Oriental* 46 ●●
1980 VERSAILLES *Oriental / Oriental* 56 ●●

JEAN-JACQUES DIENER
1998 JACQUELINE *Oriental / Oriental* 56 ●●

JEAN-LOUIS SCHERRER
1979 JEAN-LOUIS SCHERRER *Green / Vert* 23 ●●●●
1986 SCHERRER 2 *Floral Oriental / Fleuri Oriental* 48 ●●
1994 NUITS INDIENNES *Oriental / Oriental* 57 ●●●

JEAN LUC AMSLER
2000 JEAN LUC AMSLER FEMME *Floral / Florale* 36 ●●
2001 JEAN LUC AMSLER PRIVÉ FEMME
    Woody Oriental / Oriental Boisé 61 ●●●
2000 JEAN LUC AMSLER HOMME *Water / Marine* 27 ●●●
2001 JEAN LUC AMSLER PRIVÉ HOMME *Dry Woods / Boisé Cuir* 72 ●●

JEAN PATOU
1925 ADIEU SAGESSE *Floral / Florale* 30 ●●
1925 AMOUR AMOUR *Floral / Florale* 33 ●●●●
1925 QUE SAIS-JE? *Mossy Woods / Chypre Boisé* 67 ●●●
1927 CHALDÉE *Floral Oriental / Fleuri Oriental* 47 ●●●
1929 MOMENT SUPRÊME *Floral / Florale* 33 ●●●●
1930 COCKTAIL *Mossy Woods / Chypre Boisé* 66 ●
1930 JOY *Floral / Florale* 33 ●●●

1933 DIVINE FOLIE *Floral Oriental / Fleuri Oriental* 47 ●●●
1935 NORMANDIE *Soft Oriental / Oriental Doux* 53 ●●●
1936 VACANCES *Green / Vert* 23 ●●●
1938 COLONY *Mossy Woods / Chypre Boisé* 66 ●●
1946 L'HEURE ATTENDUE *Woody Oriental / Oriental Boisé* 61 ●●●
1964 CÂLINE *Soft Floral / Fleuri Aldéhydé* 42 ●●
1972 1000 *Floral / Florale* 33 ●●●●
1976 EAU DE PATOU *Citrus / Hespéridé* 17 ●●●
1987 MA LIBERTÉ* *Aromatic / Fougère* 77 ●●●
1992 SUBLIME *Soft Oriental / Oriental Doux* 53 ●●●
1998 PATOU FOR EVER *Floral / Florale* 34 ●●
1998 UN AMOUR DE PATOU *Floral / Florale* 36 ●
1980 PATOU POUR HOMME *Woody Oriental / Oriental Boisé* 63 ●●●
1994 PATOU POUR HOMME PRIVÉ *Aromatic / Fougère* 77 ●●●
1995 VOYAGEUR *Mossy Woods / Chypre Boisé* 68 ●

JEAN PAUL GAULTIER
1993 JEAN PAUL GAULTIER *Floral Oriental / Fleuri Oriental* 46 ●●
1999 FRAGILE *Floral / Florale* 31 ●●●●
1995 LE MÂLE *Woody Oriental / Oriental Boisé* 62 ●●

JESSICA McCLINTOCK
1987 JESSICA McCLINTOCK *Floral / Florale* 30 ●
1995 JESS *Floral / Florale* 33 ●●●●
1992 SCOTT McCLINTOCK *Soft Oriental / Oriental Doux* 52 ●

JIL SANDER
1980 JIL SANDER WOMAN PURE* *Soft Floral / Fleuri Aldéhydé* 42 ●
1981 JIL SANDER BATH & BEAUTY *Mossy Woods / Chypre Boisé* 67 ●●●
1982 JIL SANDER WOMAN II* *Mossy Woods / Chypre Boisé* 66 ●●
1986 JIL SANDER WOMAN III *Dry Woods / Boisé Cuir* 72 ●●
1989 JIL SANDER SUN *Floral Oriental / Fleuri Oriental* 47 ●●●
1990 JIL SANDER N° 4 *Floral Oriental / Fleuri Oriental* 46 ●
1997 JIL *Woody Oriental / Oriental Boisé* 60 ●
2000 SENSATIONS *Floral Oriental / Fleuri Oriental* 46 ●
1981 JIL SANDER MAN PURE* *Dry Woods / Boisé Cuir* 73 ●●●●
1987 JIL SANDER MAN III* *Aromatic / Fougère* 82 ●●
1989 JIL SANDER FEELING MAN *Soft Oriental / Oriental Doux* 52 ●
1993 BACKGROUND* *Woody Oriental / Oriental Boisé* 60 ●●
1999 SANDER FOR MEN *Aromatic / Fougère* 78 ●●

JIN ABE
1998 JIN ABE *Floral Oriental / Fleuri Oriental* 46 ●●

JIVAGO
1994 JIVAGO 24K WOMEN *Floral / Florale* 33 ●●●●
1998 JIVAGO 7 NOTES *Floral Oriental / Fleuri Oriental* 46 ●●
1999 MILLENNIUM HOPE WOMAN *Floral / Florale* 32 ●●
1995 JIVAGO 24k MEN *Aromatic / Fougère* 76 ●
1998 JIVAGO 7 ELEMENTS *Woody Oriental / Oriental Boisé* 62 ●●
1999 MILLENNIUM HOPE MAN *Aromatic / Fougère* 82 ●

JO MALONE
1990 NUTMEG & GINGER ♂ *Woody Oriental / Oriental Boisé* 60 ●●
1991 LIME, BASIL & MANDARIN ♂ *Citrus / Hespéridé* 17 ●●●●
1991 TUBEROSE *Floral / Florale* 31 ●●●●
1992 GRAPEFRUIT ♂ *Citrus / Hespéridé* 16 ●●
1995 AMBER & LAVENDER ♂ *Woody Oriental / Oriental Boisé* 61 ●●●
1995 FLEURS DE LA FORÊT *Mossy Woods / Chypre Boisé* 67 ●●●
1995 FRENCH LIME BLOSSOM *Floral / Florale* 30 ●
1995 GARDENIA *Floral / Florale* 30 ●●
1995 VERBENAS OF PROVENCE ♂ *Citrus / Hespéridé* 17 ●●●
1995 VETYVER ♂ *Mossy Woods / Chypre Boisé* 66 ●●
1995 WILD MUGUET *Floral / Florale* 30 ●
1996 HONEYSUCKLE & JASMINE *Floral / Florale* 38 ●●
1996 RED ROSES *Floral / Florale* 31 ●●●

JONES NEW YORK
1996 JONES NEW YORK *Green / Vert* 22 ●●

JOOP!
1987 JOOP! *Woody Oriental / Oriental Boisé* 61 ●●●●
1988 JOOP! LE BAIN *Floral Oriental / Fleuri Oriental* 47 ●●●●
1990 JOOP! NUIT D'ÉTÉ* *Woody Oriental / Oriental Boisé* 61 ●●●
1991 JOOP! BERLIN *Soft Floral / Fleuri Aldéhydé* 42 ●
1996 ALL ABOUT EVE *Woody Oriental / Oriental Boisé* 60 ●
1999 ROCOCO *Woody Oriental / Oriental Boisé* 61 ●●●

1989 JOOP! HOMME *Woody Oriental / Oriental Boisé* 63 ●●●
1992 NIGHTFLIGHT *Aromatic / Fougère* 80 ●
1997 WHAT ABOUT ADAM *Aromatic / Fougère* 80 ●

JOSEPH
1997 JOSEPH DE JOUR *Soft Floral / Fleuri Aldéhydé* 42 ●

JOURDAN → CHARLES JOURDAN

JOVAN (a selection *un choix*)
1972 JOVAN MUSK *Soft Floral / Fleuri Aldéhydé* 43 ●●●●
1992 JOVAN WHITE MUSK *Soft Oriental / Oriental Doux* 52 ●
1996 JOVAN FRESH MUSK *Floral / Florale* 32 ●
1973 JOVAN MUSK FOR MEN *Soft Floral / Fleuri Aldéhydé* 43 ●●●●
1992 JOVAN WHITE MUSK FOR MEN *Woody Oriental / Oriental Boisé* 62 ●
1998 GINSENG N.R.G *Woody Oriental / Oriental Boisé* 62 ●●

JULIO IGLESIAS
1989 ONLY *Woody Oriental / Oriental Boisé* 61 ●●●
1991 ONLY FOR MEN *Aromatic / Fougère* 77 ●●●

JUVENA
1994 DISCOVER *Aromatic / Fougère* 76 ●●

KARE
1994 EAU DE MURANO *Floral / Florale* 31 ●●●

KENZO
1988 KENZO *Floral / Florale* 32 ●●
1993 PARFUM D'ÉTÉ *Floral / Florale* 36 ●
1994 KASHÂYA *Floral Oriental / Fleuri Oriental* 46 ●
1996 L'EAU PAR KENZO *Floral / Florale* 38 ●
1996 JUNGLE: L'ÉLÉPHANT *Soft Oriental / Oriental Doux* 53 ●●●
1997 JUNGLE: LE TIGRE *Floral Oriental / Fleuri Oriental* 46 ●
1997 LE MONDE EST BEAU *Floral / Florale* 36 ●
2000 FLOWER BY KENZO *Floral Oriental / Fleuri Oriental* 46 ●●
1991 KENZO POUR HOMME *Water / Marine* 26 ●
1998 JUNGLE POUR HOMME *Woody Oriental / Oriental Boisé* 62 ●●
1999 L'EAU PAR KENZO POUR HOMME *Citrus / Hespéridé* 18 ●●

KESLING
1991 BE BOP *Floral / Florale* 32 ●●
1993 MISS BE BOP *Floral / Florale* 33 ●●●●
1994 FORMIDABLE *Floral Oriental / Fleuri Oriental* 47 ●●●
1997 C'EST MAGIQUE *Floral / Florale* 32 ●●
1997 SINAÏ *Floral Oriental / Fleuri Oriental* 46 ●
1998 ROUGE FORMIDABLE *Soft Floral / Fleuri Aldéhydé* 42 ●●
2000 DOUBLE CLICK ♀ *Citrus / Hespéridé* 16 ●
1992 BE BOP POUR HOMME *Aromatic / Fougère* 76 ●●
1995 BE BOP MAN *Dry Woods / Boisé Cuir* 72 ●●
1995 FORMIDABLE HOMME *Aromatic / Fougère* 78 ●●
1997 C'EST MAGIQUE HOMME *Aromatic / Fougère* 76 ●●
1998 BLEU FORMIDABLE *Aromatic / Fougère* 82 ●

KIRI TE KANAWA
1999 KIRI *Woody Oriental / Oriental Boisé* 61 ●●●

KITON → PALLADIO
KLEIN → CALVIN KLEIN

KNIZE
1924 KNIZE TEN *Dry Woods / Boisé Cuir* 73 ●●●

KOOKAÏ
1993 KOOKAÏ OUI-NON *Floral / Florale* 32 ●●
1996 L'EAU DE KOOKAÏ *Citrus / Hespéridé* 16 ●

KRAFT INTERNATIONAL
2001 REBEL WOMEN *Soft Floral / Fleuri Aldéhydé* 43 ●●●●
1998 REBEL ... JAMES DEAN *Aromatic / Fougère* 80 ●
2001 REBEL MEN *Aromatic / Fougère* 78 ●●

KRISTEL SAINT MARTIN
1995 PARFUM D'OR *Mossy Woods / Chypre Boisé* 66 ●●
1996 DIAMANT D'OR* *Floral Oriental / Fleuri Oriental* 46 ●●
1996 RUBIS D'OR* *Floral Oriental / Fleuri Oriental* 46 ●
1995 PARFUM D'HOMME *Aromatic / Fougère* 78 ●●

KRIZIA
1981 K de KRIZIA *Soft Floral / Fleuri Aldéhydé* 42 ●●
1986 TEATRO ALLA SCALA* *Soft Oriental / Oriental Doux* 53 ●●●
1989 MOODS* *Floral / Florale* 36 ●●
1991 KRAZY KRIZIA* *Oriental / Oriental* 56 ●●
1995 FIORI DI KRIZIA* *Floral / Florale* 32 ●
1998 SPAZIO KRIZIA DONNA *Floral Oriental / Fleuri Oriental* 47 ●●●
1999 EASY KRIZIA *Mossy Woods / Chypre Boisé* 66 ●
1984 KRIZIA UOMO *Dry Woods / Boisé Cuir* 73 ●●●●
1989 MOODS UOMO* *Woody Oriental / Oriental Boisé* 63 ●●●
1993 SPAZIO KRIZIA UOMO *Dry Woods / Boisé Cuir* 72 ●

LACOSTE
1999 LACOSTE FOR WOMEN *Floral / Florale* 36 ●
1984 LACOSTE *Aromatic / Fougère* 78 ●●
1991 LAND *Woody Oriental / Oriental Boisé* 62 ●
1996 BOOSTER *Citrus / Hespéridé* 18 ●●
1999 LACOSTE 2000 *Aromatic / Fougère* 78 ●

LAGERFELD
1982 KL *Soft Oriental / Oriental Doux* 52 ●
1994 SUN MOON STARS *Floral Oriental / Fleuri Oriental* 46 ●
2000 LAGERFELD FEMME *Citrus / Hespéridé* 17 ●●●●
1978 LAGERFELD *Woody Oriental / Oriental Boisé* 63 ●●●
1986 KL HOMME* *Oriental / Oriental* 57 ●●●
1990 PHOTO *Aromatic / Fougère* 78 ●●
1997 JAKO *Woody Oriental / Oriental Boisé* 62 ●●

LALIQUE
1992 LALIQUE *Floral Oriental / Fleuri Oriental* 48 ●●
1995 NILANG *Floral Oriental / Fleuri Oriental* 48 ●
1997 CLAIRE DE NILANG *Floral / Florale* 32 ●
1999 LE BAISER *Floral / Florale* 32 ●●
1997 LALIQUE POUR HOMME *Woody Oriental / Oriental Boisé* 62 ●●
2000 LALIQUE POUR HOMME BLEU *Woody Oriental / Oriental Boisé* 62 ●

LAMBORGHINI → TONINO LAMBORGHINI

LANCASTER
1977 EAU DE LANCASTER *Citrus / Hespéridé* 17 ●●●
1987 LANCASTER BODY & BATH *Oriental / Oriental* 56 ●
1997 SUNWATER *Floral / Florale* 36 ●

LANCETTI
1995 LANCETTI MADAME *Mossy Woods / Chypre Boisé* 67 ●●●
1997 LANCETTI EAU DE JOIE *Floral / Florale* 34 ●●
1998 LANCETTI *Soft Floral / Fleuri Aldéhydé* 43 ●●●
1995 LANCETTI MONSIEUR *Dry Woods / Boisé Cuir* 73 ●●●
1999 LANCETTI POUR HOMME *Aromatic / Fougère* 78 ●●

LANCÔME
1967 CLIMAT *Soft Floral / Fleuri Aldéhydé* 43 ●●●●
1969 Ô de LANCÔME *Citrus / Hespéridé* 17 ●●●
1978 MAGIE NOIRE *Woody Oriental / Oriental Boisé* 60 ●●
1990 TRÉSOR *Floral Oriental / Fleuri Oriental* 46 ●●
1995 POÊME *Floral Oriental / Fleuri Oriental* 47 ●●●
1998 Ô OUI *Floral / Florale* 34 ●
1999 AROMATONIC *Citrus / Hespéridé* 16 ●
2000 AROMACALM *Woody Oriental / Oriental Boisé* 61 ●●●
2000 MIRACLE *Floral / Florale* 32 ●●
1982 TROPHÈE LANCÔME* *Citrus / Hespéridé* 19 ●●●●
1996 Ô pour HOMME *Green / Vert* 22 ●●

LANVIN
1927/93 ARPÈGE *Soft Floral / Fleuri Aldéhydé* 43 ●●●●
2000 OXYGÈNE *Soft Floral / Fleuri Aldéhydé* 42 ●
1997 LANVIN L'HOMME *Aromatic / Fougère* 78 ●

LA PERLA
1987 LA PERLA *Dry Woods / Boisé Cuir* 73 ●●●
1995 IO *Mossy Woods / Chypre Boisé* 66 ●●
1998 PARFUM PRIVÉ* *Mossy Woods / Chypre Boisé* 67 ●●●
2000 ECLIX *Woody Oriental / Oriental Boisé* 60 ●
1991 GRIGIOPERLA *Aromatic / Fougère* 82 ●
2000 TOUCH GRIGIOPERLA *Woody Oriental / Oriental Boisé* 62 ●

119

LAPIDUS → TED LAPIDUS

LA PRAIRIE
1993 LA PRAIRIE *Floral / Florale* 33 ●●●●

L'ARTISAN PARFUMEUR
1978 L'EAU D'AMBRE *Oriental / Oriental* 57 ●●●
1978 MÛRE ET MUSC *Citrus / Hespéridé* 17 ●●●●
1978 TUBÉREUSE *Floral / Florale* 31 ●●●●
1978 VANILIA *Oriental / Oriental* 57 ●●●●
1979 PATCHOULI ♂ *Citrus / Hespéridé* 17 ●●●●
1982 LA HAIE FLEURIE DU HAMEAU *Floral / Florale* 31 ●●●
1990 RIVIERA PALACE *Mossy Woods / Chypre Boisé* 66 ●●
1992 MIMOSA POUR MOI *Floral / Florale* 30 ●●
1993 L'EAU DE L'ARTISAN ♂ *Citrus / Hespéridé* 17 ●●●
1993 MÛRE ET MUSC EXTRÊME *Citrus / Hespéridé* 17 ●●●●
1993 VOLEUR DE ROSES ♂ *Dry Woods / Boisé Cuir* 72 ●
1994 BOUTON D'OR* *Floral / Florale* 32 ●
1994 PREMIER FIGUIER *Mossy Woods / Chypre Boisé* 66 ●
1996 DRÔLE DE ROSE *Soft Floral / Fleuri Aldéhydé* 42 ●●
1996 THÉ POUR UN ÉTÉ ♂ *Citrus / Hespéridé* 16 ●
1999 DZING! *Dry Woods / Boisé Cuir* 73 ●●●●
1999/2000 LA CHASSE AUX PAPILLONS *Floral / Florale* 38 ●●
1999 PASSAGE D'ENFER *Dry Woods / Boisé Cuir* 72 ●●
2000 FLEUR DE CAROTTE ⓛ *Mossy Woods / Chypre Boisé* 66 ●●
2000 TEA FOR TWO *Woody Oriental / Oriental Boisé* 61 ●●●●
1978 SANTAL *Dry Woods / Boisé Cuir* 73 ●●●
1978 VETIVER *Dry Woods / Boisé Cuir* 72 ●
1982 L'EAU DU NAVIGATEUR *Dry Woods / Boisé Cuir* 73 ●●●●
1985 L'EAU DU CAPORAL *Aromatic / Fougère* 77 ●●●●
1997 MÉCHANT LOUP *Dry Woods / Boisé Cuir* 73 ●●●●
1998 NAVEGAR *Citrus / Hespéridé* 19 ●●●●

LAUDER → ESTÉE LAUDER

LAURA ASHLEY
1989 LAURA ASHLEY Nº 1 *Soft Floral / Fleuri Aldéhydé* 42 ●
1991 DILYS *Floral / Florale* 33 ●●●●
1995 L'EAU BY LAURA *Citrus / Hespéridé* 16 ●●

LAURA BIAGIOTTI
1988 ROMA *Oriental / Oriental* 56 ●●
1992 VENEZIA* *Woody Oriental / Oriental Boisé* 61 ●●●
1994 LAURA *Floral / Florale* 38 ●
1995 VENEZIA PASTELLO* *Soft Floral / Fleuri Aldéhydé* 42 ●
1996 SOTTO VOCE* *Woody Oriental / Oriental Boisé* 61 ●●●
1999 TEMPORE DONNA *Woody Oriental / Oriental Boisé* 60 ●●
1994 ROMA UOMO *Woody Oriental / Oriental Boisé* 62 ●●
1995 VENEZIA UOMO* *Woody Oriental / Oriental Boisé* 62 ●●
1999 TEMPORE UOMO *Woody Oriental / Oriental Boisé* 62 ●

LAUREN → RALPH LAUREN

LE GALION
1937 SORTILÈGE* *Soft Floral / Fleuri Aldéhydé* 43 ●●●●

LE JARDIN RETROUVÉ
1977 CHÈVREFEUILLE *Floral / Florale* 30 ●●
1977 JASMIN *Floral / Florale* 31 ●●●
1978 VERVEINE ♂ *Citrus / Hespéridé* 17 ●●●
1980 TUBÉREUSE *Floral / Florale* 31 ●●●●
1989 LYS *Floral / Florale* 30 ●●
1989 ROSE THÉ *Floral / Florale* 31 ●●●
1977 EAU DE CUIR DE RUSSIE *Dry Woods / Boisé Cuir* 72 ●●
1977 EAU DE SANDALWOOD *Woody Oriental / Oriental Boisé* 63 ●●●
1977 EAU DE VÉTYVER *Mossy Woods / Chypre Boisé* 68 ●●

LEMPICKA → LOLITA LEMPICKA

LENTHÉRIC
1967 PAGAN *Mossy Woods / Chypre Boisé* 67 ●●●
1975 TRAMP *Floral / Florale* 33 ●●●
1982 PURE SILK *Mossy Woods / Chypre Boisé* 67 ●●●
1991/2001 FLEUR *Floral / Florale* 32 ●●
1992/2000 JUST MUSK *Oriental / Oriental* 57 ●●●●
1967/2000 BLACK LABEL *Aromatic / Fougère* 77 ●●●

**LENTHÉRIC / FFC
→ FINE FRAGRANCES & COSMETICS**

LÉONARD
1970/93 FASHION *Floral Oriental / Fleuri Oriental* 46 ●●
1974 EAU FRAÎCHE *Citrus / Hespéridé* 17 ●●●
1977 TAMANGO *Soft Floral / Fleuri Aldéhydé* 42 ●●
1983 BALAHÉ *Floral Oriental / Fleuri Oriental* 47 ●●●
1989 LÉONARD DE LÉONARD* *Soft Floral / Fleuri Aldéhydé* 42 ●
1996 MISS BALAHÉ *Floral / Florale* 34 ●●
1998 FABULEUSE *Floral / Florale* 32 ●
1980 LÉONARD POUR HOMME* *Dry Woods / Boisé Cuir* 73 ●●●●
1992 MONSIEUR LÉONARD *Aromatic / Fougère* 77 ●●●●

LES COPAINS
1988/97 LES COPAINS *Floral Oriental / Fleuri Oriental* 46 ●
1999 EAU MARINE *Floral / Florale* 36 ●
1998 LES COPAINS L'HOMME *Mossy Woods / Chypre Boisé* 68 ●●
2000 LE BLEU *Aromatic / Fougère* 78 ●●

LES FLORALIES
1994 SENSES *Floral / Florale* 33 ●●●●
2000 LES FLORALIES GREEN TEA *Citrus / Hespéridé* 17 ●●●●
2000 LES FLORALIES WHITE GINGER *Citrus / Hespéridé* 16 ●
1993 INSTINCT *Aromatic / Fougère* 76 ●●

LES SENTEURS
1991 APOGÉE *Mossy Woods / Chypre Boisé* 67 ●●●

LILIAN BARONY
1995 L'EAU LILIAN *Water / Marine* 26 ●●
1997 LILIAN *Floral / Florale* 32 ●
1998 SUMMER SPLASH *Citrus / Hespéridé* 16 ●
1999 L'EAU SPORT MEN *Water / Marine* 26 ●●

LISE WATIER
1993 NEIGES *Floral / Florale* 38 ●
1999 EAU DE MER *Water / Marine* 26 ●
1997 NEIGES POUR HOMME *Citrus / Hespéridé* 18 ●●

LIZ CLAIBORNE
1986 LIZ CLAIBORNE *Floral / Florale* 32 ●
1990 REALITIES* *Floral / Florale* 34 ●●
1993 VIVID *Floral / Florale* 33 ●●●●
1996 CURVE FOR WOMEN *Floral / Florale* 32 ●
1997 LIZSPORT *Floral / Florale* 36 ●
1999 CANDIE'S *Floral / Florale* 33 ●●●
1989 CLAIBORNE FOR MEN* *Citrus / Hespéridé* 18 ●
1996 CURVE FOR MEN *Aromatic / Fougère* 76 ●
1997 CLAIBORNE SPORT *Aromatic / Fougère* 82 ●
1999 CANDIE'S MEN *Aromatic / Fougère* 78 ●

LLEWELYN
1998 STARDUST *Floral Oriental / Fleuri Oriental* 46 ●●

L'OCCITANE
1996/99 CANNELLE ORANGE ♂ *Citrus / Hespéridé* 16 ●
1996/99 FLEUR DE LOTUS *Water / Marine* 26 ●●
1996/99 LAVANDE ♂ *Aromatic / Fougère* 77 ●●●●
1999 CASSISSIER *Floral / Florale* 34 ●
1999 CÉDRAT POMELO ♂ *Citrus / Hespéridé* 16 ●●
1999 FEUILLE D'HERBE FLORALE & FRUITÉE *Mossy Woods / Chypre Boisé* 66 ●
1999 FEUILLE D'HERBE FRAÎCHE & ÉPICÉE
        Woody Oriental / Oriental Boisé 61 ●●●●
1999 FEUILLE D'HERBE FRAÎCHE & HERBACÉE *Green / Vert* 22 ●
1999 FEUILLE DE VERVEINE ♂ *Citrus / Hespéridé* 16 ●
1999 JASMIN MANDARINE *Soft Floral / Fleuri Aldéhydé* 43 ●●●
1999 MENTHE FROISSÉE *Green / Vert* 22 ●
1999 ROSE NÉROLI *Floral / Florale* 31 ●●●
1999 THÉ VERT ♂ *Citrus / Hespéridé* 16 ●●
1999 TILLEUL CHÈVREFEUILLE *Soft Floral / Fleuri Aldéhydé* 42 ●
1999 VANILLE ♂ *Soft Oriental / Oriental Doux* 53 ●●●
1990 EAU DE COLOGNE EXTRA FINE *Citrus / Hespéridé* 19 ●●●●
1991 EAU DES 4 VOLEURS *Aromatic / Fougère* 78 ●
1994 EAU DU CONTADOUR *Aromatic / Fougère* 77 ●●●
1999 EAU DU BADIAN *Citrus / Hespéridé* 18 ●●

LOEWE
1972/88 L de LOEWE *Floral / Florale 32* ●●
1985 AIRE LOEWE *Green / Vert 23* ●●●
1991 GALA LOEWE *Floral Oriental / Fleuri Oriental 46* ●●
1994 AURA LOEWE *Floral Oriental / Fleuri Oriental 46* ●
1996 GALA DE DIA *Floral / Florale 38* ●
2000 AGUA DE LOEWE ♂ *Citrus / Hespéridé 16* ●
1974 LOEWE POUR HOMME *Aromatic / Fougère 82* ●●
1987 ESENCIA LOEWE *Dry Woods / Boisé Cuir 72* ●●

LOLITA LEMPICKA
1997 LOLITA LEMPICKA *Woody Oriental / Oriental Boisé 60* ●
2000 LOLITA LEMPICKA AU MASCULIN *Woody Oriental / Oriental Boisé 62* ●●

LOMANI (a selection un choix)
1996 NETWORK ♂ *Citrus / Hespéridé 16* ●
1996 SOLYTIS *Floral Oriental / Fleuri Oriental 46* ●●
1998 CRUISER FOR WOMEN *Floral / Florale 33* ●●●●
1999 DUÉ DAY *Floral / Florale 32* ●
1999 DUÉ NIGHT *Floral / Florale 32* ●●
1999 HIGH TECH WOMEN *Floral / Florale 32* ●
2000 YES FOR WOMEN *Floral Oriental / Fleuri Oriental 46* ●
1987 LOMANI *Aromatic / Fougère 76* ●●
1993 EL PASO *Aromatic / Fougère 76* ●●
1994 DEEP BLUE *Aromatic / Fougère 80* ●
1998 CRUISER FOR MEN *Aromatic / Fougère 76* ●●
1999 HIGH TECH MEN *Mossy Woods / Chypre Boisé 68* ●●
1999 VOLCANO HOMME *Aromatic / Fougère 82* ●
2000 DUÉ CLASSIC *Aromatic / Fougère 76* ●
2000 DUÉ WILD *Woody Oriental / Oriental Boisé 62* ●●
2000 LAMBROSIO *Woody Oriental / Oriental Boisé 63* ●●●
2000 YES FOR MEN *Oriental / Oriental 56* ●●

LOUIS FÉRAUD
1997 LOVE STORY *Floral Oriental / Fleuri Oriental 47* ●●●●

L.T. PIVER
1889/1926 RÊVE D'OR *Soft Floral / Fleuri Aldéhydé 43* ●●●●
1905/91 FLORAMYE *Mossy Woods / Chypre Boisé 66* ●●
1907 POMPEÏA *Dry Woods / Boisé Cuir 73* ●●●
1939 CUIR DE RUSSIE ♂ *Dry Woods / Boisé Cuir 73* ●●●
1998 CLARTÉ *Floral / Florale 32* ●●
1998 INCLINATION *Floral / Florale 32* ●
2000 EAU DE PIVER *Woody Oriental / Oriental Boisé 61* ●●●
1850 EAU DES PRINCES *Citrus / Hespéridé 19* ●●●
1991 LAVANDE DES PRINCES *Floral / Florale 39* ●●●●
1991 VÉTYVER *Mossy Woods / Chypre Boisé 69* ●●●
1995 EAU POUR HOMME *Citrus / Hespéridé 19* ●●●●
2000 CLARTÉ FOR MEN *Aromatic / Fougère 76* ●

LUCIANO SOPRANI
1994 SOPRANI 2 *Woody Oriental / Oriental Boisé 60* ●
1995 SOLO SOPRANI ♂ *Citrus / Hespéridé 16* ●
1998 SOLO SOPRANI BLU ♂ *Aromatic / Fougère 76* ●
1999 PEOPLE DONNA *Floral / Florale 36* ●
1994 SOPRANI ACTIVE MAN *Aromatic / Fougère 80* ●●
1999 PEOPLE UOMO *Woody Oriental / Oriental Boisé 62* ●

LUCIEN LELONG
1935/97 INDISCRET *Green / Vert 22* ●●
1999 LELONG POUR FEMME *Woody Oriental / Oriental Boisé 61* ●●●

LUCKY BRAND
1997 LUCKY BRAND WOMEN'S* *Floral / Florale 38* ●
2000 LUCKY YOU FOR WOMEN *Floral / Florale 32* ●
1997 LUCKY BRAND MEN'S* *Aromatic / Fougère 80* ●
2000 LUCKY YOU FOR MEN *Mossy Woods / Chypre Boisé 68* ●●

McCLINTOCK → JESSICA McCLINTOCK
McEVOY → TRISH McEVOY

MAC
1999 ASPHALT FLOWER *Floral / Florale 33* ●●●●
1999 HYPERSOUK *Soft Oriental / Oriental Doux 53* ●●●
1999 SYNTHETIC NIRVANA *Woody Oriental / Oriental Boisé 60* ●●

MACKIE → BOB MACKIE

MADELEINE DE RAUCH
1998 BELLE DE RAUCH *Floral / Florale 33* ●●●
1998 MAN DE RAUCH *Woody Oriental / Oriental Boisé 63* ●●●●

MADELEINE MONO
1978 MADELEINE DE MADELEINE *Floral / Florale 31* ●●●●

MADELEINE VIONNET
1925/96 MADELEINE VIONNET *Floral Oriental / Fleuri Oriental 47* ●●●
1998 MV *Floral / Florale 36* ●

MAGIC HELVETIA
1994 LA BASE FOR HER *Floral / Florale 30* ●●
1994 LA BASE FOR HIM *Dry Woods / Boisé Cuir 73* ●●●●

MAÎTRE PARFUMEUR ET GANTIER
1988 AMBRE PRÉCIEUX ♂ *Oriental / Oriental 57* ●●●●
1988 EAU DE MÛRE *Citrus / Hespéridé 17* ●●●
1988 EAU DU GANTIER ♂ *Citrus / Hespéridé 17* ●●●
1988 FLEUR D'IRIS *Soft Floral / Fleuri Aldéhydé 43* ●●●
1988 FLEURS DES COMORES *Mossy Woods / Chypre Boisé 66* ●●
1988 FRAÎCHE PASSIFLORE *Citrus / Hespéridé 16* ●●
1988 FRAÎCHEUR MUSKISSIME ♂ *Citrus / Hespéridé 17* ●●●●
1988 FREEZIA D'OR *Floral / Florale 33* ●●●●
1988 JARDIN BLANC *Floral / Florale 38* ●●
1988 JASMIN *Floral / Florale 31* ●●●
1988 OR DES INDES *Oriental / Oriental 57* ●●●
1988 RACINE ♂ *Mossy Woods / Chypre Boisé 66* ●●
1988 ROSE MUSKISSIME *Floral / Florale 34* ●
1988 ROSE OPULENTE *Floral / Florale 31* ●●●
1988 SANGUINE MUSKISSIME ♂ *Citrus / Hespéridé 16* ●
1988 SOIE ROUGE *Dry Woods / Boisé Cuir 72* ●●
1988 TUBÉREUSE *Floral / Florale 31* ●●●●
1988 VOCALISE *Citrus / Hespéridé 16* ●●
1992 SECRÈTE DATURA *Oriental / Oriental 57* ●●●●
1997 CAMÉLIA CHINOIS *Green / Vert 23* ●●●●
1998 GRAIN DE PLAISIR ♂ *Mossy Woods / Chypre Boisé 66* ●
2000 BAÏMÉ ♂ *Mossy Woods / Chypre Boisé 66* ●
1988 EAU DES ÎLES *Dry Woods / Boisé Cuir 73* ●●●●
1988 GARRIGUE *Aromatic / Fougère 76* ●●
1988 IRIS BLEU GRIS *Mossy Woods / Chypre Boisé 68* ●
1988 JARDIN DU NIL *Floral / Florale 38* ●●
1988 PARFUM D'HABIT *Dry Woods / Boisé Cuir 73* ●●●●
1988 ROUTE DU VÉTIVER *Mossy Woods / Chypre Boisé 69* ●●●
1988 SANTAL NOBLE *Mossy Woods / Chypre Boisé 69* ●●●●
1988 SECRET MÉLANGE *Aromatic / Fougère 76* ●
1990 EAU POUR LE JEUNE HOMME *Citrus / Hespéridé 18* ●
1991 CENTAURE *Aromatic / Fougère 77* ●●●
1994 FRAÎCHE BADIANE *Mossy Woods / Chypre Boisé 68* ●●

MARBERT
1987 MARBERT WOMAN *Oriental / Oriental 57* ●●●
1993 SCARF *Woody Oriental / Oriental Boisé 60* ●●
1995 SUN SPIRIT* *Floral / Florale 34* ●●
1996 SCARF TAORMINA *Floral / Florale 34* ●●
1999 MARBERT WOMAN RED *Floral / Florale 34* ●
1977 MARBERT MAN *Aromatic / Fougère 82* ●●
1986 MARBERT GENTLEMAN *Mossy Woods / Chypre Boisé 68* ●●
1988 MARBERT HOMME *Dry Woods / Boisé Cuir 72* ●●
1989 MARBERT MAN PURE *Mossy Woods / Chypre Boisé 68* ●
1995 PERSONALITY *Aromatic / Fougère 77* ●●●●
1997 TYCOON *Woody Oriental / Oriental Boisé 62* ●●
1998 MARBERT MAN TOO *Aromatic / Fougère 80* ●

MARC DE LA MORANDIÈRE
1987/94 BLEU DE CHINE *Soft Oriental / Oriental Doux 53* ●●●●
1991 SISSI *Floral / Florale 33* ●●●
1994 NUAGE D'OR *Soft Floral / Fleuri Aldéhydé 43* ●●●●
1994 NUAGES D'EAU *Floral / Florale 31* ●●●
1994 THIARA *Floral Oriental / Fleuri Oriental 47* ●●●
1996 MELODIE D'AMOUR *Floral / Florale 34* ●
1999 AYAKO *Oriental / Oriental 56* ●
1999 LA PLAGE *Woody Oriental / Oriental Boisé 60* ●
1989 GENGIS KHAN *Woody Oriental / Oriental Boisé 62* ●
1992 M pour MONSIEUR *Aromatic / Fougère 78* ●
1998 M de M *Soft Oriental / Oriental Doux 52* ●●

Index des Maisons

MARCELLA BORGHESE → BORGHESE

MARIA GALLAND
2000 L'INSTANT JASMIN *Floral / Florale* 31 ●●●

MARIELLA BURANI
1992 MARIELLA BURANI *Soft Floral / Fleuri Aldéhydé* 42 ●●
1996 MARIELLA *Soft Oriental / Oriental Doux* 52 ●
1997 EAU ROSÉE *Soft Floral / Fleuri Aldéhydé* 42 ●
1999 AMULETI *Floral / Florale* 32 ●

MARILYN MIGLIN
1978 PHEROMONE *Green / Vert* 23 ●●●●
1990 DESTINY *Floral / Florale* 38 ●
1998 MYSTIC *Floral / Florale* 34 ●●
1999 GODDESS *Floral Oriental / Fleuri Oriental* 46 ●●
1999 PHEROMONE FOR MEN *Dry Woods / Boisé Cuir* 72 ●●

MARINA DE BOURBON
1994 MARINA DE BOURBON *Woody Oriental / Oriental Boisé* 60 ●
1998 MON BOUQUET *Floral / Florale* 34 ●
1999 À LA FRANÇAISE *Floral / Florale* 32 ●●
2000 L'OR DES BOURBON *Woody Oriental / Oriental Boisé* 60 ●
2000 AQUA DI AQUA *Mossy Woods / Chypre Boisé* 66 ●
1997 M de BOURBON *Aromatic / Fougère* 82 ●●
1999 BOURBON HOMME *Mossy Woods / Chypre Boisé* 69 ●●●●

MARK BIRLEY
1996 MARK BIRLEY FOR MEN *Dry Woods / Boisé Cuir* 72 ●●

MARY McFADDEN
1996 ALABASTER *Soft Floral / Fleuri Aldéhydé* 42 ●
1996 GOLD *Woody Oriental / Oriental Boisé* 60 ●

MASAKÏ MATSUSHIMA
2000 MAT; *Floral / Florale* 36 ●

MAUBOUSSIN
2000 MAUBOUSSIN *Woody Oriental / Oriental Boisé* 60 ●●

MÄURER & WIRTZ
1960 NONCHALANCE *Soft Floral / Fleuri Aldéhydé* 43 ●●●
1995 VOICE BY BETTY BARCLAY *Floral Oriental / Fleuri Oriental* 47 ●●●
1997 CYBERSP@CE ♂ *Water / Marine* 26 ●
1997 ERUPTION WOMAN *Floral Oriental / Fleuri Oriental* 46 ●●
1998 BETTY BARCLAY WOMAN *Floral / Florale* 36 ●
1999 BETTY BARCLAY WOMAN N° 2 *Floral Oriental / Fleuri Orienta* 48 ●
1999 ÉLÀ NONCHALANCE *Floral / Florale* 38 ●●
1999 FREE WORLD WOMAN *Floral / Florale* 36 ●
2000 BETTY BARCLAY WOMAN N° 3 *Floral / Florale* 33 ●●●
1959 TABAC ORIGINAL (EdC) *Soft Floral / Fleuri Aldéhydé* 42 ●●
1959 TABAC ORIGINAL (Aftershave) *Aromatic / Fougère* 78 ●●
1991 TABAC EXTREME *Aromatic / Fougère* 78 ●
1996 CULTURE by TABAC *Aromatic / Fougère* 82 ●●
1997 ERUPTION MAN *Woody Oriental / Oriental Boisé* 62 ●●
1998 X *Woody Oriental / Oriental Boisé* 62 ●
1999 CULTURE by TABAC BLUE *Aromatic / Fougère* 82 ●
1999 FREE WORLD MAN *Aromatic / Fougère* 78 ●
2000 TABAC MAN *Aromatic / Fougère* 77 ●●●●
2000 TOUCHDOWN *Dry Woods / Boisé Cuir* 72 ●●

**MAX FACTOR / H&BF
→ HEALTH & BEAUTY FOCUS**

MAXIM'S
1984 MAXIM'S DE PARIS* *Floral Oriental / Fleuri Oriental* 46 ●
1998 ORPHÉE ♂ *Aromatic / Fougère* 76 ●●
1988 MAXIM'S POUR HOMME* *Woody Oriental / Oriental Boisé* 63 ●●●●

MCM
1985 MCM OBELISK *Oriental / Oriental* 56 ●
1989 MCM BLUE PARADISE *Floral / Florale* 32 ●●
1991 MCM 1900 *Floral Oriental / Fleuri Oriental* 47 ●●●
1996 VERY M.C. ♂ *Citrus / Hespéridé* 16 ●
1998 BLACK SILVER ♂ *Aromatic / Fougère* 76 ●●
1999 MCM *Floral / Florale* 32 ●●
2001 MCM ROUGE *Floral Oriental / Fleuri Oriental* 46 ●

1986 MCM SUCCESS* *Mossy Woods / Chypre Boisé* 69 ●●●●
1993 MCM 24 MORNING* *Aromatic / Fougère* 80 ●
1993 MCM 24 EVENING* *Woody Oriental / Oriental Boisé* 63 ●●●
2000 BLUE SILVER MEN *Aromatic / Fougère* 82 ●

MEM / DANA → DANA

MENNEN
1931 MENNEN SKIN BRACER *Aromatic / Fougère* 77 ●●●

MEXX: STAR
2000 MEXX WOMAN *Floral / Florale* 34 ●
2000 MEXX MAN *Aromatic / Fougère* 76 ●●

MICHAEL KORS
2000 MICHAEL *Floral / Florale* 31 ●●●●

MICHEL GERMAIN
1994 SÉXUAL *Floral Oriental / Fleuri Oriental* 46 ●
1999 DEAUVILLE *Soft Floral / Fleuri Aldéhydé* 42 ●●
1996 SÉXUAL POUR HOMME *Woody Oriental / Oriental Boisé* 62 ●
1999 DEAUVILLE POUR HOMME *Aromatic / Fougère* 76 ●

MICHEL JORDI
1999 THE SPIRIT OF SWITZERLAND *Floral / Florale* 36 ●

MICK MICHEYL
2000 MICK MICHEYL *Floral / Florale* 34 ●●

MIGLIN → MARILYN MIGLIN

MIKHAIL BARYSHNIKOV
1989 MISHA *Mossy Woods / Chypre Boisé* 67 ●●●●
1995 BARYSHNIKOV POUR FEMME *Floral / Florale* 33 ●●●
1991 BARYSHNIKOV *Aromatic / Fougère* 76 ●●
1996 BARYSHNIKOV SPORT *Aromatic / Fougère* 80 ●

MILA SCHÖN
1980 MILA SCHÖN *Mossy Woods / Chypre Boisé* 67 ●●●
1997 SCHÖN *Floral / Florale* 34 ●●
1986 MILA SCHÖN UOMO *Green / Vert* 23 ●●●●

MILLER → NICOLE MILLER

MILLOT
1925 CRÊPE DE CHINE* *Mossy Woods / Chypre Boisé* 66 ●●

MIRA TAKLA
1990 VALLÉE DES ROIS *Floral Oriental / Fleuri Oriental* 47 ●●●

MISSONI
1981 MISSONI *Mossy Woods / Chypre Boisé* 67 ●●●●
1987 ARIA MISSONI *Floral / Florale* 32 ●●
1990 MOLTO MISSONI *Oriental / Oriental* 57 ●●●●
1993 NOI MISSONI *Citrus / Hespéridé* 16 ●●
1997 NOI DONNA *Floral Oriental / Fleuri Oriental* 46 ●●
1983 MISSONI UOMO *Dry Woods / Boisé Cuir* 73 ●●●
1990 MISSONI SPORT *Citrus / Hespéridé* 19 ●●●●
1994 OLYMPIOS *Aromatic / Fougère* 78 ●
1997 NOI UOMINI *Citrus / Hespéridé* 18 ●

MIYAKE → ISSEY MIYAKE

MOLINARD
1900/93 ORVAL *Floral / Florale* 33 ●●●
1921 HABANITA *Woody Oriental / Oriental Boisé* 61 ●●●●
1925/96 LAVANDE *Floral / Florale* 31 ●●●●
1929/93 ÎLES D'OR *Floral / Florale* 32 ●
1949 EAU FRANCE ♂ *Citrus / Hespéridé* 17 ●●●
1955/93/2000 NIRMALA *Woody Oriental / Oriental Boisé* 60 ●
1979 MOLINARD DE MOLINARD *Floral / Florale* 34 ●●
1992 EAU FRAÎCHE ♂ *Citrus / Hespéridé* 16 ●●
1993 AMBRE *Oriental / Oriental* 57 ●●●
1993 CHÈVREFEUILLE* *Floral / Florale* 30 ●●
1993 CITRON VERT* ♂ *Citrus / Hespéridé* 16 ●
1993 CLÉMENTINE *Citrus / Hespéridé* 17 ●●●
1993 MÛRE / BLACKBERRY *Citrus / Hespéridé* 17 ●●●●

1993 OEILLET*   *Floral / Florale*   31 ●●●●
1993 ORANGE-CANNELLE   *Soft Oriental / Oriental Doux*   52 ●●
1993 PATCHOULI ♂   *Mossy Woods / Chypre Boisé*   67 ●●●
1993 VANILLE   *Oriental / Oriental*   57 ●●●
1994 JASMIN   *Floral / Florale*   31 ●●●
1994 MIMOSA   *Floral / Florale*   30 ●●
1994 MISS HABANITA   *Floral / Florale*   34 ●
1994 MUGUET / LILY OF THE VALLEY   *Floral / Florale*   30 ●
1994 ROSE   *Floral / Florale*   31 ●●●
1994 VIOLETTE   *Floral / Florale*   31 ●●●●
1995 EAU LES COEURS*   *Floral / Florale*   32 ●●
1995 MUSC   *Woody Oriental / Oriental Boisé*   61 ●●●
1997 ÉCOUTE-MOI   *Floral / Florale*   33 ●●●●
1998 VANILLE FLEURIE   *Floral / Florale*   31 ●●●●
1998 VANILLE FRAÎCHEUR   *Oriental / Oriental*   56 ●●
1998 VANILLE FRUITÉE   *Oriental / Oriental*   56 ●●
1998 VANILLE MARINE   *Water / Marine*   27 ●●●●
1998 VANILLE PATCHOULI   *Woody Oriental / Oriental Boisé*   61 ●●●
1999 BASILIC FLEUR D'ORANGER   *Floral / Florale*   31 ●●●●
1999 BULLES DE FRAÎCHEUR   *Citrus / Hespéridé*   16 ●
1999 CARAMEL PAIN D'ÉPICE   *Soft Oriental / Oriental Doux*   52 ●●
1999 CHOCOLAT MENTHE   *Oriental / Oriental*   56 ●●
1999 FLEUR DE FIGUIER   *Mossy Woods / Chypre Boisé*   66 ●
1999 ORANGE CAFÉ   *Citrus / Hespéridé*   17 ●●●●
1999 POMME CANNELLE   *Mossy Woods / Chypre Boisé*   66 ●●
1999 ROSE SANTAL   *Floral / Florale*   31 ●●
2000 AUTOUR DU THÉ CLASSIQUE   *Floral / Florale*   34 ●
2000 AUTOUR DU THÉ EXOTIQUE   *Soft Floral / Fleuri Aldéhydé*   42 ●●
2000 AUTOUR DU THÉ ROMANTIQUE   *Floral / Florale*   34 ●●
2000 DOUBLE FRAÎCHEUR POUR ELLE   *Citrus / Hespéridé*   17 ●●●●
2000 UN AIR D'HABANITA   *Floral Oriental / Fleuri Oriental*   46 ●
2000 VANILLE AMBRE   *Oriental / Oriental*   57 ●●●
1935/93 MADRIGAL   *Mossy Woods / Chypre Boisé*   68 ●●
1949 VERVEINE   *Citrus / Hespéridé*   19 ●●●
1977/94 RAFALE   *Aromatic / Fougère*   78 ●●
1984 VETYVER   *Mossy Woods / Chypre Boisé*   69 ●●●
1989 TECK   *Dry Woods / Boisé Cuir*   73 ●●●
1995 BOIS PRÉCIEUX   *Mossy Woods / Chypre Boisé*   69 ●●●●
1996 MOLINARD HOMME I   *Aromatic / Fougère*   80 ●●
1996 MOLINARD HOMME II   *Woody Oriental / Oriental Boisé*   62 ●
1996 MOLINARD HOMME III   *Water / Marine*   27 ●●●
1996 VANITECK   *Dry Woods / Boisé Cuir*   73 ●●●●
2000 DOUBLE FRAÎCHEUR POUR LUI   *Citrus / Hespéridé*   19 ●●●●

MOLYNEUX

1932/95 LE CHIC*   *Soft Floral / Fleuri Aldéhydé*   42 ●●
1971 VIVRE   *Soft Floral / Fleuri Aldéhydé*   42 ●●
1977 QUARTZ   *Floral / Florale*   34 ●
1980 GAULOISE*   *Mossy Woods / Chypre Boisé*   66 ●
1990 INITIATION*   *Floral Oriental / Fleuri Oriental*   47 ●●●
1998 I LOVE YOU   *Floral / Florale*   32 ●
1999 MODERN QUARTZ   *Floral / Florale*   34 ●
1975 CAPTAIN*   *Aromatic / Fougère*   76 ●●
1988 LORD MOLYNEUX*   *Dry Woods / Boisé Cuir*   72 ●●
1996 QUARTZ POUR HOMME   *Citrus / Hespéridé*   18 ●●

MONDE NOUVEAU → UN MONDE NOUVEAU

MONSOON

1994 MONSOON   *Floral / Florale*   34 ●●
1996 SHIMÓ   *Floral Oriental / Fleuri Oriental*   46 ●●
1997 MONSOON EAU   *Water / Marine*   26 ●●

MONTANA

1986 MONTANA PARFUM DE PEAU   *Dry Woods / Boisé Cuir*   73 ●●●●
1990 MONTANA PARFUM D'ELLE*   *Mossy Woods / Chypre Boisé*   66 ●
1994 SUGGESTION EAU CUIVRÉE*   *Floral Oriental / Fleuri Oriental*   47 ●●●
1994 SUGGESTION EAU D'ARGENT*   *Floral / Florale*   36 ●●
1994 SUGGESTION EAU D'OR*   *Floral / Florale*   34 ●●
1997 JUST ME   *Woody Oriental / Oriental Boisé*   60 ●●
2000 MONTANA BLU   *Floral / Florale*   36 ●
1989 MONTANA POUR HOMME   *Woody Oriental / Oriental Boisé*   62 ●●

MONTEIL

1995 L'EAU DE MONTEIL   *Floral / Florale*   33 ●●●●

MORABITO

1987 MON CLASSIQUE   *Floral / Florale*   38 ●●
1992 TURQUOISE   *Citrus / Hespéridé*   17 ●●●●
1995 SOIR D'ÉTÉ   *Mossy Woods / Chypre Boisé*   67 ●●●
1996 MISS MORABITO   *Floral / Florale*   38 ●
1997 UN MATIN D'ÉTÉ   *Floral / Florale*   30 ●●
1998 FLEURS   *Floral / Florale*   38 ●
1998 ON AIR FEMME   *Floral / Florale*   34 ●●
1989 M de MORABITO   *Woody Oriental / Oriental Boisé*   63 ●●●●
1994 MONSIEUR MORABITO   *Aromatic / Fougère*   82 ●
1998 ON AIR HOMME   *Aromatic / Fougère*   76 ●

MORENI → POPY MORENI

MORGANE LE FAY

1997 MORGANE LE FAY   *Floral / Florale*   36 ●
2000 MORGANE LE FAY BLUE   *Woody Oriental / Oriental Boisé*   61 ●●●

MORRIS

1996 REPLAY   *Woody Oriental / Oriental Boisé*   62 ●

MOSCHINO

1987 MOSCHINO   *Oriental / Oriental*   57 ●●●
1995 CHEAP & CHIC   *Floral / Florale*   32 ●
1996 OH! DE MOSCHINO   *Soft Floral / Fleuri Aldéhydé*   42 ●
1991 MOSCHINO POUR HOMME   *Dry Woods / Boisé Cuir*   72 ●●
1997 UOMO? MOSCHINO   *Woody Oriental / Oriental Boisé*   62 ●

MUELHENS

1792 4711 ORIGINAL ♂   *Citrus / Hespéridé*   17 ●●●
1921 TOSCA   *Soft Floral / Fleuri Aldéhydé*   43 ●●●●
1976 EXTASE MUSK WOMAN   *Oriental / Oriental*   57 ●●●
1994 EXTASE DEVOTION WOMAN   *Woody Oriental / Oriental Boisé*   60 ●
1996 EXTASE BODY TALK ♂   *Citrus / Hespéridé*   16 ●
1997 EXTASE EXOTIC NATURE WOMAN   *Floral / Florale*   36 ●●
1997 VIVA DI TOSCA   *Floral Oriental / Fleuri Oriental*   47 ●●●
1998 BELLA FIRENZE   *Floral Oriental / Fleuri Oriental*   46 ●
1999 SUMATRA RAIN WOMAN   *Floral Oriental / Fleuri Oriental*   46 ●
2000 EXTASE PURE PASSION WOMAN   *Woody Oriental / Oriental Boisé*   61 ●●●
1935 IRISCH MOOS / IRISH MOSS   *Mossy Woods / Chypre Boisé*   68 ●●
1985 EXTASE MUSK MAN   *Oriental / Oriental*   57 ●●●●
1993 EXTASE MAGMA MAN   *Woody Oriental / Oriental Boisé*   63 ●●●
1993 SUMATRA RAIN MEN   *Aromatic / Fougère*   80 ●●
1995 GALILEO DE VIENTO   *Aromatic / Fougère*   78 ●●
1997 EXTASE EXOTIC NATURE MAN   *Aromatic / Fougère*   76 ●●
1997 GALILEO 21st CENTURY   *Aromatic / Fougère*   82 ●
1997 PUMA INDEPENDENCE   *Aromatic / Fougère*   82 ●
1997 SUMATRA RAIN WOOD   *Woody Oriental / Oriental Boisé*   62 ●●
1998 PUMA CHALLENGE   *Aromatic / Fougère*   80 ●●
1998 SUMATRA RAIN FRESH   *Aromatic / Fougère*   78 ●
2000 EXTASE PURE PASSION MAN   *Woody Oriental / Oriental Boisé*   62 ●●

MUGLER → THIERRY MUGLER

MULBERRY

1997 MULBERRY   *Soft Oriental / Oriental Doux*   53 ●●●
1966 MULBERRY FOR MEN   *Dry Woods / Boisé Cuir*   72 ●●

MYRURGIA (a selection   *un choix*)

1916 LAVANDA ♂   *Floral / Florale*   31 ●●●
1921 MAJA   *Soft Oriental / Oriental Doux*   53 ●●●
1996 TRIANGLE   *Floral / Florale*   34 ●●

MY VERY OWN

2000 BUTTERFLY KISSES   *Floral / Florale*   32 ●●
2000 SUNSHINE   *Floral / Florale*   36 ●
2000 GOAL   *Water / Marine*   26 ●●
2000 GRAND SLAM   *Citrus / Hespéridé*   18 ●
2000 SWISH   *Aromatic / Fougère*   78 ●
2000 TOUCH DOWN   *Aromatic / Fougère*   82 ●

NAF NAF

1991 UNE TOUCHE DE NAF NAF   *Floral / Florale*   34 ●
1995 GRAFFITI VANILLA   *Woody Oriental / Oriental Boisé*   60 ●●

NAJ-OLEARI

1989/99 NAJ-OLEARI   *Soft Floral / Fleuri Aldéhydé*   43 ●●●●

Index des Maisons

NAOMI CAMPBELL
1999 NAOMI CAMPBELL *Woody Oriental / Oriental Boisé* 61 ●●●●
2000 NAOMAGIC *Floral Oriental / Fleuri Oriental* 46 ●

NAPA VALLEY
1998 CIELO *Mossy Woods / Chypre Boisé* 66 ●
2000 BOHÈME *Mossy Woods / Chypre Boisé* 66 ●●

NAPOLEON
1999 LAPIS *Woody Oriental / Oriental Boisé* 60 ●●

NATIO
1999 U *Floral / Florale* 34 ●

NAUTICA
1997 NAUTICA WOMAN *Floral / Florale* 38 ●
1992 NAUTICA *Water / Marine* 26 ●
1997 NAUTICA COMPETITION *Woody Oriental / Oriental Boisé* 62 ●●

NAUTICA: UNILEVER COSMETICS
2000 LATITUDE LONGTITUDE *Aromatic / Fougère* 76 ●

NAUTILUS
2000 DONNA NAUTILUS *Floral / Florale* 32 ●●
1998 NAUTILUS AQUA *Water / Marine* 27 ●●●●

NAZARENO GABRIELLI
1996 NAZARENO GABRIELLI POUR FEMME
    Floral Oriental / Fleuri Oriental 46 ●●
2000 NAZARENO POUR FEMME *Floral / Florale* 34 ●●
1996 NAZARENO GABRIELLI POUR HOMME *Aromatic / Fougère* 78 ●
2000 NAZARENO POUR HOMME *Aromatic / Fougère* 80 ●●

NETWORK
1982 NOIR *Dry Woods / Boisé Cuir* 73 ●●●

NICOLE MILLER
1993 NICOLE MILLER *Floral Oriental / Fleuri Oriental* 46 ●●
1998 NICOLE *Floral / Florale* 38 ●
1994 NICOLE MILLER FOR MEN *Woody Oriental / Oriental Boisé* 62 ●●

NIKE COSMETICS
2000 NIKE WOMAN *Woody Oriental / Oriental Boisé* 60 ●
1991 NIKE *Aromatic / Fougère* 80 ●
1997 NK *Aromatic / Fougère* 82 ●

NIKI DE SAINT PHALLE
1982 NIKI DE SAINT PHALLE *Mossy Woods / Chypre Boisé* 66 ●

NIKOS
1994 SCULPTURE *Floral Oriental / Fleuri Oriental* 48 ●
1995 SCULPTURE HOMME *Woody Oriental / Oriental Boisé* 62 ●●

NINA RICCI
1946 COEUR-JOIE *Soft Floral / Fleuri Aldéhydé* 43 ●●●
1948 L'AIR DU TEMPS *Floral / Florale* 33 ●●●
1952 FILLE D'EVE *Mossy Woods / Chypre Boisé* 67 ●●●
1961 CAPRICCI *Floral / Florale* 33 ●●●
1974 FAROUCHE *Soft Floral / Fleuri Aldéhydé* 42 ●●
1980/82 FLEUR DE FLEURS *Soft Floral / Fleuri Aldéhydé* 42 ●
1987 NINA *Soft Floral / Fleuri Aldéhydé* 42 ●●
1994 DECI DELÀ *Mossy Woods / Chypre Boisé* 66 ●●
1996 LIBERTÉ ACIDULÉE (LES BELLES DE RICCI) *Floral / Florale* 32 ●
1999 AMOUR D'AMANDIER *Floral / Florale* 32 ●●
1999 DÉLICE D'ÉPICES *Floral Oriental / Fleuri Oriental* 47 ●●●
2000 BELLE DE MINUIT *Oriental / Oriental* 56 ●●
2001 PREMIER JOUR *Floral Oriental / Fleuri Oriental* 46 ●
1975 SIGNORICCI *Citrus / Hespéridé* 19 ●●●
1989 RICCI-CLUB *Woody Oriental / Oriental Boisé* 62 ●●

NINO CERRUTI → CERRUTI

NORELL
1968 NORELL *Floral / Florale* 36 ●●

OLD ENGLAND
1999 CHELSEA DREAMS *Floral / Florale* 32 ●●

OLEG CASSINI
1990 CASSINI *Mossy Woods / Chypre Boisé* 66 ●●
1998 BLACK TIE *Woody Oriental / Oriental Boisé* 60 ●
1995 CASSINI FOR MEN *Aromatic / Fougère* 76 ●

OLIVIER DE KERSAUSON
1992 LATITUDE *Aromatic / Fougère* 76 ●●
1997 LATITUDE SPORT *Water / Marine* 27 ●●●

OLIVIER STRELLI
2000 OLIVIER STRELLI *Soft Oriental / Oriental Doux* 52 ●●

OMAR SHARIF
1989 OMAR SHARIF* *Floral / Florale* 33 ●●●
1994 NUBIADE* *Woody Oriental / Oriental Boisé* 62 ●●●
1998 CONVICTION *Floral Oriental / Fleuri Oriental* 46 ●
1992 OMAR SHARIF POUR HOMME* *Aromatic / Fougère* 80 ●●
1994 IGNIS* *Dry Woods / Boisé Cuir* 73 ●●●
1999 CONVICTION MEN *Woody Oriental / Oriental Boisé* 62 ●●

ORIGINS
1995 SPRING FEVER *Floral / Florale* 34 ●●
2000 GINGER ESSENCE *Citrus / Hespéridé* 17 ●●●●

ORLANE
1983 FLEURS D'ORLANE *Floral / Florale* 38 ●
1992 EAU D'ORLANE *Citrus / Hespéridé* 16 ●
1978/80 DERRICK *Woody Oriental / Oriental Boisé* 63 ●●●

ORSAY → D'ORSAY

OSCAR DE LA RENTA
1977 OSCAR *Floral Oriental / Fleuri Oriental* 47 ●●●
1983 RUFFLES* *Floral Oriental / Fleuri Oriental* 48 ●●
1992 VOLUPTÉ *Floral Oriental / Fleuri Oriental* 46 ●●
1997 SO DE LA RENTA *Floral / Florale* 34 ●
1980 OSCAR DE LA RENTA POUR LUI *Dry Woods / Boisé Cuir* 72 ●●
1999 OSCAR FOR MEN *Dry Woods / Boisé Cuir* 72 ●●

OZBEK → RIFAT OZBEK

PACO RABANNE
1969 CALANDRE *Soft Floral / Fleuri Aldéhydé* 42 ●●
1979 MÉTAL *Soft Floral / Fleuri Aldéhydé* 42 ●
1985 LA NUIT *Dry Woods / Boisé Cuir* 73 ●●●●
1994 XS POUR ELLE *Floral / Florale* 38 ●
1996 PACO ♂ *Citrus / Hespéridé* 16 ●
1998 PACO ENERGY ♂ *Citrus / Hespéridé* 16 ●●
1999 ULTRAVIOLET *Floral Oriental / Fleuri Oriental* 46 ●
1973 PACO RABANNE POUR HOMME *Aromatic / Fougère* 78 ●●
1986 SPORT DE PACO RABANNE *Citrus / Hespéridé* 18 ●●
1988 TÉNÉRÉ *Floral / Florale* 39 ●●●●
1993 XS POUR HOMME *Aromatic / Fougère* 78 ●

PALLADIO / KITON
1997 KITON DONNA *Floral / Florale* 32 ●●
1996 KITON MEN *Mossy Woods / Chypre Boisé* 68 ●
1998 KITON NAPOLI *Woody Oriental / Oriental Boisé* 62 ●

PALOMA PICASSO
1984 PALOMA PICASSO *Mossy Woods / Chypre Boisé* 67 ●●●
1996 TENTATIONS* *Woody Oriental / Oriental Boisé* 61 ●●●
1992 MINOTAURE* *Woody Oriental / Oriental Boisé* 62 ●●

PARAH
1996 PARAH *Floral / Florale* 33 ●●●●
1998 REALLY PARAH *Soft Floral / Fleuri Aldéhydé* 42 ●●
1999 ESSENZA DI MEDITERRANEÒ DONNA *Floral / Florale* 32 ●
1999 ESSENZA DI MEDITERRANEÒ UOMO *Dry Woods / Boisé Cuir* 72 ●

PARFUMS BLEU
1975 BLUE STRATOS *Aromatic / Fougère* 80 ●
1983 GOLD *Aromatic / Fougère* 76 ●
1985 CLASSIC *Mossy Woods / Chypre Boisé* 69 ●●●
1989 ENGLISH BLAZER *Aromatic / Fougère* 76 ●●
1997 BLUE *Aromatic / Fougère* 82 ●

PARIS BLEU
1995 GALICE *Floral Oriental / Fleuri Oriental 46* ●●
1998 COEUR D'OR *Woody Oriental / Oriental Boisé 60* ●

PARLUX
1984 ANNE KLEIN* *Soft Floral / Fleuri Aldéhydé 42* ●
1985 DÉCADENCE* *Floral / Florale 38* ●●
1986 ANNE KLEIN II* *Oriental / Oriental 56* ●
1987 ANIMALE *Mossy Woods / Chypre Boisé 67* ●●●●
1988 PHANTOM OF THE OPERA* *Floral Oriental / Fleuri Oriental 48* ●●
1993 ANIMALE ANIMALE *Floral Oriental / Fleuri Oriental 46* ●●
1997 INSTINCT D'ANIMALE *Mossy Woods / Chypre Boisé 67* ●●●
2000 CHALEUR D'ANIMALE *Floral / Florale 34* ●
1993 ANIMALE FOR MEN *Aromatic / Fougère 80* ●
1994 ANIMALE ANIMALE FOR MEN *Woody Oriental / Oriental Boisé 62* ●
2000 CHALEUR D'ANIMALE POUR HOMME *Aromatic / Fougère 82* ●

PARQUET / DANA → DANA
PATOU → JEAN PATOU

PATRICIA DE NICOLAÏ
1989 COLOGNE SOLOGNE ♂ *Citrus / Hespéridé 17* ●●●
1989 LE TEMPS D'UNE FÊTE *Floral / Florale 36* ●
1989 NUMBER ONE *Floral / Florale 38* ●●
1989 ODALISQUE *Floral / Florale 38* ●
1992 VIE DE CHATEAU (CHEVERNY) ♂ *Mossy Woods / Chypre Boisé 67* ●●●
1992 EAU DE PROVENCE ♂ *Floral / Florale 31* ●●●
1992 JARDIN SECRET *Mossy Woods / Chypre Boisé 66* ●●
1992 MIMOSAÏQUE *Floral / Florale 30* ●●
1993 SACREBLEU! *Floral Oriental / Fleuri Oriental 47* ●●●
1996 JUSTE UN RÊVE *Woody Oriental / Oriental Boisé 60* ●●
1997 EAU D'ÉTÉ *Citrus / Hespéridé 16* ●●
1997 VANILLE-TONKA *Oriental / Oriental 57* ●●●
1998 ROSE-PIVOINE *Floral / Florale 31* ●●●
2000 FIG TEA *Citrus / Hespéridé 17* ●●●●
1989 NEW YORK *Woody Oriental / Oriental Boisé 62* ●●
1994 BALADIN *Dry Woods / Boisé Cuir 73* ●●●
1995 CARRÉ D'AS *Aromatic / Fougère 80* ●

PATRICK COX
2000 HIGH... (Cerise) *Citrus / Hespéridé 16* ●●
2000 HIGH... (Turquoise) *Aromatic / Fougère 78* ●

PAULINE TRIGÈRE
1973 TRIGÈRE *Soft Floral / Fleuri Aldéhydé 42* ●●

PAUL SEBASTIAN
1985 DESIGN *Soft Floral / Fleuri Aldéhydé 42* ●
1995 CASUAL *Floral / Florale 38* ●
1979 PS *Soft Oriental / Oriental Doux 53* ●●●
1995 DESIGN FOR MEN *Aromatic / Fougère 80* ●

PAUL SMITH
2000 PAUL SMITH WOMEN *Floral / Florale 34* ●
2000 PAUL SMITH MEN *Aromatic / Fougère 80* ●●

PAVAROTTI
1995 PAVAROTTI DONNA *Mossy Woods / Chypre Boisé 66* ●●
1994 LUCIANO PAVAROTTI *Dry Woods / Boisé Cuir 73* ●●●
1999 LUCIANO *Aromatic / Fougère 80* ●

PAYOT / FIVE STAR
1977 PAVLOVA *Floral / Florale 31* ●●●●

PENHALIGON'S
1911 ENGLISH FERN ♂ *Aromatic / Fougère 77* ●●●
1927 EAU DE COLOGNE ♂ *Citrus / Hespéridé 17* ●●●
1949 EAU DE VERVEINE ♂ *Citrus / Hespéridé 17* ●●●●
1963 EXTRACT OF LIMES ♂ *Citrus / Hespéridé 17* ●●●●
1976 ESPRIT DE LAVANDE ♂ *Aromatic / Fougère 76* ●
1976 GARDENIA *Floral / Florale 30* ●●
1976 LILY OF THE VALLEY *Floral / Florale 30* ●
1976 NIGHT SCENTED STOCK *Floral / Florale 31* ●●●●
1976 ORANGE BLOSSOM *Floral / Florale 31* ●●●●
1976 PRIMROSE *Floral / Florale 31* ●●●
1976 VIOLETTA *Floral / Florale 31* ●●●●
1978 BLUEBELL / WOODLAND HYACINTH *Floral / Florale 34* ●

1979 VICTORIAN POSY *Floral / Florale 33* ●●●●
1984 ELISABETHAN ROSE *Floral / Florale 31* ●●●
1987 ORMOLU *Woody Oriental / Oriental Boisé 60* ●●
1989 ESPRIT DU ROI ♂ *Citrus / Hespéridé 16* ●●
1991 CORNUBIA *Floral Oriental / Fleuri Oriental 47* ●●●
1992 EAU SANS PAREIL ♂ *Aromatic / Fougère 76* ●●
1996 QUERCUS ♂ *Citrus / Hespéridé 16* ●
1998 LP N° 9 *Floral Oriental / Fleuri Oriental 46* ●
1999 PENHALIGON'S CASTILE ♂ *Citrus / Hespéridé 17* ●●●
1872 HAMMAM BOUQUET *Woody Oriental / Oriental Boisé 63* ●●●
1902 BLENHEIM BOUQUET *Citrus / Hespéridé 19* ●●●
1911 LORDS *Citrus / Hespéridé 19* ●●●●
1989 RACQUETS FORMULA *Aromatic / Fougère 77* ●●●
1999 LP N° 9 FOR MEN *Woody Oriental / Oriental Boisé 63* ●●●

PENNY BLACK
1999 PENNY BLACK WOMAN *Floral / Florale 34* ●
1999 PENNY BLACK *Aromatic / Fougère 80* ●●

PERFUMERS GUILD
1981 CLUB COLOGNE ♂ *Citrus / Hespéridé 17* ●●●
1981 ENGLISH ROSE *Floral / Florale 31* ●●●
1981 LILY OF THE VALLEY *Floral / Florale 30* ●
1981 PROVENCE LAVENDER *Floral / Florale 31* ●●●
1982 SOCIETY *Floral / Florale 33* ●●●●
1989 WATERPERRY *Floral Oriental / Fleuri Oriental 47* ●●●
1990 SCENT OF ROMANCE ORIGINAL *Soft Oriental / Oriental Doux 53* ●●●
1990 TWENTY ONE ♂ *Citrus / Hespéridé 16* ●●●●
1990 SCENT OF FLOWERS *Floral / Florale 38* ●
1991 SCENT OF ROMANCE ST VALENTINE *Soft Floral / Fleuri Aldéhydé 43* ●●●
1992 SCENT OF ROMANCE WITH LOVE *Floral / Florale 36* ●
2000 HERITAGE ROSE *Floral / Florale 30* ●●
2000 MILLENNIUM ROSE *Soft Floral / Fleuri Aldéhydé 43* ●●●●
2000 SCENT OF ROMANCE UNFORGETTABLE *Floral / Florale 33* ●●●
1984 JB BLEND *Aromatic / Fougère 76* ●
1988 SOCIETY GENTLEMEN *Aromatic / Fougère 78* ●
1990 WATERPERRY GENTLEMEN *Aromatic / Fougère 78* ●
1999 HUNTSMAN *Mossy Woods / Chypre Boisé 68* ●

PERFUMER'S WORKSHOP
1972 TEA ROSE *Floral / Florale 31* ●●●
1987 SAMBA *Floral / Florale 34* ●●
1992 SAMBA NOVA *Mossy Woods / Chypre Boisé 66* ●
1996 SAMBA NATURAL *Water / Marine 26* ●●
1998 UNZIPPED *Woody Oriental / Oriental Boisé 60* ●
1999 SAMBA RED WOMAN *Soft Floral / Fleuri Aldéhydé 42* ●●
1999 UNZIPPED SPORT *Floral / Florale 34* ●
1999 UNZIPPED UNIVERSE *Floral Oriental / Fleuri Oriental 46* ●
2000 SAMBA HEAT WOMAN *Woody Oriental / Oriental Boisé 61* ●●●
1990 SAMBA FOR MEN *Citrus / Hespéridé 19* ●●●●
1993 SAMBA NOVA HOMME *Woody Oriental / Oriental Boisé 62* ●●
1997 SAMBA NATURAL MAN *Aromatic / Fougère 82* ●
1998 ZIPPED *Citrus / Hespéridé 18* ●●
1999 SAMBA RED MAN *Mossy Woods / Chypre Boisé 68* ●●
1999 ZIPPED SPORTS *Aromatic / Fougère 80* ●
1999 ZIPPED UNIVERSE *Woody Oriental / Oriental Boisé 62* ●●
2000 SAMBA HEAT MAN *Woody Oriental / Oriental Boisé 62* ●

PERFUMES Y DISEÑO
2000 MONTECRISTO *Dry Woods / Boisé Cuir 72* ●●

PERRY ELLIS
1985/96 PERRY ELLIS FOR WOMEN *Soft Floral / Fleuri Aldéhydé 42* ●●
1993 360° FOR WOMEN *Floral / Florale 32* ●●
1996 AMERICA FOR WOMEN *Floral / Florale 32* ●
2000 PERRY ELLIS PORTFOLIO *Floral / Florale 38* ●
1985/96 PERRY ELLIS FOR MEN *Dry Woods / Boisé Cuir 73* ●●●
1995 360° FOR MEN *Aromatic / Fougère 80* ●
1996 AMERICA FOR MEN *Aromatic / Fougère 80* ●
1997 PERRY ELLIS RESERVE *Aromatic / Fougère 80* ●
1999 PERRY ELLIS PORTFOLIO FOR MEN *Aromatic / Fougère 76* ●

PHILIPPE VENET
1965/96 VENET *Floral Oriental / Fleuri Oriental 47* ●●●
1998 EAU DE COUTURE *Soft Floral / Fleuri Aldéhydé 43* ●●●●
2000 COUTURE POUR ELLE *Woody Oriental / Oriental Boisé 60* ●
2000 COUTURE POUR LUI *Woody Oriental / Oriental Boisé 62* ●

PICOT / LENTHÉRIC → LENTHÉRIC

PIERRE BALMAIN
1947/90 VENT VERT *Green / Vert 23* ●●●
1953/92 JOLIE MADAME *Woody Oriental / Oriental Boisé 60* ●●
1967 MISS BALMAIN *Dry Woods / Boisé Cuir 73* ●●●
1980 IVOIRE *Soft Floral / Fleuri Aldéhydé 42* ●
1998 BALMAIN *Mossy Woods / Chypre Boisé 66* ●
2000 EAU D'IVOIRE *Floral / Florale 34* ●
1964/90 MONSIEUR BALMAIN *Citrus / Hespéridé 19* ●●●●
1983 ÉBÈNE *Aromatic / Fougère 78* ●●

PIERRE CARDIN
1981 CHOC *Mossy Woods / Chypre Boisé 66* ●
1990 ROSE CARDIN *Mossy Woods / Chypre Boisé 67* ●●●
1995 OPHÉLIE *Soft Floral / Fleuri Aldéhydé 43* ●●●
2000 MONTE CARLO *Oriental / Oriental 56* ●●
2000 YSEULT *Citrus / Hespéridé 17* ●●●●
1965/86 BLEU MARINE *Woody Oriental / Oriental Boisé 62* ●
1972 PIERRE CARDIN POUR MONSIEUR *Soft Oriental / Oriental Doux 52* ●
1987 PIERRE CARDIN MUSK* *Aromatic / Fougère 77* ●●●●
1992 ENIGME *Aromatic / Fougère 82* ●●
1995 INSATIABLE *Aromatic / Fougère 76* ●
1996 CENTAURE CUIR AMBRE *Woody Oriental / Oriental Boisé 62* ●●
1996 CENTAURE CUIR BLANC *Mossy Woods / Chypre Boisé 68* ●●
1996 CENTAURE CUIR CASAQUE *Aromatic / Fougère 80* ●●
1996 CENTAURE CUIR ÉTALON *Dry Woods / Boisé Cuir 73* ●●●
1996 CENTAURE CUIR FOUGÈRE *Aromatic / Fougère 76* ●
1996 SPORTIF *Aromatic / Fougère 80* ●
1998 CENTAURE DIAMANT NOIR *Aromatic / Fougère 76* ●●
1998 CENTAURE TÊTE D'OR *Aromatic / Fougère 76* ●●
2000 TRISTAN *Dry Woods / Boisé Cuir 73* ●●●●

PIGUET → ROBERT PIGUET

PINO SILVESTRE: MAVIVE
1996 GREEN GENERATION ♂ *Aromatic / Fougère 76* ●●
1998 GREEN GENERATION HER *Floral / Florale 32* ●
1955 PINO SILVESTRE ORIGINAL *Mossy Woods / Chypre Boisé 69* ●●●
1992 ICE WATER* *Aromatic / Fougère 82* ●
1998 GREEN GENERATION HIM *Aromatic / Fougère 76* ●
1998 PINO SILVESTRE EXTREME *Citrus / Hespéridé 19* ●●●●

PIVER → L.T. PIVER

POI
1995 VERDI 800 *Woody Oriental / Oriental Boisé 63* ●●●

POLICE
1998 POLICE *Aromatic / Fougère 77* ●●●

POPY MORENI
1996 POPY MORENI *Woody Oriental / Oriental Boisé 60* ●
1998 POPY MORENI DE FÊTE *Floral / Florale 36* ●●
1999 LE CIRQUE DE POPY MORENI *Soft Floral / Fleuri Aldéhydé 42* ●

PRESCRIPTIVES
1986 CALYX *Floral / Florale 32* ●
1998 FLIRT *Floral / Florale 34* ●●
2000 PRESCRIPTIVES POTION *Floral / Florale 36* ●●

PRINCE MATCHABELLI (a selection *un choix*)
1952 WIND SONG *Floral / Florale 33* ●●●
1970 CACHET (Original) *Dry Woods / Boisé Cuir 73* ●●●

PRISCILLA PRESLEY
1990 MOMENTS *Woody Oriental / Oriental Boisé 61* ●●●
1993 EXPERIENCES *Floral / Florale 33* ●●●●
1996 INDIAN SUMMER *Floral Oriental / Fleuri Oriental 46* ●
1998 ROSES AND MORE *Floral / Florale 31* ●●●
1999 GOLDEN MOMENT *Floral Oriental / Fleuri Oriental 46* ●

PUIG → ANTONIO PUIG

PUPA (a selection *un choix*)
1996 FIORILU EN FLEURS *Floral / Florale 32* ●●
1997 PLUMES *Floral / Florale 34* ●

RABANNE → PACO RABANNE

RALPH LAUREN
1978 LAUREN *Floral / Florale 32* ●●
1979 TUXEDO* *Mossy Woods / Chypre Boisé 67* ●●●
1990 SAFARI *Soft Floral / Fleuri Aldéhydé 42* ●
1996 POLO SPORT WOMAN *Water / Marine 26* ●●
1998 ROMANCE *Floral / Florale 33* ●●●
2000 RALPH *Floral / Florale 34* ●
1978 POLO *Dry Woods / Boisé Cuir 72* ●●
1979 CHAPS *Woody Oriental / Oriental Boisé 63* ●●●
1985 CHAPS MUSK *Woody Oriental / Oriental Boisé 63* ●●●
1991 POLO CREST *Dry Woods / Boisé Cuir 72* ●●
1992 SAFARI FOR MEN *Aromatic / Fougère 76* ●
1994 POLO SPORT *Aromatic / Fougère 82* ●
1998 POLO SPORT EXTREME *Dry Woods / Boisé Cuir 72* ●●
1999 ROMANCE MEN *Aromatic / Fougère 80* ●

RAPHAËL
1947 RÉPLIQUE* *Mossy Woods / Chypre Boisé 67* ●●●

RAVELLO
1997 RAVELLO *Floral Oriental / Fleuri Oriental 47* ●●●

RED PEARL
1999 RED PEARL *Floral Oriental / Fleuri Oriental 46* ●

RÉGINE'S
1989 RÉGINE'S *Woody Oriental / Oriental Boisé 61* ●●●
1992 ZOA *Floral / Florale 34* ●●
1995 PALACE *Soft Floral / Fleuri Aldéhydé 42* ●●
1991 JIMMY'Z *Woody Oriental / Oriental Boisé 62* ●●
1993 RÉGINE'S FOR MEN *Woody Oriental / Oriental Boisé 62* ●

RÉMY LATOUR
1989 SI TENDRE *Soft Floral / Fleuri Aldéhydé 42* ●
1993 LUNE D'ÉTÉ *Woody Oriental / Oriental Boisé 60* ●
1994 SI FLEURI *Floral / Florale 36* ●●
1998 L'ÉLUE *Floral Oriental / Fleuri Oriental 46* ●●
1990 MANÈS *Woody Oriental / Oriental Boisé 62* ●●
1994 KRYIAZ *Aromatic / Fougère 80* ●
1996 CIGAR *Woody Oriental / Oriental Boisé 62* ●●
1996 CIGARILLO *Dry Woods / Boisé Cuir 73* ●●●●
1997 MANÈS ICE *Aromatic / Fougère 78* ●
1999 PRESSURE *Aromatic / Fougère 82* ●●

RÉMY MARQUIS
1999 MARQUIS POUR FEMME *Woody Oriental / Oriental Boisé 60* ●
1999 RÉMY FOR WOMAN *Floral / Florale 34* ●●
1999 MARQUIS *Aromatic / Fougère 80* ●
1999 RÉMY *Woody Oriental / Oriental Boisé 62* ●●

RENATO BALESTRA
1997 ORO POUR FEMME *Mossy Woods / Chypre Boisé 66* ●●
1997 ARGENTO POUR HOMME *Mossy Woods / Chypre Boisé 69* ●●●

RÉVILLON
1953/94 DETCHÉMA *Soft Floral / Fleuri Aldéhydé 43* ●●●●
1981 TURBULENCES *Mossy Woods / Chypre Boisé 67* ●●●●
1994 ANOUCHKA *Mossy Woods / Chypre Boisé 66* ●●
1998 EAU DE RÉVILLON *Floral / Florale 36* ●
1984 FRENCH LINE* *Dry Woods / Boisé Cuir 73* ●●●●
1995 R *Mossy Woods / Chypre Boisé 68* ●

REVLON
1955 INTIMATE* *Mossy Woods / Chypre Boisé 66* ●
1970 MOONDROPS *Floral / Florale 33* ●●●●
1973 CHARLIE *Floral / Florale 34* ●●
1973 CIARA *Oriental / Oriental 57* ●●●●
1975 JONTUE *Floral / Florale 31* ●●●●
1978 ENJOLI *Floral / Florale 31* ●●●●
1984 ENJOLI MIDNIGHT *Soft Oriental / Oriental Doux 53* ●●●
1984 FOREVER KRYSTLE *Floral Oriental / Fleuri Oriental 47* ●●●
1985 MAROC* *Mossy Woods / Chypre Boisé 67* ●●●●
1987 XI'A XI'ANG* *Floral Oriental / Fleuri Oriental 46* ●●
1990 UNFORGETTABLE *Woody Oriental / Oriental Boisé 61* ●●●●
1993 CHARLIE RED *Floral / Florale 32* ●●

1994 CHARLIE WHITE *Water / Marine 26* ●
1994 FIRE & ICE *Oriental / Oriental 56* ●●
1995 CHARLIE GOLD *Floral Oriental / Fleuri Oriental 46* ●
1995 CIARA FEMME FATALE* *Floral Oriental / Fleuri Oriental 46* ●●
1995 LASTING *Floral / Florale 32* ●●
1996 CHERISH* *Floral / Florale 32* ●
1996 FIRE & ICE COOL *Citrus / Hespéridé 16* ●
1996 JONTUE MOONLIGHT* *Floral / Florale 38* ●
1997 CHARLIE SUNSHINE *Floral / Florale 32* ●
1997 CHARLIE WHITE MUSK *Soft Floral / Fleuri Aldéhydé 42* ●
1997 SHE* *Floral / Florale 34* ●●
1998 CHARLIE SILVER *Floral / Florale 32* ●
1999 FIRE & ICE SMOULDER FOR HER *Woody Oriental / Oriental Boisé 60* ●
1999 UNFORGETTABLE TOO *Floral Oriental / Fleuri Oriental 46* ●●
2000 ROUGE DE REVLON *Floral Oriental / Fleuri Oriental 46* ●●
2000 URBAN ENERGY *Floral / Florale 34* ●
2001 SKINLIGHTS *Citrus / Hespéridé 16* ●
1958/89 THAT MAN *Citrus / Hespéridé 19* ●●●●
1965 PUB *Aromatic / Fougère 77* ●●●
1994 FIRE & ICE FOR MEN *Aromatic / Fougère 80* ●
1999 FIRE & ICE SMOULDER FOR HIM *Mossy Woods / Chypre Boisé 68* ●●

REYNALD KATZ
1998 REYNALD KATZ ♂ *Citrus / Hespéridé 16* ●

RICCI → NINA RICCI

RIFAT OZBEK
1995 OZBEK *Floral / Florale 31* ●●●
1999 OZBEK 1001 *Oriental / Oriental 56* ●

RITZ
1935 JEAN NATÉ *Aromatic / Fougère 77* ●●●

ROBERT PIGUET
1944 BANDIT *Dry Woods / Boisé Cuir 73* ●●●
1948 FRACAS *Floral / Florale 31* ●●●●

ROBERTA DI CAMERINO
1998 ROBERTA DI CAMERINO *Floral Oriental / Fleuri Oriental 46* ●
1998 ROBERTA DI CAMERINO POUR HOMME *Aromatic / Fougère 76* ●

ROBERTO CAPUCCI
1963 PARCE QUE!* *Soft Floral / Fleuri Aldéhydé 43* ●●●
1974 YENDI* *Soft Floral / Fleuri Aldéhydé 43* ●●●●
1987 CAPUCCI DE CAPUCCI *Woody Oriental / Oriental Boisé 60* ●●
1999 OPERA III *Woody Oriental / Oriental Boisé 60* ●
1968 CAPUCCI POUR HOMME *Citrus / Hespéridé 18* ●●
1985 R de CAPUCCI* *Aromatic / Fougère 78* ●
1999 OPERA IV *Mossy Woods / Chypre Boisé 68* ●●

ROBERTO VERINO
1992 VERINO *Floral Oriental / Fleuri Oriental 46* ●●
1995 EAU DE VERINO *Floral / Florale 36* ●
2000 VERINO POUR HOMME *Aromatic / Fougère 78* ●●

ROCCOBAROCCO
1994 ROCCOBAROCCO TRE *Floral / Florale 34* ●●
1995 SILVER JEANS FEMME *Floral / Florale 34* ●
1997 GOLD JEANS FEMME *Citrus / Hespéridé 16* ●
1997 PIAZZA DI SPAGNA *Floral / Florale 36* ●
1998 BLACK JEANS FEMME *Floral / Florale 33* ●●●●
1989 ROCCOBAROCCO* *Aromatic / Fougère 77* ●●●●
1995 SILVER JEANS HOMME *Aromatic / Fougère 76* ●
1997 GOLD JEANS HOMME *Aromatic / Fougère 82* ●●
1998 BLACK JEANS HOMME *Woody Oriental / Oriental Boisé 60* ●●
1998 PIAZZA DI SPAGNA UOMO *Aromatic / Fougère 82* ●

ROCHAS
1944/89 FEMME *Mossy Woods / Chypre Boisé 67* ●●●
1960/89 MADAME ROCHAS *Soft Floral / Fleuri Aldéhydé 43* ●●●●
1970 EAU DE ROCHAS *Citrus / Hespéridé 17* ●●●
1978 MYSTÈRE *Woody Oriental / Oriental Boisé 60* ●●
1984 LUMIÈRE (Original)* *Floral / Florale 38* ●
1984/2000 LUMIÈRE (New) *Soft Floral / Fleuri Aldéhydé 42* ●●
1987 BYZANCE *Floral Oriental / Fleuri Oriental 48* ●●
1994 TOCADE *Floral Oriental / Fleuri Oriental 47* ●●●

1995 BYZANTINE* *Floral Oriental / Fleuri Oriental 48* ●
1996 FLEUR D'EAU *Floral / Florale 36* ●
1997 TOCADILLY* *Floral / Florale 34* ●●
1998 ALCHIMIE *Floral Oriental / Fleuri Oriental 46* ●●
1948 MOUSTACHE *Mossy Woods / Chypre Boisé 68* ●●
1969 MONSIEUR ROCHAS *Aromatic / Fougère 77* ●●●
1980 MACASSAR *Dry Woods / Boisé Cuir 73* ●●●●
1990 GLOBE* *Aromatic / Fougère 80* ●●
1993 EAU DE ROCHAS HOMME *Citrus / Hespéridé 19* ●●●●
1999 ROCHAS MAN *Woody Oriental / Oriental Boisé 62* ●●

RODIER
1998 RODIER *Woody Oriental / Oriental Boisé 60* ●
1999 COLÈRE DE RODIER *Woody Oriental / Oriental Boisé 60* ●
1999 GOURMANDISE DE RODIER *Citrus / Hespéridé 16* ●
1999 ORGUEIL DE RODIER *Floral Oriental / Fleuri Oriental 46* ●
1999 PARESSE DE RODIER *Soft Floral / Fleuri Aldéhydé 42* ●
2000 PASSION DE FEMME *Dry Woods / Boisé Cuir 72* ●
1999 PASSION D'HOMME *Woody Oriental / Oriental Boisé 62* ●●

ROGER & GALLET
1806 JEAN-MARIE FARINA ♂ *Citrus / Hespéridé 17* ●●●
1991 BOUQUET IMPÉRIAL ♂ *Citrus / Hespéridé 17* ●●●●
1991 ROGER & GALLET EXTRA-VIEILLE ♂ *Citrus / Hespéridé 17* ●●●
1991 LAVANDE ROYALE *Floral / Florale 31* ●●●
1992 NATURE SYSTEM ♂ *Citrus / Hespéridé 16* ●●
1993 POUR UNE FEMME *Floral / Florale 38* ●
1999 EAU POUR SOI *Floral / Florale 32* ●
2000 EAU DE THÉ VERT ♂ *Citrus / Hespéridé 16* ●
1974/91 VÉTYVER *Mossy Woods / Chypre Boisé 69* ●●●
1980 L'HOMME *Aromatic / Fougère 76* ●●
1985 OPEN *Aromatic / Fougère 82* ●●
1993 POUR L'HOMME *Citrus / Hespéridé 18* ●●

ROMEO GIGLI
1989 ROMEO *Floral / Florale 34* ●●
1994 G GIGLI* *Soft Floral / Fleuri Aldéhydé 42* ●
1999 DI ROMEO GIGLI *Soft Floral / Fleuri Aldéhydé 43* ●●●●
1991 GIGLI PER UOMO *Woody Oriental / Oriental Boisé 62* ●●
1995 SUD EST *Aromatic / Fougère 82* ●

ROSINE
1991 LA ROSE DE ROSINE *Soft Floral / Fleuri Aldéhydé 43* ●●●●
1993 LA COUPE D'OR *Floral Oriental / Fleuri Oriental 46* ●●
1994 MEA CULPA *Floral / Florale 38* ●●
1996 LE MUGUET DE ROSINE *Floral / Florale 30* ●
1997 ROSE D'ÉTÉ *Floral / Florale 36* ●
1997 ROSEBERRY *Soft Floral / Fleuri Aldéhydé 42* ●●
2000 ROSE D'ARGENT *Floral / Florale 31* ●●●

ROYAL COPENHAGEN
1970 ROYAL COPENHAGEN *Woody Oriental / Oriental Boisé 63* ●●●
1976 ROYAL COPENHAGEN MUSK *Soft Oriental / Oriental Doux 53* ●●●●
1996 ROYAL COPENHAGEN SPORT* *Aromatic / Fougère 82* ●
1999 VIKING *Aromatic / Fougère 80* ●

ROYAL DOULTON
1998 DOULTON *Floral Oriental / Fleuri Oriental 46* ●●

ROYAL SECRET
1958 ROYAL SECRET *Oriental / Oriental 57* ●●●
1964 GALORÉ *Floral Oriental / Fleuri Oriental 47* ●●●
1990 ROMANCE *Floral / Florale 33* ●●●●
1999 ROYAL SECRET II *Woody Oriental / Oriental Boisé 60* ●●
1999 ROYAL SECRET FOR MEN* *Woody Oriental / Oriental Boisé 62* ●●

RYKIEL → SONIA RYKIEL
SABATINI → GABRIELA SABATINI
SAINT LAURENT → YVES SAINT LAURENT

SALVADOR DALI
1983 SALVADOR DALI *Soft Oriental / Oriental Doux 53* ●●●
1991 LAGUNA *Floral Oriental / Fleuri Oriental 46* ●
1994 DALISSIME *Floral / Florale 32* ●●
1995 EAU DE DALI *Floral / Florale 32* ●
1996 DALIMIX ♂ *Citrus / Hespéridé 16* ●
1997 DALIMIX GOLD ♂ *Green / Vert 22* ●

House Index

1997 LE ROY SOLEIL *Soft Oriental / Oriental Doux* 52 ●●
1999 DALIMANIA *Floral Oriental / Fleuri Oriental* 46 ●●
2000 DALIFLOR *Floral / Florale* 32 ●
1987 SALVADOR DALI POUR HOMME *Woody Oriental / Oriental Boisé* 62 ●●
1992 SALVADOR *Aromatic / Fougère* 82 ●●
1998 LE ROY SOLEIL HOMME *Mossy Woods / Chypre Boisé* 68 ●●

SALVATORE FERRAGAMO
1998 SALVATORE FERRAGAMO *Floral / Florale* 34 ●●
1999 SALVATORE FERRAGAMO POUR HOMME
     Mossy Woods / Chypre Boisé 68 ●

SAMBA → PERFUMER'S WORKSHOP
SANDER → JIL SANDER

SCAASI
1989 SCAASI *Floral / Florale* 34 ●●

SCANNON
1966 KANØN *Woody Oriental / Oriental Boisé* 63 ●●●

SCAPA OF SCOTLAND
1991 SCAPA *Citrus / Hespéridé* 16 ●●
1999 INTENSE DE SCAPA *Citrus / Hespéridé* 17 ●●●●
1994 SCAPA POUR HOMME* *Aromatic / Fougère* 78 ●●

SCHERRER → JEAN-LOUIS SCHERRER

SCHIAPARELLI
1937/97 SHOCKING *Oriental / Oriental* 57 ●●●
1937/97 ZUT *Woody Oriental / Oriental Boisé* 60 ●

SCHIAPPARELLI PIKENZ
1995 JOHNNY LAMBS *Woody Oriental / Oriental Boisé* 62 ●●

SCHÖN → MILA SCHÖN

SEA WORLD
1998 IMPLICITE *Soft Floral / Fleuri Aldéhydé* 42 ●
1998 IMPLICITE HOMME *Mossy Woods / Chypre Boisé* 68 ●●

SEBASTIAN → PAUL SEBASTIAN

SERGE LUTENS
1993 AMBRE SULTAN ♂ *Soft Oriental / Oriental Doux* 53 ●●●●
2000 À LA NUIT *Floral / Florale* 31 ●●●
2000 ARABIE ♂ *Woody Oriental / Oriental Boisé* 61 ●●●●
2000 DOUCE AMÈRE ♂ *Woody Oriental / Oriental Boisé* 60 ●●
2000 SA MAJESTÉ LA ROSE *Floral / Florale* 30 ●●

SERGIO TACCHINI
1998 SERGIO TACCHINI DONNA *Water / Marine* 26 ●●
2000 O•ZONE WOMAN *Citrus / Hespéridé* 17 ●●●●
1987 SERGIO TACCHINI *Aromatic / Fougère* 76 ●
1993 SERGIO TACCHINI SPORT EXTREME* *Aromatic / Fougère* 82 ●
1996 SERGIO TACCHINI UOMO *Aromatic / Fougère* 78 ●●
2000 O•ZONE MAN *Citrus / Hespéridé* 19 ●●●●

SEVE BALLESTEROS
1992 ROYAL GREEN *Aromatic / Fougère* 80 ●

SHISEIDO
1964 ZEN (Original) *Floral / Florale* 33 ●●●
1976 INOUÏ *Green / Vert* 23 ●●●
1980 MURASAKI *Soft Floral / Fleuri Aldéhydé* 42 ●
1986 SPIRIT OF ZEN *Floral / Florale* 38 ●●
1992 FEMINITÉ DU BOIS *Woody Oriental / Oriental Boisé* 61 ●●●
1997 RELAXING FRAGRANCE *Floral / Florale* 36 ●
1997 VOCALISE *Floral Oriental / Fleuri Oriental* 46 ●
1999 ENERGIZING FRAGRANCE *Soft Floral / Fleuri Aldéhydé* 42 ●●
2000 ZEN (New) *Mossy Woods / Chypre Boisé* 66 ●
1979 TACTICS *Green / Vert* 23 ●●●●
1993 BASALA *Aromatic / Fougère* 77 ●●●●

SHULTON / H&BF → HEALTH & BEAUTY FOCUS
SHULTON / PARFUMS BLEU → PARFUMS BLEU

SHU UEMURA
1988/99 PARFUM ALLIÉ BEATS 14 *Green / Vert* 22 ●●
1988/99 PARFUM ALLIÉ CRYSTAL 32 *Floral / Florale* 36 ●
1988/99 PARFUM ALLIÉ DELICIOUS 62 *Woody Oriental / Oriental Boisé* 61 ●●●
1988/99 PARFUM ALLIÉ DREAM 45 *Soft Floral / Fleuri Aldéhydé* 42 ●●
1988/99 PARFUM ALLIÉ FOREST 02 *Aromatic / Fougère* 76 ●●
1988/99 PARFUM ALLIÉ MARIA 66 *Floral Oriental / Fleuri Oriental* 48 ●
1988/99 PARFUM ALLIÉ MELLOW 51 *Floral / Florale* 34 ●●
1988/99 PARFUM ALLIÉ PASTEL 43 *Floral / Florale* 38 ●
1988/99 PARFUM ALLIÉ SPLASH 24 *Citrus / Hespéridé* 16 ●●
1988/99 PARFUM ALLIÉ SWING 36 *Floral / Florale* 36 ●
1989 SHU UEMURA *Mossy Woods / Chypre Boisé* 66 ●●
1999 SHU UEMURA 029 ♂ *Aromatic / Fougère* 76 ●

SHULTON / P&G
1937 OLD SPICE *Soft Oriental / Oriental Doux* 53 ●●●
1996 OLD SPICE WHITEWATER *Aromatic / Fougère* 80 ●●

SISLEY
1974 EAU DE CAMPAGNE ♂ *Green / Vert* 23 ●●●
1990 EAU DU SOIR *Mossy Woods / Chypre Boisé* 67 ●●●

SLAVA ZAÏTSEV
1992 MAROUSSIA *Floral Oriental / Fleuri Oriental* 47 ●●●
1996 AUTHENTIC MAROUSSIA *Floral Oriental / Fleuri Oriental* 48 ●

SMALTO → FRANCESCO SMALTO

SO COSMETICS
1994 SO...? *Woody Oriental / Oriental Boisé* 61 ●●●
1997 SO...? INSPIRED *Floral / Florale* 34 ●
2000 SO...? WILD *Floral / Florale* 34 ●
1998 SO HIM *Aromatic / Fougère* 82 ●
2000 SO MAX *Aromatic / Fougère* 78 ●

SONIA RYKIEL
1993 LE PARFUM *Woody Oriental / Oriental Boisé* 60 ●●
1997 SONIA RYKIEL *Woody Oriental / Oriental Boisé* 60 ●
1998 L'EAU DE SONIA RYKIEL *Floral / Florale* 32 ●
2000 RYKIEL ROSE *Floral / Florale* 34 ●●
1999 RYKIEL HOMME *Aromatic / Fougère* 82 ●

SOPRANI → LUCIANO SOPRANI

S.T.DUPONT
1998 S.T.DUPONT FEMME *Floral / Florale* 34 ●
2000 SIGNATURE POUR FEMME *Floral Oriental / Fleuri Oriental* 46 ●●
1998 S.T.DUPONT HOMME *Dry Woods / Boisé Cuir* 73 ●●●●
2000 SIGNATURE POUR HOMME *Woody Oriental / Oriental Boisé* 62 ●

ST JOHN
1994 ST JOHN *Floral Oriental / Fleuri Oriental* 47 ●●●●
1998 WHITE CAMELLIA *Floral / Florale* 38 ●

STENDHAL
1960 CHARTREUSE DE PARME *Floral / Florale* 31 ●●●●

STÉPHANIE DE MONACO
1989 STÉPHANIE *Woody Oriental / Oriental Boisé* 61 ●●●
1991 L'INSAISISSABLE *Floral / Florale* 32 ●●

SUCCÈS DE PARIS
1994 DREAMING PRINCESS *Floral Oriental / Fleuri Oriental* 46 ●●
1995 BEST LADY *Floral / Florale* 33 ●●●
1995 FUJIYAMA ♂ *Citrus / Hespéridé* 16 ●
1997 L'EAU DE SUCCÈS* *Floral / Florale* 32 ●●
1999 POLEMIC! *Floral Oriental / Fleuri Oriental* 46 ●
2000 IRENA GREGORI *Floral Oriental / Fleuri Oriental* 48 ●
1995 BEST MAN *Woody Oriental / Oriental Boisé* 62 ●

SULKA
1998 BURL *Woody Oriental / Oriental Boisé* 63 ●●●●

SWANK / REGENCY
1964 JADE EAST *Aromatic / Fougère* 77 ●●●

SWISS ARMY
1996 SWISS ARMY *Aromatic / Fougère* 80 ●

TACCHINI → SERGIO TACCHINI

TED BAKER
1999 TED BAKER WOMAN *Soft Floral / Fleuri Aldéhydé* 42 ●
1998 TED BAKER SKINWEAR *Citrus / Hespéridé* 19 ●●●●
2000 ENDURANCE *Aromatic / Fougère* 76 ●

TED LAPIDUS
1984 CRÉATION *Mossy Woods / Chypre Boisé* 66 ●
1992 FANTASME *Floral Oriental / Fleuri Oriental* 46 ●●
1997 FOU D'ELLE *Floral / Florale* 32 ●●
1987 LAPIDUS POUR HOMME *Aromatic / Fougère* 77 ●●●●
1999 TED *Woody Oriental / Oriental Boisé* 62 ●●

TERRY ELLIS
1997 SOUTHERN EXPOSURE *Citrus / Hespéridé* 16 ●●

THIERRY MUGLER
1992 ANGEL *Woody Oriental / Oriental Boisé* 60 ●
1998 ANGEL INNOCENT *Woody Oriental / Oriental Boisé* 60 ●
1996 A*MEN / ANGEL MEN *Woody Oriental / Oriental Boisé* 60 ●●

TIFFANY
1987 TIFFANY *Floral / Florale* 33 ●●●●
1995 TRUESTE *Soft Floral / Fleuri Aldéhydé* 42 ●
1999 SHEER TIFFANY *Floral / Florale* 38 ●
1989 TIFFANY FOR MEN *Woody Oriental / Oriental Boisé* 63 ●●●
1998 TIFFANY FOR MEN SPORT *Green / Vert* 22 ●

TOCCA
1998 EAU DE TOUCH *Floral / Florale* 30 ●●

TODD OLDHAM
1995 TODD OLDHAM* *Woody Oriental / Oriental Boisé* 60 ●

TOMMY HILFIGER
1996 TOMMY GIRL *Floral / Florale* 36 ●
1999 FREEDOM FOR HER *Floral / Florale* 38 ●
1995 TOMMY *Aromatic / Fougère* 78 ●
1998 HILFIGER ATHLETICS *Citrus / Hespéridé* 18 ●
1999 FREEDOM FOR HIM *Aromatic / Fougère* 78 ●●

TONINO LAMBORGHINI
2000 LAMBORGHINI POUR FEMME *Floral / Florale* 32 ●
1999 LAMBORGHINI POUR HOMME *Aromatic / Fougère* 78 ●●

TOSCA / MUELHENS → MUELHENS

TOVA BORGNINE (a selection *un choix*)
1982 TOVA *Soft Floral / Fleuri Aldéhydé* 43 ●●●●

TRIGÈRE → PAULINE TRIGÈRE

TRISH McEVOY
1998 #1 GRAPEFRUIT & YELLOW FREESIA *Citrus / Hespéridé* 17 ●●●●
1998 #2 JASMINE & ROSE HONEY *Green / Vert* 22 ●
1999 #3 SNOWDROP & CRYSTAL FLOWERS *Floral / Florale* 36 ●
2000 #4 GARDENIA MUSK *Floral / Florale* 30 ●●
2000 #6 MANDARIN & GINGER LILY *Floral / Florale* 32 ●
2000 #7 BASIL TONIC *Citrus / Hespéridé* 16 ●
2000 #8 CITRUS PETALS *Citrus / Hespéridé* 17 ●●●●
2000 #9 BLACKBERRY & VANILLA MUSK *Woody Oriental / Oriental Boisé* 60 ●
2000 #10 LAVENDER SPICE *Aromatic / Fougère* 76 ●●

TRUSSARDI
1982 TRUSSARDI *Dry Woods / Boisé Cuir* 73 ●●●
1989 ACTION* *Green / Vert* 22 ●●
1993 DONNA TRUSSARDI *Mossy Woods / Chypre Boisé* 67 ●●●
1997 LIGHT HER *Floral / Florale* 32 ●●
1999 PYTHON *Woody Oriental / Oriental Boisé* 61 ●●●
1990 ACTION UOMO* *Aromatic / Fougère* 80 ●
1993 ACTION SPORT *Citrus / Hespéridé* 19 ●●●●
1995 L'UOMO TRUSSARDI *Aromatic / Fougère* 82 ●
1997 LIGHT HIM *Woody Oriental / Oriental Boisé* 62 ●

1999 TRUSSARDI UOMO FRESH *Dry Woods / Boisé Cuir* 72 ●●

TSUMURA
1988 SANTA FE FOR MEN *Woody Oriental / Oriental Boisé* 62 ●

TUFI DUEK
2000 FORUM *Oriental / Oriental* 56 ●●

TUVACHÉ / COTY → COTY

ULRIC DE VARENS
1994 VARENSIA *Mossy Woods / Chypre Boisé* 66 ●●
1995 PLEINE LUNE *Woody Oriental / Oriental Boisé* 60 ●
1996 RUE PEROGLÈSE *Mossy Woods / Chypre Boisé* 66 ●●
1997 EAU DE VARENS N° 2 ♂ *Citrus / Hespéridé* 16 ●
1997 EAU DE VARENS N° 3 ♂ *Citrus / Hespéridé* 16 ●●
1998 EAU DE VARENS N° 4 ♂ *Citrus / Hespéridé* 17 ●●●●
1999 U de V POUR ELLE *Floral / Florale* 34 ●
2000 RECTOVERSO LOLLIPOP TOFFEE *Woody Oriental / Oriental Boisé* 60 ●●
2000 RECTOVERSO MANDARIN MUSK *Citrus / Hespéridé* 16 ●●
2000 RECTOVERSO SUN SEA *Floral / Florale* 38 ●
2000 RECTOVERSO SWEETY FRUITY *Floral / Florale* 34 ●
1993 U de V *Aromatic / Fougère* 78 ●
1995 VERSION HOMME* *Mossy Woods / Chypre Boisé* 68 ●●
1999 U de V N° 2 *Woody Oriental / Oriental Boisé* 62 ●●
2000 U de V FUN *Aromatic / Fougère* 80 ●

ULTIMA II
1990 U II SHEER SCENT *Mossy Woods / Chypre Boisé* 66 ●
1994 HEAD OVER HEELS *Floral / Florale* 32 ●
1996 MADLY *Floral / Florale* 32 ●●

UNGARO
1977/90 UNGARO *Woody Oriental / Oriental Boisé* 61 ●●●●
1983 DIVA *Mossy Woods / Chypre Boisé* 67 ●●●●
1987/92 SENSO *Floral / Florale* 34 ●●
1997 FLEUR DE DIVA *Floral / Florale* 36 ●
2001 DESNUDA *Woody Oriental / Oriental Boisé* 60 ●●
1993 UNGARO POUR L'HOMME III *Aromatic / Fougère* 78 ●

UN MONDE NOUVEAU
1993/98 CHERRY MUSK *Floral / Florale* 32 ●●
1993 SAVAGE VANILLA *Woody Oriental / Oriental Boisé* 60 ●●
1993/98 WHITE SPELL *Floral / Florale* 38 ●
1995/98 LOVIN' GIRL *Citrus / Hespéridé* 16 ●●

VALENTIN YUDASHKIN
1999 VALENTIN YUDASHKIN *Floral Oriental / Fleuri Oriental* 46 ●

VALENTINO
1977/86 VALENTINO *Floral / Florale* 34 ●●
1991 VENDETTA* *Woody Oriental / Oriental Boisé* 60 ●
1997 VERY VALENTINO *Oriental / Oriental* 56 ●
1991 VENDETTA POUR HOMME* *Dry Woods / Boisé Cuir* 72 ●●
1999 VERY VALENTINO POUR HOMME *Woody Oriental / Oriental Boisé* 62 ●●

VALERIA MAZZA
1998 VALERIA *Floral / Florale* 36 ●●

VAN CLEEF & ARPELS
1976 FIRST *Soft Floral / Fleuri Aldéhydé* 43 ●●●●
1987 GEM *Woody Oriental / Oriental Boisé* 61 ●●●●
1993 VAN CLEEF *Floral Oriental / Fleuri Oriental* 46 ●●
1994 MISS ARPELS *Floral / Florale* 34 ●
1999 BIRMANE *Floral / Florale* 32 ●●
1978 VAN CLEEF & ARPELS POUR HOMME *Dry Woods / Boisé Cuir* 73 ●●●●
1989 TSAR *Aromatic / Fougère* 78 ●
1998 EAU DU TSAR *Aromatic / Fougère* 80 ●

VAN GILS
1988 VAN GILS *Aromatic / Fougère* 77 ●●●●
1997 BETWEEN SHEETS *Aromatic / Fougère* 78 ●

VANDERBILT → GLORIA VANDERBILT

VENTILO
1997 VENTILO *Floral Oriental / Fleuri Oriental* 46 ●●

1998 L'ÉTÉ DE VENTILO *Floral Oriental / Fleuri Oriental 46* ●
1998 L'HOMME DE VENTILO *Dry Woods / Boisé Cuir 73* ●●●●

VENTURI → GIAN MARCO VENTURI
VERINO → ROBERTO VERINO

VERSACE
1982 GIANNI VERSACE *Mossy Woods / Chypre Boisé 67* ●●●●
1989 V'E VERSACE* *Mossy Woods / Chypre Boisé 66* ●●
1991 VERSUS DONNA* *Floral Oriental / Fleuri Oriental 46* ●●
1994 RED JEANS *Floral / Florale 34* ●●
1995 BABY ROSE JEANS *Floral / Florale 38* ●
1995 VERSACE'S BLONDE *Floral / Florale 31* ●●●●
1996 YELLOW JEANS* *Floral / Florale 34* ●
1997 WHITE JEANS* *Mossy Woods / Chypre Boisé 67* ●●●
1998 V/S WOMAN *Floral / Florale 34* ●
2000 METAL JEANS WOMEN *Floral Oriental / Fleuri Oriental 48* ●
2000 VERSACE ESSENCE EMOTIONAL *Soft Floral / Fleuri Aldéhydé 42* ●●
2000 VERSACE ESSENCE ETHEREAL *Floral / Florale 36* ●
2000 VERSACE ESSENCE EXCITING *Floral / Florale 30* ●●
2001 VERSACE WOMAN *Mossy Woods / Chypre Boisé 66* ●●
1984 VERSACE L'HOMME *Woody Oriental / Oriental Boisé 63* ●●●
1990 VERSUS UOMO* *Woody Oriental / Oriental Boisé 62* ●
1994 BLUE JEANS *Woody Oriental / Oriental Boisé 60* ●●
1995 BABY BLUE JEANS *Citrus / Hespéridé 19* ●●●
1996 GREEN JEANS* *Aromatic / Fougère 78* ●
1996 THE DREAMER *Woody Oriental / Oriental Boisé 62* ●●
1997 BLACK JEANS* *Aromatic / Fougère 76* ●●
2000 V/S MAN *Woody Oriental / Oriental Boisé 62* ●
2000 METAL JEANS MEN *Water / Marine 26* ●

VICKY TIEL
1990 VICKY TIEL ORIGINALÉ *Floral / Florale 33* ●●●●
1994 SIRÈNE *Floral Oriental / Fleuri Oriental 46* ●●
1997 VÉNUS DE L'AMOUR *Floral Oriental / Fleuri Oriental 47* ●●●
1999 ÉTHÉRÉ *Floral / Florale 36* ●
1998 ULYSSE *Woody Oriental / Oriental Boisé 62* ●

VICTOR
1946 SILVESTRE *Mossy Woods / Chypre Boisé 69* ●●●
1949 ACQUA DI SELVA *Mossy Woods / Chypre Boisé 69* ●●●

VICTORIA'S SECRET (a selection *un choix*)
2000 DREAM ANGELS DIVINE *Soft Floral / Fleuri Aldéhydé 42* ●●
2000 DREAM ANGELS HALO *Floral / Florale 31* ●●●●
2000 DREAM ANGELS HEAVENLY *Floral Oriental / Fleuri Oriental 46* ●●

VISARI
1999 FLEURAGE *Soft Floral / Fleuri Aldéhydé 42* ●●

VITTADINI → ADRIENNE VITTADINI

VIVIENNE WESTWOOD
1998 BOUDOIR *Floral Oriental / Fleuri Oriental 47* ●●●
2000 LIBERTINE *Mossy Woods / Chypre Boisé 66* ●

VUARNET
2000 DUO POUR ELLE *Floral / Florale 32* ●
1999 VUARNET *Aromatic / Fougère 78* ●
2000 DUO POUR HOMME *Mossy Woods / Chypre Boisé 68* ●●

WEIL
1928 ZIBELINE *Mossy Woods / Chypre Boisé 67* ●●●
1933/96 SECRET DE VÉNUS *Woody Oriental / Oriental Boisé 61* ●●●
1945 ANTILOPE *Mossy Woods / Chypre Boisé 67* ●●●
1961/93 WEIL EAU DE FRAÎCHEUR ♂ *Citrus / Hespéridé 16* ●
1971 WEIL DE WEIL *Green / Vert 23* ●●●
1984/91 BAMBOU *Floral / Florale 32* ●●
1995 FLEUR DE WEIL* *Floral / Florale 32* ●
1980/97 WEIL POUR HOMME *Aromatic / Fougère 82* ●●
1986 KIPLING *Woody Oriental / Oriental Boisé 62* ●●

WILKES BASHFORD
1998 WILKES SAN FRANCISCO ♂ *Aromatic / Fougère 76* ●

WILLIAMS
1935 AQUA VELVA ICE BLUE *Mossy Woods / Chypre Boisé 68* ●●

WOODS OF WINDSOR (a selection *un choix*)
1974 LAVENDER *Floral / Florale 31* ●●●
1974 WILD ROSE *Floral / Florale 31* ●●●
1978 LILY OF THE VALLEY *Floral / Florale 30* ●
1982 FORGET ME NOT *Soft Floral / Fleuri Aldéhydé 43* ●●●
1997 MIMOSA *Floral / Florale 30* ●●
1998 VIOLET *Floral / Florale 31* ●●●●
1999 FREESIA *Floral / Florale 30* ●●
1981 FOR GENTLEMEN *Mossy Woods / Chypre Boisé 69* ●●●

WORTH
1924/85/2000 DANS LA NUIT *Woody Oriental / Oriental Boisé 61* ●●●
1925/95 SANS ADIEU *Water / Marine 26* ●●
1925/2000 VERS LE JOUR *Floral / Florale 34* ●
1932 JE REVIENS *Soft Floral / Fleuri Aldéhydé 43* ●●●●
1934/2000 VERS TOI *Soft Floral / Fleuri Aldéhydé 43* ●●●●
1977 MISS WORTH *Floral / Florale 33* ●●●●
1981 WORTH POUR HOMME *Aromatic / Fougère 78* ●●

XAN KIM
1999 MERGE ♂ *Aromatic / Fougère 76* ●

YARDLEY
1873 ENGLISH LAVENDER *Floral / Florale 31* ●●●
1913 APRIL VIOLETS *Floral / Florale 31* ●●●●
1973 YOU'RE THE FIRE FOR WOMEN *Soft Oriental / Oriental Doux 53* ●●●
1980/94 LILY OF THE VALLEY *Floral / Florale 30* ●
1982/88 ESP STAYFAST *Floral / Florale 33* ●●●●
1984 ENGLISH FINE COLOGNE ♂ *Citrus / Hespéridé 17* ●●●
1995 WHITE LAVENDER *Floral / Florale 34* ●●
1996 BAROQUE *Floral Oriental / Fleuri Oriental 46* ●●
1996 IMPERIAL VETYVER ♂ *Mossy Woods / Chypre Boisé 67* ●●●
1996 SANDALWOOD ♂ *Woody Oriental / Oriental Boisé 61* ●●●
1997 ENGLISH ROSE *Floral / Florale 31* ●●●
2000 LAVENDER INSPIRATIONS: GINGER & LIME *Citrus / Hespéridé 16* ●●
2000 LAVENDER INSPIRATIONS: JUNIPER & ROSE *Floral / Florale 31* ●●●●
2000 LAVENDER INSPIRATIONS: SEAWEED & ALOE *Water / Marine 26* ●●
2000 NARCISSUS *Floral / Florale 38* ●
1989 YOU'RE THE FIRE FOR MEN *Dry Woods / Boisé Cuir 73* ●●●
1992 YARDLEY ORIGINAL *Aromatic / Fougère 80* ●

YARDLEY / FFC
→ FFC – FINE FRAGRANCES & COSMETICS
YARDLEY / PARFUMS BLEU → PARFUMS BLEU

YOHJI YAMAMOTO
1996 YOHJI *Oriental / Oriental 56* ●●
1998 YOHJI ESSENTIAL *Mossy Woods / Chypre Boisé 66* ●●
1999 YOHJI HOMME *Aromatic / Fougère 77* ●●●●

YVES SAINT LAURENT
1964 Y *Mossy Woods / Chypre Boisé 66* ●
1971 RIVE GAUCHE *Soft Floral / Fleuri Aldéhydé 42* ●●
1977 OPIUM *Soft Oriental / Oriental Doux 53* ●●●
1983 PARIS *Floral / Florale 31* ●●●
1993 YVRESSE (CHAMPAGNE) *Mossy Woods / Chypre Boisé 66* ●
1998 IN LOVE AGAIN* Ⓛ *Floral / Florale 32* ●
1999 BABY DOLL PARIS *Floral / Florale 32* ●
1999 VICE VERSA* Ⓛ *Floral / Florale 34* ●●
1971 YSL POUR HOMME *Citrus / Hespéridé 19* ●●●●
1981 KOUROS *Aromatic / Fougère 77* ●●●●
1988 JAZZ *Aromatic / Fougère 76* ●
1993 KOUROS FRAÎCHEUR *Aromatic / Fougère 78* ●●
1995 OPIUM POUR HOMME *Woody Oriental / Oriental Boisé 62* ●●
1998 LIVE JAZZ *Aromatic / Fougère 82* ●
2000 BODY KOUROS *Woody Oriental / Oriental Boisé 62* ●

ZAHAROFF
1997 ZAHAROFF *Floral Oriental / Fleuri Oriental 46* ●
1999 ZAHAROFF POUR HOMME *Woody Oriental / Oriental Boisé 63* ●●●●

ZEGNA → ERMENEGILDO ZEGNA

Parfums
du Monde

Fragrances
of the World

Publisher *Editeur*
Fragrance Editions
PO Box 14
Blakehurst
Sydney 2221
Australia

Fragrance evaluation
Michael Edwards
in consultation with the perfumers
and/or senior evaluators of the Houses

Evaluation des parfums
Michael Edwards
avec l'aide des créateurs de parfums
et/ou les principaux évaluateurs des
maisons de parfumerie

Technical consultant
Conseiller technique
Guy Robert

Editor *Editrice*
Fiona Stewart

Coordination
Margaret Khoury

Art direction
Direction artistique
Béatrice Torrente, Patrick Lébédeff
Emphase, Paris

Images
Coordination
Victoria Meppem,
Vogue Australia
Photographs *Photographies*
Isamu Sawa
Art direction *Direction artistique*
Simone Elder
Flowers *Fleurs*
Summers Floral

Translation *Traduction*
Catherine Donzel
Brigitte Carcenac de Torné

Production
Peter Bowen, Jackie Welch
Production Art Services, Sydney
K&H Lithographics, Sydney

Printer *Imprimeur*
The Pot Still Press, Sydney

Perfume Legends

Critical acclaim for Michael Edwards's book

'This book is unique, nothing else
is comparable'
Edmond Roudnitska,
celebrated French perfumer

'Magnificent ... the world's leading writer on the
subject'
The Observer

'A fascinating book for anyone with even a passing
interest in perfume. Charting all the great scents
since the launch of Guerlain's *Jicky* in 1889 to
Mugler's *Angel* in 1992, this tells the story of some
of the world's most famous fragrances. Edwards's
passion for the subject makes this more a great
read than just a reference book. Information value:
Outstanding.'
Harpers & Queen

'Michael Edwards's book is marvellously
documented. It is an invaluable contribution to the
history of modern perfumery. I am particularly
proud to appear among the legends, and can't wait
to read the next two *Perfume Legends*:
The Rise of American Fragrances and *Men &
Men's Fragrances.*'
Pierre Dinand, designer of the Opium, Ysatis,
Obsession and Pleasures bottles

*Accueil enthousiaste fait au livre de Michael
Edwards traduit par Guy Robert*

« *Ce livre est tout à fait unique, il n'en existe aucun
qui lui soit comparable* »
Edmond Roudnitska,
le parfumeur le plus célèbre

« *La 'Bible' des parfums* »   ***Le Figaro***

« *Ex-cep-tion-nel! Signé Michael Edwards, cet
album* Parfums de Légende *est une petite oeuvre
d'art que tous les amoureux du parfum se doivent
de posséder.*

*Voilà, en effet, un livre extraordinaire. Pour la
première fois, les parfumeurs, les couturiers, les
créateurs de flacons et les dirigeants des grandes
maisons de parfums parlent de leur art comme ils
ne l'ont jamais fait.*

*Un voyage fascinant dans l'univers des parfums au
travers de leur histoire, du savoir-faire français,
illustré par une iconographie superbe et rare, des
photographies, des croquis, des dessins et des
documents d'archives.*

Pour le prix d'une eau de toilette, Parfums de
Légende *est un livre-révélation à consulter -
presque - comme un incunable.* »
Paris Match

ISBN 0 9587419 6 4
Copyright © 2001 Michael Edwards

ORDER FORM

	Order Units	USA $	Canada $	France FF	UK £	EU €	NZ $*	AUS $*	
Fragrances of the World 2001		54.50	81.50	395	37.50	60.22	90	79	
Fragrances of the World 2001 + Fragrance Adviser CD ROM (English version)		149.50	224.50	995	99.50	151.69	305	265	
Perfume Legends Hard cover English edition		120.00	180.00	–	75.00	–	175	159	
Parfums de Légende Soft cover French edition		–	POA	245	–	37.35	POA	POA	
Fragrances of the World 2002 Parfums du Monde Released March 2002		54.50	81.50	395	37.50	60.22	90	79	
Add postage + packing per book		9.50	13.50	80	9.50	12.20	20	10	
Please ✓ currency ❏ US $ ❏ CAN $ ❏ FF ❏ UK£ ❏ EU € ❏ NZ $ ❏ AUS $								TOTAL	

*Prices include GST

Please charge . . . . to my ❏ MasterCard ❏ Visa Card

CARD NUMBER

Expiry date / Cardholder

Signature

Billing Address

DELIVER TO (please print and allow up to 21 days for delivery)

Name

Address

City / State / Zip or Postcode

Country   Tel/Fax #

E-mail

ORDER FORM

	Order Units	USA $	Canada $	France FF	UK £	EU €	NZ $*	AUS $*	
Fragrances of the World 2001		54.50	81.50	395	37.50	60.22	90	79	
Fragrances of the World 2001 + Fragrance Adviser CD ROM (English version)		149.50	224.50	995	99.50	151.69	305	265	
Perfume Legends Hard cover English edition		120.00	180.00	–	75.00	–	175	159	
Parfums de Légende Soft cover French edition		–	POA	245	–	37.35	POA	POA	
Fragrances of the World 2002 Parfums du Monde Released March 2002		54.50	81.50	395	37.50	60.22	90	79	
Add postage + packing per book		9.50	13.50	80	9.50	12.20	20	10	
Please ✓ currency ❏ US $ ❏ CAN $ ❏ FF ❏ UK£ ❏ EU € ❏ NZ $ ❏ AUS $								TOTAL	

*Prices include GST

Please charge . . . . to my ❏ MasterCard ❏ Visa Card

CARD NUMBER

Expiry date / Cardholder

Signature

Billing Address

DELIVER TO (please print and allow up to 21 days for delivery)

Name

Address

City / State / Zip or Postcode

Country   Tel/Fax #

E-mail

ORDER FORM

	Order Units	USA $	Canada $	France FF	UK £	EU €	NZ $*	AUS $*	
Fragrances of the World 2001		54.50	81.50	395	37.50	60.22	90	79	
Fragrances of the World 2001 + Fragrance Adviser CD ROM (English version)		149.50	224.50	995	99.50	151.69	305	265	
Perfume Legends Hard cover English edition		120.00	180.00	–	75.00	–	175	159	
Parfums de Légende Soft cover French edition		–	POA	245	–	37.35	POA	POA	
Fragrances of the World 2002 Parfums du Monde Released March 2002		54.50	81.50	395	37.50	60.22	90	79	
Add postage + packing per book		9.50	13.50	80	9.50	12.20	20	10	
Please ✓ currency ❏ US $ ❏ CAN $ ❏ FF ❏ UK£ ❏ EU € ❏ NZ $ ❏ AUS $								TOTAL	

*Prices include GST

Please charge . . . . to my ❏ MasterCard ❏ Visa Card

CARD NUMBER

Expiry date / Cardholder

Signature

Billing Address

DELIVER TO (please print and allow up to 21 days for delivery)

Name

Address

City / State / Zip or Postcode

Country   Tel/Fax #

E-mail

TO ORDER

USA and Canada	Please telephone 1 800 426 8986 *or* fax this order form to (847) 677 1338
European Union	Please complete and fax this order form to +61 2 9546 8067 *or*
	e-mail orders@fragrance-editions.com *or*
	post to: Fragrance Editions PO Box 14, Blakehurst, 2221, Sydney, Australia
Australia and New Zealand	Please complete and fax this order form to 02 9546 8067 (+61 2 9546 8067) *or*
	e-mail orders@fragrance-editions.com *or*
	post to: Fragrance Editions PO Box 14, Blakehurst, 2221, Sydney, Australia

Other countries	For current prices, please fax +61 2 9546 8067 *or* e-mail orders@fragrance-editions.com
Quantity discounts and queries	Please fax +61 2 9546 8067 *or* e-mail orders@fragrance-editions.com

Please tick here if you would like to receive more information on:

❏ Perfume Legends

❏ Fragrance Adviser CD-ROM Software

TO ORDER

USA and Canada	Please telephone 1 800 426 8986 *or* fax this order form to (847) 677 1338
European Union	Please complete and fax this order form to +61 2 9546 8067 *or*
	e-mail orders@fragrance-editions.com *or*
	post to: Fragrance Editions PO Box 14, Blakehurst, 2221, Sydney, Australia
Australia and New Zealand	Please complete and fax this order form to 02 9546 8067 (+61 2 9546 8067) *or*
	e-mail orders@fragrance-editions.com *or*
	post to: Fragrance Editions PO Box 14, Blakehurst, 2221, Sydney, Australia

Other countries	For current prices, please fax +61 2 9546 8067 *or* e-mail orders@fragrance-editions.com
Quantity discounts and queries	Please fax +61 2 9546 8067 *or* e-mail orders@fragrance-editions.com

Please tick here if you would like to receive more information on:

❏ Perfume Legends

❏ Fragrance Adviser CD-ROM Software

TO ORDER

USA and Canada	Please telephone 1 800 426 8986 *or* fax this order form to (847) 677 1338
European Union	Please complete and fax this order form to +61 2 9546 8067 *or*
	e-mail orders@fragrance-editions.com *or*
	post to: Fragrance Editions PO Box 14, Blakehurst, 2221, Sydney, Australia
Australia and New Zealand	Please complete and fax this order form to 02 9546 8067 (+61 2 9546 8067) *or*
	e-mail orders@fragrance-editions.com *or*
	post to: Fragrance Editions PO Box 14, Blakehurst, 2221, Sydney, Australia

Other countries	For current prices, please fax +61 2 9546 8067 *or* e-mail orders@fragrance-editions.com
Quantity discounts and queries	Please fax +61 2 9546 8067 *or* e-mail orders@fragrance-editions.com

Please tick here if you would like to receive more information on:

❏ Perfume Legends

❏ Fragrance Adviser CD-ROM Software